This is No. 714 of Everyman's Library

Everyman, I will go with thee, and be thy guide,
In thy most need to go by thy side.

EVERYMAN'S LIBRARY
EDITED BY ERNEST RHYS

ORATORY

BRITISH ORATIONS
HISTORICAL & POLITICAL
INTRODUCTION BY "THE
MEMBER FOR BARCHESTER"

BRITISH HISTORICAL
AND POLITICAL ORATIONS

FROM THE 12th TO THE 20th CENTURY

LONDON: J. M. DENT & SONS LTD.
NEW YORK: E. P. DUTTON & CO. INC

BOOK
PRODUCTION
WAR ECONOMY
STANDARD

INTRODUCTION

ORATORY is the lay-clerk of history, and this book, unlike most of its kind, attempts to trace the line of national and political events in the speeches they helped to inspire. The chronicle that depends on the spoken word is bound however to have its gaps, for at times the great occasion comes and the orator is not there, or if he does appear he proves too voluble or pedantic for the matter in hand. But in the main it is true that the crisis, the moment of reform or reaction, will find its voice, and the eloquence of the spokesman is often a sure sign of the force of the event.

When John Ball spoke to the rebels at Blackheath or when Peter Wentworth in 1576 declared the Liberty of the Commons, when Fox told the same Commons that "every blow you strike in America is against yourselves" or, to hark back again, when James I. spoke to the Parliament on the State of Monarchy with an accent that the Kaiser might envy him— we feel that the hour and the man were in tune. At such times the emphatic word is the clue to the yet more emphatic move-ment in the commonwealth.

The want of a Hansard or a *Daily Mercury* makes the account difficult when carried some centuries away from news-papers and the daily reporter. We are lucky to have Ethel-red's speech to the pious invaders of Britain, who followed St. Augustine over in the sixth century; and because of its brevity we are inclined to reckon it with John Ball's speech and Lincoln's famous terse enunciation of democracy, as among the models of what we may call the epitome speech. William of Normandy's address to his troops before the Battle of Hastings sounds like a more sophisticated item, which had gone through its changes, like the ballad of Patrick Spens, before it found a scribe.

A long breach has to be patched up before we touch then the beginning of the hard struggle between the Lion and the Unicorn, the Crown and the Commons. Queen Elizabeth is the opener of the debate, so far as our account goes, and there is that in her words which tells she is the monarch of expressive men. Her idiom is touched—shall we say ?—with Elizabethan conceit; and Francis Bacon seems to expect it of her as he stands at her elbow. His own speeches in parliament gave her much offence at one time: we have chosen a characteristic one in which he is protesting against the increase of taxation. Peter Wentworth follows, and speaks on the liberty of parliament with a directness that has often been missed in our Westminster rhetoric, while it has always been a merit of English speaking at its best. How different the eloquence of King Jamie—"that soul of a casuist in a king"; according to a French critic his Star Chamber speech contains the full formula of the "Rex sacer Dei," which was to be the snare of the house of Stuart and of its noblest son. Charles the First's address to his troops at Worcester may be ranked with Elizabeth's to the men at Tilbury; both ring with pride and courage; but Elizabeth's lacks her own accent, and we prefer the speech we have taken from her.

The worst of royal oratory is that you are apt to miss in it the temperament of the speaker; but you have the personal touch strongly marked again in Cromwell. The rhetorical note is carried to a pitch of fantasy by my Lord Belhaven in his protest against the Union of England and Scotland, while the echoes of the struggle between Army and Parliament, in Cromwell's time, are to be heard in the speech of William Pulteney, Earl of Bath: an old discussion which was revived under other terms only last year, when the threatened rebellion of Ulster led to a question of the army's right to civil independence. We have another note from "Liberty Wilkes," that revolutionary dilettante, who was a surprisingly cautious speaker when he had a critical audience before him. But Wilkes was not a born orator, like Burke, who comes next in the list, a true master of the instrument.

He to be sure, by his noble personality, his fine brain, his rhetoric, his sense of the event and his power in voicing it, affirmed the classic tradition and began a new one. Rich, ample, fluid language gathered in architectured periods, was never employed to the like effect. His masterpiece was his huge oration on conciliation with America, which would have had a place in this anthology, but that it is already to be had in another volume of the series.[1] Even so, one passage, toward the close of the speech, must be given to keep the

[1] Everyman's Library: *Burke's American Speeches.*

record of the men who have spoken for English liberty. It relates the anti-revolutionary Burke to John Ball and to John Bright; and socialism and labour, and to the latest voice of man or woman seeking to liberate their kind.

"England, Sir, is a nation which still I hope respects, and formerly adored, her freedom. The colonists emigrated from you when this part of your character was most predominant, and they took this bias and direction the moment they parted from your hands. They are therefore not only devoted to liberty, but to liberty according to English ideas and on English principles. Abstract liberty, like other mere abstractions, is not to be found. Liberty inheres in some sensible object; and every nation has formed to itself some favourite point, which by way of eminence becomes the criterion of their happiness. It happened you know, Sir, that the great contests for freedom in this country were from the earliest times chiefly upon the question of taxing. Most of the contests in the ancient commonwealths turned primarily on the right of election of magistrates, or on the balance among the several orders of the state. The question of money was not with them so immediate. But in England it was otherwise. On this point of taxes the ablest pens and most eloquent tongues have been exercised; the greatest spirits have acted and suffered. In order to give the fullest satisfaction concerning the importance of this point, it was not only necessary for those who in argument defended the excellence of the English constitution to insist on this privilege of granting money as a dry point of fact, and to prove that the right had been acknowledged in ancient parchments and blind usages to reside in a certain body called a House of Commons. They went much further; they attempted to prove, and they succeeded, that in theory it ought to be so, from the particular nature of a House of Commons, as an immediate representative of the people, whether the old records had delivered this oracle or not. They took infinite pains to inculcate, as a fundamental principle, that in all monarchies the people must in effect themselves, mediately or immediately, possess the power of granting their own money, or no shadow of liberty could subsist. The colonies draw from you, as with their life-blood, these ideas and principles."

From Burke, Chatham, and Fox—the magic gambler in politics as in money—to the younger Pitt, we are at the turn of the eighteenth century, when the power of the voice was

supreme in the Commons. Was it Macaulay who said that
parliamentary government is government by speaking, and
that that power might exist without judgment, without
knowledge, without the ruler's philosophy or the statesman's wisdom? The younger Pitt was the type of the parliamentary kind—"the minion, the child, the spoiled child of
the House of Commons." There he was unequalled in his
day; a man who from a babe was fed on eloquence by his
father with Demosthenes for a dry-nurse. The relation of
the master-speaker to the event, and oratory to history, is
well seen in the concurrent speeches and episodes, fired by
revolution, reform and war, during the last decades of the
eighteenth and the first of the nineteenth century. At times
the interest of the debate between Fox and Pitt, their blasts
and counterblasts, rather leads us to neglect the events for
the men. Three other causes, vitally affecting national
affairs and constitutional rights, are touched in the speeches
of Grattan on Ireland, Sheridan on the Warren Hastings trial,
in which he was on the side of the angels and against British
injury to India, and Lord Erskine in defence of the printer of
Paine's *Rights of Man*. The Fall of Napoleon is signalised by
the Tory wit, Canning, in his seriously conceived Liverpool
speech; the Great Reform Bill is admirably explained by
Macaulay, while Catholic Rights have their spokesman in
Daniel O'Connell and Jewish Disabilities in Sheil—two of the
most eloquent of the Irish orators. A stage further brings us
to the repeal of the Corn Laws and the "Hungry Forties,"
where Peel, a belated convert to the reform, uses the unanswerable argument of necessity. When John Bright, the
greatest of peace-pleaders, comes on the scene, we have for the
sake of history taken his memorable speech on Peace with
Russia, instead of the often-quoted Crimean speech in which
the Angel of Death figured. A remarkable oration of Disraeli's
passing from banter to a final note of eloquence, and Gladstone's encyclopædic First Midlothian Speech, bring on the
record to our day. The late Joseph Chamberlain is among the
last of the great Victorian parliamentarians; and if we have
hesitated between one of his earlier speeches—that for instance
in which he attacked the House of Lords at Denbigh in 1884
—and a later one with the Imperial Federation motive in it.
and decided on the second of the two, it is because this adds
a fresh argument—the present war being in view—to the
colonial account of Great Britain.

The idea of the yet freer and greater Britain that might have been is admirably stated in a speech of Lord Rosebery's, which may be quoted here since there is no room for it elsewhere in the book:—

" One cannot but pause for a moment to reflect that but for a small incident—the very ordinary circumstance of the acceptance of a peerage—this Empire might have been incalculably greater. Had the elder Pitt, when he became First Minister, not left the House of Commons, he would probably have retained his sanity and his authority. He would have prevented, or suppressed, the reckless budget of Charles Townshend, have induced George III. to listen to reason, have introduced representatives from America into the Imperial Parliament, and preserved the thirteen American colonies to the British Crown. Is it fanciful to dwell for a moment on what might have happened? The Reform Bill which was passed in 1832 would probably have been passed much earlier; for the new blood of America would have burst the old vessels of the Constitution. It would have provided for some self-adjusting system of representation, such as now prevails in the United States, by which increasing population is proportionately represented. And at last, when the Americans became the majority, the seat of Empire would perhaps have been moved solemnly across the Atlantic, and Britain have become the historical shrine and the European outpost of the world empire.

" What an extraordinary revolution it would have been had it been accomplished! The greatest known without bloodshed; the most sublime transference of power in the history of mankind. Our conceptions can scarcely picture the procession across the Atlantic, the greatest sovereign in the greatest fleet in the universe, Ministers, Government, Parliament departing solemnly for the other hemisphere, not, as in the case of the Portuguese sovereigns emigrating to Brazil, under the spur of necessity, but under the vigorous embrace of the younger world. It is well to bridle the imagination, lest it become fantastic and extravagant.

" Moreover, it is a result to which we can scarcely acclimatise ourselves, even in idea. But the other effects might have been scarcely less remarkable. America would have hung on the skirts of Britain and pulled her back out of European complications. She would have profoundly affected the foreign policy of the mother country in the direction of peace. Her influence in our domestic policy would have been scarcely less potent. It might probably have appeased and even contented Ireland. The ancient constitution of Great Britain would have been rendered more comprehensive and more elastic. On the other hand, the American yearning for liberty would have taken a different form; it would have blended with other traditions and flowed into other moulds. And, above all, had there been no Separation, there would have been no War of Independence, no War of 1812, with all the bitter memories that these have left on American soil. To secure that priceless boon I could have been satisfied to see the British Federal Parliament sitting in Columbia Territory. It is difficult indeed to dam the flow of ideas in dealing with so pregnant a possibility. But I restrain myself, because I know that I am dreaming, and that an historical dream, though not a bad relaxation in itself, should not be allowed to become a nightmare."

The present writer can only recall his own experience when he tries to mark some of the later and contemporary stages of the art. He has heard Mr. Gladstone in London, and Colonel Robert Ingersoll in New York, and the late William Morris, burly and nervous, debating on a Hammersmith platform with George Bernard Shaw; has been in Trafalgar Square when free-speech and open eloquence led to police riot and arrests; has heard the late Joseph Cowen and Lord Morley at Newcastle, and Mr. Lloyd George in Wales; has met Mr. Chesterton in a debate on Witches and Night Fears, been converted to women's suffrage by a speech of Mrs. Despard's, and fallen under the spell of Rabindranath Tagore's voice. And when finally he compares the old oratory with the new, he is led to ask if the day of the great oration is not over, because the day of the rhetorician is over? We talk now, we hardly make orations; and the change may be seen in the natural colloquial style of Mr. Lloyd George, as compared, let us say, with the older parliamentary mode of Lord Rosebery, the greatest of surviving orators, or Mr. Winston Churchill. What is to be inferred from it? That the House of Parliament is on the eve of change, and that in the future it will talk less and do more? That perhaps is too much to say; but Westminster may yet see its two State Chambers resolve themselves into Houses of Enactment, and be content that its members shall do most of their real talking down in the country.

In order to round off the chronicle, a supplement of three notable speeches on the World War is added. The full record of our own time, and of those who have voiced its needs and its great political reforms, would demand a volume in itself.

" THE MEMBER FOR BARCHESTER."

BIBLIOGRAPHY

Select British Eloquence, edited by Channcey A. Goodrich, New York and London, 1852; British Eloquence of the Nineteenth Century, London and Glasgow, 1855–58; Treasure of British Eloquence, edited by Robert Cochrane, Edinburgh, 1879; Representative British Orations, edited by Charles Kendall Adams, New York, 1884 (3 vols.); Political Orations, from Wentworth to Macaulay, edited with introduction by William Clarke, 1889 (Camelot Series); Modern Political Orations, edited by Leopold Wagner, 1896; The Book of Public Speaking, Arthur Charles Fox-Davies, London, 1913 (5 vols.). For Speeches of John Bright, Burke, Macaulay, and William Pitt, see bibliographies in Everyman's Library, Vols. 252, 340, 399, 145. See also History of Oratory, H. Hardwicke, New York, 1896; Art of the Orator, Edgar R. Jones, M.P. (preface by Rt. Hon. D. Lloyd George, M.P.), 1912. The publishers' acknowledgments are due to the *Manchester Guardian* and the *Daily Chronicle* for their reports of speeches by Mr. Asquith, Mr. Lloyd George, and Mr. Redmond.

CONTENTS

BRITISH ORATIONS

THE COMING OF CHRISTIANITY

ETHELBERT

Isle of Thanet: 597

Speech to Augustine and his followers on their Mission to Convert England

[The meeting must have been remarkable. The Saxon king, " the Son of the Ash-tree," with his wild soldiers round, seated on the bare ground on one side—on the other side, with a huge silver cross borne before him (crucifixes were not yet introduced), and beside it a large picture of Christ painted and gilded, after the fashion of those times on an upright board, came up from the shore Augustine and his companions; chanting, as they advanced, a solemn Litany, for themselves and for those to whom they came. He, as we are told, was a man of almost gigantic stature,[1] head and shoulders taller than anyone else; with him were Lawrence, who afterwards succeeded him as Archbishop of Canterbury, and Peter, who became the first Abbot of St. Augustine's. They and their companions, amounting altogether to forty, sat down at the King's command, and the interview began.

Neither, we must remember, could understand the other's language. Augustine could not understand a word of Anglo-Saxon; and Ethelbert, we may be tolerably sure, could not speak a word of Latin. But the priests whom Augustine had brought from France as knowing both German and Latin, now stepped forward as interpreters; the King heard it all attentively, and then gave this most characteristic answer, bearing upon it a stamp of truth which it is impossible to doubt:]

Your words are fair, and your promises—but because they are new and doubtful, I cannot give my assent to them, and leave the customs which I have so long observed, with the whole Anglo-Saxon race. But because you have come hither as strangers from a long distance, and as I seem to myself to have seen clearly, that what you yourselves believed to be true and good, you wish to impart to us, we do not wish to molest you; nay, rather we are anxious to receive you hospitably, and to give you all that is needed for your support, nor do you hinder you from joining all whom you can to the faith of your religion.

[1] Acta Sanct. 399.

[Such an answer, simple as it was, really seems to contain the seeds of all that is excellent in the English character—exactly what a king should have said on such an occasion—exactly what, under the influence of Christianity, has grown up into all our best institutions. There is the natural dislike to change, which Englishmen still retain; there is the willingness at the same time to listen favourably to anything which comes recommended by the energy and self-devotion of those who urge it; there is, lastly, the spirit of moderation and toleration, and the desire to see fair play, which is one of our best gifts, and which, I hope, we shall never lose. We may, indeed, well be thankful not only that we had an Augustine to convert us, but that we had an Ethelbert for our King.]

STANLEY'S MEMORIALS OF CANTERBURY.

THE RAGE OF BATTLE

DUKE WILLIAM OF NORMANDY

ADDRESS TO HIS ARMY BEFORE THE BATTLE OF HASTINGS
1066

NORMANS! bravest of nations! I have no doubt of your courage, and none of your victory, which never by any chance or obstacle escaped your efforts. If indeed you had, once only, failed to conquer, there might be a need now to inflame your courage by exhortation; but your native spirit does not require to be roused. Bravest of men, what could the power of the Frankish king effect with all his people, from Lorraine to Spain, against Hastings my predecessor? What he wanted of France he took, and gave to the king only what he pleased. What he had, he held as long as it suited him, and relinquished it only for something better. Did not Rollo my ancestor, founder of our nation, with our fathers conquer at Paris the king of the Franks in the heart of his kingdom, nor had the king of the Franks any hope of safety until he humbly offered his daughter and possession of the country, which, after you, is called Normandy.

Did not your fathers capture the king of the Franks at Rouen, and keep him there until he restored Normandy to Duke Richard, then a boy; with this condition, that, in every conference between the king of France and the Duke of Normandy, the duke should wear his sword, while the king should not be permitted to carry a sword nor even a dagger. This concession

your fathers compelled the great king to submit to, as binding
for ever.   Did not the same duke lead your fathers to Mirmande,
at the foot of the Alpes, and enforce submission from the lord of
the town, his son-in-law, to his own wife, the duke's daughter?
Nor was it enough for you to conquer men, he conquered the
devil himself, with whom he wrestled, cast down and bound
him with his hands behind his back, and left him a shameful
spectacle to angels.   But why do I talk of former times?   Did
not you, in our own time, engage the Franks at Mortemer?   Did
not the Franks prefer flight to battle, and use their spurs?   While
you—Ralph, the commander of the Franks having been slain—
reaped the honour and the spoil as the natural result of your
usual success.   Ah! let any one of the English whom, a hundred
times, our predecessors, both Danes and Normans, have defeated
in battle, come forth and show that the race of Rollo ever suffered a defeat from his time until now, and I will withdraw
conquered.   Is it not, therefore, shameful that a people accustomed to be conquered, a people ignorant of war, a people even
without arrows, should proceed in order of battle against you,
my brave men?   Is it not a shame that king Harold, perjured
as he was in your presence, should dare to show his face to you?
It is amazing to me that you have been allowed to see those
who, by a horrible crime, beheaded your relations and Alfred my
kinsman, and that their own heads are still on their shoulders.
Raise your standards, my brave men, and set neither measure nor
limit to your merited rage.   May the lightning of your glory
be seen and the thunders of your onset heard from East to West,
and be ye the avengers of noble blood.

FROM HENRY OF HUNTINGDON'S CHRONICLE.

BONDMEN AND FREEMEN

JOHN BALL

ADDRESS TO THE REBELS AT BLACKHEATH
1381

When Adam delved and Eve span,
Who was then the gentleman?

FROM the beginning all men by nature were created alike, and
our bondage or servitude came in by the unjust oppression of
naughty men.   For if God would have had any bondmen from
the beginning, he would have appointed who should be bond,

and who free. And therefore I exhort you to consider that now the time is come, appointed to us by God, in which ye may (if ye will) cast off the yoke of bondage, and recover liberty. I counsel you therefore well to bethink yourselves, and to take good hearts unto you, that after the manner of a good husband that tilleth his ground, and riddeth out thereof such evil weeds as choke and destroy the good corn, you may destroy first the great lords of the realm, and after, the judges and lawyers, and questmongers, and all other who have undertaken to be against the commons. For so shall you procure peace and surety to yourselves in time to come; and by despatching out of the way the great men, there shall be an equality in liberty, and no difference in degrees of nobility; but a like dignity and equal authority in all things brought in among you.

THE QUEEN AND THE ROYAL SUCCESSION

ELIZABETH

PALACE OF WESTMINSTER: 5 Nov. 1566

[The address was read by Bacon.

After grateful acknowledgments of the general government of the queen the two Houses desired, first, to express their wish that her highness would be pleased to marry " where it should please her, with whom it should please her, and as soon as it should please her."

Further, as it was possible that her highness might die without children, her faithful subjects were anxious to know more particularly the future prospects of the realm. Much as they wished to see her married, the settlement of the succession was even more important, " carrying with it such necessity that without it they could not see how the safety of her royal person or the preservation of her imperial crown and realm could be or should be sufficiently and certainly provided for." " Her late illness (the queen had been unwell again), the amazedness that most men of understanding were by fruit of that sickness brought unto," and the opportunity of making a definite arrangement while Parliament was sitting, were the motives which induced them to be more urgent than they would otherwise have cared to be. History and precedent alike recommended a speedy decision. They hoped that she might live to have a child of her own; but she was mortal, and should she die before her subjects knew to whom their allegiance was due, a civil war stared them in the face. The decease of a prince leaving the realm without a government was the most frightful disaster which could befall the commonwealth; with the vacancy of the throne all writs were suspended, all commissions were void, law itself was dead. Her Majesty was not ignorant of these things. If she refused to provide a remedy " it would be a dangerous burden before God upon her majesty ! " They had therefore felt it to be their duty to present this address; and on their knees they implored her to consider it and to give them an answer before the session closed.

Elizabeth had prepared her answer; as soon as Bacon ceased, she drew herself up and spoke as follows:]

IF the order of your cause had matched the weight of your matter, the one might well have craved reward, and the other much the sooner be satisfied. But when I call to mind how far from dutiful care, yea rather how nigh a traitorous trick this tumbling cast did spring, I muse how men of wit can so hardly use that gift they hold. I marvel not much that bridle-less colts do not know their rider's hand whom bit of kingly rein did never snaffle yet. Whether it was fit that so great a cause as this should have had this beginning in such a public place as that, let it be well weighed. Must all evil bodings that might be recited be found little enough to hap to my share ? Was it well meant, think you, that those that knew not how fit this matter was to be granted by the prince, would prejudicate their prince in aggravating the matter ? so all their arguments tended to my careless care of this my dear realm.

[So far she spoke from a form which remains in her own hand-writing.[1] She continued perhaps in the same style; but her words remain only in the Spanish of de Silva.]

She was not surprised at the Commons, she said; they had small experience and had acted like boys; but that the Lords should have gone along with them she confessed had filled her with wonder. There were some among them who had placed their swords at her disposal when her sister was on the throne, and had invited her to seize the crown; she knew but too well that if she allowed a successor to be named, there would be found men who would approach him or her with the same encouragement to disturb the peace of the realm. If she pleased she could name the persons to whom she alluded. When time and circumstances would allow she would see to the matter of their petition before they asked her; she would be sorry to be forced into doing anything which in reason and justice she was bound to do; and she concluded with a request that her words should not be misinterpreted.

[1] Answer to the Parliament by the Queen; Autograph: *Domestic MSS., Elizabeth*, vol. xli. *Rolls House.*

[So long as she was speaking to the lay peers she controlled her temper; but her passion required a safety-valve, and she rarely lost an opportunity of affronting and insulting her bishops.

Turning sharp round where Grindal and Pilkington were standing—]

And you *doctors*, she said—it was her pleasure to ignore their right to a higher title; you I understand make long prayers about this business. One of you dared to say in times past that I and my sister were bastards; and you must needs be interfering in what does not concern you. Go home and amend your own lives and set an honest example in your families. The Lords in Parliament should have taught you to know your places; but if they have forgotten their duty I will not forget mine. Did I so choose I make the impertinence of the whole set of you an excuse to withdraw my promise to marry; but for the realm's sake I am resolved that I will marry; and I will take a husband that will not be to the taste of some of you. I have not married hitherto out of consideration for you, but it shall be done now, and you who have been so urgent with me will find the effects of it to your cost. Think you the prince who will be my consort will feel himself safe with such as you, who thus dare to thwart and cross your natural queen?

FROUDE'S HISTORY OF QUEEN ELIZABETH.

ON THE LIBERTY OF THE COMMONS

PETER WENTWORTH

HOUSE OF COMMONS: 8 FEBRUARY, 1576

MR. SPEAKER,—I find in a little volume these words, in effect: " Sweet is the name of Liberty, but the thing itself a value beyond all inestimable treasure." So much the more it behoveth us lest we, contenting ourselves with the sweetness of the name, lose and forego the thing, being of the greatest value that can come unto this noble realm. The inestimable treasure is the use of it in this House. And, therefore, I do think it needful to put you in remembrance that this honourable assembly are assembled and come together here in this place for three special causes of most weighty and great importance. The first and principal is to make and abrogate such laws as may be most for the preservation of our noble sovereign; the second

. . .; the third is to make or abrogate such laws as may be the chiefest surety, safe-keeping, and enrichment of this noble realm of England. So that I do think that the part of the faithful-hearted subject is to do his endeavour to remove all stumbling-blocks out of the way that may impair or any manner of way hinder these good and godly causes of this our coming together. I was never of Parliament but the last, and the last session, at both of which times I saw the liberty of free speech, the which is the only salve to heal all the sores of this Commonwealth, so much and so many ways infringed, and so many abuses offered to this honourable council, as hath much grieved me, even of very conscience and love to my prince and State. Wherefore, to avoid the like, I do deem it expedient to open the commodities that grow to the prince and the whole State by free speech used in this place; at least, so much as my simple wit can gather it, the which is very little in respect of that that wise heads can say therein, and so it is of more force. First, all matters that concern God's honour, through free speech, shall be propagated here and set forward, and all things that do hinder it removed, repulsed, and taken away. Next, there is nothing commodious, profitable, or any way beneficial for the prince or State but faithful and loving subjects will offer it to this place. Thirdly, all things discommodious, perilous, or hurtful to the prince or State shall be prevented, even so much as seemeth good to our merciful God to put into our minds, the which no doubt shall be sufficient if we do earnestly call upon Him and fear Him (for Solomon saith, " The fear of God is the beginning of wisdom. Wisdom breatheth life into her children, receiveth them that seek her, and will go beside them in the way of righteousness "), so that our minds shall be directed to all good, needful, and necessary things, if we call upon God with faithful hearts. Fourthly, if the envious do offer anything hurtful or perilous, what inconvenience doth grow thereby? Verily, I think none; nay, will you have me to say my simple opinion thereof—much good cometh thereof. How, forsooth? Why, by the darkness of the night the brightness of the sun showeth more excellent and clear; and how can truth appear and conquer until falsehood and all subtleties that should shadow and darken it are found out? For it is offered in this place as a piece of fine needlework to them that are most skilful therein, for there cannot be a false stitch (God aiding us) but will be found out. Fifthly, this good cometh thereof—a wicked purpose may the easier be prevented when it is known. Sixthly, an evil man can do the less harm when it is known. Seventhly, sometime it happeneth that a good man will in this place (for argument sake) prefer an evil cause, both for that he would have a doubtful truth to be opened and manifested, and also the evil prevented. So that to this point I conclude, that in this House, which is termed a place of free speech, there is nothing so necessary for the preservation of the prince and State as free speech; and without this it is a scorn and mockery to call it a Parliament House, for in truth it is none but a very school of flattery and dissimulation, and so a fit place to serve the devil and his angels in, and not to glorify God and benefit the Commonwealth.

Now to the impediments thereof, which, by God's grace and my little experience, I will utter plainly and faithfully. I will use the words of Elcha—" Behold, I am as the new wine which has no vent, and bursteth the new vessels in sunder; therefore, I will speak that I may have a vent. I will open my lips and make answer. I will regard no manner of person, no man will I spare; for if I go about to please men, I know not how soon my Maker will take me away." My text is vehement, which, by God's sufferance, I mean to observe, hoping therewith to offend none; for that of very justice none ought to be offended for seeking to do good and saying of the truth.

Amongst other, Mr. Speaker, two things do great hurt in this place, of which I do mean to speak. The one is a rumour which runneth about the House, and this it is—" Take heed what you do; the Queen liketh not such matter; whoever preferreth it, she will be offended with him." Or the contrary—" Her Majesty liketh of such matter; whoever speaketh against it, she will be much offended with him." The other—sometimes a message is brought into the House, either of commanding or inhibiting, very injurious to the freedom of speech and consultation. I would to God, Mr. Speaker, that these two were burned in hell—I mean rumours and messages, for wicked they undoubtedly are. The reason is, the devil was the first author of them, from whom proceedeth nothing but wickedness. Now I will set down reasons to prove them wicked. For if we be in hand with anything for the advancement of God's glory, were it not wicked to say the Queen liketh not of it, or commandeth that we shall not deal in it? Greatly were these speeches to her Majesty's dishonour; and an hard opinion were it, Mr. Speaker, that these things should enter into her Majesty's thought. Much more wicked were it that her Majesty should like or command anything against God or hurtful to herself and the State. The Lord grant that this thing may be far from her Majesty's heart! Here this may be objected—that, if the Queen's Majesty have intelligence of anything perilous or beneficial to her Majesty's person or the State, would you not have her Majesty give knowledge thereof to the House, whereby her peril may be prevented and her benefit provided for? God forbid! Then were her Majesty in worse case than any of her subjects. And, in the beginning of our speech, I showed it to be a special cause of our assembling; but my intent is, that nothing should be done to God's dishonour, to her Majesty's peril, or the peril of the State. And, therefore, I will show the inconveniences that grow of these two. First, if we follow not the prince's mind, Solomon saith: "The king's displeasure is a messenger of death." This is a terrible thing to weak nature; for who is able to abide the fierce countenance of his prince? But if we will discharge our consciences, and be true to God and prince and State, we must have due consideration of the place and the occasion of our coming together, and especially have regard unto the matter wherein we both shall serve God and our prince and State faithfully, and not dissembling as eye-pleasers, and so justly avoid all displeasures both to God and our prince; for Solomon saith, "In the way of the righteous there is life." As for any other way, it is the path to death. So that, to avoid everlasting death and condemnation with the high and mighty God, we ought to proceed in every cause according to the matter, and not according to the prince's mind. And now I will show you a reason to prove it perilous always to follow the prince's mind. Many a time it falleth out that a prince may favour a cause perilous to himself and the whole State. What are we then if we follow the prince's mind? Are we not unfaithful unto God, our prince, and State? Yes, truly; we are chosen of the whole realm, of a special trust and confidence by them reposed in us, to foresee all such inconveniences. Then I will set down my opinion herein; that is to say, he that dissembleth to her Majesty's peril to be accounted as a hateful enemy, for that he giveth unto her Majesty a detestable Judas's kiss; and he that contrarieth her mind to her preservation, yea, though her Majesty would be much offended with him, is to be judged an approved lover. For " faithful are the wounds of a lover," saith Solomon; "but the kisses of an enemy are deceitful." "And 'tis better," saith Antisthenes, " to fall amongst ravens than amongst flatterers; for ravens do but devour the dead corpse, and flatterers the living." And it is both traitorous and hellish, through flattery, to seek to devour our natural prince; and that do flatterers. Therefore, let them leave it with shame enough.

Now to another great matter that riseth of this grievous rumour. What is it, forsooth? Whatsoever thou art that pronounceth it, thou doth pronounce thy own discredit. Why so? For that thou doth what lieth in thee to pronounce the prince to be perjured, the which we neither will nor may believe. For we ought not, without too manifest proof, to credit any dishonour to our anointed. No; we ought not without it to think any evil of her Majesty, but rather to hold him a liar, what credit soever he be of; for the Queen's Majesty is the head of the law, and must of necessity maintain the law, for by the law her Majesty is made justly our queen, and by it she is most chiefly maintained. Hereunto agreeth the most excellent words of Bracton (*De Legibus Angliæ*, lib. i. cap. 7), who saith, "The king hath no peer nor equal in his kingdom." He hath no equal, for otherwise he might lose his authority of commanding, since that an equal hath no power of commandment over an equal. The king ought not to be under man, but under God, and under the law, because the law maketh him a king. Let the king, therefore, attribute that the law attributeth unto him, that is, dominion and power; for he is not a king in whom will and not the law doth rule; and therefore he ought to be under the law. I pray you mark the reason why my authority saith the king ought to be under the law; for, saith he, "He is God's vicegerent upon earth;" that is, His lieutenant, to execute and do His will, the which is law or justice, and thereunto was her Majesty sworn at her coronation, as I have heard learned men in this place sundry times affirm. Unto which I doubt not her Majesty will, for her honour and conscience' sake, have special regard; for free speech and conscience in this place are granted by a special law, as that without the which the prince and State cannot be preserved or maintained. So that I would wish that every man that feareth God, regardeth the prince's honour, or esteemeth his own credit, to fear at all times hereafter to pronounce any such horrible speeches so much to the prince's dishonour, for in so doing he showeth himself an open enemy to her Majesty, and so worthy to be contemned of all faithful hearts. Yet there is another inconvenience that riseth of this wicked rumour. The utterers thereof seem to put into our heads that the Queen's

Majesty both conceived an evil opinion, diffidence, and mistrust in us, her faithful and loving subjects; for, if she hath not, her Majesty would wish that all things dangerous to herself should be laid open before us, assuring herself that loving subjects as we are would, without schooling and direction, with careful mind to our powers, prevent and withstand all perils that might happen unto her Majesty. And this opinion I doubt not but her Majesty hath conceived of us; for undoubtedly there was never prince that had faithfuller hearts than her Majesty hath here, and surely there were never subjects had more cause heartily to love their prince for her quiet government than we have. So that he that raiseth this rumour still increaseth but discredit in seeking to sow sedition as much as lieth in him between our merciful Queen and us her loving and faithful subjects, the which, by God's grace, shall never lie in his power; let him spit out all his venom, and therewithal show out his malicious heart. Yet I have collected sundry reasons to prove this a hateful and detestable rumour, and the utterer thereof to be a very Judas to our noble Queen. Therefore, let any hereafter take heed how he publish it, for as a very Judas unto her Majesty, and an enemy to the whole State, we ought to accept him.

Now, the other was a message, Mr. Speaker, brought the last session into the House that we should not deal in any matters of religion, but first to receive from the bishops. Surely this was a doleful message; for it was as much as to say, "Sirs, ye shall not deal in God's causes; no! ye shall no wise seek to advance His glory!" And, in recompense of your unkindness, God in His wrath will look upon your doings that the chief cause that ye were called together for, the which is the preservation of their prince, shall have no success. If some one of this House had presently made this interpretation of this said message, had he not seemed to have the spirit of prophecy? Yet, truly, I assure you, Mr. Speaker, there were divers of this House that said with grievous hearts, immediately upon the message, that God of His justice could not prosper the session. And let it be holden for a principle, Mr. Speaker, that council that cometh not together in God's name cannot prosper. For God saith, "Where two or three are gathered together in my name, there am I in the midst amongst them." Well, God, even the great and mighty God, whose name is the Lord of Hosts, great in council and infinite in thought, and who is the only good Director of all Hearts, was the last session shut out of doors! But what fell out of it, forsooth? His great indignation was therefore poured upon

this House; for He did put into the Queen's Majesty's heart
to refuse good and wholesome laws for her own preservation,
the which caused many faithful hearts for grief to burst out
with sorrowful tears and moved all Papists, traitors to God
and her Majesty, who envy good Christian government, in their
sleeves to laugh all the whole Parliament House to scorn.   And
shall I pass over this weighty matter so lightly?   Nay!   I will
discharge my conscience and duties to God, my prince, and
country.   So certain it is, Mr. Speaker, that none is without
fault, no, not our noble Queen, sith then her Majesty hath committed great fault, yea, dangerous faults to herself.

Love, even perfect love, void of dissimulation, will not suffer
me to hide them to her Majesty's peril, but to utter them to her
Majesty's safety.   And these they are: It is a dangerous thing
in a prince unkindly to abuse his or her nobility and people; and
it is a dangerous thing in a prince to oppose or bend herself
against her nobility and people, yea, against most loving and
faithful nobility and people.   And how could any prince more
unkindly entreat, abuse, and oppose herself against her nobility
and people than her Majesty did the last Parliament?   Did she
call of purpose to prevent traitorous perils to her person, and
for no other cause?   Did not her Majesty send unto us two bills,
willing us to make choice of that we liked best for her safety,
and thereof to make a law, promising her Majesty's assent
thereunto?   And did we not first choose the one, and her
Majesty refused it, yielding no reason; nay, yielding great
reasons why she ought to have yielded to it?   Yet did we
nevertheless receive the other, and, agreeing to make a law
thereof, did not her Majesty in the end refuse all our travails?
And did not we, her Majesty's faithful nobility and subjects,
plainly and openly decipher ourselves unto her Majesty and
our hateful enemies, and hath not her Majesty left us all open
to their revenge?   Is this a just recompense in our Christian
Queen for our just dealings?   The heathen do requite good for
good; then how much more is it to be expected in a Christian
prince?   And will not this her Majesty's handling, think you,
Mr. Speaker, make cold dealing in any of her Majesty's subjects
toward her again?   I fear it will.   And hath it not caused
many already, think you, Mr. Speaker, to seek a salve for the
head that they have broken?   I fear it hath; and many more
will do the like, if it be not prevented in time.   And hath it not
marvellously rejoiced and encouraged the hollow hearts of her
Majesty's hateful enemies and traitorous subjects?   No doubt

but it hath. And I beseech God that her Majesty may do all things that may grieve the hearts of her enemies, and may joy the hearts that unfeignedly love her Majesty; and I beseech the same God to endue her Majesty with His wisdom, whereby she may discern faithful advice from traitorous, sugared speeches, and to send her Majesty a melting, yielding heart unto sound counsel, that will may not stand for a reason; and then her Majesty will stand where her enemies have fallen; for no estate will stand where the prince will not be governed by advice. And I doubt not but that some of her Majesty's council have dealt plainly and faithfully with her Majesty herein. If any have, let it be a sure sign to her Majesty to know them for approved subjects; and whatsoever they be that did persuade her Majesty so unkindly to entreat, abuse, and to oppose herself against her nobility and people, or commend her Majesty for so doing, let it be a sure token to her Majesty to know them for sure traitors and underminers of her Majesty's life, and remove them out of her Majesty's presence and favour; for, the more cunning they are the more dangerous are they unto her Majesty. But was this all? No; for God would not vouchsafe that His Holy Spirit should all that session descend upon our bishops; so that in that session nothing was done to the advancement of His glory. I have heard of old Parliament men that the tarnishment of the Pope and Popery and the restoring of true religion had their beginning from this House, and not from the bishops; and I have heard that few laws for religion had their foundation from them. And I do surely think—before God I speak it!—that the bishops were the cause of that doleful message. And I will show you what moveth me so to think. I was, amongst others, the last Parliament, sent unto the Bishop of Canterbury for the Articles of Religion that then passed this House. He asked us why we did put out of the book the homilies, consecrating of bishops, and such like. "Surely, sir," said I, "because we were so occupied with other things that we had no time to examine them how they agreed with the Word of God." "What!" said he, "surely you mistook the matter; you will refer yourself wholly to us therein?" "No! by the faith I bear to God," said I, "we will pass nothing until we understand what it is; for that were but to make you popes. Make you popes who list," said I, "for we will make you none." And sure, Mr. Speaker, the speech seemed to me a pope-like speech; and I fear lest our bishops do attribute this of the Pope's canons unto themselves, " *papa non potest errare* "; for surely, if they did not, they would reform things amiss, and not to spurn against God's people for writing therein as they do. But I can tell them news: they do but kick against the pricks; for undoubtedly they both have and do err; for God will reveal His truth maugre the hearts of them and all His enemies; for great is the truth, and it will prevail. And, to say the truth, it is an error to think that God's spirit is tied only in them; for the Heavenly Spirit saith: " First seek the kingdom of God and the righteousness thereof, and all these things (meaning temporal) shall be given you." These words were not spoken to the bishops only, but to all. And the writ, Mr. Speaker, that we are called up by, is chiefly to deal in God's cause, so that our commission, both from God and our prince, is to deal in God's causes. Therefore, the accepting of such messages, and taking them in good part, do highly offend God, and is the acceptation of the breach of the liberties of this honourable council. For is it not all one thing to say, sirs, " you shall deal in such matters only," as to say " you shall not deal in such matters "? and is as good to have fools and flatterers in the House as men of wisdom, grave judgment, faithful hearts, and sincere consciences; for they, being taught what they shall do, can give their consents as well as others. Well, " He that hath an office," saith Saint Paul, " let him wait on his office," or give diligent attendance on his office. It is a great and special part of our office, Mr. Speaker, to maintain the freedom and consultation of speech; for by this good laws that do set forth God's glory, and for the preservation of the prince and State, are made. Saint Paul, in the same place, saith: " Hate that which is evil, cleave unto that which is good." Then with Saint Paul I do advise you all here present, yea, and heartily and earnestly desire you, from the bottom of your hearts, to hate all messengers, tale-carriers, or any other thing, whatsoever it be, that any way infringes the liberties of this honourable council; yea, hate it or them as poisonous unto our Commonwealth, for they are venomous beasts that do use it. Therefore, I say unto you again and again, " Hate that which is evil, and cling unto that which is good." And thus, being loving and faithful-hearted, I do wish to be conceived in fear of God and of love of our prince and State; for we are incorporated into this place to serve God and all England, and not to be time-servers, as humour-feeders, as cancers that would pierce the bone, or as flatterers that would fain beguile all the world, and so worthy to be condemned both

of God and man; but let us show ourselves a people endued
with faith, I mean a lively faith that bringeth forth good works,
and not as dead. And these good works I wish to break forth
in this sort, not only in hating the enemies before spoken
against, but also in openly reproving them as enemies to God,
our prince, and State, that do use them, for they are so. Therefore, I would have none spared or forborne that shall from
henceforth offend herein, of what calling soever he be; for
the higher place he hath the more harm he may do. Therefore,
if he will not eschew offences, the higher I wish him hanged.
I speak this in charity, Mr. Speaker; for it is better that one
should be hanged than that this noble State should be subverted.
Well, I pray God with all my heart to turn the hearts of all
the enemies of our prince and State, and to forgive them that
wherein they have offended; yea, and to give them grace
to offend therein no more. Even so, I do heartily beseech God
to forgive us for holding our peace when we have heard any
inquiry offered to this honourable council; for surely it is no
small offence, Mr. Speaker, for we offend therein against God,
our prince, and State, and abuse the confidence by them reposed
in us. Wherefore God, for His great mercies' sake, grant that
we may from henceforth show ourselves neither bastards nor
dastards therein, but that as rightly-begotten children we may
sharply and boldly reprove God's enemies, our princes, and
State; and so shall every one of us discharge our duties in this
our high office, wherein He hath placed us, and show ourselves
haters of evil and cleavers to that that is good to the setting
forth of God's glory and honour, and to the preservation of our
noble Queen and Commonwealth, for these are the marks that
we ought only in this place to shoot at. I am thus earnest—I
take God to witness, for conscience' sake—love unto my prince
and Commonwealth, and for the advancement of justice; "for
justice," saith an ancient father, "is the prince of all virtues,"
yea, the safe and faithful guard of man's life, for by it empires,
kingdoms, people, and cities, be governed, the which, if it be
taken away, the society of man cannot long endure. And a
king, saith Solomon, "that sitteth in the throne of judgment,
and looketh well about him, chaseth away all evil"; in the
which State and throne God, for His great mercies' sake, grant
that our noble Queen may be heartily vigilant and watchful;
for surely there was a great fault committed both in the last
Parliament and since also that was, as faithful hearts as any
were unto the prince and State received most displeasure, the

which is but a hard point in policy to encourage the enemy, to discourage the faithful-hearted, who of fervent love cannot dissemble, but follow the rule of Saint Paul, who saith, "Let love be without dissimulation."

Now to another great fault I found the last Parliament, committed by some of this House also, the which I would desire of them all might be left. I have seen right good men in other causes, although I did dislike them in that doing, sit in an evil matter against which they had most earnestly spoken. I mused at it, and asked what it meant, for I do think it a shameful thing to serve God, their prince, or country, with the tongue only and not with the heart and body. I was answered that it was a common policy in this House to mark the best sort of the same, and either to sit or arise with them. That same common policy I would gladly have banished this House, and have grafted in the stead thereof either to rise or sit as the matter giveth cause; "for the eyes of the Lord behold all the earth, to strengthen all the hearts of them that are whole with him." These be God's own words; mark them well, I heartily beseech you all; for God will not receive half-part; He will have the whole. And again, He misliketh these two-faced gentlemen, and here be many eyes that will to their great shame behold their double-dealing that use it. Thus I have holden you long with my rude speech, the which since it tendeth wholly with pure conscience to seek the advancement of God's glory, our honourable sovereign's safety, and to the sure defence of this noble isle of England, and all by maintaining of the liberties of this honourable council, the fountain from whence all these do spring—my humble and hearty suit unto you all is to accept my good-will, and that this that I have here spoken out of conscience and great zeal unto my prince and State may not be buried in the pit of oblivion, and so no good come thereof.

SPEECH ON THE THREE SUBSIDIES

FRANCIS BACON (AFTERWARDS LORD VERULAM)

HOUSE OF COMMONS: 1593

MR. FRANCIS BACON assented to three subsidies, but not to the payment under six years; and to this propounded three reasons, which he desired might be answered.

First. Impossibility or difficulty.

Second. Danger and discontent.

Third. A better manner of supply than subsidy.

For impossibility, the poor men's rent is such as they are not able to yield it, and the general commonalty is not able to pay so much upon the present. The gentlemen must sell their plate and the farmers their brass pots ere this will be paid. And as for us, we are here to search the wounds of the realm and not to skin them over; wherefore we are not to persuade ourselves of their wealth more than it is.

The danger is this: we breed discontent in the people. And in a cause of jeopardy, her Majesty's safety must consist more in the love of her people than in their wealth. And therefore we ought not to give them cause of discontentment. In granting these subsidies thus we run into perils. The first: in putting two payments into one, we make it a double subsidy; for it maketh 4s. in the pound a payment. The second is, that this being granted in this sort, other princes hereafter will look for the like; so we shall put an ill precedent upon ourselves and to our posterity; and in histories it is to be observed that of all nations the English care not to be subject, base, taxable, etc.

The manner of supply may be by levy or imposition when need shall most require. So when her Majesty's coffers are empty, they may be imbursed by these means.

THE STATE OF MONARCHY & THE DIVINE RIGHT OF KINGS

JAMES I (OF ENGLAND)

WHITEHALL: 21 MARCH, 1609

THE State of Monarchy is the supremest thing upon earth; for Kings are not only God's Lieutenants upon earth, and sit upon God's throne, but even by God himself they are called Gods. There be three principal similitudes that illustrate the state of Monarchy. One taken out of the word of God and the two other out of the grounds of Policy and Philosophy. In the Scriptures Kings are called Gods, and so their power after a certain relation compared to the Divine power. Kings are also compared to Fathers of families: for a King is truly *Parens patriae*, the politic father of his people. And lastly, Kings are compared to the head of this microcosm of the body of man.

Kings are justly called Gods, for that they exercise a manner or resemblance of Divine power upon earth. For if you will consider the Attributes to God, you shall see how they agree in the person of a King. God hath power to create, or destroy, make or unmake at his pleasure, to give life or send death, to judge all, and to be judged nor accountable to none. To raise low things, and to make high things low at his pleasure, and to God are both soul and body due. And the like power have Kings: they make and unmake their subjects: they have power of raising, and casting down: of life and of death: Judges over all their subjects, and in all causes, and yet accountable to none but God only. They have power to exalt low things, and abase high things, and make of their subjects like men at the Chess. A pawn to take a Bishop or a Knight, and to cry up or down any of their subjects, as they do their money. And to the King is due both the affection of the soul, and the service of the body of his subjects: And therefore that reverend Bishop here amongst you, though I hear that by divers he was mistaken or not well understood, yet did he preach both learnedly and truly anent this point concerning the power of a King. For what he spake of a King's power in *Abstracto*, is most true in Divinity. For to Emperors, or Kings that are Monarchs, their subjects' bodies and goods are due for their defence and maintenance. But if I had been in his place, I would only have added two words, which would have cleared all: For after I had told as a Divine, what was due by the subjects to their Kings in general, I would then have concluded as an Englishman, showing this people, that as in general all subjects were bound to relieve their King; so to exhort them, that as we lived in a settled state of a Kingdom which was governed by his own fundamental Laws and Orders, that according thereunto, they were now (being assembled for this purpose in Parliament) to consider how to help such a King as now they had; and that according to the ancient form, and order established in this Kingdom: putting so, a difference between the general power of a King in Divinity, and the settled and established state of this Crown, and Kingdom. And I am sure that the Bishop meant to have done the same, if he had not been straitened by time, which in respect of the greatness of the presence preaching before me, and such an auditory, he durst not presume upon.

As for the Father of a family, they had of old under the Law of Nature *Patriam potestatem*, which was *Potestatem vitae et necis* over their children or family, (I mean such Fathers of families as were the lineal heirs of those families whereof Kings did originally come:) for Kings had their first original from them, who planted and spread themselves in *Colonies* through the world. Now a Father may dispose of his Inheritance to his children, at his pleasure: yea even, disinherit the eldest upon just occasions, and prefer the youngest, according to his liking; make them beggars, or rich at his pleasure; restrain or banish out of his presence, as he finds them give cause of offense, or restore them in favour again with the penitent sinner. So may the King deal with his subjects.

And lastly, as for the head of the natural body, the head hath the power of directing all the members of the body to that use which the judgement in the head thinks most convenient. It may apply sharp cures, or cut off corrupt members, let blood in what proportion it thinks fit, and as the body may spare, but yet is all this power ordained by God *Ad aedificationem, non ad destructionem*. For although God have power as well of destruction, as of creation or maintenance; yet will it not agree with the wisdom of God, to exercise his power in the destruction of nature, and overturning the whole frame of things, since his creatures were made, that his glory might thereby be the better expressed. So were he a foolish father that would disinherit or destroy his children without a cause, or leave off the carefull education of them. And it were an idle head that would in place of physic so poison or phlebotomize the body as might breed a dangerous distemper or destruction thereof.

But now in these our times we are to distinguish between the state of Kings in their first original, and between the state of settled Kings and Monarchs, that do at this time govern in civil Kingdoms. For even as God, during the time of the Old Testament, spake by Oracles, and wrought by Miracles, yet how soon it pleased him to settle a *Church* which was bought, and redeemed by the blood of his only son *Christ*, then was there a cessation of both. He ever after governing his people and Church within the limits of his revealed will. So in the first original of Kings, whereof some had their beginning by Conquest, and some by election of the people, their wills at that time served for Law; yet how soon Kingdoms began to be settled in civility and policy, then did Kings set down their minds by Laws, which are properly made by the King only, but at the rogation of the people, the King's grant being obtained thereunto. And so the King became to be *Lex loquens*, after a sort, binding himself by a double oath to the observation of the fundamental Laws of his Kingdom: *Tacitly*, as by being a King, and so bound to protect as well the people as the Laws of his Kingdom. And *Expressly*, by his oath at his Coronation: So as every just King in a settled Kingdom is bound to observe that paction made to his people by his Laws, in framing his government agreeable thereunto, according to that paction which God made with Noe after the deluge, *Hereafter seed-time, and harvest, cold and heat, summer and winter, and day and night shall not cease so long as the earth remains*. And therefore a King governing in a settled Kingdom, leaves to be a King, and degenerates into a Tyrant as soon as he leaves off to rule according to his Laws. In which case the King's conscience may speak unto him, as the poor widow said to Philip of Macedon; either govern according to your Law, *Aut ne Rex sis*. And though no Christian man ought to allow rebellion of people against their Prince, yet doth God never leave Kings unpunished when they transgress these limits; for in that same psalm where God saith to Kings, *Vos dii estis*, he immediately thereafter concludes, *But ye shall die like men*. The higher we are placed, the greater shall our fall be. *Ut casus sic dolor:* the taller the trees be, the more in danger of the wind; and the tempest beats forest upon the highest mountains. Therefore all Kings that are not tyrants, or perjured, will be glad to bound themselves within the limits of their Laws; and they that persuade them the contrary, are vipers, and pests, both against them and the commonwealth. For it is a great difference between a King's government in a settled State, and what Kings in their original power might do in *Individuo vago*. As for my part, I thank God, I have ever given good proof, that I never had intention to the contrary. And I am sure to go to my grave with that reputation and comfort, that never King was in all his time more careful to have his Laws duly observed, and himself to govern thereafter, than I.

I conclude then this point touching the power of Kings with this Axiom of Divinity, that as to dispute what God may do, is blasphemy, but *quid vult Deus*, that divines may lawfully, and do ordinarily dispute and discuss; for to dispute *A posse ad esse* is both against logic and divinity: so is it sedition in subjects to dispute what a King may do in the height of his power. But just Kings will ever be willing to declare what they will do, if they will not incur the curse of God. I will not be content that my power be disputed upon, but I shall ever be willing to make the reason appear of all my doings, and rule my actions according to my Laws.

THE STATE OF ENGLAND, 1628

SIR JOHN ELIOT

HOUSE OF COMMONS: 3 JUNE, 1628

WE sit here, Sir, as the great Council of the King, and, in that capacity, it is our duty to take into consideration the state and affairs of the kingdom, and when there is occasion to give a true representation of them, by way of counsel and advice, with what we conceive necessary or expedient to be done.

In this consideration, I confess many a sad thought hath affrighted me, and that not only in respect of our dangers from abroad (which yet I know are great, as they have been often pressed and dilated to us), but in respect of our disorders here at home, which do enforce those dangers, and by which they are occasioned. For I believe I shall make it clear to you, that both at first the cause of these dangers were our disorders, and our disorders now are yet our greatest dangers; that not so much the potency of our enemies, as the weakness of ourselves, doth threaten us, so that the saying of one of the Fathers may be assumed by us, *Non tam potentia sua quam negligentia nostra*— "Not so much by their power as by our neglect." Our want of true devotion to Heaven, our insincerity and doubting in religion, our want of councils, our precipitate actions, the insufficiency or unfaithfulness of our generals abroad, ignorance and corruption of our ministers at home, the impoverishing of the sovereign, the oppression and depression of the subject, the exhausting of our treasures, the waste of our provisions, consumption of our ships, destruction of our men—these make the advantage of our enemies, not the reputation of their arms; and if in these there be not reformation, we need no foes abroad. Time itself will ruin us.

To show this more fully, I believe you will all hold it necessary that what I say, should not seem an aspersion on the state or imputation on the government, as I have known such motions misinterpreted. But far is this from me to propose, who have none but clear thoughts of the excellency of the King; nor can I have other ends but the advancement of his Majesty's glory. I shall desire a little of your patience extraordinary, as I lay upon the particulars, which I shall do with what brevity I may, answerable to the importance of the cause and the necessity now upon us; yet with such respect and observation to the time, as I hope it shall not be thought troublesome.

I. For the first, then, our insincerity and doubling in religion, is the greatest and most dangerous disorder of all others. This hath never been unpunished; and of this we have many strong examples of all states and in all times to awe us. What testimony doth it want? Will you have authority of books? Look on the collections of the Committee for Religion; *there* is too clear an evidence. See there the commission procured for composition with the papists of the North! Mark the proceedings thereupon, and you will find them to little less amounting than a toleration in effect: the slight payments, and the easiness of them, will likewise show the favour that is intended. Will you have proofs of *men?* Witness the hopes, witness the presumptions, witness the reports of all the papists generally. Observe the dispositions of commanders, the trust of officers, the confidence in secretaries to employments in this kingdom, in Ireland, and elsewhere. These will all show that it hath too great a certainty. And to this add but the incontrovertible evidence of that All-powerful Hand, which we have felt so sorely, that gave it full assurance, for as the heavens oppose themselves to our impiety, so it is we that first opposed the heavens.

II. For the second, our want of councils, that great disorder in a state under which there can not be stability. If effects may show their causes (as they are often a perfect demonstration of them) our misfortunes, our disasters serve to prove our deficiencies in council, and the consequences they draw with them. If reason be allowed in this dark age, the judgment of dependencies and foresight of contingencies in affairs, do confirm my position. For, if we view ourselves at home, are we in strength, are we in reputation, equal to our ancestors? If we view ourselves abroad, are our friends as many? Are our enemies no more? Do our friends retain their safety and possessions? Do not our enemies enlarge themselves, and gain from them and us? To what council owe we the loss of the Palatinate, where we sacrificed both our honour and our men sent thither, stopping those greater powers appointed for the service, by which it might have been defended? What council gave direction to the late action, whose wounds are yet bleeding, I mean the expedition to Rhé, of which there is yet so sad a memory in all men? What design for us, or advantage to our state, could that impart?

You know the wisdom of your ancestors, and the practice of their times, how they preserved their safeties. We all know, and have as much cause to doubt [i.e. distrust or guard against] as they had, the greatness and ambition of that kingdom, *which the Old World could not satisfy*. Against this greatness and ambition, we likewise know the proceedings of that princess, that never-to-be-forgotten, excellent Queen Elizabeth, whose name, without admiration, falls not into mention even with her enemies. You know how she advanced herself, and how she advanced the nation in glory and in state; how she depressed her enemies, and how she upheld her friends; how she enjoyed a full security, and made those our scorn who now are made our terror.

Some of the principles she built on were these; and if I mistake, let reason and our statesmen contradict me.

First, to maintain, in what she might, a unity in France, that the kingdom, being at peace within itself, might be a bulwark to keep back the power of Spain by land.

Next, to preserve an amity and league between that state and us, that so we might come in aid of the Low Countries [Holland], and by that means receive their ships, and help them by sea.

This triple cord, so working between France, the States [Holland], and England, might enable us, as occasion should require, to give assistance unto others. And by this means, as the experience of that time doth tell us, we were not only free from those fears that now possess and trouble us, but then our names were fearful to our enemies. See now what correspondency our action had with this. Try our conduct by these rules. It did induce, as a necessary consequence, a division in France between the Protestants and their king, of which there is too woful and lamentable experience. It hath made an absolute breach between that state and us, and so entertains us against France, and France in preparation against us, that we have nothing to promise to our neighbours, nay, hardly to ourselves. Next, observe the *time* in which it was attempted, and you shall find it not only varying from those principles, but directly contrary and opposite to those ends; and such, as from the issue and success, rather might be thought a conception of Spain than begotten here with us.

[Here there was an interruption made by Sir Humphrey May, Chancellor of the Duchy, and of the Privy Council, expressing a dislike; but the House ordered Sir John Eliot to go on, whereupon he proceeded thus:]

Mr. Speaker, I am sorry for this interruption, but much more sorry if there hath been occasion on my part. And, as I shall submit myself wholly to your judgment, to receive what censure you may give me, if I have offended, so, in the integrity of my intentions and the clearness of my thoughts, I must still retain this confidence, *that no greatness shall deter me from the duties I owe to the service of my king and country; but that, with a true English heart, I shall discharge myself as faithfully and as really to the extent of my poor power, as any man whose honours or whose offices most strictly oblige him.*

You know the dangers of Denmark, and how much they concern us; what in respect of our alliance and the country; what in the importance of the Sound; what an advantage to our enemies the gain thereof would be! What loss, what prejudice to us by this disunion; we breaking in upon France, France enraged by us, and the Netherlands at amazement between both. Neither could we intend to aid that luckless king [Christian IV., of Denmark], whose loss is our disaster.

Can those, [the King's ministers] that express their trouble at the hearing of these things, and have so often told us in this place of their knowledge in the conjunctures and disjunctions of affairs—can they say they advised in this? Was this an act of council, Mr. Speaker? I have more charity than to think it; and unless they make confession of it themselves, I can not believe it.

III. For the next, the insufficiency and unfaithfulness of our generals (that great disorder abroad), what shall I say? I wish there were not cause to mention it; and, but for the apprehension of the danger that is to come, if the like choice hereafter be not prevented, I could willingly be silent. But my duty to my sovereign, my service to this House, and the safety and honour of my country, are above all respects; and what so nearly trenches to the prejudice of these must not, shall not, be forborne.

At Cadiz, then, in that first expedition we made, when we arrived and found a conquest ready—the Spanish ships, I mean, fit for the satisfaction of a voyage, and of which some of the chiefest then there, themselves have since assured me, that the satisfaction would have been sufficient, either in point of honour or in point of profit—*why was it neglected?* Why was it not achieved, it being granted on all hands how feasible it was?

Afterward, when, with the destruction of some of our men, and the exposure of others, who (though their fortune since has not been such), by chance, came off safe—when, I say, with the loss of our serviceable men, that unserviceable fort was gained, and the whole army landed, *why was there nothing done?* Why was there nothing *attempted?* If nothing was intended, wherefore did they land? If there *was* a service, wherefore were they shipped again? Mr. Speaker, it satisfies me too much [i.e. I am over-satisfied] in this case—when I think of their dry and hungry march into that drunken quarter (for so the soldiers termed it), which was the period [termination] of their journey—that divers of our men being left as a sacrifice to the enemy, *that labor was at an end.*

For the next undertaking, at Rhé, I will not trouble you much; only this, in short. Was not that whole action carried against the judgment and opinion of those officers that were of the council? Was not the first, was not the last, was not all in the landing—in the intrenching—in the continuance there—in the assault—in the retreat—without their assent? Did any advice take place of such as were of the council? If there should be made a particular inquisition thereof, these things will be manifest and more. I will not instance the manifesto that was made, giving the reason of these arms; nor by whom, nor in what manner, nor on what grounds it was published, nor what effects it hath wrought, drawing, as it were, almost the whole world into league against us. Nor will I mention the leaving of the wines, the leaving of the salt, which were in our possession, and of a value, as it is said, to answer much of our expense. Nor will I dwell on that great wonder (which no Alexander or Cæsar ever did), the enriching of the enemy by courtesies when our soldiers wanted help; nor the private intercourse and parleys with the fort, which were continually held. What they intended may be read in the success; and upon due examination thereof, they would not want their proofs.

For the last voyage to Rochelle, there need no observations, it is so fresh in memory; nor will I make an inference or corollary on all. Your own knowledge shall judge what truth or what sufficiency they express.

IV. For the next, the ignorance and corruption of our ministers, where can you miss of instances? If you survey the court, if you survey the country; if the church, if the city be examined; if you observe the bar, if the bench, if the ports, if the shipping, if the land, if the seas—all these will render you variety of proofs; and that in such measure and proportion as shows the greatness of our disease to be such that, if there be not some speedy application for remedy, our case is almost desperate.

Fifthly, Mr. Speaker, I fear I have been too long in these particulars that are past, and am unwilling to offend you; therefore in the rest I shall be shorter, and as to that which concerns the impoverishing of the King, no other arguments will I use than such as all men grant.

The exchequer, you know, is empty, and the reputation thereof gone; the ancient lands are sold; the jewels pawned; the plate engaged; the debts still great; almost all charges, both ordinary and extraordinary, borne up by projects! What poverty can be greater? What necessity so great? What perfect English heart is not almost dissolved into sorrow for this truth?

Sixthly, For the oppression of the subject, which, as I remember, is the next particular I proposed, it needs no demonstration. The whole kingdom is a proof; and for the exhausting of our treasures, that very oppression speaks it. What waste of our provisions, what consumption of our ships, what destruction of our men there hath been. Witness that expedition to Algiers—witness that with Mansfeldt—witness that to Cadiz—witness the next—witness that to Rhé—witness the last (I pray God we may never have-more such witnesses)—witness, likewise, the Palatinate—witness Denmark—witness the Turks—witness the Dunkirkers—witness all! What losses we have sustained! How we are impaired in munitions, in ships, in men!

It is beyond contradiction that we were never so much weakened, nor ever had less hope how to be restored.

These, Mr. Speaker, are our dangers; these are they who do threaten us, and these are, like the Trojan horse, brought in cunningly to surprise us. In these do lurk the strongest of our enemies, ready to issue on us; and if we do not speedily expel them, these are the signs, these are the invitations to others! These will so prepare their entrance that we shall have no means left of refuge or defence. If we have these enemies at home, how can we strive with those that are abroad? If we be free from these, no other can impeach us. Our ancient English virtue (like the old Spartan valour), cleared from these disorders

—our being in sincerity of religion and once made friends with Heaven; having maturity of councils, sufficiency of generals, incorruption of officers, opulency in the King, liberty in the people, repletion in treasure, plenty of provisions, reparation of ships, preservation of men—our ancient English virtue, I say, thus rectified, will secure us; and unless there be a speedy reformation in these, I know now not what hopes or expectations we can have.

These are the things, sir, I shall desire to have taken into consideration; that as we are the great council of the kingdom, and have the apprehension of these dangers, we may truly represent them unto the King, which I conceive we are bound to do by a triple obligation—of duty to God, of duty to his Majesty, and of duty to our country.

And, therefore, I wish it may so stand with the wisdom and judgment of the House, that these things may be drawn into the body of a remonstrance, and in all humility expressed, with a prayer to his Majesty, that for the safety of himself, for the safety of the kingdom, and for the safety of religion, he will be pleased to give us time to make perfect inquisition thereof, or to take them into his own wisdom, and there give them such timely reformation as the necessity and justice of the case doth import.

And thus, sir, with a large affection and loyalty to his Majesty, and with a firm duty and service to my country, I have suddenly (and it may be with some disorder) expressed the weak apprehensions I have, wherein, if I have erred, I humbly crave your pardon, and so submit myself to the censure of the House.

DEFENCE AGAINST IMPEACHMENT FOR HIGH TREASON

THOMAS WENTWORTH, EARL OF STRAFFORD

HOUSE OF LORDS: 13 APRIL, 1641

MY LORDS,—This day I stand before you, charged with high treason. The burden of the charge is heavy, yet far the more so because it hath borrowed the authority of the House of Commons. If they were not interested, I might expect a no less easy, than I do a safe issue. But let neither my weakness plead my innocence, nor their power my guilt. If your Lordships will conceive of my defences as they are in themselves, without reference to either party—and I shall endeavour so to present them—I hope to go hence as clearly justified by you, as I now am in the testimony of a good conscience by myself.

My Lords, I have all along, during this charge, watched to see that poisoned arrow of treason, which some men would fain have feathered in my heart; but, in truth, it hath not been in my quickness to discover any such evil yet within my breast, though now, perhaps, by sinister information, sticking to my clothes.

They tell me of a two-fold treason—one against the Statute, another by the common law; this direct, that consecutive; this individual, that accumulative; this in itself, that by way of construction.

As to this charge of treason, I must and do acknowledge that if I had the least suspicion of my own guilt, I would save your Lordships the pains. I would cast the first stone. I would pass the first sentence of condemnation against myself. And whether it be so or not, I now refer to your Lordships' judgment and deliberation. You, and you only, under the care and protection of my gracious master, are my judges. I shall ever celebrate the providence and wisdom of your noble ancestors, who have put the keys of life and death, so far as concerns you and your posterity, into your own hands. None but your own selves, my Lords, know the rate of your noble blood; none but yourselves must hold the balance in disposing of the same. . . .

If that one article had been proved against me, it contained more weighty matter than all the charges besides. It would not only have been treason, but villainy, to have betrayed the trust of his Majesty's army. But, as the managers have been sparing, by reason of the times, as to insisting on that article, I have resolved to keep the same method, and not utter the least expression which might disturb the happy agreement intended between the two kingdoms. I only admire how I, being an incendiary against the Scots in the twenty-third article, am become a confederate with them in the twenty-eighth article! How could I be charged for betraying Newcastle, and also for fighting with the Scots at Newburne, since fighting against them was no possible means of betraying the town into their hands, but rather to hinder their passage thither! I never advised war any further than, in my poor judgment, it concerned the very life of the King's authority, and the safety and honour of his kingdom. Nor did I ever see that any advantage could be made by a war in Scotland, where nothing could be gained but hard blows. For my part, I honour that nation, but I wish they may ever be under their own climate. I have no desire that they should be too well acquainted with the better soil of England.

My Lords, you see what has been alleged for this constructive, or rather destructive, treason. For my part, I have not the judgment to conceive that such treason is agreeable to the fundamental grounds either of reason or of law. Not of reason, for how can that be treason in the lump or mass, which is not so in any of its parts? or how can that make a thing treasonable which is not so in itself? Not of law, since neither statute, common law nor practice hath, from the beginning of the government, ever mentioned such a thing.

It is hard, my Lords, to be questioned upon a law which cannot be shown! Where hath this fire lain hid for so many hundred years, without smoke to discover it, till it thus bursts forth to consume me and my children? My Lords, do we not live under laws? and must we be punished by laws before they are made? Far better were it to live by no laws at all, but to be governed by those characters of virtue and discretion which Nature hath stamped upon us, than to put this necessity of divination upon a man, and to accuse him of a breach of law before it is a law at all! If a waterman upon the Thames split his boat by grating upon an anchor, and the same have no buoy appended to it, the owner of the anchor is to pay the loss; but if a buoy be set there, every man passeth upon his own peril. Now, where is the mark, where is the token set upon the crime to declare it to be high treason?

My Lords, be pleased to give that regard to the peerage of England as never to expose yourselves to such moot points, such constructive interpretations of law. If there must be a trial of wits, let the subject matter be something else than the lives and honour of peers! It will be wisdom for yourselves and your posterity to cast into the fire those bloody and mysterious volumes of constructive and arbitrary treason, as the primitive Christians did their books of curious arts, and betake yourselves to the plain letter of the law and statute, which telleth what is, and what is not, treason, without being ambitious to be more learned in the art of killing than our forefathers. These gentlemen tell us that they speak in defence of the Commonwealth against my arbitrary laws. Give me leave to say I speak in defence of the Commonwealth against their arbitrary treason!

It is now full two hundred and forty years since any man was touched for this alleged crime to this height before myself. Let us not awaken those sleeping lions to our destruction, by taking up a few musty records that have lain by the walls for so many ages, forgotten or neglected.

My Lords, what is my present misfortune may be for ever yours! It is not the smallest part of my grief that not the crime of treason, but my other sins, which are exceeding many, have brought me to this bar; and, except your Lordships' wisdom provide against it, the shedding of my blood may make way for the tracing out of yours. You, your estates, your posterity, lie at the stake!

For my poor self, if it were not for your Lordships' interest, and the interest of a saint in heaven, who hath left me here two pledges on earth, I should never take the pains to keep up this ruinous cottage of mine. It is loaded with such infirmities that, in truth, I have no great pleasure to carry it about with me any longer. Nor could I ever leave it at a fitter time than this, when I hope that the better part of the world would perhaps think that by my misfortunes I had given a testimony of my integrity to my God, my King, and my country. I thank God I count not the afflictions of the present life to be compared to that glory which is to be revealed in the time to come!

My Lords! my Lords! my Lords! something more I had intended to say, but my voice and my spirit fail me. Only I do, in all humility and submission, cast myself down at your Lordships' feet, and desire that I may be a beacon to keep you from shipwreck. Do not put such rocks in your own way, which no prudence, no circumspection, can eschew or satisfy, but by your utter ruin!

And so, my Lords, even so, with all tranquillity of mind, I submit myself to your decision. And whether your judgment in my case—I wish it were not the case of you all—be for life or for death, it shall be righteous in my eyes, and shall be received with a *Te Deum laudamus*, we give God the praise.

LIBERTY AND DISCIPLINE

CHARLES I

Address to his Troops at Wellington: 1642

[His majesty caused his military orders for the discipline and gov ernment of the army to be read at the head of each regiment; and then, which is not fit ever to be forgotten, putting himself in the middle, where he might be best heard, not much unlike the emperor Trajan, who, when he made Sura great marshal of the empire, gave him a sword, saying, " Receive this sword of me; and if I command as I ought, employ it in my defence; if I do otherwise, draw it against me and take my life from me,"[1] his majesty made this speech to his soldiers:]

Gentlemen, you have heard these orders read: it is your part, in your several places, to observe them exactly. The time cannot be long before we come to action, therefore you have the more reason to be careful: and I must tell you, I shall be very severe in the punishing of those, of what condition soever, who transgress these instructions. I cannot suspect your courage and resolution; your conscience and your loyalty hath brought you hither, to fight for your religion, your King, and the laws of the land. You shall meet with no enemies but traitors, most of them Brownists, Anabaptists, and atheists; such who desire to destroy both Church and State, and who have already condemned you to ruin for being loyal to us. That you may see what use I mean to make of your valour, if it please God to bless it with success, I have thought fit to publish my resolution to you in a Protestation; which when you have heard me make, you will believe you cannot fight in a better quarrel; in which I promise to live and die with you.

[The Protestation his majesty was then pleased to make was in these words:]

I do promise in the presence of Almighty God, and as I hope for his blessing and protection, that I will, to the utmost of my power, defend and maintain *the true reformed Protestant religion established in the Church of England*, and, by the grace of God, in the same will live and die.

[1] Aur. Victor, *De Caesaribus*, c. xi

I desire to govern by the *known laws of the land,* and that the *liberty and property of the subject* may be by them preserved with the same care as my own just rights. And if it please God, by his blessing upon his army, raised for my necessary defence, to preserve me from this rebellion, I do solemnly and faithfully promise, in the sight of God, to maintain the just *privileges and freedom of Parliament,* and to govern by the *known laws of the land* to my utmost power ; and particularly, to observe inviolably *the laws consented to by me this Parliament.* In the mean while, if this time of war, and the great necessity and straits I am now driven to, beget any violation of these, I hope it shall be imputed by God and men to the authors of this war, and not to me, who have so earnestly laboured for the preservation of the peace of this kingdom.

When I willingly fail in these particulars, I will expect no aid or relief from any man, or protection from Heaven. But in this resolution, I hope for the cheerful assistance of all good men, and am confident of God's blessing.

[This Protestation, and the manner and solemnity of making it, gave not more life and encouragement to the little army than it did comfort and satisfaction to the gentry and inhabitants of those parts; into whom the Parliament had infused, that, if his majesty prevailed by force, he would with the same power abolish all those good laws which had been made this Parliament; so that they looked upon this Protestation as a more ample security for their enjoying the benefit of those Acts than the royal assent he had before given. And a more general and passionate expression of affection cannot be imagined than he received by the people of those counties of Derby Stafford, and Shropshire, as he passed, or a better reception than he found at Shrewsbury, into which town he entered on Tuesday the 20th of September.]

PROTECTOR AND PARLIAMENT

OLIVER CROMWELL

HOUSE OF COMMONS: 22 JAN. 1655

GENTLEMEN,—I perceive you are here as the House of Parliament, by your Speaker whom I see here, and by your faces which are in a great measure known to me.

When I first met you in this room, it was to my apprehension the hopefullest day that ever mine eyes saw, as to the considerations of this world. For I did look at, as wrapt-up in you together with myself, the hopes and the happiness of,—though not of the greatest,—yet a very great " People "; and the best People in the world. And truly and unfeignedly I thought it so: as a People that have the highest and clearest profession amongst them of the greatest glory, namely, Religion: as a People that have been, like other Nations, sometimes up and sometimes down in our honour in the world, but yet never so low but we might measure with other Nations:—and a People that have had a stamp upon them from God; God having, as it were, summed-up all our former honour and glory in the things that *are* of glory to Nations, in an Epitome, within these Ten or Twelve years last past! So that we knew one another at home, and are well known abroad.

And if I be not very much mistaken, we were arrived,—as I, and truly I believe as many others, did think,—at a very safe port; where we might sit down and contemplate the Dispensations of God and our Mercies; and might know our Mercies not to have been like to those of the Ancients,—who did make out their peace and prosperity, as they thought, by their own endeavours; who could not say, as we, That all ours were let down to us from God Himself! Whose appearances and providences amongst us are not to be outmatched by any Story. Truly this was our condition. And I know nothing else we had to do, save as Israel was commanded in that most excellent Psalm of David: " The things which we have heard and known, and our fathers have told us, we will not hide them from our children; showing to the generation to come the praises of the Lord, and His strength, and His wonderful works that He hath done. For He established a Testimony in Jacob, and appointed a Law in Israel; which He commanded our fathers that they should make known to their children; that the generation to come might know them, even the children which should be born, who should arise and declare them to *their* children: that they might set their hope in God, and not forget the works of God, but keep His commandments."[1]

This I thought had been a song and a work worthy of England, whereunto you might happily have invited them,—had you had hearts unto it. You had this opportunity fairly delivered unto you. And if a history shall be written of these Times and Transactions, it will be said, it will not be denied, that these things that I have spoken are true! This talent was put into your hands. And I shall recur to that which I said at the first: I came with very great joy and contentment and comfort, the first time I met you in this place. But we and these Nations are, for the present, under some disappointment!—If I had proposed to have played the Orator,—which I never did affect, nor do, nor I hope shall,—I doubt not but upon easy suppositions, which I am persuaded every one among you will grant, we did meet upon such hopes as these.

I met you a second time here: and I confess, at that meeting I had much abatement of my hopes, though not a total frustration. I confess that that which damped my hopes so soon was somewhat that did look like a parricide. It is obvious enough unto you that the then management of affairs did savour of a Not owning,—too-too much savour, I say, of a Not owning of the Authority that called you hither. But God left us not without an expedient that gave a second possibility—Shall I say possibility? It seemed to me a probability—of recovering out of that dissatisfied condition we were all then in, towards some mutuality of satisfaction. And therefore by that Recognition, suiting with the Indenture that returned you hither; to which afterwards was also added your own Declaration,[2] conformable to, and in acceptance of, that expedient:—thereby, I say, you had, though with a little check, another opportunity renewed unto you to have made this Nation as happy as it could have been if everything had smoothly run on from that first hour of your meeting. And indeed,—you will give me liberty of my thoughts and hopes,—I did think, as I have formerly found in that way that I have been engaged in as a soldier, That some

[1] Psalm lxxviii, 3-7.
[2] *Commons Journals* (vii, 368), September 14, 1654.

affronts put upon us, some disasters at the first, have made way for very great and happy successes; and I did not at all despond but the stop put upon you, in like manner, would have made way for a blessing from God. That Interruption being, as I thought, necessary to divert you from violent and destructive proceedings; to give time for better deliberations;—whereby leaving the Government as you found it, you might have proceeded to have made those good and wholesome Laws which the People expected from you, and might have answered the Grievances, and settled those other things proper to you as a Parliament: for which you would have had thanks from all that intrusted you.

What hath happened since that time I have not taken public notice of; as declining to intrench on Parliament privileges. For sure I am you will all bear me witness, That from your entering into the House upon the Recognition, to this very day, you have had no manner of interruption or hindrance of mine in proceeding to what blessed issue the heart of a good man could propose to himself,—to this very day none. You see you have me very much locked up, as to what you have transacted among yourselves, from that time to this. But some things I shall take liberty to speak of to you.

As I may not take notice what you have been doing; so I think I have a very great liberty to tell you That I do not know what you have been doing! I do not know whether you have been alive or dead. I have not once heard from you all this time; I have not: and that you all know. If that be a fault that I have not, surely it hath not been mine! —If I have had any melancholy thoughts, and have sat down by them,—why might it not have been very lawful for me to think that I was a Person judged unconcerned in all these businesses? I can assure you I have not so reckoned myself! Nor did I reckon myself unconcerned in you. And so long as any just patience could support my expectation, I would have waited to the uttermost to have received from you the issue of your consultations and resolutions.—I have been careful of your safety, and the safety of those that you represented, to whom I reckon myself a servant.

But what messages have I disturbed you withal? What injury or indignity hath been done, or offered, either to your persons or to any privileges of Parliament, since you sat? I looked at myself as strictly obliged by my Oath, since your recognising the Government in the authority of which you were called hither and sat, To give you all possible security, and to keep you from any unparliamentary interruption. Think you I could not say more upon this subject, if I listed to expatiate thereupon? But because my actions plead for me, I shall say no more of this. I say, I have been caring for *you*, for your quiet sitting; caring for your privileges, as I said before, that they might not be interrupted; have been seeking of God, from the great God a blessing upon you, and a blessing upon these Nations. I have been consulting if possibly I might, in any-thing, promote, in my place, the real good of this Parliament, of the hopefulness of which I have said so much unto you. And I did think it to be my business rather to see the utmost issue, and what God would produce by you, than unseasonably to intermeddle with you.

But, as I said before, I have been caring for you, and for the peace and quiet of these Nations: indeed I have; and that I shall a little presently manifest unto you. And it leadeth me to let you know somewhat,—which, I fear, I fear, will be, through some interpretation, a little too justly put upon *you;* whilst you have been employed as you have been, and,—in all that time expressed in the Government, in that Government, I say in that Government,—have brought forth nothing that you yourselves say *can* be taken notice of without infringement of your privileges.[1] I will tell you somewhat, which, if it be not news to you, I wish you had taken very serious consideration of. If it be news, I wish I had acquainted you with it sooner. And yet if any man will ask me why I did it not, the reason is given already: Because I did make it my business to give you no interruption.

There be some trees that will not grow under the shadow of other trees: There be some that choose,—a man may say so by way of allusion,—to thrive under the shadow of other trees. I will tell you what hath thriven,—I will not say what you have *cherished*, under your shadow; that were too hard. Instead of Peace and Settlement,—instead of mercy and truth being brought together, and righteousness and peace kissing each

[1] An embarrassed sentence; characteristic of his Highness. "You have done nothing noticeable upon this 'Somewhat' that I am about to speak of,—nor, indeed, it seems upon *any* Somewhat,—and *this* was one you may, without much 'interpretation,' be blamed for doing nothing upon." "Government" means *Instrument of Government:* "the time expressed" therein is *Five Months*,—now, by my way of calculating it, expired! Which may account for the embarrassed iteration of the phrase, on his Highness's part.—(*Carlyle's note.*)

other, by your reconciling the Honest People of these Nations, and settling the woful distempers that are amongst us; which had been glorious things and worthy of Christians to have proposed,—weeds and nettles, briers and thorns have thriven under your shadow! Dissettlement and division, discontent and dissatisfaction; together with real dangers to the whole,—have been more multiplied within these five months of your sitting, than in some years before! Foundations have also been laid for the future renewing of the Troubles of these Nations by all the enemies of them abroad and at home. Let not these words seem too sharp: for they are true as any mathematical demonstrations are or can be. I say, the enemies of the peace of these Nations abroad and at home, the discontented humours throughout these Nations,—which products I think no man will grudge to call by that name, of briers and thorns,—*they* have nourished themselves under your shadow!

And that I may clearly be understood: They have taken their opportunities from your sitting, and from the hopes they had, which with easy conjecture they might take up and conclude that there would be no Settlement; and they have framed their designs, preparing for the execution of them accordingly. Now whether,—which appertains not to me to judge of, on their behalf,—they had any occasion ministered for this, and from whence they had it, I list not to make any scrutiny or search. But I will say this: I think they had it not from me. I am sure they had not from me. From whence they had, is not my business now to discourse: but *that* they had, is obvious to every man's sense. What preparations thay have made, to be executed in such a season as they thought fit to take their opportunity from: that I know, not as men know things by conjecture, but by certain demonstrable knowledge. That they have been for some time past furnishing themselves with arms; nothing doubting but they should have a day for it; and verily believing that, whatsoever their former disappointments were, they should have more done for them by and from our own divisions, than they were able to do for themselves. I desire to be understood that, in all I have to say of this subject, you will take it that I have no reservation in my mind,—as I have not,—to mingle things of guess and suspicion with things of fact; but " that " the things I am telling of are fact; things of evident demonstration.

These weeds, briers and thorns,—they have been preparing, and have brought their designs to some maturity, by the advantages given to them, as aforesaid, from your sittings and proceedings. But by the Waking Eye that watched over that Cause that God will bless, they have been, and yet are, disappointed. And having mentioned that Cause, I say, that slighted Cause,—let me speak a few words in behalf thereof; though it may seem too long a digression. Whosoever despiseth it, and will say, It is *non Causa pro Causa,* " a Cause without a Cause," —the All-searching Eye before mentioned will find out that man; and will judge him, as one that regardeth not the works of God nor the operations of His hands ! For which God hath threatened that He will cast men down, and not build them up. That man who, because he can dispute, will tell us he knew not when the Cause began, nor where it is; but modelleth it according to his own intellect; and submits not to the Appearances of God in the World; and therefore lifts up his heel against God, and mocketh at all His providences; laughing at the observations, made up not without reason and the Scriptures, and by the quickening and teaching Spirit which gives life to these other;— calling such observations " enthusiasms ": such men, I say, no wonder if they " stumble and fall backwards, and be broken and snared and taken,"[1] by the things of which they are so wilfully and maliciously ignorant ! The Scriptures say, " The Rod has a voice, and He will make Himself known by the judgments which He executeth." And do we not think He will, and does, by the providences of mercy and kindness which He hath for His People and their just liberties; " whom He loves as the apple of His eye " ? Doth He not by them manifest Himself ? And is He not thereby also seen giving kingdoms for them, " giving men for them, and people for their lives,"—as it is in Isaiah Forty-third ?[2] Is not this as fair a lecture and as clear speaking, as anything our dark reason, left to the letter of the Scriptures, can collect from them ? By this voice has God spoken very loud on behalf of His People, by judging their enemies in the late War, and restoring them a liberty to worship, with the freedom of their consciences, and freedom in estates and persons when they do so. And thus we have found the Cause of God by the works of God; which are the testimony of God. Upon which rock whosoever splits shall suffer shipwreck. But it is your glory,—and it is mine, if I have any in the world concerning the Interest of those that have an interest in a better world,—

---

[1] Isaiah xxviii, 13.
[2] Isaiah xliii, 3, 4.

it is my glory that I know a Cause which yet we have *not* lost; but do hope we shall take a little pleasure rather to lose our lives than lose! But you will excuse this long digression.

I say unto you, Whilst you have been in the midst of these Transactions, that Party, that Cavalier Party,—I could wish some of them had thrust-in here, to have heard what I say,—have been designing and preparing to put this Nation in blood again, with a witness. But because I am confident there are none of that sort here, therefore I shall say the less to that. Only this I must tell you: They have been making great preparations of arms; and I do believe it will be made evident to you that they have raked-out many thousands of arms, even all that this City could afford, for divers months last past. But it will be said, "May we not arm ourselves for the defence of our houses? Will anybody find fault for that?" Not for that. But the reason for *their* doing so hath been as explicit, and under as clear proof, as the fact of doing so. For which I hope, by the justice of the land, some will, in the face of the Nation, answer it with their lives: and then the business will be pretty well out of doubt.—Banks of money have been framing, for these and other suchlike uses. Letters have been issued with Privy-seals, to as great Persons as most are in the Nation, for the advance of money,—which "Letters" have been discovered to us by the Persons themselves. Commissions for Regiments of horse and foot, and command of Castles, have been likewise given from Charles Stuart, since your sitting. And what the general insolences of that Party have been, the Honest People have been sensible of, and can very well testify.

It hath not only been thus. But as in a quinsy or pleurisy, where the humour fixeth in one part, give it scope, all " disease " will gather to that place, to the hazarding of the whole; and it is natural to do so till it destroy life in that person on whomsoever this befalls. So likewise will *these* diseases take accidental causes of aggravation of their distemper. And this was that which I did assert, That they have taken accidental causes for the growing and increasing of those distempers,—as much as would have been in the natural body if timely remedy were not applied. And indeed things were come to that pass,—in respect of which I shall give you a particular account,—that no mortal physician, if the Great Physician had not stepped in, could have cured the distemper. Shall I lay this upon your account, or my own? I am sure I can lay it upon God's account: That if He had not stepped in, the disease had been mortal and destructive!

And what is all this? "What are these new diseases that have gathered to this point?" Truly I must needs still say: "A company of men like briers and thorns"; and worse, if worse can be. Of another sort than those before mentioned to you. These also have been and yet are endeavouring to put us into blood and into confusion; more desperate and dangerous confusion than England ever yet saw. And I must say, as when Gideon commanded his son to fall upon Zeba and Zalmunna, and slay them, they thought it more noble to die by the hand of a man than of a stripling,—which shows there is some contentment in the hand by which a man falls: so it is some satisfaction if a Commonwealth must perish, that it perish by men, and not by the hands of persons differing little from beasts! That if it must needs suffer, it should rather suffer from rich men than from poor men, who, as Solomon says, "when they oppress, leave nothing behind them, but are as a sweeping rain." Now such as these also are grown up under your shadow. But it will be asked, What have they done? I hope, though they pretend "Commonwealth's Interest," they have had no encouragement from you; but have, as in the former case, rather taken it than that you have administered any cause unto them for so doing. "Any cause" from delays, from hopes that this Parliament would not settle, from Pamphlets mentioning strange Votes and Resolves of yours; which I hope did abuse you! But thus you see that, whatever the grounds were, these have been the effects. And thus I have laid these things before you; and you and others will be easily able to judge how far you are concerned.

"What these men have done?" They also have laboured to pervert, where they could, and as they could, the Honest-meaning People of the Nation. They have laboured to engage some in the Army:—and I doubt not that only they, but some others also, very well known to you, have helped to this work of debauching and dividing the Army. They have, they have! I would be loath to say Who, Where, and How? much more loath to say they were any of your own number. But I can say: Endeavours have been made to put the Army into a distemper, and to feed that which is the worst humour in the Army. Which though it was not as mastering humour, yet these took advantage from delay of the Settlement, and the practices before mentioned, and the stopping of the pay of the Army, to run us into Free-quarter, and to bring us into the inconveniences most to be feared and avoided.—What if I am able to make it appear in fact, That some amongst you have run into the City of London, to persuade to Petitions and Addresses to you for reversing your own Votes that you have passed? Whether these practices were in favour of your Liberties, or tended to beget hopes of Peace and Settlement from you; and whether debauching the Army in England, as is before expressed, and starving it, and putting it upon Free-quarter, and occasioning and necessitating the greatest part thereof in Scotland to march into England, leaving the remainder thereof to have their throats cut there; and kindling by the rest a fire in our own bosoms, were for the advantage of affairs here, let the world judge!

This I tell you also: That the correspondence held with the Interest of the Cavaliers, by that Party of men called Levellers, who call themselves Commonwealth's-men, is in our hands. Whose Declarations were framed to that purpose, and ready to be published at the time of their projected common Rising; whereof, "I say," we are possessed; and for which we have the confession of themselves now in custody; who confess also they built their hopes upon the assurance they had of the Parliament's not agreeing to a Settlement;—whether these humours have not nourished themselves under your boughs, is the subject of my present discourse; and I think I shall say not amiss, if I affirm it to be so. And I must say it again, That that which hath been their advantage, thus to raise disturbance, had been by the loss of those golden opportunities which God hath put into your hands for Settlement. Judge you whether these things were thus, or not, when you first sat down. I am sure things were not thus! There was a very great peace and sedateness throughout these Nations; and great expectations of a happy Settlement. Which I remembered to you at the beginning in my Speech; and hoped that you would have entered on your business as you found it.

There was a Government already in the possession of the People,—I say a Government in the possession of the People, for many months. It hath now been exercised near Fifteen Months: and if it were needful that I should tell you *how* it came into their possession, and how willingly they received it; how all Law and Justice were distributed from it, in every respect, as to life, liberty and estate; how it was owned by

God, as being the dispensation of His providence after Twelve
Years War; and sealed and witnessed unto by the People,—
I should but repeat what I said in my last Speech unto you
in this place: and therefore I forbear. When you were
entered upon this Government; ravelling into it—You know
I took no notice what you were doing—If you had gone upon
that foot of account, To have made such good and wholesome
provisions for the Good of the People of these Nations as were
wanted; for the settling of such matters in things of Religion as
would have upheld and given countenance to a Godly Ministry,
and yet as would have given a just liberty to godly men of
different judgments,—" to " men of the same faith with them
that you call the Orthodox Ministry in England, as it is well
known the Independents are, and many under the form of Bap-
tism, who are sound in the faith, and though they may perhaps
be different in judgment in some lesser matters, yet as true
Christians both looking for salvation only by faith in the blood
of Christ, men professing the fear of God, and having recourse
to the name of God as to a strong tower,—I say you might have
had opportunity to have settled peace and quietness amongst
all professing Godliness; and might have been instrumental
if not to have healed the breaches, yet to have kept the Godly
of all judgments from running one upon another; and by
keeping them from being overrun by a Common Enemy,
" have " rendered them and these Nations both secure, happy
and well satisfied.

Are these things done; or any things towards them? Is
there not yet upon the spirits of men a strange itch? Nothing
will satisfy them unless they can press their finger upon their
brethren's consciences, to pinch them there. To do this was
no part of the Contest we had with the Common Adversary.
For " indeed " Religion was not the thing at first contested for
" at all ":[1] but God brought it to that issue at last; and gave it
unto us by way of redundancy; and at last it proved to be that
which was most dear to us. And wherein consisted this more
than in obtaining that liberty from the tyranny of the Bishops
to all species of Protestants to worship God according to their
own light and consciences? For want of which many of our
brethren forsook their native countries to seek their bread
from strangers, and to live in howling wildernesses; and for

[1] Power of the Militia was the point upon which the actual War
began. A statement not false ; yet truer in form than it is in essence.
—(Carlyle.)

which also many that remained here were imprisoned, and
otherwise abused and made the scorn of the Nation. Those
that were sound in the faith, how proper was it for them to
labour for liberty, for a just liberty, that men might not be
trampled upon for their consciences! Had not they themselves laboured, but lately, under the weight of persecution?
And was it fit for them to sit heavy upon others? Is it ingenuous to ask liberty, and not to give it? What greater hypocrisy
than for those who were oppressed by the Bishops to become
the greatest oppressors themselves, so soon as their yoke was
removed? I could wish that they who call for liberty now also
had not too much of that spirit, if the power were in their
hands!—As for profane persons, blasphemers, such as preach
sedition; the contentious railers, evil-speakers, who seek by
evil words to corrupt good manners; persons of loose conversation,—punishment from the Civil Magistrate ought to
meet with these. Because, if they pretend conscience; yet
walking disorderly and not according but contrary to the
Gospel, and even to natural lights,—they are judged of all.
And their sins being open, make them subjects of the Magistrate's sword, who ought not to bear it in vain.—The discipline
of the Army *was* such, that a man would not be suffered to
remain there, of whom we could take notice he was guilty of
such practices as these.

And therefore how happy would England have been, and you
and I, if the Lord had led you on to have settled upon such
good accounts as these are, and to have discountenanced such
practices as the other, and left men in disputable things free to
their own consciences! Which was well provided for by the
" Instrument of " Government; and liberty left to provide
against what was apparently evil. Judge you, Whether the
contesting for things that were provided for by this Government
hath been profitable expense of time, 'for the good of these
Nations! By means whereof you may see you have wholly
elapsed your time, and done just nothing!—I will say this to
you, in behalf of the Long Parliament: That, had such an
expedient as this Government been proposed to them; and
could they have seen the Cause of God thus provided for; and
been, by debates, enlightened in the grounds " of it," whereby
the difficulties might have been cleared " to them," and the
reason of the whole enforced, and the circumstances of time
and persons, with the temper and disposition of the People,
and affairs both abroad and at home when it was undertaken

might have been well weighed "by them": I think in my conscience,—well as they were thought to love their seats,—they would have proceeded in another manner than you have done! And *not* have exposed things to these difficulties and hazards they now are at; nor given occasion to leave the People so dissettled as they now are. Who, I dare say, in the soberest and most judicious part of them, did expect, not a question, but a doing of things in pursuance of the "Instrument of" Government. And if I be not misinformed, very many of you came up with this satisfaction; having had time enough to weigh and consider the same.

And when I say "such an expedient as this Government,"—wherein I dare assert there is a just Liberty to the People of God, and the just Rights of the People in these Nations provided for,—I can put the issue thereof upon the clearest reason; whatsoever any go about to suggest to the contrary. But this not being the time and place of such an averment, "I forbear at present." For satisfaction's sake herein, enough is said in a Book entituled "*A State of the Case of the Commonwealth*," published in January, 1653. And for myself, I desire not to keep my place in this Government an hour longer than I may preserve England in its just rights, and may protect the People of God in such a just Liberty of their Consciences as I have already mentioned. And therefore if this Parliament have judged things to be otherwise than as I have stated them,—it had been huge friendliness between persons who had such a reciprocation in so great concernments to the public, for *them* to have convinced me in what particulars therein my error lay! Of which I never yet had a word from you! But if, instead thereof, your time has been spent in setting-up somewhat else, upon another bottom than this stands "upon,"—it looks as if the laying grounds for a *quarrel* had rather been designed than to give the People *settlement*. If it be thus, it's *well* your labours have not arrived to any maturity at all!

This Government called you hither; the constitution thereof being limited so,—a Single Person and a Parliament. And this was thought most agreeable to the general sense of the Nation;—having had experience enough, by trial, of other conclusions; judging this most likely to avoid the extremes of Monarchy on the one hand, and of Democracy on the other;—and yet not to found *Dominium in Gratia* "either." And if so, then certainly to make the Authority more than a mere notion, it was requisite that it should be as it is in this

" Frame of " Government; which puts it upon a true and equal balance. It has been already submitted to the judicious, true and honest People of this Nation, Whether the balance be not equal? And what their judgment is, is visible—by submission to it; by acting upon it; by restraining their Trustees from meddling with it. And it neither asks nor needs any better ratification? But when Trustees in Parliament shall, by experience, find any evil in any parts of this " Frame of " Government, " a question " referred by the Government itself to the consideration of the Protector and Parliament,—of which evil or evils Time itself will be the best discoverer:—how can it be reasonably imagined that a Person or Persons, coming in by election, and standing under such obligations, and so limited, and so necessitated by oath to govern for the People's good, and to make *their* love, under God, the best underpropping and only safe footing:—how can it, I say, be imagined that the present or succeeding Protectors will refuse to agree to alter any such thing in the Government as may be found to be for the good of the People? Or to recede from anything which he might be convinced casts the balance too much to the Single Person? And although, for the present, the keeping-up and having in his power the Militia seems the hardest " condition," yet if the power of the Militia should be yielded up at such a time as this, when there is as much need of it to keep this Cause (now most evidently impugned by all Enemies), as there was to *get* it " for the sake of this Cause ":—what would become of us all! Or if it should not be equally placed in him and the Parliament, but yielded up *at any time*—it determines his power either for doing the good he ought, or hindering Parliaments from perpetuating themselves; from imposing what Religion they please on the consciences of men, or what Government they please upon the Nation. Thereby subjecting us to dissettlement in every Parliament, and to the desperate consequences thereof. And if the Nation *shall* happen to fall into a blessed Peace, how easily and certainly will their charge be taken off, and their forces be disbanded! And then where will the danger be to have the Militia thus stated? What if I should say: If there *be* a disproportion, or disequality as to the power, it is on the other hand!—

And if this be so, Wherein have you had cause to quarrel? What demonstrations have you held forth to settle me to your opinion? I would you had made me so happy as to have let me known your grounds! I have made a free and ingenuous confession of my faith to *you*. And I could have wished it had been in your hearts to have agreed that some friendly and cordial debates might have been toward mutual conviction. Was there none amongst you to move such a thing? No fitness to listen to it? No desire of a right understanding? If it be not folly in me to listen to Town-talk, such things *have* been proposed; and rejected, with stiffness and severity, once and again. Was it not likely to have been more advantageous to the good of this Nation? I will say this to you for myself; and to that I have my conscience as a thousand witnesses, and I have my comfort and contentment in it; and I have the witness too of divers here, who I think truly would scorn to own me in a lie: That I would not have been averse to any alteration, of the good of which I might have been convinced. Although I could not have agreed to the taking it off the foundation on which it stands; namely, the acceptance and consent of the People.

I will not presage what you have been about, or doing, in all this time. Nor do I love to make conjectures. But I must tell you this: That as I undertook this Government in the simplicity of my heart and as before God, and to do the part of an honest man, and to be true to the Interest,—which in my conscience " I think " is dear to many of you; though it is not always understood what God in His wisdom may hide from us, as to Peace and Settlement:—so I can say that no particular interest, either of myself, estate, honour or family, are, or have been, prevalent with me to this undertaking. For if you had, upon the old Government, offered me this one, this one thing,—I speak as thus advised, and before God; as having been to this day of this opinion; and this hath been my constant judgment, well known to many who hear me speak:—if, " I say," this one thing had been inserted, this one thing, That the Government should have been placed in my Family hereditary, I would have rejected it! And I could have done no other according to my present conscience and light. I will tell you my reason;—though I cannot tell what God *will* do with me, nor with you, nor with the Nation, for throwing away precious opportunities committed to us.

This hath been my principle; and I liked it, when this Government came first to be proposed to me, That it puts us off that hereditary way. Well looking that God hath declared what Government He delivered to the Jews; and that He placed it upon such Persons as had been instrumental for the Conduct and Deliverance of His People. And considering that Promise in *Isaiah*, " That God would give Rulers as at the first, and Judges as at the beginning," I did not know but that God might " now " begin,—and though, at present, with a most unworthy person; yet, as to the future, it might be after this manner; and I thought this might usher it in! I am speaking as to my judgment against making Government hereditary. To have men chosen, for their love to God, and to Truth and Justice; and not to have it hereditary. For as it is in the *Ecclesiastes:* " Who knoweth whether he may beget a fool or a wise man? " Honest or not honest, whatever they be, they must come in, on that plan; because the Government is made a patrimony!—And this I perhaps do declare with too much earnestness; as being my own concernment;—and know not what place it may have in your hearts, and in those of the Good People in the Nation. But however it be, I have comfort in this my truth and plainness.

I have thus told you my thoughts; which truly I have declared to you in the fear of God, as knowing He will not be mocked; and in the strength of God, as knowing and rejoicing that I am supported in my speaking;—especially when I do not form or frame things without the compass of integrity and honesty; so that my own conscience gives me not the lie to what I say. And then in what I say, I can rejoice.

Now to speak a word or two to you. Of that, I must profess in the name of the same Lord, and wish there had been no cause that I should have thus spoken to you! I told you that I came with joy the first time; with some regret the second; yet now I speak with most regret of all! I look upon you as having among you many persons that I could lay down my life individually for. I could, through the grace of God, desire to lay down my life for you. So far am I from having an unkind or unchristian heart towards you in your particular capacities; I have this indeed as a work most incumbent upon me: this of speaking these things to you. I consulted what might be my duty in such a day as this; casting up all considerations. I must confess, as I told you, that I did think occasionally, This Nation had suffered extremely in the respects mentioned; as also in the disappointment of their expectations of that justice which was due to them by your sitting thus long. " Sitting thus long "; and what have you brought forth? I did not nor cannot comprehend what it is. I would be loath to call it a Fate; that were too paganish a word. But there hath been Something in it that we had not in our expectations.

I did think also, for myself, That I am like to meet with difficulties; and that this Nation will not, as it is fit it should not, be deluded with *pretexts* of Necessity in that great business of raising of Money. And were it not that I can make some dilemmas upon which to resolve some things of my conscience, judgment and actions, I should shrink at the very prospect of my encounters. Some of them are general, some are more special. Supposing this Cause or this Business must be carried on, it is either of God or of man. If it be of man, I would I had never touched it with a finger. If I had not had a hope fixed in me that this Cause and this Business was of God, I would many years ago have run from it. If it be of God, He will bear it up. If it be of man, it will tumble; as everything that hath been of man since the world began hath done. And what are all our Histories, and other Traditions of Actions in former times, but God manifesting Himself, that He hath shaken, and tumbled down and trampled upon, everything that He had not planted? And as this is, so let the All-wise God deal with it. If this be of human structure and invention, and if it be an old Plotting and Contriving to bring things to this Issue, and that they are not the Births of Providence,—then they will tumble. But if the Lord take pleasure in England, and if He will do us good,—He is very able to bear us up! Let the difficulties be whatsoever they will, we shall in His strength be able to encounter with them. And I bless God I have been inured to difficulties; and I never found God failing when I trusted in Him. I can laugh and sing, in my heart, when I speak of these things to you or elsewhere. And though some may think it is an hard thing To raise Money without Parliamentary Authority upon this Nation; yet I have another argument to the Good People of this Nation, if they would be safe, and yet have no better principle: Whether they prefer the having of their will though it be their destruction, rather than comply with things of Necessity? That will excuse me. But I should wrong my native country to suppose this.

For I look at the People of these Nations as the blessing of the Lord: and they are a People blessed by God. They have been so; and they will be so, by reason of that immortal seed which hath been, and is, among them; those Regenerated Ones in the land, of several judgments; who are all the Flock of Christ, and lambs of Christ. " His," though perhaps under many unruly passions, and troubles of spirit; whereby they give disquiet to themselves and others: yet they are not so to God; since to us He is a God of other patience; and He will own the least of Truth in the hearts of His People. And the People being the blessing of God, they will not be so angry but they will prefer their safety to their passions, and their real security to forms, when Necessity calls for Supplies. Had they not well been acquainted with this principle, they had never seen this day of Gospel Liberty.

But if any man shall object, " It is an easy thing to talk of Necessities when men create Necessities: would not the Lord Protector make himself great and his family great? Doth not he make these Necessities? And then he will come upon the People with his argument of Necessity! "—This was something hard indeed. But I have *not* yet known what it is to " make Necessities," whatsoever the thoughts or judgments of men are. And I say this, not only to this Assembly, but to the world, That the man liveth not who can come to me and charge me with having, in these great Revolutions, " made Necessities." I challenge even all that fear God. And as God hath said, " My glory I will not give unto another," let men take heed and be twice advised how they call His Revolutions, the things of God, and His working of things from one period to another,— how, I say, they call them Necessities of men's creation! For by so doing, they do vilify and lessen the works of God, and rob Him of His glory; which He hath said He will not give unto another, nor suffer to be taken from Him! We know what God did to Herod, when he was applauded and did not acknowledge God. And God knoweth what He will do with men, when they call His Revolutions human designs, and so detract from His glory. These issues and events have not been forecast; but were sudden Providences in things: whereby carnal and worldly men are enraged; and under and at which, many, and I fear some good men, have murmured and repined, because disappointed of their mistaken fancies. But still all these things have been the wise disposings of the Almighty; though instruments have had their passions and frailties. And I think it is an honour to God to acknowledge the Necessities to have been of God's imposing, when truly they have been so, as indeed they have. Let us take our sin in our actions to ourselves; it's much more safe than to judge things so contingent, as if there were not a God that ruled the Earth!

We know the Lord hath poured this Nation from vessel to vessel, till He poured it into your lap, when you came first together. I am confident that it came so into your hands; and was not judged by you to be from counterfeited or feigned Necessity, but by Divine Providence and Dispensation. And this I speak with more earnestness, because I speak for God and not for men. I would have any man to come and tell of the Transactions that have been, and of those periods of time wherein God hath made these Revolutions; and find where he can fix a feigned Necessity! I could recite particulars, if either my strength would serve me to speak, or yours to hear. If that you would resolve the great Hand of God in His great Dispensations, you would find that there is scarce a man who fell off, at any period of time when God had any work to do, who can give God or His work at this day a good word.

"It was," say some, "the cunning of the Lord Protector,"—I take it to myself,—"it was the craft of such a man, and his plot, that hath brought it about!" And, as they say in other countries, "There are five or six cunning men in England that have skill; they do all these things." Oh, what blasphemy is this! Because men that are without God in the world, and walk not with Him, know not what it is to pray or believe, and to receive returns from God, and to be spoken unto by the Spirit of God,—who speaks without a Written Word sometimes, yet according to it! God hath spoken heretofore in divers manners. Let Him speak as He pleaseth. Hath He not given us liberty, nay, is it not our duty, To go to the Law and the Testimony? And there we shall find that there *have* been impressions, in extraordinary cases, as well without the Written Word as with it. And therefore there is no difference in the thing thus asserted from truths generally received,—except we will exclude the Spirit; without whose concurrence all other teachings are ineffectual. He doth speak to the hearts and consciences of men; and leadeth them to His Law and Testimony, and there "also" He speaks to them: and so gives them double teachings. According to that of Job: "God speaketh once, yea twice"; and to that of David: "God hath spoken once, yea twice have I heard this." These men that live upon their *mumpsimus* and *sumpsimus,* their Masses and Service-books, their dead and carnal worship,—no marvel if they be strangers to God, and to the works of God, and to spiritual dispensations. And because *they* say and believe thus, must we do so too? We, in this land, have been otherwise instructed; even by the Word, and Works, and Spirit of God.

To say that men bring forth these things when God doth them,—judge you if God will bear this? I wish that every sober heart, though he hath had temptations upon him of deserting this Cause of God, yet may take heed how he provokes and falls into the hands of the Living God by such blasphemies as these! According to the Tenth of the *Hebrews:* " If we sin wilfully after that we have received the knowledge of the truth, there remains no more sacrifice for sin."   " A terrible word." It was spoken to the Jews who, having professed Christ, apostatised from Him. What then? Nothing but a fearful " falling into the hands of the Living God ! "—They that shall attribute to this or that person the contrivances and production of those mighty things God hath wrought in the midst of us; and " fancy " that they have not been the Revolutions of Christ Himself, " upon whose shoulders the government is laid,"—they speak against God, and they fall under His hands without a Mediator. That is, if we deny the Spirit of Jesus Christ the glory of all His works in the world; by which He rules kingdoms, and doth administer, and is the rod of His strength,—we provoke the Mediator: and He may say: I will leave you to God, I will not intercede for you; let Him tear you to pieces! I will leave thee to fall into God's hands; thou deniest me my sovereignty and power committed to me; I will not intercede nor mediate for thee; thou fallest into the hands of the Living God !—Therefore whatsoever you may judge men for, howsoever you may say, " This is cunning, and politic, and subtle,"—take heed again, I say, how you judge of His Revolutions as the product of men's inventions !—I may be thought to press too much upon this theme. But I pray God it may stick upon your hearts and mine. The worldly-minded man knows nothing of this, but is a stranger to it; and thence his atheisms, and murmurings at instruments, yea, repining at God Himself. And no wonder; considering the Lord hath done such things amongst us as have not been known in the world these thousand years, and yet notwithstanding is not owned by us !

There is another Necessity, which you have put upon us, and we have not sought. I appeal to God, Angels and Men,—if I shall " now " raise money according to the Article in the Government, whether I am not compelled to do it ! Which " Government " had power to call you hither; and did:—and instead of seasonably providing for the Army, you have laboured to overthrow the Government, and the Army is now upon Free-quarter! And you would never so much as let me hear a tittle from you concerning it. Where is the fault? Has it not been as if you had a purpose to put this extremity upon us and the Nation? I hope this was not in your minds. I am not willing to judge so:—but such is the state into which we are reduced. By the designs of some in the Army who are now in custody, it was designed to get as many of them as possible,—through discontent for want of money, the Army being in a barren country, near thirty weeks behind in pay, and upon other specious pretences,—to march for England out of Scotland; and, in discontent, to seize their General there [General Monk], a faithful and honest man, that so another [Colonel Overton] might head the Army. And all this opportunity taken from your delays. Whether will this be a thing of feigned Necessity? What could it signify, but " The Army are in discontent already; and we will make them live upon stones; we will make them cast-off their governors and discipline?" What can be said to this? I list not to unsaddle myself, and put the fault upon your backs. Whether it hath been for the good of England, whilst men have been talking of this thing or the other, and pretending liberty and many good words,—whether it has been as it should have been? I am confident you cannot think it has. The Nation will not think so. And if the worst should be made of things, I know not what the Cornish men nor the Lincolnshire men may think, or other Counties; but I believe they will all think *they are not safe*. A temporary suspension of " caring for the greatest liberties and privileges " (if it were so, which is denied) would not have been of such damage as the not providing against Free-quarter hath run the Nation upon. And if it be my " liberty " to walk abroad in the fields, or to take a journey, yet it is not my wisdom to do so when my house is on fire!

I have troubled you with a long Speech; and I believe it may not have the same resentment with all that it hath with some. But because that is unknown to me, I shall leave it to God;—and conclude with this: That I think myself bound, as in my duty to God, and to the People of these Nations for their safety and good in every respect,—I think it my duty to tell you that it is not for the profit of these Nations, nor for common and public good, for you to continue here any longer. And therefore I do declare unto you, That I do dissolve this Parliament.

ON THE UNION OF ENGLAND AND SCOTLAND

JOHN HAMILTON, LORD BELHAVEN

SCOTTISH PARLIAMENT HOUSE: 2 NOV. 1706

MY LORD CHANCELLOR,—When I consider the affair of a union betwixt the two nations, as expressed in the several articles thereof, and now the subject of our deliberation at this time, I find my mind crowded with a variety of melancholy thoughts; and I think it my duty to disburden myself of some of them by laying them before, and exposing them to the serious consideration of, this honourable House.

I think I see a free and independent kingdom delivering up that which all the world hath been fighting for since the days of Nimrod; yea, that for which most of all the empires, kingdoms, states, principalities, and the dukedoms of Europe are at this time engaged in the most bloody and cruel wars; to wit, a power to manage their own affairs by themselves, without the assistance and counsel of any other.

I think I see a national Church, founded upon a rock, secured by a claim of right, hedged and fenced about by the strictest and most pointed legal sanctions that sovereignty could contrive, voluntarily descending into a plain, upon an equal level with Jews, Papists, Socinians, Arminians, Anabaptists, and other sectaries.

I think I see the noble and honourable peerage of Scotland, whose valiant predecessors led armies against their enemies upon their own proper charges and expense, now divested of their followers and vassalages; and put upon such an equal foot with their vassals, that I think I see a petty English exciseman receive more homage and respect than what was paid formerly to their *quondam* MacCallammores.

I think I see the present peers of Scotland, whose noble ancestors conquered provinces, overran countries, reduced and subjected towns and fortified places; exacted tribute through the greatest part of England, now walking in the Court of Requests, like so many English attorneys; laying aside their walking swords when in company with the English peers, lest their self-defence should be found murder.

I think I see the honourable estate of barons, the bold assertors of the nation's rights and liberties in the worst of times, now setting a watch upon their lips, and a guard upon their tongues, lest they may be found guilty of *scandalum magnatum*, a speaking evil of dignities.

I think I see the royal state of burghers walking their desolate streets, hanging down their heads under disappointments, wormed out of all the branches of their old trade, uncertain what hand to turn to, necessitated to become prentices to their unkind neighbours; and yet, after all, finding their trade so fortified by companies, and secured by prescriptions, that they despair of any success therein.

I think I see our learned judges laying aside their pratiques and decisions, studying the common law of England, gravelled with *certioraris, nisi priuses*, writs of error, verdicts, injunctions, demurs, etc., and frightened with appeals and avocations, because of the new regulations and rectifications they may meet with.

I think I see the valiant and gallant soldiery either sent to learn the plantation trade abroad, or at home petitioning for a small subsistence, as a reward of their honourable exploits; while their old corps are broken, the common soldiers left to beg, and the youngest English corps kept standing.

I think I see the honest industrious tradesman loaded with new taxes and impositions, disappointed of the equivalents, drinking water in place of ale, eating his saltless pottage, petitioning for encouragement to his manufactures, and answered by counter petitions.

In short, I think I see the laborious ploughman, with his corn spoiling upon his hands for want of sale, cursing the day of his birth, dreading the expense of his burial, and uncertain whether to marry or do worse.

I think I see the incurable difficulties of the landed men, fettered under the golden chain of " equivalents," their pretty daughters petitioning for want of husbands, and their sons for want of employment.

I think I see our mariners delivering up their ships to their Dutch partners; and what through presses and necessity, earning their bread as underlings in the Royal English Navy !

But above all, my Lord, I think I see our ancient mother, Caledonia, like Cæsar, sitting in the midst of our senate, ruefully looking round about her, covering herself with her royal garment, attending the fatal blow, and breathing out her last with an *et tu quoque mi fili!*

Are not these, my Lord, very afflicting thoughts? And yet they are but the least part suggested to me by these dishonour-able articles. Should not the consideration of these things vivify these dry bones of ours? Should not the memory of our noble predecessors' valour and constancy rouse up our drooping spirits? Are our noble predecessors' souls got so far into the English cabbage-stalk and cauliflowers, that we should show the least inclination that way? Are our eyes so blinded, are our ears so deafened, are our hearts so hardened, are our tongues so faltered, are our hands so fettered, that in this our day—I say, my Lord, in this *our* day—we should not mind the things that concern the very being and well-being of our ancient kingdom, before the day be hid from our eyes?

No, my Lord, God forbid! Man's extremity is God's oppor-tunity: He is a present help in time of need—a deliverer, and that right early! Some unforeseen providence will fall out, that may cast the balance; some Joseph or other will say, "Why do ye strive together, since ye are brethren?" None can destroy Scotland save Scotland's self. Hold your hands from the *pen*, and you are secure! There will be a Jehovah-Jireh; and some ram will be caught in the thicket, when the bloody knife is at our mother's throat. Let us then, my Lord, and let our noble patriots behave themselves like men, and we know not how soon a blessing may come!

I design not at this time to enter into the merits of any one particular article. I intend this discourse as an introduction to what I may afterward say upon the whole debate, as it falls in before this honourable House; and therefore, in the further prosecution of what I have to say, I shall insist upon a few par-ticulars, very necessary to be understood before we enter into the detail of so important a matter.

I shall therefore, in the first place, endeavour to encourage a free and full deliberation, without animosities and heats. In the next place, I shall endeavour to make an inquiry into the nature and source of the unnatural and dangerous divisions that are now on foot within this isle, with some motives showing that it is our interest to lay them aside at this time. And all this with all deference, and under the correction of this honourable House.

My Lord Chancellor, the greatest honour that was done unto a Roman was to allow him the glory of a triumph; the greatest and most dishonourable punishment was that of a parricide. He that was guilty of parricide was beaten with rods upon his naked body till the blood gushed out of all the veins of his body; then he was sewed up in a leathern sack called a *culeus*, with a cock, a viper, and an ape, and thrown headlong into the sea.

My Lord, patricide is a greater crime than parricide, all the world over.

In a triumph, my Lord, when the conqueror was riding in his triumphal chariot, crowned with laurels, adorned with trophies, and applauded with huzzas, there was a monitor appointed to stand behind him to warn him not to be high-minded nor puffed up with overweening thoughts of himself; and to his chariot were tied a whip and a bell, to remind him that, notwithstanding all his glory and grandeur, he was accountable to the *people* for his administration, and would be punished as other men if found guilty.

The greatest honour among *us*, my Lord, is to represent the sovereign's sacred person [as High Commissioner] in Parliament; and in one particular it appears to be greater than that of a triumph, because the whole legislative power seems to be entrusted with him. If he give the royal assent to an act of the estates, it becomes a law obligatory upon the subject, though contrary to or without any instructions from the sovereign. If he refuse the royal assent to a vote in Parliament, it cannot be a law, though he has the sovereign's particular and positive instructions for it.

His Grace the Duke of Queensberry, who now represents her Majesty in this session of Parliament, hath had the honour of that great trust as often, if not more, than any Scotchman ever had. He hath been the favourite of two successive sovereigns; and I cannot but commend his constancy and perseverance, that, notwithstanding his former difficulties and unsuccessful attempts, and maugre some other specialities not yet determined, his Grace has yet had the resolution to undertake the most unpopular measure last. If his Grace succeed in this affair of a union, and that it prove for the happiness and welfare of the nation, then he justly merits to have a statue of gold erected for himself; but if it shall tend to the entire destruction and abolition of our nation, and that we, the nation's trustees, shall go into it, then I must say that a whip and a bell, a cock, a viper, and an ape are but too small punishments for any such bold unnatural undertaking and complaisance.

1. That I may pave the way, my Lord, to a full, calm, and free reasoning upon this affair, which is of the last consequence unto this nation, I shall mind this honourable House that we are

the successors of those noble ancestors who founded our monarchy, framed our laws, amended, altered, and corrected them from time to time, as the affairs and circumstances of the nation did require, without the assistance or advice of any foreign power or potentate, and who, during the time of two thousand years, have handed them down to us, a free independent nation, with the hazard of their lives and fortunes. Shall not we, then, argue for that which our progenitors have purchased for us at so dear a rate, and with so much immortal honour and glory? God forbid! Shall the hazard of a father unbind the ligaments of a dumb son's tongue? and shall we hold our peace when our *patria*, our country, is in danger? I say this, my Lord, that I may encourage every individual member of this House to speak his mind freely. There are many wise and prudent men among us who think it not worth their while to open their mouths; there are others who can speak very well, and to good purpose, who shelter themselves under the shameful cloak of silence, from a fear of the frowns of great men and parties. I have observed, my Lord, by my experience, the greatest number of speakers in the most trivial affairs; and it will always prove so while we come not to the right understanding of the oath *de fideli*, whereby we are bound not only to give our vote but our *faithful advice* in Parliament, as we should answer to God. And in our ancient laws the representatives of the honourable barons and the royal boroughs are termed " spokesmen." It lies upon your Lordships, therefore, particularly to take notice of such whose modesty makes them bashful to speak. Therefore I shall leave it upon you, and conclude this point with a very memorable saying of an honest private gentleman to a great queen, upon occasion of a state project, contrived by an able statesman, and the favourite to a great king, against a peaceful obedient people, because of the diversity of their laws and constitutions: " If at this time thou hold thy peace, salvation shall come to the people from another place, but thou and thy house shall perish." I leave the application to each particular member of this House.

2. My Lord, I come now to consider our divisions. We are under the happy reign, blessed be God, of the best of queens, who has no evil design against the meanest of her subjects; who loves all her people, and is equally beloved by them again; and yet, that under the happy influence of our most excellent Queen, there should be such divisions and factions, more dangerous and threatening to her dominions than if we were under an arbitrary government, is most strange and unaccountable. Under an

*C⁷¹⁴

arbitrary prince all are willing to serve, because all are under a necessity to obey, whether they will or not. He chooses, therefore, whom he will, without respect to either parties or factions; and if he think fit to take the advice of his councils or parliaments, every man speaks his mind freely, and the prince receives the faithful advice of his people, without the mixture of self-designs. If he prove a good prince, the government is easy; if bad, either death or a revolution brings a deliverance, whereas here, my Lord, there appears no end of our misery, if not prevented in time. Factions are now become independent, and have got footing in councils, in parliaments, in treaties, in armies, in incorporations, in families, among kindred; yea, man and wife are not free from their political jars.

It remains, therefore, my Lord, that I inquire into the nature of these things; and since the names give us not the right idea of the thing, I am afraid I shall have difficulty to make myself well understood.

The names generally used to denote the factions are Whig and Tory; as obscure as that of Guelfs and Ghibellines; yea, my Lord, they have different significations, as they are applied to factions in each kingdom. A Whig in England is a heterogeneous creature: in Scotland he is all of a piece. A Tory in England is all of a piece, and a statesman: in Scotland he is quite otherwise— an anti-courtier and anti-statesman.

A Whig in England appears to be somewhat like Nebuchadnezzar's image, of different metals, different classes, different principles, and different designs; yet, take them altogether, they are like a piece of some mixed drugget of different threads; some finer, some coarser, which, after all, make a comely appearance and an agreeable suit. Tory is like a piece of loyal home-made English cloth, the true staple of the nation, all of a thread; yet if we look narrowly into it, we shall perceive a diversity of colours, which, according to the various situations and positions, make various appearances. Sometimes Tory is like the moon in its full; as appeared in the affair of the Bill of Occasional Conformity. Upon other occasions, it appears to be under a cloud, and as if it were eclipsed by a greater body; as it did in the design of calling over the illustrious Princess Sophia. However, by this we may see their designs are to outshoot Whig in his own bow.

Whig, in Scotland, is a true blue Presbyterian, who, without considering time or power, will venture his all for the Kirk, but something less for the State. The greatest difficulty is how to describe a Scotch Tory. Of old, when I knew them first, Tory was an honest-hearted, comradish fellow, who, provided he was maintained and protected in his benefices, titles, and dignities, by the State, was the less anxious who had the government of the Church. But now, what he is since *jure divino* came in fashion, and that Christianity, and by consequence salvation, comes to depend upon Episcopal ordination, I profess I know not what to make of him; only this I must say, that he endeavours to do by opposition that which his brother in England endeavours by a more prudent and less scrupulous method.

Now, my Lord, from these divisions there has got up a kind of aristocracy, something like the famous triumvirate at Rome. They are a kind of undertakers and pragmatic statesmen, who, finding their power and strength great, and answerable to their designs, will make bargains with our gracious sovereign; they will serve her faithfully, but upon their own terms; they must have their own instruments, their own measures. This man must be turned out, and that man put in, and then they will make her the most glorious queen in Europe.

Where will this end, my Lord? Is not her Majesty in danger by such a method? Is not the monarchy in danger? Is not the nation's peace and tranquillity in danger? Will a change of parties make the nation more happy? No, my Lord. The seed is sown that is like to afford us a perpetual increase. It is not an annual herb, it takes deep root; it seeds and breeds; and if not timely prevented by her Majesty's royal endeavours, will split the whole island in two.

3. My Lord, I think, considering our present circumstances at this time, the Almighty God has reserved this great work for us. We may bruise this hydra of division, and crush this cockatrice's egg. Our neighbours in England are not yet fitted for any such thing; they are not under the afflicting hand of Providence, as we are. Their circumstances are great and glorious; their treaties are prudently managed, both at home and abroad; their generals brave and valorous, their armies successful and victorious; their trophies and laurels memorable and surprising; their enemies subdued and routed, their strongholds besieged and taken. Sieges relieved, marshals killed and taken prisoners, provinces and kingdoms are the results of their victories. Their royal navy is the terror of Europe; their trade and commerce extended through the universe, encircling the whole habitable world, and rendering their own capital city the emporium

for the whole inhabitants of the earth. And which is yet more than all these things, the subjects freely bestowing their treasure upon their sovereign; and above all, these vast riches, the sinews of war, and without which all the glorious success had proved abortive, these treasures are managed with such faithfulness and nicety, that they answer seasonably all their demands, though at never so great a distance. Upon these considerations, my Lord, how hard and difficult a thing will it prove to persuade our neighbours to a self-denying bill.

'Tis quite otherwise with us, my Lord, as we are an obscure, poor people, though formerly of better account, removed to a distant corner of the world, without name, and without alliances; our posts mean and precarious; so that I profess I don't think any one post in the kingdom worth the briguing [seeking] after, save that of being Commissioner to a long session of a factious Scotch Parliament, with an antedated commission, and that yet renders the rest of the ministers more miserable. What hinders us then, my Lord, to lay aside our divisions, to unite cordially and heartily together in our present circumstances, when our all is at stake? Hannibal, my Lord, is at our gates—Hannibal is come within our gates—Hannibal is come the length of this table —he is at the foot of the throne. He will demolish the throne if we take not notice. He will seize upon these regalia. He will take them as our *spolia opima*, and whip us out of this House, never to return again.

For the love of God, then, my Lord, for the safety and welfare of our ancient kingdom, whose sad circumstances I hope we shall yet convert into prosperity and happiness! We want no means if we unite. God blessed the peacemakers. We want neither men nor sufficiency of all manner of things necessary to make a nation happy. All depends upon management. *Concordia res parvæ crescunt*—small means increase by concord. I fear not these Articles, though they were ten times worse than they are, if we once cordially forgive one another, and that according to our proverb, " Bygones be bygones," and fair play for time to come. For my part, in the sight of God, and in the presence of this honourable House, I heartily forgive every man, and beg that they may do the same to me. And I do most humbly propose that his Grace my Lord Commissioner may appoint an *Agape*, may order a love feast for this honourable House, that we may lay aside all self-designs, and after our fasts and humiliations, may have a day of rejoicing and thankfulness; may eat our meat with gladness, and our bread with a merry heart. Then shall we sit each man under his own fig-tree, and the voice of the turtle shall be heard in our land, a bird famous for constancy and fidelity.

My Lord, I shall pause here, and proceed no further in my discourse, till I see if his Grace my Lord Commissioner will receive any humble proposals for removing misunderstandings among us, and putting an end to our fatal divisions. Upon my honour, I have no other design; and I am content to beg the favour upon my bended knees.

(*A pause, during which no response was made.*)

My Lord Chancellor, I am sorry that I must pursue the thread of my sad and melancholy story. What remains is more afflictive than what I have already said. Allow me then to make this meditation—that if our posterity, after we are all dead and gone, shall find themselves under an ill-made bargain, and shall have recourse of our records for the names of the managers who made that treaty by which they have suffered so much, they will certainly exclaim: " Our nation must have been reduced to the last extremity at the time of this treaty! All our great chieftains, all our noble peers, who once defended the rights and liberties of the nation, must have been killed, and lying dead on the bed of honour, before the nation could ever condescend to such mean and contemptible terms! Where were the great men of the noble families—the Stewarts, Hamiltons, Grahams, Campbells, Johnstons, Murrays, Homes, Kers? Where were the two great officers of the Crown, the Constable and the Marischal of Scotland? Certainly all were extinguished, *and now we are slaves for ever!* "

But the English records; how will they make their posterity reverence the names of those illustrious men who made that treaty, and for ever brought under those fierce, warlike, and troublesome neighbours, who had struggled so long for independency, shed the best blood of their nation, and reduced a considerable part of their country to become waste and desolate!

I see the English Constitution remaining firm—the same two Houses of Parliament; the same taxes, customs, and excise; the same trade in companies, the same municipal laws, while all ours are either subjected to new regulations, or annihilated for ever! And for what? Only that we may have the honour to pay their old debts; and may have some few persons present [in Parliament] as witnesses to the validity of the deed, when they are pleased to contract more!

Good God! What? *Is* this an entire surrender?

My Lord, I find my heart so full of grief and indignation, that I must beg pardon not to finish the last part of my discourse: but pause that I may drop a tear as the prelude to so sad a story!

THE ARMY AND THE PARLIAMENT

WILLIAM PULTENEY, EARL OF BATH

HOUSE OF COMMONS: 1746

SIR,—We have heard a great deal about Parliamentary armies, and about an army continued from year to year. I have always been, sir, and always shall be, against a standing army of any kind. To me it is a terrible thing, whether under that of Parliamentary or any other designation. A standing army is still a standing army, whatever name it is called by. They are a body of men distinct from the body of the people; they are governed by different laws; and blind obedience, and an entire submission to the orders of their commanding officers, is their only principle. The nations around us, sir, are always enslaved and have been enslaved by these very means; by means of their standing armies they have every one lost their liberties. It is, indeed, impossible that the liberties of the people can be preserved in any country where a numerous standing army is kept up. Shall we, then, take any of our measures from the examples of our neighbours? No, sir, on the contrary, from their misfortunes we ought to learn to avoid those rocks on which they have split.

It signifies nothing to tell me that our army is commanded by such gentlemen as cannot be supposed to join in any measure for enslaving their country. It may be so. I hope it is so! I have a very good opinion of many gentlemen now in the army. I believe they would not join in any such measures. But their lives are uncertain, nor can we be sure how long they may be continued in command; they may be all dismissed in a moment, and proper tools of power put in their room. Besides, sir, we know the passions of men; we know how dangerous it is to trust the best of men with too much power. Where was there a braver army than that under Julius Cæsar? Where was there ever an army that had served their country more faithfully? That army was commanded generally by the best citizens of Rome, by men of great fortune and figure in their country; yet *that* army enslaved their country. The affections of the soldiers towards their country, the honour and integrity of the under officers, are not to be depended on. By the military law, the administration of justice is so quick, and the punishment so severe, that neither officer nor soldier dares offer to dispute the orders of his supreme commander; he must not consult his own inclinations. If an officer were commanded to pull his own father out of this House, he must do it; he dares not disobey; immediate death would be the sure consequence of the least grumbling. And if an officer were sent into the Court of Requests, accompanied by a body of musqueteers with screwed bayonets, and with orders to tell us what we ought to do, and how we were to vote, I know what would be the duty of this House; I know it would be our duty to order the officer to be taken and hanged up at the door of the lobby. But, sir, I doubt much if such a spirit could be found in the House, or in any House of Commons that will ever be in England.

Sir, I talk not of imaginary things. I talk of what has happened to an English House of Commons, and from an English army; and not only from an English army, but an army that was raised by that very House of Commons, an army that was paid by them, and an army that was commanded by generals appointed by them. Therefore, do not let us vainly imagine that an army raised and maintained by authority of Parliament will always be submissive to them. If an army be so numerous as to have it in their power to overawe Parliament, they will be submissive as long as the Parliament does nothing to disoblige their favourite general; but when that case happens, I am afraid that, in place of Parliament's dismissing the army, the army will dismiss the Parliament, as they have done heretofore. Nor does the legality or illegality of the Parliament, or of the army, alter the case. For with respect to that army, according to their way of thinking, the Parliament dismissed by them was a legal Parliament; they were an army raised and maintained according to law, and at first they were raised, as they imagined, for the preservation of those liberties which they afterwards destroyed.

It has been urged, sir, that whoever is for the Protestant succession must be for continuing the army; for that very reason I am against continuing the army. I know that neither the Protestant succession in his most illustrious house, or any succession, can ever be safe so long as there is a standing army in the country. Armies, sir, have no regard to hereditary successions. The first two Cæsars at Rome did pretty well, and found means to keep their armies in tolerable subjection, because the generals and officers were all their own creatures. But how did it fare with their successors? Was not every one of them named by the army without any regard to hereditary right, or to any right? A cobbler, a gardener, or any man who happened to raise himself in the army, and could gain their affections, was made Emperor of the world. Was not every succeeding Emperor raised to the throne, or tumbled headlong into the dust, according to the mere notion or mad phrenzy of the soldiers?

We are told this army is desired to be continued but for one year longer, or for a limited term of years. How absurd is this distinction! Is there any army in the world continued for any term of years? Does the most absolute monarch tell his army that he is to continue them any number of years, or any number of months?

How long have we already continued our army from year to year? And if it thus continues, wherein will it differ from the standing armies of those countries which have already submitted their necks to the yoke? We are now come to the Rubicon. Our army is now to be reduced, or never will. From his Majesty's own mouth we are assured of a profound tranquillity abroad, and we know there is one at home. If this is not a proper time, if these circumstances do not afford us a safe opportunity of reducing at least a part of our regular forces, we never can expect to see any reduction. This nation, overburdened with debts and taxes, must be loaded with the heavy charge of perpetually supporting a numerous standing army; and remain for ever exposed to the danger of having its liberties and privileges trampled upon by any future king or ministry, who shall take in their head to do so, and shall take a proper care to model the army for that purpose.

BRISTOL SPEECHES

EDMUND BURKE

I.

SPEECH AT HIS ARRIVAL AT BRISTOL BEFORE THE ELECTION IN THAT CITY

1774

GENTLEMEN,—I am come hither to solicit in person, that favour which my friends have hitherto endeavoured to pro- cure for me, by the most obliging, and to me the most honour- able, exertions.

I have so high an opinion of the great trust which you have to confer on this occasion; and, by long experience, so just a diffidence in my abilities to fill it in a manner adequate even to my own ideas, that I should never have ventured of myself to intrude into that awful situation. But since I am called upon by the desire of several respectable fellow-subjects, as I have done at other times, I give up my fears to their wishes. Whatever my other deficiencies may be, I do not know what it is to be wanting to my friends.

I am not fond of attempting to raise public expectation by great promises. At this time, there is much cause to consider, and very little to presume. We seem to be approaching to a great crisis in our affairs, which calls for the whole wisdom of the wisest among us, without being able to assure ourselves, that any wisdom can preserve us from many and great inconveniences. You know I speak of our unhappy contest with America. I confess, it is a matter on which I look down as from a precipice. It is difficult in itself, and it is rendered more intricate by a great variety of plans of conduct. I do not mean to enter into them. I will not suspect a want of good intention in framing them. But however pure the intentions of their authors may have been, we all know that the event has been unfortunate. The means of recovering our affairs are not obvious. So many great questions of commerce, of finance, of constitution, and of policy, are involved in this American deliberation, that I dare engage for nothing, but that I shall give it, without any predilection to former opinions, or any sinister bias whatsoever, the most honest and impartial consideration of which I am capable. The public has a full right to it; and this great city, a main pillar in the commercial interest of Great Britain, must totter on its base by the slightest mistake with regard to our American measures.

Thus much, however, I think it not amiss to lay before you; That I am not, I hope, apt to take up or lay down my opinions lightly. I have held, and ever shall maintain, to the best of my power, unimpaired and undiminished, the just, wise, and necessary constitutional superiority of Great Britain. This is necessary for America as well as for us. I never mean to depart from it. Whatever may be lost by it, I avow it. The forfeiture even of your favour, if by such a declaration I could forfeit it, though the first object of my ambition, never will make me disguise my sentiments on this subject.

But,—I have ever had a clear opinion, and have ever held a constant correspondent conduct, that this superiority is consistent with all the liberties a sober and spirited American ought to desire. I never mean to put any colonist, or any human creature, in a situation not becoming a free-man. To reconcile British superiority with American liberty shall be my great object, as far as my little faculties extend. I am far from thinking that both, even yet, may not be preserved.

When I first devoted myself to the public service, I considered how I should render myself fit for it; and this I did by endeavouring to discover what it was that gave this country the rank it holds in the world. I found that our prosperity and dignity arose principally, if not solely, from two sources; our constitution, and commerce. Both these I have spared no study to understand, and no endeavour to support.

The distinguishing part of our constitution is its liberty. To preserve that liberty inviolate, seems the particular duty and proper trust of a member of the House of Commons. But the liberty, the only liberty I mean, is a liberty connected with order; that not only exists along with order and virtue, but which cannot exist at all without them. It inheres in good and steady government, as in its substance and vital principle.

The other source of our power is commerce, of which you are so large a part, and which cannot exist, no more than your liberty, without a connexion with many virtues. It has ever been a very particular and a very favourite object of my study, in its principles, and in its details. I think many here are acquainted with the truth of what I say. This I know, that I have ever had my house open, and my poor services ready, for traders and manufacturers of every denomination. My favourite ambition is to have those services acknowledged. I now appear before you to make trial, whether my earnest endeavours have been so wholly oppressed by the weakness of my abilities, as to be rendered insignificant in the eyes of a great trading city; or whether you choose to give a weight to humble abilities, for the sake of the honest exertions with which they are accompanied. This is my trial to-day. My industry is not on trial. Of my industry I am sure, as far as my constitution of mind and body admitted.

When I was invited by many respectable merchants, freeholders, and freemen of this city, to offer them my services, I had just received the honour of an election at another place, at a very great distance from this. I immediately opened the matter to those of my worthy constituents who were with me, and they unanimously advised me not to decline it. They told me, that they had elected me with a view to the public service: and as great questions relative to our commerce and colonies were imminent, that in such matters I might derive authority and support from the representation of this great commercial city; they desired me therefore to set off without delay, very well persuaded that I never could forget my obligations to them, or to my friends, for the choice they had made of me. From that time to this instant I have not slept; and if I should have the honour of being freely chosen by you, I hope I shall be as far from slumbering or sleeping when your service requires me to be awake, as I have been in coming to offer myself a candidate for your favour.

II.

SPEECH TO THE ELECTORS OF BRISTOL

On his being declared by the Sheriffs, duly elected one of the representatives in Parliament for that city, on Thursday, the 3rd of November, 1774

GENTLEMEN,—I cannot avoid sympathising strongly with the feelings of the gentleman who has received the same honour that you have conferred on me. If he, who has bred and passed his whole life amongst you; if he, who through the easy gradations of acquaintance, friendship, and esteem, has obtained the honour, which seems of itself, naturally and almost insensibly, to meet with those, who, by the even tenor of pleasing manners and social virtues, slide into the love and confidence of their fellow-citizens;—if he cannot speak but with great emotion on this subject, surrounded as he is on all sides with his old friends; you will have the goodness to excuse me, if my real, unaffected embarrassment prevents me from expressing my gratitude to you as I ought.

I was brought hither under the disadvantage of being unknown, even by sight, to any of you. No previous canvass was made for me. I was put in nomination after the poll was opened. I did not appear until it was far advanced. If, under all these accumulated disadvantages, your good opinion has carried me to this happy point of success; you will pardon me, if I can only say to you collectively, as I said to you individually, simply, and plainly, I thank you—I am obliged to you—I am not insensible of your kindness.

This is all that I am able to say for the inestimable favour you have conferred upon me. But I cannot be satisfied, without saying a little more in defence of the right you have to confer such a favour. The person that appeared here as counsel for the candidate, who so long and so earnestly solicited your votes, thinks proper to deny, that a very great part of you have any votes to give. He fixes a standard period of time in his own imagination, not what the law defines, but merely what the convenience of his client suggests, by which he would cut off, at one stroke, all those freedoms which are the dearest privileges of your corporation; which the common law authorises; which your magistrates are compelled to grant; which come duly authenticated into this court; and are saved in the clearest words, and with the most religious care and tenderness, in that very act of parliament, which was made to regulate the elections by freemen, and to prevent all possible abuses in making them.

I do not intend to argue the matter here. My learned counsel has supported your cause with his usual ability; the worthy sheriffs have acted with their usual equity, and I have no doubt, that the same equity, which dictates the return, will guide the final determination. I had the honour, in conjunction with many far wiser men, to contribute a very small assistance, but, however, some assistance, to the forming the judicature which is to try such questions. It would be unnatural in me to doubt the justice of that court, in the trial of my own cause, to which I have been so active to give jurisdiction over every other.

I assure the worthy freemen, and this corporation, that, if

the gentleman perseveres in the intentions which his present
warmth dictates to him, I will attend their cause with diligence,
and I hope with effect. For, if I know anything of myself, it
is not my own interest in it, but my full conviction, that induces
me to tell you—*I think there is not a shadow of doubt in the
case.*

I do not imagine that you find me rash in declaring myself,
or very forward in troubling you. From the beginning to the
end of the election, I have kept silence in all matters of discussion. I have never asked a question of a voter on the other
side, or supported a doubtful vote of my own. I respected
the abilities of my managers; I relied on the candour of the
court. I think the worthy sheriffs will bear me witness, that
I have never once made an attempt to impose upon their reason,
to surprise their justice, or to ruffle their temper. I stood
on the hustings (except when I gave my thanks to those who
favoured me with their votes) less like a candidate, than an
unconcerned spectator of a public proceeding. But here
the face of things is altered. Here is an attempt for a general
massacre of suffrages; an attempt, by a promiscuous carnage
of *friends* and *foes*, to exterminate above two thousand votes,
including *seven hundred polled for the gentleman himself, who
now complains,* and who would destroy the friends whom he
has obtained, only because he cannot obtain as many of them
as he wishes.

How he will be permitted, in another place, to stultify and
disable himself, and to plead against his own acts, is another
question. The law will decide it. I shall only speak of it as
it concerns the propriety of public conduct in this city. I do
not pretend to lay down rules of decorum for other gentlemen.
They are best judges of the mode of proceeding that will recommend them to the favour of their fellow-citizens. But I confess
I should look rather awkward, if I had been the *very first to
produce the new copies of freedom,* if I had persisted in producing
them to the last; if I had ransacked, with the most unremitting
industry and the most penetrating research, the remotest
corners of the kingdom to discover them; if I were then, all
at once, to turn short, and declare, that I had been sporting all
this while with the right of election; and that I had been drawing
out a poll, upon no sort of rational grounds, which disturbed the
peace of my fellow-citizens for a month together—I really, for
my part, should appear awkward under such circumstances.

It would be still more awkward in me, if I were gravely to

look the sheriffs in the face, and to tell them, they were not to determine my cause on my own principles; not to make the return upon those votes upon which I had rested my election. Such would be my appearance to the court and magistrates.

But how should I appear to the *voters* themselves? If I had gone round to the citizens entitled to freedom, and squeezed them by the hand—" Sir, I humbly beg your vote—I shall be eternally thankful—may I hope for the honour of your support?—Well!—come—we shall see you at the council-house." —If I were then to deliver them to my managers, pack them into tallies, vote them off in court, and when I heard from the bar—" Such a one only! and such a one for ever!—he's my man!"—" Thank you, good Sir—Hah! my worthy friend! thank you kindly—that's an honest fellow—how is your good family?" Whilst these words were hardly out of my mouth, if I should have wheeled round at once, and told them—" Get you gone, you pack of worthless fellows! you have no votes —you are usurpers! you are intruders on the rights of real freemen! I will have nothing to do with you! you ought never to have been produced at this election, and the sheriffs ought not to have admitted you to poll."

Gentlemen, I should make a strange figure if my conduct had been of this sort. I am not so old an acquaintance of yours as the worthy gentleman. Indeed I could not have ventured on such kind of freedoms with you. But I am bound, and I will endeavour, to have justice done to the rights of freemen; even though I should, at the same time, be obliged to vindicate the former[1] part of my antagonist's conduct against his own present inclinations.

I owe myself, in all things, to *all* the freemen of this city. My particular friends have a demand on me that I should not deceive their expectations. Never was cause or man supported with more constancy, more activity, more spirit. I have been supported with a zeal indeed and heartiness in my friends, which (if their object had been at all proportioned to their endeavours) could never be sufficiently commended. They supported me upon the most liberal principles. They wished that the members for Bristol should be chosen for the city, and for their country at large, and not for themselves.

So far they are not disappointed. If I possess nothing else, I am sure I possess the temper that is fit for your service. I

[1] Mr. Brickdale opened his poll, it seems, with a tally of those very kind of freemen, and voted many thousands of them.

know nothing of Bristol, but by the favours I have received, and the virtues I have seen exerted in it.

I shall ever retain, what I now feel, the most perfect and grateful attachment to my friends—and I have no enmities; no resentment. I never can consider fidelity to engagements, and constancy in friendships, but with the highest approbation; even when those noble qualities are employed against my own pretensions. The gentleman, who is not so fortunate as I have been in this contest, enjoys, in this respect, a consolation full of honour both to himself and to his friends. They have certainly left nothing undone for his service.

As for the trifling petulance, which the rage of party stirs up in little minds, though it should show itself even in this court, it has not made the slightest impression on me. The highest flight of such clamorous birds is winged in an inferior reign of the air. We hear them, and we look upon them, just as you, gentlemen, when you enjoy the serene air on your lofty rocks, look down upon the gulls that skim the mud of your river, when it is exhausted of its tide.

I am sorry I cannot conclude without saying a word on a topic touched upon by my worthy colleague. I wish that topic had been passed by at a time when I have so little leisure to discuss it. But since he has thought proper to throw it out, I owe you a clear explanation of my poor sentiments on that subject.

He tells you that "the topic of instructions has occasioned much altercation and uneasiness in this city;" and he expresses himself (if I understand him rightly) in favour of the coercive authority of such instructions.

Certainly, gentlemen, it ought to be the happiness and glory of a representative to live in the strictest union, the closest correspondence, and the most unreserved communication with his constituents. Their wishes ought to have great weight with him; their opinion, high respect; their business, unremitted attention. It is his duty to sacrifice his repose, his pleasures, his satisfactions, to theirs; and above all, ever, and in all cases, to prefer their interest to his own. But his unbiassed opinion, his mature judgment, his enlightened conscience, he ought not to sacrifice to you, to any man, or to any set of men living. These he does not derive from your pleasure; no, nor from the law and the constitution. They are a trust from Providence, for the abuse of which he is deeply answerable. Your representative owes you, not his industry only, but his judgment; and he betrays, instead of serving you, if he sacrifices it to your opinion.

My worthy colleague says, his will ought to be subservient to yours. If that be all, the thing is innocent. If government were a matter of will upon any side, yours, without question, ought to be superior. But government and legislation are matters of reason and judgment, and not of inclination; and what sort of reason is that, in which the determination precedes the discussion; in which one set of men deliberate, and another decide; and where those who form the conclusion are perhaps three hundred miles distant from those who hear the arguments?

To deliver an opinion, is the right of all men; that of constituents is a weighty and respectable opinion, which a representative ought always to rejoice to hear; and which he ought always most seriously to consider. But *authoritative* instructions; *mandates* issued, which the member is bound blindly and implicitly to obey, to vote, and to argue for, though contrary to the clearest conviction of his judgment and conscience,— these are things utterly unknown to the laws of this land, and which arise from a fundamental mistake of the whole order and tenor of our constitution.

Parliament is not a *congress* of ambassadors from different and hostile interests; which interests each must maintain, as an agent and advocate, against other agents and advocates; but parliament is a *deliberative* assembly of *one* nation, with *one* interest, that of the whole; where, not local purposes, not local prejudices, ought to guide, but the general good, resulting from the general reason of the whole. You choose a member indeed; but when you have chosen him, he is not member for Bristol, but he is a member of *parliament*. If the local constituent should have an interest, or should form an hasty opinion, evidently opposite to the real good of the rest of the community, the member for that place ought to be as far, as any other, from any endeavour to give it effect. I beg pardon for saying so much on this subject. I have been unwillingly drawn into it; but I shall ever use a respectful frankness of communication with you. Your faithful friend, your devoted servant, I shall be to the end of my life: a flatterer you do not wish for. On this point of instructions, however, I think it scarcely possible we ever can have any sort of difference. Perhaps I may give you too much, rather than too little, trouble.

From the first hour I was encouraged to court your favour,

to this happy day of obtaining it, I have never promised you anything but humble and persevering endeavours to do my duty. The weight of that duty, I confess, makes me tremble; and whoever well considers what it is, of all things in the world, will fly from what has the least likeness to a positive and precipitate engagement. To be a good member of parliament is, let me tell you, no easy task; especially at this time, when there is so strong a disposition to run into the perilous extremes of servile compliance or wild popularity. To unite circumspection with vigour, is absolutely necessary; but it is extremely difficult. We are now members for a rich commercial *city*; this city, however, is but a part of a rich commercial *nation*, the interests of which are various, multiform, and intricate. We are members for that great nation, which however is itself but part of a great *empire*, extended by our virtue and our fortune to the farthest limits of the east and of the west All these wide-spread interests must be considered; must be compared; must be reconciled, if possible. We are members for a *free* country; and surely we all know, that the machine of a free constitution is no simple thing; but as intricate and as delicate as it is valuable. We are members in a great and ancient *monarchy;* and we must preserve religiously the true legal rights of the sovereign, which form the key-stone that binds together the noble and well-constructed arch of our empire and our constitution. A constitution made up of balanced powers must ever be a critical thing. As such I mean to touch that part of it which comes within my reach. I know my inability, and I wish for support from every quarter. In particular I shall aim at the friendship, and shall cultivate the best correspondence, of the worthy colleague you have given me.

I trouble you no further than once more to thank you all; you, gentlemen, for your favours; the candidates, for their temperate and polite behaviour; and the sheriffs, for a conduct which may give a model for all who are in public stations.

ON AMERICAN POLICY

LORD CHATHAM

House of Lords: 20 January, 1775.

As I have not the honour of access to his Majesty, I will endeavour to transmit to him, through the constitutional channel of this House, my ideas of America, to rescue him from the misadvice of his present ministers. I congratulate your lordships that the business is at last entered upon by the noble lords laying the papers before you. As I suppose your lordships too well apprized of their contents, I hope I am not premature in submitting to you my present motion—

"That an humble address be presented to his Majesty, humbly to desire and beseech his Majesty that, in order to open the way towards a happy settlement of the dangerous troubles in America, by beginning to allay ferments and soften animosities there; and, above all, for preventing in the meantime any sudden and fatal catastrophe at Boston, now suffering under the daily irritation of an army before their eyes posted in their town: it may graciously please his Majesty that immediate orders be despatched to General Gage for removing his Majesty's forces from the town of Boston as soon as the rigour of the season, and other circumstances indispensable to the safety and accommodation of the said troops, may render the same practicable."

I wish, my lords, not to lose a day in this urgent, pressing crisis; an hour now lost in allaying ferments in America may produce years of calamity. For my own part, I will not desert for a moment the conduct of this weighty business from the first to the last, unless nailed to my bed by the extremity of sickness. I will give it unremitted attention; I will knock at the door of this sleeping and confounded ministry; and will rouse them to a sense of their important danger.

When I state the importance of the Colonies to this country, and the magnitude of danger hanging over this country from the present plan of misadministration practised against them, I desire not to be understood to argue for a reciprocity of indulgence between England and America. I contend not for indulgence, but justice to America; and I shall ever contend that the Americans justly owe obedience to us in a limited degree—they owe obedience to our ordinances of trade and navigation; but let the line be skilfully drawn between the objects of those ordinances and their private, internal property; let the sacredness of their property remain inviolate; let it be taxable only by their own consent, given in their provincial assemblies, else it will cease to be property. As to the metaphysical refinements, attempting to show that the Americans are equally free from obedience and commercial restraints as from taxation for revenue, as being unrepresented here, I pronounce them as futile, frivolous, and groundless.

When I urge this measure of recalling the troops from Boston, I urge it on this pressing principle—that it is necessarily preparatory to the restoration of your peace and the establishment of your prosperity. It will then appear that you are disposed to treat amicably and equitably; and to consider, revise, and repeal, if it should be found necessary, as I affirm it will, those violent acts and declarations which have disseminated confusion throughout your Empire.

Resistance to your acts was necessary, as it was just; and your vain declarations of the omnipotence of Parliament, and your imperious doctrines of the necessity of submission, will be found equally impotent to convince, or to enslave, your fellow-subjects in America, who feel that that tyranny, whether ambitioned by an individual part of the legislature, or the bodies who comprise it, is equally intolerable to British subjects.

The means of enforcing this thraldom are found to be as ridiculous and weak in practice as they are unjust in principle. Indeed, I cannot but feel the most anxious sensibility for the situation of General Gage and the troops under his command; thinking him, as I do, a man of humanity and understanding, and entertaining, as I ever will, the highest respect, the warmest love, for the British troops. Their situation is truly unworthy; penned up—pining in inglorious inactivity. They are an army of impotence. You may call them an army of safety and guard, but they are in truth an army of impotence and contempt; and, to make the folly equal to the disgrace, they are an army of irritation and vexation. But I find a report creeping abroad, that ministers censure General Gage's inactivity; let them censure him—it becomes them—it becomes their justice and their honour. I mean not to censure his inactivity; it is a prudent and necessary inaction; but it is a miserable condition, where disgrace is prudence, and where it is necessary to be contemptible. This tameness, however contemptible, cannot be censured; for the first drop of blood shed in civil and unnatural war might be *immedicabile pulnus.*

I therefore urge and conjure your lordships immediately to adopt this conciliating measure. I will pledge myself for its immediately producing conciliatory effects by its being thus well timed; but if you delay till your vain hope shall be accomplished of triumphantly dictating reconciliation, you delay for ever. But admitting that this hope, which in truth is desperate, should be accomplished, what do you gain by the imposition of your victorious amnity? You will be untrusted and unthanked. Adopt, then, the grace while you have the opportunity of reconcilement, or at least prepare the way. Allay the ferment prevailing in America, by removing the obnoxious hostile cause —obnoxious and unserviceable, for their merit can be only inaction. *Non dimicare et vincere*—their victory can never be by exertions. Their force would be most disproportionately exerted against a brave, generous, and united people, with arms in their hands, and courage in their hearts—three millions of people, the genuine descendants of a valiant and pious ancestry, driven to those deserts by the narrow maxims of a superstitious tyranny. And is the spirit of persecution never to be appeased? Are the brave sons of those brave forefathers to inherit their sufferings, as they have inherited their virtues? Are they to sustain the infliction of the most impressive and unexampled severity, beyond the accounts of history or description of poetry. "*Rhadamanthus habet durissima regna, castigatque, auditique.*" So says the wisest poet and perhaps the wisest statesman and politician. But our ministers say, the Americans must not be heard. They have been condemned unheard. The indiscriminate hand of vengeance has lumped together innocent and guilty, with all the formalities of hostility has blocked up the town (Boston), and reduced to beggary and famine thirty thousand inhabitants.

But his Majesty is advised that the union in America cannot last. Ministers have more eyes than I, and should have more ears; but with all the information I have been able to procure, I can pronounce it a union, solid, permanent, and effectual. Ministers may satisfy themselves and delude the public with the report of what they call commercial bodies in America. They are not commercial; they are your packers and factors; they live upon nothing—for I call commission nothing. I mean the ministerial authority for this American intelligence; the runners for government, who are paid for their intelligence. But these are not the men, nor this the influence, to be considered in America when we estimate the firmness of their union. Even to extend the question, and to take in the really mercantile circle, will be totally inadequate to the consideration. Trade indeed increases the wealth and glory of a country; but its real strength and stamina are to be looked for amongst the cultivators of the land; in their simplicity of life is found the simpleness of virtue;—the integrity and courage of freedom. These true, genuine sons of the earth are invincible; and they surround and hem in the mercantile bodies; even if these bodies, which supposition I totally disclaim, could be supposed disaffected to the cause of liberty. Of this general spirit existing in the British nation (for so I wish to distinguish the real and genuine Americans from the pseudo-traders I have described), of this spirit of independence animating the nation of America, I have the most authentic information. It is not new among them; it is, and has ever been, their established principle, their confirmed persuasion; it is their nature and their doctrine.

I remember some years ago, when the repeal of the Stamp Act was in agitation, conversing in a friendly confidence with a person of undoubted respect and authenticity on that subject; and he assured me with a certainty which his judgment and opportunity gave him, that these were the prevalent and steady principles of America—that you might destroy their towns, and cut them off from the superfluities, perhaps the conveniences of life; but that they were prepared to despise your power, and would not lament their loss, whilst they have— what, my lords?—their woods and their liberty. The name of my authority, if I am called upon, will authenticate the opinion irrefragably. (It was Dr. Franklin.)

If illegal violences have been, as it is said, committed in America, prepare the way, open the door of possibility, for acknowledgment and satisfaction; but proceed not to such coercion, such prescription; cease your indiscriminate inflictions; amerce not thirty thousand; oppress not three millions, for the fault of forty or fifty individuals. Such severity of injustice must for ever render incurable the wounds you have already given your colonies; you irritate them to unappeasable rancour. What though you march from town to town, and from province to province; though you should be able to secure the obedience of the country you leave behind you in your progress, to grasp the dominion of eighteen hundred miles of continent, populous in numbers possessing valour, liberty and resistance?

This resistance to your arbitrary system of taxation might have been foreseen; it was obvious from the nature of things, and of mankind; and above all, from the Whiggish spirit flourishing in that country. The spirit which now resists your taxation in America is the same which formerly opposed loans, benevolences, and ship-money in England; the same spirit which called all England on its legs, and by the Bill of Rights vindicated the English constitution; the same spirit which established the great fundamental, essential maxim of your liberties—that no subject of England shall be taxed but by his own consent.

This glorious spirit of Whiggism animates three millions in America, who prefer poverty with liberty to gilded chains and sordid affluence; and who will die in defence of their rights as men, as freemen. What shall oppose this spirit, aided by the congenial flame growing in the breasts of every Whig in England, to the amount, I hope, of double the American numbers? Ireland they have to a man. In that country, joined as it is with the cause of colonies, and placed at their head, the distinction I contend for is and must be observed. This country superintends and controls their trade and navigation; but they tax themselves. And this distinction between external and internal control is sacred and insurmountable; it is involved in the abstract nature of things. Property is private, individual, absolute. Trade is an extended and complicated consideration; it reaches as far as ships can sail or winds can blow; it is a great and various machine. To regulate the numberless movements of its several parts, and combine them with effect, for the good of the whole, requires the superintending wisdom and energy of the supreme power in the empire. But this supreme power has no effect towards internal taxation, for it does not exist in that relation; there is no such thing, no such idea in this constitution, as a supreme power operating upon property. Let this distinction remain for ever ascertained; taxation is theirs, commercial regulation is ours. As an American, I would recognize to England her supreme right of regulating commerce and navigation; as an Englishman by birth and principle, I recognize to the Americans their supreme unalienable right to their property—a right which they are justified in the defence of to the last extremity. To maintain this principle is the common cause of the Whigs on the other side of the Atlantic, and on this. " 'Tis liberty to liberty engaged," that they will defend themselves, their families, and their country. In this great cause they are immovably allied; it is the alliance of God and nature— immutable, eternal, fixed as the firmament of heaven.

To such united force, what force shall be opposed? What, my lords? A few regiments in America, and seventeen or eighteen thousand men at home! The idea is too ridiculous to take up a moment of your lordships' time. Nor can such a rational and principled union be resisted by the tricks of office or ministerial manœuvre. Laying of papers on your table, or counting numbers on a division, will not avert or postpone the hour of danger; it must arrive, my lords, unless these fatal Acts are done away; it must arrive in all its horrors, and then these boastful ministers, spite of all their confidence, and all their manœuvres, shall be forced to hide their heads. They shall be forced to a disgraceful abandonment of their present measures and principles, which they avow but cannot defend measures which they presume to attempt, but cannot hope to effectuate. They cannot, my lords, they cannot stir a step; they have not a move left; they are checkmated.

But it is not repealing this Act of Parliament, it is not repealing a piece of parchment, that can restore America to our bosom; you must repeal her fears and her resentments; and you may then hope for her love and gratitude. But now, insulted with an armed force posted at Boston, irritated with an hostile array before her eyes, her concessions, if you could force them, would be suspicious and insecure; they will be *irato animo;* they will not be the sound, honourable passions of freemen, they will be dictates of fear, and extortions of force. But it is more than evident that you cannot force them, united as they are, to your unworthy terms of submission—it is impossible; and when I hear General Gage censured for inactivity, I must retort with indignation on those whose intemperate measures and improvident councils have betrayed him into his present situation. His situation reminds me, my lords, of the answer of a French general in the civil wars of France—Monsieur Condé opposed to Monsieur Turenne. He was asked how it happened that he did not take his adversary prisoner, as he was often very near him: " *J'ai peur,*" replied Condé very honestly, " *J'ai peur qu'il ne me prenne* " (I'm afraid he'll take me).

When your lordships look at the papers transmitted us from America, when you consider their decency, firmness, and wisdom, you cannot but respect their cause, and wish to make it your own. For myself, I must declare and avow that in all my reading and observation—and it has been my favourite study: I have read Thucydides, and have studied and admired the master-states of the world—that for solidity of reasoning, force of sagacity, and wisdom of conclusion, under such a complication of difficult circumstances, no nation or body of men can stand in preference to the General Congress at Philadelphia. I trust it is obvious to your lordships, that all attempts to impose servitude upon such men, to establish despotism over such a mighty continental nation, must be vain, must be fatal. We shall be forced ultimately to retract; let us restrain while we can, not when we must. I say we must necessarily undo these violent oppressive Acts; they must be repealed—you will repeal them; I pledge myself for it, that you will in the end repeal them; I stake my reputation on it:—I will consent to be taken for an idiot, if they are not finally repealed. Avoid, then, this humiliating, disgraceful necessity. With a dignity becoming your exalted situation, make the first advances to concord, to peace, and happiness; for that is your true dignity, to act with prudence and justice. That you should first concede is obvious, from sound and rational policy. Concession comes with better grace and more salutary effect from superior power; it reconciles superiority of power with the feelings of men, and establishes solid confidence on the foundations of affection and gratitude.

So thought a wise poet and a wise man in political sagacity, the friend of Mæcenas, and the eulogist of Augustus—to him the adopted son and successor, the first Cæsar, to him the master of the world, he wisely urged this conduct of prudence and dignity: " *Tuque puer, tu parce; projice tela manu.*"

Every motive, therefore, of justice and of policy, of dignity and prudence, urges you to allay the ferment in America—by a removal of your troops from Boston, by a repeal of your Acts of Parliament, and by demonstration of amicable dispositions towards your Colonies. On the other hand, every danger and every hazard impend to deter you from perseverance in your present ruinous measures—foreign war hanging over your heads by a slight and brittle thread; France and Spain watching your conduct, and waiting for the maturity of your errors; with a vigilant eye to America, and the temper of your Colonies, more than to their own concerns, be they what they may.

To conclude, my lords, if the ministers thus persevere in misadvising and misleading the King, I will not say that they can alieniate the affections of his subjects from his crown; but I will affirm that they will make the crown not worth his wearing. I will not say that the King is betrayed; but I will pronounce that the kingdom is undone.

THE COMMONS AND ITS RIGHTS

JOHN WILKES

HOUSE OF COMMONS: 1776

[On the Motion that Leave be Given to Bring in a Bill for a Just and Equal Representation of the People of England in Parliament, 1776].

ALL wise governments and well-regulated states have been particularly careful to mark and correct the various abuses which a considerable length of time almost necessarily creates. Among these, one of the most striking and important in our country is the present unfair and inadequate state of the representation of the people of England in Parliament. It is now become so partial and unequal, from the lapse of time, that I believe almost every gentleman in the House will agree with me in the necessity of its being taken into our most serious consideration, and of our endeavouring to find a remedy for this great and growing evil.

I wish, sir, my slender abilities were equal to a thorough investigation of this momentous business; very diligent and well-meant endeavours have not been wanting to trace it from the first origin. The most natural and perfect idea of a free government is, in my mind, that of the people themselves assembling to determine by what laws they choose to be governed, and to establish the regulations they think necessary for the protection of their property and liberty against all violence and fraud. Every member of such a community would submit with alacrity to the observance of whatever had been enacted by himself, and assist with spirit in giving efficacy and vigour to laws and ordinances which derived all their authority from his own approbation and concurrence. In small inconsiderable states, this mode of legislation has been happily followed, both in ancient and modern times. The extent and populousness of a great empire seems scarcely to admit it without confusion or tumult, and therefore, our ancestors, more wise in this than the ancient Romans, adopted the representation of the many by a few, as answering more fully the true ends of government. Rome was enslaved from inattention to this very circumstance, and by one other fatal act, which ought to be a strong warning to the people, even against their own representatives here—the leaving power too long in the hands of the same persons, by which the armies of the republic became the armies of Sylla, Pompey, and Cæsar. When all the burghers of Italy obtained the freedom of Rome, and voted in public assemblies, their multitudes rendered the distinction of the citizen of Rome, and the alien, impossible. Their assemblies and deliberations became disorderly and tumultuous. Unprincipled and ambitious men found out the secret of turning them to the ruin of the Roman liberty and the commonwealth. Among us this evil is avoided by representation, and yet the justice of this principle is preserved. Every Englishman is supposed to be present in Parliament, either in person or by deputy chosen by himself; and therefore the resolution of Parliament is taken to be the resolution of every individual, and to give to the public the consent and approbation of every free agent of the community.

According to the first formation of this excellent constitution, so long and so justly our greatest boast and best inheritance, we find that the people thus took care no laws should be enacted, no taxes levied, but by their consent, expressed by their representatives in the great council of the nation. The mode of representation in ancient times being tolerably adequate and proportionate, the sense of the people was known by that of Parliament; their share of power in the legislature was preserved, and founded in equal justice; at present it is become insufficient, partial, and unjust. From so pleasing a view as that of the equal power which our ancestors had, with great wisdom and care, modelled for the commons of this realm, the present scene gives us not very venerable ruins of that majestic and beautiful fabric, the English constitution.

As the whole seems in disorder and confusion, all the former union and harmony of the parts are lost and destroyed. It appears, sir, from the writs remaining in the king's remembrancer's office in the exchequer, that no less than twenty-two towns sent members to the Parliaments in the 23d, 25th, and 26th, of King Edward I., which have long ceased to be represented. The names of some of them are scarcely known to us, such as those of Canebrig and Bamburgh in Northumberland, Pershore and Brem in Worcestershire, Jarvall and Tykhull in Yorkshire. What a happy fate, sir, has attended the boroughs of Gatton and Old Sarum, of which, although *ipsæ periere ruinæ*, the names are familiar to us; the clerk regularly calls them over, and four respectable gentlemen represent their departed greatness, as knights of coronation represent Aquitaine and Normandy! The little town of Banbury, *petite ville grand renom*, as Rabelais says of Chinon, has, I believe, only seventeen electors, and a chancellor of the exchequer. Its influence and weight, on a division, I have often seen overpower the united force of the members for London, Bristol, and several of the most opulent counties. East Grinstead too, I think, has only about thirty electors, yet gives a seat among us to that brave, heroic lord, at the head of a great department, now very military, who has fully determined to conquer America, but not in Germany. It is not, sir, my purpose to weary the patience of the House by the researches of an antiquarian into the ancient state of our representation, and its variations at different periods. I shall only remark shortly on what passed in the reign of Henry VI. and some of his successors. In that reign, Sir John Fortescue, his chancellor, observed that the House of Commons consisted of more than 300 chosen men. Various alterations were made by succeeding kings till James II., since which period no change has happened. Great abuses, it must be owned, contrary to the primary ideas of the English constitution, were committed by our former princes, in giving the right of representation to several paltry boroughs, because the places were poor, and dependent on them, or on a favourite overgrown peer. The landmarks of the constitution have often been removed. The marked partiality to Cornwall, which single county still sends, within one, as many members as the whole kingdom of Scotland, is striking, and arose from its yielding to the Crown in tin and lands a larger hereditary revenue than any other English county, as well as from this duchy being in the Crown, and giving an amazing command and influence. By such acts of our princes the constitution was wounded in its most vital parts. Henry VIII. restored two members, Edward VI. twenty, Queen Mary four, Queen Elizabeth twelve, James I. sixteen, Charles I. eighteen; in all seventy-two. The alterations by creation in the same period were more considerable; for Henry VIII. created thirty-three, Edward VI. twenty-eight, Queen Mary seventeen, Queen Elizabeth forty-eight, James I. eleven; in all 137. Charles I. made no creation of this kind. Charles II. added two for the county, and two for the city of Durham, and two for Newmarket-on-Trent. This House is at this hour composed of the same representation it was at his demise, notwithstanding the many and important changes which have since happened; it becomes us therefore to inquire, whether the sense of Parliament can be now, on solid grounds, from the present representation, said to be the sense of the nation, as in the time of our forefathers. I am satisfied, sir, the sentiments of the people cannot be justly known at this time, from the resolutions of a Parliament, composed as the present is, even though no undue influence was practised after the return of the members to the House; even supposing for a moment the influence of all the baneful arts of corruption to be suspended, which, for a moment, I believe they have not been, under the present profligate administration. Let us examine, sir, with exactness and candour, of what the efficient parts of the House are composed, and what proportion they bear on the large scale to the body of the people of England, who are supposed to be represented.

The southern part of this island, to which I now confine my ideas, consists of about five millions of people, according to the most received calculation. I will state by what number the majority of this House is elected, and I suppose the largest number present of any recorded in our journals, which was in the famous year 1741. In that year the three largest divisions appear in our journals. The first is that on the 21st of January, when the numbers were 253 to 250; the second on the 25th day of the same month, 236 to 235; the third on the 9th of March, 242 to 242. In these divisions the members of Scotland are included; but I will state my calculations only for England, because it gives the argument more force. The division, therefore, I adopt is that of January 21st; the number of members present on that day were 503. Let me, however, suppose the number of 254 to be the majority of members who will ever be able to attend in their places. I state it high, from the accidents of sickness, service in foreign parts, travelling, and necessary avocations. From the majority of electors in the boroughs which returned members to this House, it has been demonstrated that this number of 254 members are actually elected by no more than

5,723 persons, generally the inhabitants of Cornish and other boroughs, and perhaps not the most respectable part of the community. Is our sovereign, then, to learn the sense of his whole people from these few persons? Are these the men to give laws to this vast empire, and to tax this wealthy nation? I do not mention all the tedious calculations, because gentlemen may find them at length in the works of the incomparable Dr. Price, in Postlethwaite, and in Burgh's " Political Disquisitions." Figures afford the clearest demonstration, incapable of cavil or sophistry. Since Burgh's calculation, only one alteration has happened; I allude to the borough of Shoreham, in Sussex; for by the Act of 1771, all the freeholders of forty shillings per annum, in the neighbouring rape or hundred of Bramber, are admitted to vote for that borough, but many of the old electors were disfranchised. It appears, likewise, that fifty-six of our members are elected by only 364 persons. Lord Chancellor Talbot supposed that the majority of this House was elected by 50,000 persons, and he exclaimed against the injustice of that idea. More accurate calculators than his lordship, and the unerring rules of political arithmetic, have shown the injustice to be vastly beyond what his lordship even suspected. When we consider, sir, that the most important powers of this House, the levying taxes on, and enacting laws for five millions of persons, is thus usurped and unconstitutionally exercised by the small number I have mentioned, it becomes our duty to the people to restore to them their clear rights, their original share in the legislature. The ancient representation of this kingdom, we find, was founded by our ancestors in justice, wisdom, and equality. The present state of it would be continued by us in folly, obstinacy, and injustice. The evil has been complained of by some of the wisest patriots our country has ever produced. I shall beg leave to give that close reasoner, Mr. Locke's ideas, in his own words. He says, in the treatise on civil government: " Things not always changing equally, and private interests often keeping up customs and privileges, when the reasons of them are ceased, it often comes to pass, that in Governments where part of the legislature consists of representatives chosen by the people, that in tract of time this representation becomes very unequal and disproportionate to the reasons it was at first established upon. To what gross absurdities the following of a custom, when reason has left it, may lead, we may be satisfied, when we see the bare name of a town, of which there remains not so much as the ruins, where scarce so much housing as a sheep-cot, or more inhabitants than a shep-herd, is to be found, sends as many representatives to the grand assembly of law-makers, as a whole county, numerous in people and powerful in riches. This strangers stand amazed at, and every one must confess, needs a remedy." After so great an authority as that of Mr. Locke, I shall not be treated on this occasion as a mere visionary, and the propriety of the motion I shall have the honour of submitting to the House will scarcely be disputed. Even the members for such places as Old Sarum and Gatton, who I may venture to say at present *stant nominis umbræ*, will, I am persuaded, have too much candour to com-plain of the right of their few constituents, if indeed they have constituents, if they are not self-created, self-elected, self-exis-tent, of this pretended right being transferred to the county, while the rich and populous manufacturing towns of Birmingham, Manchester, Leeds, Sheffield, and others, may have at least an equitable share in the formation of those laws by which they are governed. My idea, sir, in this case, as to the wretched and depopulated towns and boroughs in general, I own is amputation. I say with Horace, *Inutiles ramos amputans, feliciores inserit.* This is not, sir, the first attempt of the kind to correct, although in an inconsiderable degree, this growing evil. Proceedings of a similar nature were had among us above a century past. The clerk will read from our journals what passed on the 26th of March, 1668, on a bill to enable the county palatine of Durham to send two knights for the county, and two citizens for the city of Durham.

The clerk reads: In a book of authority, " Anchitell Grey's Debates," we have a more particular account of what passed in the House on that occasion. He says that " Sir Thomas Meres moved, that the shires may have an increase of knights, and that some of the small boroughs, where there are but few electors, may be taken away; and a bill was brought in for that purpose." " On a division the bill was rejected, 65 to 50." This, however, alludes only to the bill then before the House, respecting the county and city of Durham. I desire to add the few remarkable words of Sir Thomas Strickland in this debate, because I have not seen them quoted on the late important American questions: " The county palatine of Durham was never taxed in Parliament, by ancient privilege, before King James's time, and so needed no representatives; but now being taxed, it is but reasonable they should have them." Such sentiments, sir, were promulgated in this House even so long ago as the reign of Charles II. I am aware, sir, that the power *de jure* of the legislature to disfranchise a number of boroughs, upon the general grounds of improving the constitution, has been doubted; and gentlemen will ask, whether a power is lodged in the representative to destroy his immediate constituent? Such a question is best answered by another. How originated the right, and upon what grounds was it gained? Old Sarum and Gatton, for instance, were populous towns when the right of representation was first given them. They are now desolate, and therefore ought not to retain a privilege which they acquired only by their extent and populousness. We ought in everything, as far as we can, to make the theory and practice of the constitution coincide, and the supreme legislative body of a state must surely have this power inherent in them. It was *de facto* lately exercised to its full extent by this House in the case of Shoreham, with universal approbation: for near a hundred corrupt voters were disfranchised, and about twice that number of freeholders admitted from the county of Sussex. It will be objected, I foresee, that a time of perfect calm and peace throughout this vast empire is the most proper to propose internal regulations of this importance; and that while intestine discord rages in the whole northern continent of America, our attention ought to be fixed upon the most alarming object, and all our efforts employed to extinguish the devouring flame of a civil war. In my opinion, sir, the American war is, in this truly critical area, one of the strongest arguments for the regulations of our representation, which I now submit to the House. During the rest of our lives, likewise, I may venture to prophecy, America will be the leading feature of this age. In our late disputes with the Americans, we have always taken it for granted that the people of England justified all the iniquitous, cruel, arbitrary, and mad proceedings of administration, because they had the approbation of the majority of this House. The absurdity of such an argument is apparent; for the majority of this House, we know, speak only the sense of 5,723 persons, even supposing, according to the constitutional custom of our ancestors, the constituent had been consulted on this great national point as he ought to have been. We have seen in what manner the acquiescence of a majority here is obtained. The people in the southern part of this island amount to upwards of five millions, the sense, therefore, of five millions cannot be ascertained by the opinion of not six thousand, even supposing it had been collected. The Americans with great reason insist that the present war is carried on contrary to the sense of the nation, by a ministerial junto, and an arbitrary faction, equally hostile to the rights of Englishmen and the claims of Americans. The various addresses to the throne from the most numerous bodies, praying that the sword may be returned to the scabbard, and all hostilities cease, confirm this assertion. The capital of our country has repeatedly declared, by various public acts, its abhorrence of the present unnatural civil war, begun on principles subversive of our constitution.

Our history furnishes frequent instances of the sense of Parliament running directly counter to the sense of the nation. It was notoriously of late the case in the business of the Middlesex election. I believe the fact to be equally certain in the grand American dispute, at least as to the actual hostilities now carrying on against our brethren and fellow-subjects. The proposal before us will bring the case to an issue, and from a fair and equal representation of the people, America may at length distinguish the real sentiments of freemen and Englishmen. I do not mean, sir, at this time, to go into a tedious detail of all the various proposals which have been made for redressing this irregularity in the representation of the people. I will not intrude on the indulgence of the House, which I have always found so favourable to me. When the bill is brought in, and sent to a committee, it will be the proper time to examine all the minutiæ of this great plan, and to determine on the propriety of what ought now to be done, as well as of what formerly was actually accomplished. The journals of Cromwell's Parliaments prove that a more equal representation was settled, and carried by him into execution. That wonderful, comprehensive mind embraced the whole of this powerful empire. Ireland was put on a par with Scotland, and each kingdom sent thirty members to Parliament, which consisted likewise of 400 from England and Wales, and was to be triennial. Our colonies were then a speck on the face of the globe; now they cover half the New World. I will at this time, sir, only throw out general ideas, that every free agent in this kingdom should, in my wish, be represented in Parliament; that the metropolis, which contains in itself a ninth part of the people, and the counties of Middlesex, York, and others, which so greatly abound with inhabitants, should receive an increase in their representation; that the mean and insignificant boroughs, so emphatically styled the rotten part of our constitution, should be lopped off, and the electors in them thrown into the counties; and the rich, populous, trading towns, Birmingham, Manchester, Sheffield, Leeds, and others, be permitted to send deputies to the great council of the nation. The disfranchising of the mean, venal, and dependent boroughs, would be laying the axe to the root of corruption and treasury influence, as well as aristocratical tyranny. We ought equally to guard against those who sell themselves, or whose lords sell them. Burgage tenures, and private property in a share of the legislature, are monstrous absurdities in a free state, as well as an insult to common sense. I wish, sir, an English Parliament to speak the free, unbiassed sense of the body of the English people, and of every man among us, of each individual who may be justly supposed to be comprehended in a fair majority.

The meanest mechanic, the poorest peasant and day-labourer, has important rights respecting his personal liberty, that of his wife and children, his property, however inconsiderable, his wages, his earnings, the very price and value of each day's hard labour, which are in many trades and manufactures regulated by the power of Parliament. Every law relative to marriage, to the protection of a wife, sister, or daughter, against violence and brutal lust, to every contract or agreement with a rapacious or unjust master, interest the manufacturer, the cottager, the servant, as well as the rich subjects of the state. Some share, therefore, in the power of making those laws which deeply interest them, and to which they are expected to pay obedience, should be referred even to this inferior, but most useful set of men in the community; and we ought always to remember this important truth, acknowledged by every free state—that all government is instituted for the good of the mass of the people to be governed; that they are the original fountain of power, and even of revenue, and in all events, the last resource. The various instances of partial injustice throughout this kingdom will likewise become the proper subjects of inquiry in the course of the bill before the committee, such as the many freeholds in the city of London, which are not represented in this House. These freeholds being within the particular jurisdiction of the city, are excluded from giving a vote in the county of Middlesex, and by Act of Parliament only liverymen can vote for Members of Parliament in London. These, and other particulars, I leave. I mention them now to show the necessity of a new regulation of the representation of this kingdom. My inquiries, sir, are confined to the southern part of the island. Scotland I leave to the care of its own careful and prudent sons. I hope they will spare a few moments from the management of the arduous affairs of England and America, which at present so much engross their time, to attend to the state of representation among their own people, if they have not all emigrated to this warmer and more fruitful climate. I am almost afraid that the forty-five Scottish gentlemen among us represent themselves. Perhaps in my plan for the improvement of the representation of England, almost all the natives of Scotland may be included. I shall only remark, that the proportion of representation between the two countries cannot be changed. In the twenty-second article of the Treaty of Union, the number of forty-five is to be the representative body in the Parliament of Great Britain for the northern part of this island. To increase the members for England and Wales beyond the number of which the English Parliament consisted at the period of that treaty, in 1706, would be a breach of public faith, and a violation of a solemn treaty between two independent states. My proposition has for its basis the preservation of that compact, the proportional share of each kingdom in the legislative body remaining exactly according to its establishment. The monstrous injustice and glaring partiality of the present representation of the commons of England has been fully stated, and is, I believe, almost universally acknowledged, as well as the necessity of our recurring to the great leading principle of our free constitution, which declares this House of Parliament to be only a delegated power from the people at large. Policy, no less than justice, calls our attention to this momentous point; and reason, not custom, ought to be our guide in a business of this consequence, where the rights of a free people are materially interested. Without a true representation of the commons our constitution is essentially defective, our Parliament is a delusive name, a mere phantom, and all other remedies to recover the pristine purity of the form of government established by our ancestors, would be ineffectual; even the shortening the period of Parliaments, and a place and pension bill, both which I highly approve, and think absolutely necessary. I therefore flatter myself, sir, that I have the concurrence of the House with the motion which I have now the honour of making, " That leave be given to bring in a bill for a just and equal representation of the people of England in Parliament."

ON IRISH RIGHTS

HENRY GRATTAN

DUBLIN: IRISH HOUSE OF COMMONS: 19 APRIL, 1780

SIR,—I have entreated an attendance on this day, that you might, in the most public manner, deny the claim of the British Parliament to make law for Ireland, and with one voice lift up your hands against it.

If I had lived when the 9th of William took away the woollen manufacture, or when the 6th of George the First declared this country to be dependent, and subject to laws to be enacted by the Parliament of England, I should have made a covenant with my own conscience to seize the first moment of rescuing my country from the ignominy of such acts of power; or, if I had a son, I should have administered to him an oath that he would consider himself a person separate and set apart for the discharge of so important a duty; upon the same principle am I now come to move a declaration of right, the first moment occurring, since my time, in which such a declaration could be made with any chance of success, and without aggravation of oppression.

Sir, it must appear to every person that, notwithstanding the import of sugar and export of woollens, the people of this country are not satisfied—something remains; the greater work is behind; the public heart is not well at ease. To promulgate our satisfaction; to stop the throats of millions with the votes of Parliament; to preach homilies to the volunteers; to utter invectives against the people under pretence of affectionate advice, is an attempt, weak, suspicious, and inflammatory.

You cannot dictate to those whose sense you are entrusted to represent; your ancestors, who sat within these walls, lost to Ireland trade and liberty; you, by the assistance of the people, have recovered trade, you still owe the kingdom liberty; she calls upon you to restore it.

The ground of public discontent seems to be, " we have gotten commerce, but not freedom ": the same power which took away the export of woollens and the export of glass may take them away again; the repeal is partial, and the ground of repeal is upon a principle of expediency.

Sir, expedient is a word of appropriated and tyrannical import; expedient is an ill-omened word, selected to express the reservation of authority, while the exercise is mitigated; expedient is the ill-omened expression of the Repeal of the American stamp act. England thought it expedient to repeal that law; happy had it been for mankind, if, when she withdrew the exercise, she had not reserved the right! To that reservation she owes the loss of her American empire, at the expense of millions, and America the seeking of liberty through a sea of bloodshed. The repeal of the woollen act, similarly circumstanced, pointed against the principle of our liberty, present relaxation, but tyranny in reserve, may be a subject for illumination to a populace, or a pretence for apostacy to a courtier, but cannot be the subject of settled satisfaction to a freeborn, an intelligent, and an injured community. It is therefore they consider the free trade as a trade *de facto*, not *de jure*, a licence to trade under the Parliament of England, not a free trade under the charters of Ireland, as a tribute to her strength; to maintain which, she must continue in a state of armed preparation, dreading the approach of a general peace, and attributing all she holds dear to the calamitous condition of the British interest in every quarter of the globe. This dissatisfaction, founded upon a consideration of the liberty we have lost, is increased when they consider the opportunity they are losing; for if this nation, after the death-wound given to her freedom, had fallen on her knees in anguish, and besought the Almighty to frame an occasion in which a weak and injured people might recover their rights, prayer could not have asked, nor God have furnished, a moment more opportune for the restoration of liberty, than this in which I have the honour to address you.

England now smarts under the lesson of the American war; the doctrine of Imperial legislature she feels to be pernicious; the revenues and monopolies annexed to it she has found to be untenable, she lost the power to enforce it; her enemies are a host, pouring upon her from all quarters of the earth; her armies are dispersed; the sea is not hers; she has no minister, no ally, no admiral, none in whom she long confides, and no general whom she has not disgraced; the balance of her fate is in the hands of Ireland; you are not only her last connection, you are the only nation in Europe that is not her enemy. Besides, there does, of late, a certain damp and spurious supineness overcast her arms and councils, miraculous as that vigour which has lately inspirited yours;—for with you everything is the reverse; never was there a Parliament in Ireland so possessed of the confidence of the people; you are the greatest political assembly now sitting in the world; you are at the head of an immense army; nor do we only possess an unconquerable force, but a certain unquenchable public fire, which has touched all ranks of men like a visitation.

Turn to the growth and spring of your country, and behold and admire it; where do you find a nation who, upon whatever concerns the rights of mankind, expresses herself with more truth or force, perspicuity or justice? not the set phrase of scholastic men, not the tame unreality of court addresses, not the vulgar raving of a rabble, but the genuine speech of liberty, and the unsophisticated oratory of a free nation.

See her military ardour, expressed not only in 40,000 men, conducted by instinct as they were raised by inspiration, but manifested in the zeal and promptitude of every young member of the growing community. Let corruption tremble; let the enemy, foreign or domestic, tremble; but let the friends of liberty rejoice at these means of safety and this hour of redemption. Yes, there does exist an enlightened sense of rights, a young appetite for freedom, a solid strength, and a rapid fire, which not only put a declaration of right within your power, but put it out of your power to decline one. Eighteen counties are at your bar; they stand there with the compact of Henry, with the charter of John, and with all the passions of the people. "Our lives are at your service, but our liberties—we received them from God; we will not resign them to man." Speaking to you thus, if you repulse these petitioners, you abdicate the privileges of Parliament, forfeit the rights of the kingdom, repudiate the instruction of your constituents, bilge the sense of your country, palsy the enthusiasm of the people, and reject that good which not a minister, not a Lord North, not a Lord Buckinghamshire, not a Lord Hillsborough, but a certain providential conjuncture, or rather the hand of God, seems to extend to you. Nor are we only prompted to this when we consider our strength; we are challenged to it when we look to Great Britain. The people of that country are now waiting to hear the Parliament of Ireland speak on the subject of their liberty; it begins to be made a question in England whether the principal persons wish to be free: it was the delicacy of former parliaments to be silent on the subject of commercial restrictions, lest they should show a knowledge of the fact, and not a sense of the violation; you have spoken out, you have shown a knowledge of the fact, and not a sense of the violation. On the contrary, you have returned thanks for a partial repeal made on a principle of power; you have returned thanks as for a favour, and your exultation has brought your charters as well as your spirit into question, and tends to shake to her foundation your title to liberty: thus you do not leave your rights where you found them. You have done too much not to do more; you have gone too far not to go on; you have brought yourselves into that situation, in which you must silently abdicate the rights of your country, or publicly restore them. It is very true you may feed your manufacturers, and landed gentlemen may get their rents, and you may export woollen, and may load a vessel with baize, serges, and kerseys, and you may bring back again directly from the plantations, sugar, indigo, specklewood, beetle-root, and panellas. But liberty, the foundation of trade, the charters of the land, the independency of Parliament, the securing, crowning, and the consummation of everything, are yet to come. Without them the work is imperfect, the foundation is wanting, the capital is wanting, trade is not free, Ireland is a colony without the benefit of a charter, and you are a provincial synod without the privileges of a parliament.

I read Lord North's proposition; I wish to be satisfied, but I am controlled by a paper, I will not call it a law, it is the sixth of George the First. [The paper was read.] I will ask the gentlemen of the long robe is this the law? I ask them whether it is not practice? I appeal to the judges of the land, whether they are not in a course of declaring that the Parliament of Great Britain, naming Ireland, binds her? I appeal to the magistrates of justice, whether they do not, from time to time, execute certain acts of the British Parliament? I appeal to the officers of the army, whether they do not fine, confine, and execute their fellow-subjects by virtue of the Mutiny Act, an act of the British Parliament; and I appeal to this House whether a country so circumstanced is free. Where is the freedom of trade? where is the security of property? where is the liberty of the people? I here, in this Declamatory Act, see my country proclaimed a slave! I see every man in this house enrolled a slave! I see the judges of the realm, the oracles of the law, borne down by an unauthorised foreign power, by the authority of the British Parliament against the law! I see the magistrates prostrate, and I see Parliament witness of these infringements, and silent (silent or employed to preach moderation to the people, whose liberties it will not restore)! I therefore say, with the voice of 3,000,000 of people, that, notwithstanding the import of sugar, beetle-wood and panellas, and the export of woollens and kerseys, nothing is safe, satisfactory, or honourable, nothing except a declaration of right. What! are you, with 3,000,000 of men at your back, with charters in one hand and arms in the other, afraid to say you are a free people? Are you, the greatest House of Commons that ever sat in Ireland, that want but this one act to equal that English House of Commons that passed the Petition of Right, or that other that passed the Declaration of Right, are you afraid to tell that British Parliament you are a free people? Are the cities and the instructing counties, who have breathed a spirit that would have done honour to old Rome when Rome did honour to mankind, are they to be free by connivance? Are the military associations, those bodies whose origin, progress, and deportment have transcended, equalled at least, anything in modern or ancient story—is the vast line of northern army, are they to be free by connivance? What man will settle among you? Where is the use of the Naturalisation Bill? What man will settle among you? who will leave a land of liberty and a settled government for a kingdom controlled by the Parliament of another country, whose liberty is a thing by stealth, whose trade a thing by permission, whose judges deny her charters, whose Parliament leaves everything at random; where the chance of freedom depends upon the hope, that the jury shall despise the judge stating a British act, or a rabble stop the magistrate executing it, rescue your abdicated privileges, and save the constitution by trampling on the government, by anarchy and confusion?

But I shall be told that these are groundless jealousies, and that the principal cities, and more than one half of the counties of the kingdom, are misguided men, raising those groundless jealousies. Sir, let me become, on this occasion, the people's advocate, and your historian; the people of this country were possessed of a code of liberty similar to that of Great Britain but lost it through the weakness of the kingdom and the pusillanimity of its leaders. Having lost our liberty by the usurpation of the British Parliament, no wonder we became a prey to her ministers; and they did plunder us with all the hands of all the harpies, for a series of years, in every shape of power, terrifying our people with the thunder of Great Britain, and bribing our leaders with the rapine of Ireland. The kingdom became a plantation, her Parliament, deprived of its privileges, fell into contempt; and, with the legislature, the law, the spirit of liberty, with her forms, vanished. If a war broke out, as in 1778, and an occasion occurred to restore liberty and restrain rapine, Parliament declined the opportunity; but, with an active servility and trembling loyalty, gave and granted, without regard to the treasure we had left, or the rights we had lost. If a partial separation was made upon a principle of expediency, Parliament did not receive it with the tranquil dignity of an august assembly, but with the alacrity of slaves.

The principal individuals, possessed of great property but no independency, corrupted by their extravagance, or enslaved by their following a species of English factor against an Irish people, more afraid of the people of Ireland than the tyranny of England, proceeded to that excess that they opposed every proposition to lessen profusion, extend trade, or promote liberty; they did more, they supported a measure which, at one blow, put an end to all trade; they did more, they brought you to a condition which they themselves did unanimously acknowledge a state of impending ruin; they did this, talking as they are now talking, arguing against trade as they now argue against liberty, threatening the people of Ireland with the power of the British nation, and imploring them to rest satisfied with the ruins of their trade, as they now implore them to remain satisfied with the wreck of their constitution.

The people thus admonished, starving in a land of plenty, the victim of two Parliaments, of one that stopped their trade, the other that fed on their constitution, inhabiting a country where industry was forbid, or towns swarming with begging manufacturers, and being obliged to take into their own hands that part of government which consists in protecting the subject, had recourse to two measures, which, in their origin, progress, and consequence, are the most extraordinary to be found in any age or in any country—viz., a commercial and a military association. The consequence of these measures was instant; the enemy that hung on your shores departed, the Parliament asked for a free trade, and the British nation granted the trade, but withheld the freedom. The people of Ireland are, therefore, not satisfied; they ask for a constitution; they have the authority of the wisest men in this house for what they now demand. What have these walls, for this last century, resounded? The usurpation of the British Parliament, and the interference of the privy council. Have we taught the people to complain, and do we now condemn their insatiability, because they desire us to remove such grievances, at a time in which nothing can oppose them, except the very men by whom these grievances were acknowledged?

Sir, we may hope to dazzle with illumination, and we may sicken with addresses, but the public imagination will never rest, nor will her heart be well at ease—never! so long as the Parliament of England exercises or claims a legislation over this country: so long as this shall be the case, that very free trade, otherwise a perpetual attachment, will be the cause of new discontent; it will create a pride to feel the indignity of bondage; it will furnish a strength to bite your chain, and the liberty withheld will poison the good communicated.

The British Minister mistakes the Irish character: had he intended to make Ireland a slave, he should have kept her a beggar; there is no middle policy; win her heart by the restoration of her right, or cut off the nation's right hand; greatly emancipate, or fundamentally destroy. We may talk plausibly to England, but so long as she exercises a power to bind this country, so long are the nations in a state of war; the claims of the one go against the liberty of the other, and the sentiments of the latter go to oppose those claims to the last drop of her blood. The English opposition, therefore, are right; mere trade will not satisfy Ireland—they judge of us by other great nations, by the nation whose political life has been a struggle for liberty; they judge of us with a true knowledge of, and just deference for, our character—that a country enlightened as Ireland, chartered as Ireland, armed as Ireland, and injured as Ireland, will be satisfied with nothing less than liberty.

I admire that public-spirited merchant (Alderman Horan) who spread consternation at the Custom-house, and, despising the example which great men afforded, determined to try the question, and tendered for entry what the British Parliament prohibits the subject to export, some articles of silk, and sought at his private risk the liberty of his country; with him I am convinced it is necessary to agitate the question of right. In vain will you endeavour to keep it back, the passion is too natural, the sentiment is too irresistible; the question comes on of its own vitality—you must reinstate the laws.

There is no objection to this resolution, except fears; I have examined your fears; I pronounce them to be frivolous. I might deny that the British nation was attached to the idea of binding Ireland; I might deny that England was a tyrant at heart; and I might call to witness the odium of North and the popularity of Chatham, her support of Holland, her contributions to Corsica, and the charters communicated to Ireland; but ministers have traduced England to debase Ireland; and politicians, like priests, represent the power they serve as diabolical, to possess with superstitious fears the victim whom they design to plunder. If England is a tyrant, it is you have made her so: it is the slave that makes the tyrant, and then murmurs at the master whom he himself has constituted. I do allow, on the subject of commerce, England was jealous in the extreme, and I do say it was commercial jealousy, it was the spirit of monopoly (the woollen trade and the act of navigation had made her tenacious of a comprehensive legislative authority), and having now ceded that monopoly, there is nothing in the way of your liberty except your own corruption and pusillanimity; and nothing can prevent your being free except yourselves. It is not in the disposition of England; it is not in the interest of England; it is not in her arms. What! can 8,000,000 of Englishmen, opposed to 20,000,000 of French, to 7,000,000 of Spanish, to 3,000,000 of Americans, reject the alliance of 3,000,000 in Ireland? Can 8,000,000 of British men, thus outnumbered by foes, take upon their shoulders the expense of an expedition to enslave you? Will Great Britain, a wise and magnanimous country, thus tutored by experience and wasted by war, the French navy riding her Channel, send an army to Ireland, to levy no tax, to enforce no law, to answer no end whatsoever, except to spoliate the charters of Ireland, and enforce a barren oppression? What! has England lost thirteen provinces? has she reconciled herself to this loss, and will she not be reconciled to the liberty of Ireland? Take notice, that the very constitution which I move you to declare, Great Britain herself offered to America: it is a very instructive proceeding in the British history. In 1778 a commission went out, with powers to cede to the thirteen provinces of America, totally and radically, the legislative authority claimed over her by the British Parliament and the Commissioners, pursuant to their powers, did offer to all, or any, of the American States the total surrender of the legislative authority of the British Parliament. I will read you their letter to the Congress. Here the letter was read, surrendering the power as aforesaid.]

What! has England offered this to the resistance of America, and will she refuse it to the loyalty of Ireland? Your fears then are nothing but an habitual subjugation of mind; that subjugation of mind which made you, at first, tremble at every great measure of safety; which made the principal men amongst us conceive the commercial association would be a war; that fear, which made them imagine the military association had a tendency to treason, which made them think a short money-bill would be a public convulsion; and yet these measures have not only proved to be useful but are held to be moderate, and the Parliament that adopted them praised, not for its unanimity only, but for its temper also. You now wonder that you submitted for so many years to the loss of the woollen trade and the deprivation of the glass trade; raised above your former abject state in commerce, you are ashamed at your past pusillanimity; so when you have summoned a boldness which shall assert the liberties of your country—raised by the act, and reinvested, as you will be, in the glory of your ancient rights and privileges, you will be surprised at yourselves, who have so long submitted to their violation. Moderation is but a relative term; for nations, like men, are only safe in proportion to the spirit they put forth, and the proud contemplation with which they survey themselves. Conceive yourselves a plantation, ridden by an oppressive government, and everything you have done is but a fortunate frenzy: conceive yourselves to be what you are, a great, a growing, and a proud nation, and a declaration of right is no more than the safe exercise of your indubitable authority.

But though you do not hazard disturbance by agreeing to this resolution, you do most exceedingly hazard tranquillity by rejecting it. Do not imagine that the question will be over when this motion shall be negatived. No; it will recur in a vast variety of shapes and diversity of places. Your constituents have instructed you in great numbers, with a powerful uniformity of sentiment, and in a style not the less awful because full of respect. They will find resources in their own virtue, if they have found none in yours. Public pride and conscious liberty, wounded by repulse, will find ways and means of vindication. You are in that situation in which every man, every hour of the day, may shake the pillars of the state; every court may swarm with the question of right; every quay and wharf with prohibited goods: what shall the Judges, what the Commissioners, do upon this occasion? Shall they comply with the laws of Ireland, and against the claims of England, and stand firm where you have capitulated? shall they, on the other hand, not comply, and shall they persist to act against the law? will you punish them if they do so? will you proceed against them for not showing a spirit superior to your own? On the other hand, will you not punish them? Will you leave liberty to be trampled on by those men? Will you bring them and yourselves, all constituted orders, executive power, judicial power, and parliamentary authority, into a state of odium, impotence, and contempt; transferring the task of defending public right into the hands of the populace, and leaving it to the judges to break the laws, and to the people to assert them? Such would be the consequence of false moderation, of irritating timidity, of inflammatory palliatives, of the weak and corrupt hope of compromising with the court, before you have emancipated the country.

I have answered the only semblance of a solid reason against the motion; I will remove some lesser pretences, some minor impediments; for instance, first, that we have a resolution of the same kind already on our Journals, it will be said; but how often was the great charter confirmed? not more frequently than your rights have been violated. In one solitary resolution, declaratory of your right, sufficient for a country whose history, from the beginning unto the end, has been a course of violation? The fact is, every new breach is a reason for a new repair; every new infringement should be a new declaration; lest charters should be overwhelmed with precedents to their prejudice, a nation's right obliterated, and the people themselves lose the memory of their own freedom.

I shall hear of ingratitude: I name the argument to despise it and the men who make use of it: I know the men who use it are not grateful, they are insatiate; they are public extortioners who would stop the tide of public prosperity, and turn it to the channel of their own emolument: I know of no species of gratitude which should prevent my country from being free, no gratitude which should oblige Ireland to be the slave of England. In cases of robbery and usurpation, nothing is an object of gratitude except the thing stolen, the charter spoliated. A nation's liberty cannot, like her treasures, be meted and parcelled out in gratitude; no man can be grateful or liberal of his conscience, nor woman of her honour, nor nation of her liberty: there are certain unimpartable, inherent, invaluable properties not to be alienated from the person, whether body politic or body natural. With the same contempt do I treat that charge which says that Ireland is insatiable; saying, that Ireland asks nothing but that which Great Britain has robbed her of, her rights and privileges; to say that Ireland will not be satisfied with liberty, because she is not satisfied with slavery, is folly. I laugh at that man who supposes that Ireland will not be content with a free trade and a free constitution; and would any man advise her to be content with less?

I shall be told that we hazard the modification of the law of Poynings' and the Judges' Bill, and the Habeas Corpus Bill, and the Nullum Tempus Bill; but I ask, have you been for years begging for these little things, and have not you yet been able to obtain them? and have you been contending against a little body of eighty men in Privy Council assembled, convocating themselves into the image of a parliament, and ministering your high office? and have you been contending against one man, an humble individual, to you a Leviathan— the English Attorney-General—who advises in the case of Irish bills, and exercises legislation in his own person, and makes your parliamentary deliberations a blank, by altering your bills or suppressing them? and have you not yet been able to conquer this little monster? Do you wish to know the reason? I will tell you: because you have not been a parliament, nor your country a people. Do you wish to know the remedy?— be a parliament, become a nation, and these things will follow in the train of your consequence. I shall be told that titles are shaken, being vested by force of English acts; but in answer to that, I observe, time may be a title, acquiescence a title, forfeiture a title, but an English act of parliament certainly cannot: it is an authority which, if a judge would charge, no jury would find, and which all the electors in Ireland have already disclaimed unequivocally, cordially, and universally. Sir, this is a good argument for an act of title, but no argument against a declaration of right. My friend who sits above me (Mr. Yelverton) has a Bill of Confirmation; we do not come unprepared to Parliament. I am not come to shake property, but to confirm property and restore freedom. The nation begins to form; we are moulding into a people; freedom asserted, property secured, and the army (a mercenary band) likely to be restrained by law. Never was such a revolution accomplished in so short a time, and with such public tranquillity. In what situation would those men who call themselves friends of constitution and of government have left you?

They would have left you without a title, as they state it, to your estates, without an assertion of your constitution, or a law for your army; and this state of unexampled private and public insecurity, this anarchy raging in the kingdom for eighteen months, these mock moderators would have had the presumption to call peace.

I shall be told that the judges will not be swayed by the resolution of this House. Sir, that the judges will not be borne down by the resolutions of Parliament, not founded in law, I am willing to believe; but the resolutions of this House, founded in law, they will respect most exceedingly. I shall always rejoice at the independent spirit of the distributors of the law, but must lament that hitherto they have given no such symptom. The judges of the British nation, when they adjudicated against the laws of that country, pleaded precedent and the prostration and profligacy of a long tribe of subservient predecessors, and were punished. The judges of Ireland, if they should be called upon, and should plead sad necessity, the thraldom of the times, and, above all, the silent fears of Parliament, they no doubt will be excused: but when your declarations shall have protected them from their fears; when you shall have emboldened the judges to declare the law according to the charter, I make no doubt they will do their duty; and your resolution, not making a new law, but giving new life to the old ones, will be secretly felt and inwardly acknowledged, and there will not be a judge who will not perceive, to the innermost recess of his tribunal, the truth of your charters and the vigour of your justice.

The same laws, the same charters, communicate to both kingdoms, Great Britain and Ireland, the same rights and privileges; and one privilege above them all is that communicated by Magna Charta, by the 25th of Edward the Third, and by a multitude of other statutes, "not to be bound by any act except made with the archbishops, bishops, earls, barons, and freemen of the commonalty," viz., of the parliament of the realm. On this right of exclusive legislation are founded the Petition of Right, Bill of Right, Revolution, and Act of Settlement. The King has no other title to his crown than that which you have to your liberty; both are founded, the throne and your freedom, upon the right vested in the subject to resist by arms, notwithstanding their oaths of allegiance, any authority attempting to impose acts of power as laws, whether that authority be one man or a host, the second James, or the British Parliament!

Every argument for the House of Hanover is equally an argument for the liberties of Ireland: the Act of Settlement is an act of rebellion, or the declaratory statute of the 6th of George the First an act of usurpation; for both cannot be law.

I do not refer to doubtful history, but to living record; to common charters; to the interpretation England has put upon these charters—an interpretation not made by words only, but crowned by arms; to the revolution she had formed upon them, to the king she has deposed, and to the king she has established; and, above all, to the oath of allegiance solemnly plighted to the House of Stuart, and afterwards set aside, in the instance of a grave and moral people absolved by virtue of these very charters.

And as anything less than liberty is inadequate to Ireland, so is it dangerous to Great Britain. We are too near the British nation, we are too conversant with her history, we are too much fired by her example, to be anything less than her equal; anything less, we should be her bitterest enemies—an enemy to that power which smote us with her mace, and to that constitution from whose blessings we were excluded: to be ground as we have been by the British nation, bound by her parliament, plundered by her crown, threatened by her enemies, insulted with her protection, while we returned thanks for her condescension, is a system of meanness and misery which has expired in our determination, as I hope it has in her magnanimity.

There is no policy left for Great Britain but to cherish the remains of her empire, and do justice to a country who is determined to do justice to herself, certain that she gives nothing equal to what she received from us when we gave her Ireland.

With regard to this country, England must resort to the free principles of government, and must forego that legislative power which she has exercised to do mischief to herself; she must go back to freedom, which, as it is the foundation of her constitution, so is it the main pillar of her empire; it is not merely the connection of the crown, it is a constitutional annexation, an alliance of liberty, which is the true meaning and mystery of the sisterhood, and will make both countries one arm and one soul, replenishing from time to time, in their immortal connection, the vital spirit of law and liberty from the lamp of each other's light; thus combined by the ties of common interest, equal trade and equal liberty, the constitution of both countries may become immortal, a new and milder empire may arise from the errors of the old, and the British nation assume once more her natural station—the head of mankind.

That there are precedents against us I allow—acts of power I would call them, not precedent; and I answer the English pleading such precedents, as they answered their kings when they urged precedents against the liberty of England: Such things are the weakness of the times; the tyranny of one side, the feebleness of the other, the law of neither; we will not be bound by them; or rather, in the words of the declaration of right, "no doing judgment, proceeding, or anywise to the contrary, shall be brought into precedent or example." Do not then tolerate a power—the power of the British Parliament over this land, which has no foundation in utility or necessity, or empire, or the laws of England, or the laws of Ireland, or the laws of nature, or the laws of God—do not suffer it to have a duration in your mind.

Do not tolerate that power which blasted you for a century, that power which shattered your loom, banished your manufactures, dishonoured your peerage, and stopped the growth of your people; do not, I say, be bribed by an export of woollen, or an import of sugar, and permit that power which has thus withered the land to remain in your country and have existence in your pusillanimity.

Do not suffer the arrogance of England to imagine a surviving hope in the fears of Ireland; do not send the people to their own resolves for liberty, passing by the tribunals of justice and the high court of parliament; neither imagine that, by any formation of apology, you can palliate such a commission to your hearts, still less to your children, who will sting you with their curses in your grave for having interposed between them and their Maker, robbing them of an immense occasion, and losing an opportunity which you did not create, and can never restore.

Hereafter, when these things shall be history, your age of thraldom and poverty, your sudden resurrection, commercial redress, and miraculous armament, shall the historian stop at liberty, and observe—that here the principal men among us fell into mimic trances of gratitude—they were awed by a weak ministry, and bribed by an empty treasury—and when liberty was within their grasp, and the temple opened her folding doors, and the arms of the people clanged, and the zeal of the nation urged and encouraged them on, that they fell down, and were prostituted at the threshold.

I might, as a constituent, come to your bar and demand my liberty. I do call upon you, by the laws of the land and their violation, by the instruction of eighteen counties, by the arms, inspiration, and providence of the present moment, tell us the rule by which we shall go—assert the law of Ireland—declare the liberty of the land.

I will not be answered by a public lie, in the shape of an amendment; neither, speaking for the subjects' freedom, am I to hear of faction. I wish for nothing but to breathe, in this our island, in common with my fellow-subjects, the air of liberty. I have no ambition, unless it be the ambition to break your chain, and contemplate your glory. I never will be satisfied so long as the meanest cottager in Ireland has a link of the British chain clanking to his rags; he may be naked, he shall not be in iron; and I do see the time is at hand, the spirit is gone forth, the declaration is planted; and though great men should apostatise, yet the cause will live; and though the public speaker should die, yet the immortal fire shall outlast the organ which conveyed it, and the breath of liberty, like the word of the holy man, will not die with the prophet, but survive him.

I shall move you, " That the King's most excellent Majesty, and the Lords and Commons of Ireland, are the only power competent to make laws to bind Ireland."

TRIAL OF WARREN HASTINGS

RICHARD BRINSLEY SHERIDAN

HOUSE OF LORDS: JUNE 1788

[Sheridan had taken ill, and retired to try if in the fresh air he could recover, so that he might conclude all he had to say upon the evidence on the second charge. Some time after, Mr. Fox informed their Lordships that Mr. Sheridan was much better, but that he felt he was not sufficiently so to be able to do justice to the subject he had in hand. Sheridan therefore made this concluding speech on a later day.]

MY LORDS, permit me to remind you, that, when I had last the honour of addressing you, I concluded with submitting to the Court the whole of the correspondence, as far as it could be obtained, between the principal and agents in the nefarious plot carried on against the nabob vizier and the begums of Oude. These letters demand of the Court the most grave and deliberate attention, as containing not only a narrative of that foul and unmanly conspiracy, but also a detail of the motives and ends for which it was formed, and an exposition of the trick and quibble, the prevarication and the untruth with which it was then acted, and is now attempted to be defended. It will here be naturally inquired, with some degree of surprise, how the private correspondence which thus establishes the guilt of its authors came to light? This was owing to a mutual resentment which broke out about the middle of December 1782 between the parties. Mr. Middleton, on the one hand, became jealous of the abatement of Mr. Hastings' confidence; and the governor-general was incensed at the tardiness with which the resident proceeded.

From this moment, shyness and suspicion between the principal and the agent took place. Middleton hesitated about the expediency of resuming the *jaghires*, and began to doubt whether the advantage would be equal to the risk. Mr. Hastings, whether he apprehended that Middleton was retarded by any return of humanity or sentiments of justice, by any secret combination with the begum and her son, or a wish to take the *lion's share* of the plunder to himself, was exasperated at the delay. Middleton represented the unwillingness of the nabob to execute the measure—the low state of his finances—that his troops were mutinous for want of pay—that his life had been in danger from an insurrection among them—and that in this moment of distress he had offered £100,000, in addition to a like sum paid before, as an equivalent for the resumption which was demanded of him. Of this offer, however, it now appears, *the nabob knew nothing!* In conferring an obligation, my Lords, it is sometimes contrived, from motives of delicacy, that the name of the donor shall be concealed from the person obliged; but here it was reserved for Middleton to refine this sentiment of delicacy, so as to leave the person *giving utterly ignorant of the favour he bestowed!*

But notwithstanding these little differences and suspicions, Mr. Hastings and Mr. Middleton, on the return of the latter to Calcutta in October 1782, lived in the same style of friendly collusion and fraudulent familiarity as formerly. After, however, an intimacy of about six months, the governor-general very unexpectedly arraigns his friend before the Board at Calcutta. It was on this occasion that the prisoner, rashly for himself, but happily for the purposes of justice, produced these letters. Whatever, my Lords, was the meaning of this proceeding — whether it was a juggle to elude inquiry, or whether it was intended to make an impression at Fyzabad—whether Mr. Hastings drew up the charge, and instructed Mr. Middleton how to prepare the defence; or whether the accused composed the charge, and the accuser the defence, there is discernible in the transaction the same habitual collusion in which the parties lived, and the prosecution ended, as we have seen, in a rhapsody, a repartee, and a poetical quotation by the prosecutor!

The *private letters*, my Lords, are the only part of the correspondence thus providentially disclosed, which is deserving of attention. They were written in the confidence of private communication, without any motives to palliate and colour facts, or to mislead. The counsel for the prisoner have, however, chosen to rely on the *public* correspondence, prepared, as appears on the very face of it, for the concealment of fraud and the purpose of deception. They, for example, dwelt on a letter from Mr. Middleton, dated December 1781, which intimates some supposed contumacy of the begums; and this they thought countenanced the proceedings which afterward took place, and particularly the resumption of the *jaghires;* but, my Lords, you cannot have forgotten, that both Sir Elijah Impey and Mr. Middleton declared, in their examination at your bar, that the letter was totally false. Another letter, which mentions " the determination of the nabob to resume the *jaghires*," was also dwelt upon with great emphasis; but it is in evidence that the nabob, on the contrary, could not, by any means, be induced to sanction the measure; that it was not indeed, till Mr. Middleton had actually issued his own *Perwannas* [warrants] for the collection of the rents, that the prince, to avoid a state of the lowest degradation, consented to give it the appearance of his act.

In the same letter, the resistance of the begums to the seizure of their treasures is noticed as an instance of *female levity*, as if their defence of the property assigned for their subsistence was a matter of censure, or that they merited a reproof for feminine lightness, because they urged an objection to being *starved!*

The opposition, in short, my Lords, which was *expected* from the princesses, was looked to as a justification of the proceedings which afterward happened. There is not, in the *private* letters, the slightest intimation of the anterior rebellion, which by prudent *afterthought* was so greatly magnified. There is not a syllable of those dangerous machinations which were to dethrone the nabob, nor of those sanguinary artifices by which the English were to be extirpated. It is indeed said, that if such measures were rigorously pursued, as had been set on foot, the people might be driven from murmurs to resistance, and rise up in arms against their oppressors.

Where then, my Lords, is the proof of this mighty rebellion? It is contained alone, where it is natural to expect it, in the *fabricated* correspondence between Middleton and Hastings, and in the affidavits collected by Sir Elijah Impey!

The gravity of the business on which the chief justice was employed on this occasion contrasted with the vivacity, the rapidity, and celerity of his movements, is exceedingly curious. At one moment he appeared in Oude, at another in Chunar, at a third in Benares, procuring testimony, and in every quarter exclaiming like Hamlet's Ghost, "SWEAR!" To him might also have been applied the words of Hamlet to the Ghost, "What, Truepenny! are you there?" But the similitude goes no further. He was never heard to give the injunction:

> "Taint not thy mind, nor let thy soul contrive
> Against thy *mother* aught!"

It is, my Lords, in some degree worthy of your observation, that not one of the private letters of Mr. Hastings has at any time been disclosed. Even Middleton, when all confidence was broken between them by the production of his private correspondence at Calcutta, either feeling for his own safety, or sunk under the fascinating influence of his master, did not dare attempt a retaliation! The letters of Middleton, however, are sufficient to prove the situation of the nabob, when pressed to the resumption of the *jaghires*. He is there described as being sometimes lost in sullen melancholy—at others, agitated beyond expression, exhibiting every mark of agonised sensibility. Even Middleton was moved by his distresses to interfere for a temporary respite, in which he might become more reconciled to the measure. " I am fully of opinion," said he, " that the despair of the nabob must impel him to violence. I know, also, that the violence must be fatal to himself; but yet I think, that with his present feelings, he will disregard all consequences."

Mr. Johnson, the assistant resident, also wrote to the same purpose. The words of his letter are memorable. " He thought it would require a *campaign* to execute the orders for the resumption of the *jaghires !* " A campaign against whom? Against the nabob, our friend and ally, who had *voluntarily* given the order ! ! This measure, then, which we have heard contended was for his good and the good of his country, could truly be only enforced by a campaign! Such is British justice! such is British humanity! Mr. Hastings guarantees to the allies of the company their prosperity and his protection. The former he secures by sending an army to plunder them of their wealth and to desolate their soil. The latter produces the misery and the ruin of the protected. His is the protection which the vulture gives to the lamb, which covers while it devours its prey; which, stretching its baleful pinions and hovering in mid air, disperses the kites and lesser birds of prey, and saves the innocent and helpless victim from all talons but its own.

It is curious, my Lords, to remark, that in the correspondence of these creatures of Mr. Hastings, and in their earnest endeavours to dissuade him from the resumption of the *jaghires*, not a word is mentioned of the measure being contrary to honour— to faith; derogatory to national character; unmanly or unprincipled. Knowing the man to whom they were writing, their only arguments were, that it was contrary to *policy* and to *expediency*. Not one word do they mention of the just claims which the nabob had to the gratitude and friendship of the English. Not one syllable of the treaty by which we were bound to protect him. Not one syllable of the relation which subsisted between him and the princesses they were about to plunder. Not one syllable is hinted of justice or mercy. All which they addressed to him was the apprehension that the money to be procured would not be worth the danger and labour with which it must be attended. There is nothing, my Lords, to be found in the history of human turpitude; nothing in the nervous delineations and penetrating brevity of Tacitus; nothing in the luminous and luxuriant pages of Gibbon, or of any other historian, dead or living, who, searching into measures and characters with the rigour of truth, presents to our abhorrence depravity in its blackest shapes, which can equal, in the grossness of the guilt, or in the hardness of heart with which it was conducted, or in low and grovelling motives, the acts and character of the prisoner. It was he who, in the base desire of stripping two helpless women, could stir the son to rise up in vengeance against them; who, when that son had certain touches of nature in his breast, certain feelings of an awakened conscience, could accuse him of entertaining peevish objections to the plunder and sacrifice of his mother; who, having finally divested him of all thought, all reflection, all memory, all conscience, all tenderness and duty as a son, all dignity as a monarch; having destroyed his character and depopulated his country, at length brought him to violate the dearest ties of nature, in countenancing the destruction of his parents. This crime, I say, has no parallel or prototype in the Old World or the New, from the day of original sin to the present hour. The victims of his oppression were confessedly destitute of all power to resist their oppressors. But their debility, which from other bosoms would have claimed some compassion, at least with respect to the mode of suffering, with him only excited the ingenuity of torture. Even when every feeling of the nabob was subdued; when, as we have seen, my Lords, nature made a last, lingering, feeble stand within his breast; even then, that cold spirit of malignity, with which his doom was fixed, returned with double rigour and sharper acrimony to its purpose, and compelled the child to inflict on the parent that destruction of which he was himself reserved to be the final victim.

Great as this climax, in which, my Lords, I thought the pinnacle of guilt was attained, there is yet something still more transcendently flagitious. I particularly allude to his [Hastings'] infamous letter, falsely dated the 15th of February 1782, in which, at the very moment that he had given the order for the entire destruction of the begums, and for the resumption of the *jaghires*, he expresses to the nabob the warm and lively interest which he took in his welfare; the sincerity and ardour of his friendship; and that, though his presence was eminently wanted at Calcutta, he could not refrain from coming to his assistance, and that in the meantime he had sent four regiments to his aid; so deliberate and cool, so hypocritical and insinuating, is the villainy of this man! What heart is not exasperated by the malignity of a treachery so barefaced and dispassionate? At length, however, the nabob was on his guard. He could not be deceived by this mask. The offer of the four regiments developed to him the object of Mr. Hastings. He perceived the daggar bunglingly concealed in the hand, which was treacherously extended as if to his assistance. From this moment the last faint ray of hope expired in his bosom. We accordingly find no further confidence of the nabob in the prisoner. Mr. Middleton now swayed his iron sceptre without control. The *jaghires* were seized. Every measure was carried. The nabob, mortified, humbled, and degraded, sunk into insignificance and contempt. This letter was sent at the very time when the troops surrounded the walls of Fyzabad; and then began a scene of horrors, which, if I wished to inflame your Lordships' feelings, I should only have occasion minutely to describe—to state the violence committed on that palace which the piety of the kingdom had raised for the retreat and seclusion of the objects of its pride and veneration! It was in these shades, rendered sacred by superstition, that innocence reposed. Here venerable age and helpless infancy found an asylum! If we look, my Lords, into the whole of this most wicked transaction, from the time when this treachery was first conceived, to that when, by a series of artifices the most execrable, it was brought to a completion, the prisoner will be seen standing aloof, indeed, but not inactive. He will be discovered reviewing his agents, rebuking at one time the pale conscience of Middleton, at another relying on the stouter villainy of Hyder Beg Cawn. With all the calmness of veteran delinquency, his eye will be seen ranging through the busy prospect, piercing the darkness of subordinate guilt, and disciplining with congenial adroitness the agents of his crimes and the instruments of his cruelty.

The feelings, my Lords, of the several parties at the time will be most properly judged of by their respective correspondence. When the bow [younger] begum, despairing of redress from the nabob, addressed herself to Mr. Middleton, and reminded him of the guarantee which he had signed, she was instantly promised that the amount of her *jaghire* should be made good, though he said he could not interfere with the sovereign decision of the nabob respecting the lands. The deluded and unfortunate woman " thanked God that Mr. Middleton was at hand for her relief." At this very instant he was directing every effort to her destruction; for he had actually written the orders which were to take the collection out of the hands of her agents! But let it not be forgotten, my Lords, when the begum was undeceived, when she found that British faith was no protection—when she found that she should leave the country, and prayed to the God of nations not to grant His peace to those who remained behind —there was still no charge of rebellion, no recrimination made to all her reproaches for the broken faith of the English; that, when stung to madness, she asked " how long would be her reign," there was no mention of her disaffection. The stress is therefore idle, which the counsel for the prisoner have strove to lay on these expressions of an injured and enraged woman. When, at last, irritated beyond bearing, she denounced infamy on the heads of her oppressors, who is there that will not say that she spoke in a *prophetic* spirit; and that what she then predicted has not, even to its last letter, been accomplished? But did Mr. Middleton, even to this violence, retort any particle of accusation? No! he sent a *jocose* reply, stating that he had received such a letter under her seal, but that from its contents, he could not suspect it to come from her; and begged therefore that she would endeavour to detect the *forgery!* Thus did he add to foul injuries the vile aggravation of a *brutal jest.* Like the tiger he showed the savageness of his nature by grinning at his prey, and fawning over the last agonies of his unfortunate victim!

The letters, my Lords, were then enclosed to the nabob, who, no more than the rest, made any attempt to justify himself by imputing any criminality to the begums. He only sighed a hope that his conduct to his parents had drawn no shame upon his head; and declared his intention to punish, not any disaffection in the begums, but some officious servants who had dared to foment the misunderstanding between them and himself. A letter was finally sent to Mr. Hastings, about six days before the seizure of the treasures from the begums, declaring their innocence; and referring the governor-general, in proof of it, to Captain Gordon, whose life they had protected, and whose safety should have been their justification. This inquiry was never made. It was looked on as unnecessary, because the conviction of their innocence was too deeply impressed already.

The counsel, my Lords, in recommending an attention to the public in reference to the private letters, remarked particularly that one of the latter should not be taken in evidence, because it was evidently and abstractedly private, relating the anxieties of Mr. Middleton on account of the illness of his son. This is a singular argument indeed. The circumstance, however, undoubtedly merits strict observation, though not in the view in which it was placed by the counsel. It goes to show that some, at least, of the persons concerned in these transactions felt the force of those ties which their efforts were directed to tear asunder; that those who could ridicule the respective attachment of a mother and a son; who could prohibit the reverence of the son to the mother; who could deny to maternal debility the protection which filial tenderness should afford, were yet sensible of the straining of those chords by which they are connected. There is something in the present business, with all that is horrible to create aversion, so vilely loathsome as to excite disgust. It is, my Lords, surely superfluous to dwell on the sacredness of the ties which those aliens to feeling, those apostates to humanity, thus divided. In such an assembly as the one before which I speak, there is not an eye but must look reproof to this conduct, not a heart but must anticipate its condemnation. *Filial piety!* It is the primal bond of society. It is that instinctive principle which, panting for its proper good, soothes, unbidden, each sense and sensibility of man. It now quivers on every lip. It now beams from every eye. It is that gratitude which, softening under the sense of recollected good, is eager to own the vast, countless debt it never, alas! can pay, for so many long years of unceasing solicitudes, honourable self-denials, life-preserving cares. It is that part of our practice where duty drops its awe, where reverence refines into love. It asks no aid of memory. It needs not the deductions of reason. Pre-existing, paramount over all, whether moral law or human rule, few arguments can increase, and none can diminish it. It is the sacrament of our nature; not only the duty, but the indulgence of man. It is the first great privilege. It is among his last most endearing delights. It causes the bosom to glow with reverberated love. It requites the visitations of nature, and returns the blessings that have been received. It fires emotion into vital principle. It changes what was instinct into a master passion; sways all the sweetest energies of man; hangs over each vicissitude of all that must pass away; and aids the melancholy virtues in their last sad tasks of life, to cheer the languors of decrepitude and age, and

" Explore the thought, explain the aching eye! "

But, my Lords, I am ashamed to consume so much of your Lordships' time in attempting to give a cold picture of this sacred impulse, when I behold so many breathing testimonies of its influence around me; when every countenance in this assembly is beaming, and erecting itself into the recognition of this universal principle!

The expressions contained in the letter of Mr. Middleton, of tender solicitude for his son, have been also mentioned, as a proof of the amiableness of his affections. I confess that they do not tend to raise his character in my estimation. Is it not rather an aggravation of his guilt, that he, who thus felt the anxieties of a parent, and who, consequently, must be sensible of the reciprocal feelings of a child, could be brought to tear asunder, and violate in others, all those dear and sacred bonds? Does it not enhance the turpitude of the transaction, that it was not the result of idiotic ignorance or brutal indifference? I aver that his guilt is increased and magnified by these considerations. His criminality would have been less had he been insensible to tenderness —less, if he had not been so thoroughly acquainted with the true quality of paternal love and filial duty.

The *jaghires* being seized, my Lords, the begums were left without the smallest share of that pecuniary compensation promised by Mr. Middleton as an equivalent for the resumption. And as tyranny and injustice, when they take the field, are always attended by their camp followers, paltry pilfering and petty insult, so in this instance the goods taken from the princesses were sold at a mock sale at an inferior value. Even gold and jewels, to use the language of the begums, instantly lost their value when it was known that they came from them. Their ministers were imprisoned, to extort the deficiency which this fraud occasioned; and every mean art was employed to justify a continuance of cruelty toward them. Yet this was small to the frauds of Mr. Hastings. After extorting upward of £600,000, he forebade Mr. Middleton to come to a *conclusive settlement* with the princesses. He knew that the treasons of our allies in India had their origin solely in the wants of the Company. He could not, therefore, say that the begums were entirely innocent, until he had consulted the General Record of Crimes, *the Cash Account of Calcutta!* His prudence was fully justified by the event; for there was actually found a balance of *twenty-six lacs* more against the begums, which £260,000 worth of treason had never been dreamed of before. " Talk not to us," said the governor-general, "of their guilt or innocence, but as it suits the Company's *credit!*

We will not try them by the Code of Justinian, nor the Institutes of Timur. We will not judge them either by British laws, or their local customs! No! we will try them by the *Multiplication Table ;* we will find the guilty by the *Rule of Three ;* and we will condemn them according to the unerring rules of—COCKER's *Arithmetic !* "

My Lords, the prisoner has said in his defence, that the cruelties exercised toward the begums were not of his order. But in another part of it he avows, " that whatever were their distresses, and whoever was the agent in the measure, it was, in his opinion, reconcilable to justice, honour, and sound policy." By the testimony of Major Scott, it appears, that though the defence of the prisoner was not drawn up by himself, yet that this paragraph he wrote with his *own proper hand.* Middleton, it seems, had confessed his share in these transactions with some degree of compunction, and solicitude as to the consequences. The prisoner observing it, cries out to him: " Give me the pen; I will defend the measure as just and necessary. I will take something upon myself. Whatever part of the load you cannot bear, my *unburdened* character shall assume! Your conduct I will crown with my irresistible approbation. Do you find *memory* and I will find *character*, and thus twin warriors we will go into the field, each in his proper sphere of action, and assault, repulse, and contumely shall all be set at defiance."

If I could not prove, my Lords, that those acts of Mr. Middleton were in reality the acts of Mr. Hastings, I should not trouble your Lordships by combating them; but as this part of his criminality can be incontestably ascertained, I appeal to the assembled legislators of this realm to say whether these acts were justifiable on the score of *policy*. I appeal to all the august presidents in the courts of British justice, and to all the learned ornaments of the profession, to decide whether these acts were reconcilable to *justice*. I appeal to the reverend assemblage of prelates feeling for the general interests of humanity and for the honour of the religion to which they belong, to determine whether these acts of Mr. Hastings and Mr. Middleton were such as a Christian ought to perform, or a man to avow.

My Lords, with the ministers of the nabob [Bahar Ally Cawn and Jewar Ally Cawn] was confined in the same prison that arch-rebel Sumshire Khan, against whom so much criminality has been charged by the counsel for the prisoner. We hear, however, of no inquiry having been made concerning his treason, though so many were held respecting the *treasures* of the others. With all his guilt, he was not so far noticed as to be deprived of his *food*, to be complimented with *fetters*, or even to have the satisfaction of being *scourged*, but was *cruelly* liberated from a dungeon, and *ignominiously* let loose on his parole!

Here Sheridan read the following order from Mr. Middleton to Lieutenant Rutledge in relation to the begums' ministers, dated 28th January 1782:
" SIR,—When this note is delivered to you by Hoolas Roy, I have to desire that you order the two prisoners to be put *in irons, keeping them from all food, etc., agreeably to my instructions of yesterday.* NATH. MIDDLETON."

The begums' ministers, on the contrary, to extort from them the disclosure of the place which concealed the treasures, were, according to the evidence of Mr. Holt, after being fettered and imprisoned, led out on a scaffold, and this array of terrors proving unavailing, the *meek*-tempered Middleton, as a *dernier ressort*, menaced them with a confinement in the fortress of Chunargar. Thus, my lords, was a British garrison made the *climax of cruelties* To English arms, to English officers, around whose banners humanity has ever entwined her most glorious wreath, how will this sound? It was in this fort, where the British flag was flying, that these helpless prisoners were doomed to deeper dungeons, heavier chains, and severer punishments. Where that flag was displayed which was wont to cheer the depressed, and to dilate the subdued heart of misery, these venerable but unfortunate men were fated to encounter every aggravation of horror and distress. It, moreover, appears that they were both cruelly flogged, though one was above seventy years of age. Being charged with disaffection, they vindicated their innocence— " Tell us where are the remaining treasures," was the reply. " It is only treachery to your immediate sovereigns, and you will then be fit associates for the representatives of British faith and British justice in India!" O Faith! O Justice! I conjure you by your sacred names to depart for a moment from this place, though it be your peculiar residence; nor hear your names profaned by such a sacrilegious combination as that which I am now compelled to repeat—where all the fair forms of nature and art, truth and peace, policy and honour, shrink back aghast from the deleterious shade—where all existences, nefarious and vile, have sway—where, amid the black agents on one side and Middleton with Impey on the other, the great figure of the piece —characteristic in his place, aloof and independent from the puny profligacy in his train, but far from idle and inactive, turning a malignant eye on all mischief that awaits him; the multiplied apparatus of temporising expedients and intimidating instruments, now cringing on his prey, and fawning on his vengeance—now quickening the limping pace of craft, and forcing every stand that retiring nature can make to the heart; the attachments and the decorums of life; each emotion of tenderness and honour; and all the distinctions of national pride; with a long catalogue of crimes and aggravations beyond the reach of thought for human malignity to perpetrate or human vengeance to punish; *lower* than *perdition—blacker* than *despair!*

It might, my Lords, have been hoped, for the honour of the human heart, that the begums were themselves exempted from a share in these sufferings, and that they had been wounded only through the sides of their ministers. The reverse of this, however, is the fact. Their palace was surrounded by a guard, which was withdrawn by Major Gilpin to avoid the growing resentments of the people, and replaced by Mr. Middleton, through his fears of that "dreadful responsibility" which was imposed upon him by Mr. Hastings. The women, also, of the khord mahal, who were not involved in the begums' supposed crimes; who had raised no *sub-rebellion* of their own; and who, it has been proved, lived in a distinct dwelling, were causelessly implicated, nevertheless, in the same punishment. Their residence surrounded with guards, they were driven to despair by famine, and when they poured forth in sad procession, were beaten with bludgeons, and forced back by the soldiery to the scene of madness which they had quitted. These are acts, my Lords, which, when told, need no comment. I will not offer a single syllable to awaken your Lordships' feelings; but leave it to the facts which have been stated to make their own impression.

The inquiry which now only remains, my Lords, is, whether Mr. Hastings is to be answerable for the crimes committed by his agents? It has been fully proved that Mr. Middleton signed the treaty with the superior begum in October 1778. He also acknowledged signing some others of a different date, but could not *recollect* the authority by which he did it! These treaties were recognised by Mr. Hastings, as appears by the evidence of Mr. Purling, in the year 1780. In that of October 1778, the *jaghire* was secured, which was allotted for the support of the women in the khord mahal. But still the prisoner pleads that he is not accountable for the cruelties which were exercised. His is the plea which tyranny, aided by its prime minister, treachery, is always sure to set up. Mr. Middleton has attempted to strengthen this ground by endeavouring to claim the whole infamy in these transactions, and to monopolise the guilt! He dared even to aver, that he had been condemned by Mr. Hastings for the ignominious part he had acted. He dared to avow this, because Mr. Hastings was on his trial, and he thought he never would be arraigned; but in the face of this Court, and before he left the bar, he was compelled to confess that it was for the *lenience*, and not the *severity* of his proceedings, that he had been reproved by the prisoner.

It will not, I trust, be concluded that because Mr. Hastings has not marked every passing shade of guilt, and because he has only given the bold outline of cruelty, he is therefore to be acquitted. It is laid down by the law of England, that law which is the perfection of reason, that a person ordering an act to be done by his agent is answerable for that act with all its consequences, " Quod facit per alium, facit per se." Middleton was appointed, in 1777, the confidential agent, the *second self* of Mr. Hastings. The governor-general ordered the measure. Even if he never saw, nor heard afterward of its consequences, he was therefore answerable for every pang that was inflicted, and for all the blood that was shed. But he did hear, and that instantly, of the whole. He wrote to accuse Middleton of forbearance and of neglect! He commanded him to work upon the hopes and fears of the princesses, and to leave no means untried, until, to speak his own language, which was better suited to the banditti of a cavern, " he obtained possession of the secret hoards of the old ladies." He would not allow even of a delay of two days to smooth the compelled approaches of a son to his mother, on this occasion! His orders were peremptory. After this, my Lords, can it be said that the prisoner was ignorant of the acts, or not culpable for their consequences? It is true, he did not direct the guards, the famine, and the bludgeons; he did not weigh the fetters, nor number the lashes to be inflicted on his victims; but yet he is just as guilty as if he had borne an active and personal share in each transaction. It is as if he had commanded that the heart should be torn from the bosom, and enjoined that no blood should follow. He is in the same degree accountable to the *law*, to his *country*, to his *conscience*, and to his GOD!

The prisoner has endeavoured also to get rid of a part of his guilt, by observing that he was but one of the supreme council, and that all the rest had sanctioned those transactions with their approbation. Even if it were true that others did participate in

the guilt, it cannot tend to diminish his criminalty. But the
fact is, that the council erred in nothing so much as in a repre-
hensible credulity given to the declarations of the governor-
general. They knew not a word of those transactions until they
were finally concluded. It was not until the January following
that they saw the mass of falsehood which had been published
under the title of " Mr. Hastings' Narrative." They were, then,
unaccountably duped to permit a letter to pass, dated the 29th
of November, intended to seduce the directors into a belief that
they had received intelligence at that time, which was not the
fact. These observations, my Lords, are not meant to cast any
obloquy on the council; they undoubtedly were deceived; and
the deceit practised on them is a decided proof of his consciousness of guilt. When tired of corporeal infliction, Mr. Hastings
was gratified by insulting the understanding. The coolness and
reflection with which this act was managed and concerted raises
its enormity and blackens its turpitude. It proves the prisoner
to be that monster in nature, a *deliberate and reasoning tyrant !*
Other tyrants of whom we read, such as a Nero, or a Caligula, were
urged to their crimes by the impetuosity of passion. High rank
disqualified them from advice, and perhaps equally prevented
reflection. But in the prisoner we have a man born in a state
of mediocrity; bred to mercantile life; used to system; and
accustomed to regularity; who was accountable to his masters,
and therefore was compelled to think and to deliberate on every
part of his conduct. It is this cool deliberation, I say, which
renders his crimes more horrible, and his character more
atrocious.

When, my Lords, the Board of Directors received the advices
which Mr. Hastings thought proper to transmit, though un-
furnished with any other materials to form their judgment, they
expressed very strongly their doubts, and properly ordered an
inquiry into the circumstances of the alleged disaffection of the
begums, declaring it, at the same time, to be a debt which was
due to the honour and justice of the British nation. This inquiry,
however, Mr. Hastings thought it absolutely necessary to elude.
He stated to the council, in answer, " that it would revive those
animosities that subsisted between the begums and the nabob
[Asoph Dowlah], which had then subsided. If the former were
inclined to appeal to a foreign jurisdiction, they were the best
judges of their own feeling, and should be left to make their own
complaint." All this, however, my Lords, is nothing to the
magnificent paragraph which concludes this communication.

" Besides," says he, " I hope it will not be a departure from official language to say, that the *majesty of justice* ought not to be approached without solicitation. She ought not to descend to inflame or provoke, but to withhold her judgment until she is called on to determine." What is still more astonishing is, that Sir John Macpherson, who, though a man of sense and honour, is rather Oriental in his imagination, and not learned in the sublime and beautiful from the immortal leader of this prosecution, was caught by this bold, bombastic quibble, and joined in the same words, " That the *majesty of justice* ought not to be approached without solicitation." But, my Lords, do you, the judges of this land, and the expounders of its rightful laws—do you approve of this mockery and call it the character of justice, which takes the *form of right* to excite wrong? No, my Lords, justice is not this halt and miserable object; it is not the ineffective bawble of an Indian pagod; it is not the portentous phantom of despair; it is not like any fabled monster, formed in the eclipse of reason, and found in some unhallowed grove of superstitious darkness and political dismay! No, my Lords. In the happy reverse of all this, I turn from the disgusting caricature to the real image! *Justice* I have now before me august and pure! The abstract idea of all that would be perfect in the spirits and the aspirings of men!—where the mind rises; where the heart expands; where the countenance is ever placid and benign; where her favourite attitude is to stoop to the unfortunate; to hear their cry and to help them; to rescue and relieve, to succour and save; majestic, from its mercy; venerable, from its utility; uplifted, without pride; firm, without obduracy; beneficent in each preference; lovely, though in her frown!

On that justice I rely : deliberate and sure, abstracted from all party purpose and political speculation; not on words, but on facts. You, my Lords, who hear me, I conjure, by those rights which it is your best privilege to preserve; by that fame which it is your best pleasure to inherit; by all those feelings which refer to the first term in the series of existence, the original compact of our nature, our controlling rank in the creation. This is the call on all to administer to truth and equity, as they would satisfy the laws and satisfy themselves, with the most exalted bliss possible or conceivable for our nature; the self-approving consciousness of virtue, when the condemnation we look for will be one of the most ample mercies accomplished for mankind since the creation of the world! My Lords, I have done.

THE LIBERTY OF THE PRESS
(DEFENCE OF TOM PAINE)

HENRY, LORD ERSKINE

COURT OF KING'S BENCH: 18 DEC. 1792

GENTLEMEN OF THE JURY,—The Attorney-General, in that part of his address which referred to a letter supposed to have been written to him from France, exhibited signs of strong sensibility and emotion. I do not, I am sure, charge him with acting a part to seduce you; on the contrary, I am persuaded, from my own feelings, and from my acquaintance with my friend from our childhood upwards, that HE expressed himself as he felt. But, gentlemen, if he felt those painful embarrassments, you may imagine what MINE must be: he can only feel for the august character whom he represents in this place as a subject for his Sovereign, too far removed by custom from the intercourses which generate affections to produce any other sentiments than those that flow from a relation common to us all: but it will be remembered that I stand in the same relation towards another great person more deeply implicated by this supposed letter; who, not restrained from the cultivation of personal attachments by those qualifications which must always secure them, has exalted my duty to a Prince into a warm and honest affection between man and man. Thus circumstanced, I certainly should have been glad to have had an earlier opportunity of knowing correctly the contents of this letter, and whether (which I positively deny) it proceeded from the defendant. Coming thus suddenly upon us, I see but too plainly the impression it has made upon *you*, who are to try the cause, and I feel its weight upon *myself*, who am to conduct it; but this shall neither detach me from my duty, nor enervate me (if I can help it) in the discharge of it.

If the Attorney-General be well founded in the commentaries he has made to you upon the book which he prosecutes; if he be warranted by the law of England in repressing its circulation, from the illegal and dangerous matters contained in it; if that suppression be, as he avows it, and as in common sense it must be, the sole object of the prosecution, the public has great reason to lament that this letter should have been at all brought into the service of the cause. It is no part of the charge upon the record; it had no existence for months after the work was composed and published; it was not written by the defendant, if written by him at all, till after he had been in a manner insultingly expelled from the country by the influence of Government; it was not even written till he had become the subject of another country. It cannot, therefore, by any fair inference, decipher the mind of the author when he composed his work; still less can it affect the construction of the language in which it is written. The introduction of this letter at all is, therefore, not only a departure from the charge, but a dereliction of the object of the prosecution, which is to condemn *the book*: since, if the condemnation of the author is to be obtained, *not by the work itself*, but by *collateral matter*, not even existing when it was written, nor known to its various publishers throughout the kingdom, how can a verdict upon *such* grounds condemn the work, or criminate *other* publishers, strangers to the collateral matter on which the conviction may be obtained to-day? I maintain, therefore, upon every principle of sound policy, as it affects the interests of the Crown, and upon every rule of justice, as it affects the author of *The Rights of Man*, that the letter should be wholly dismissed from your consideration.

Gentlemen, the Attorney-General has thought it necessary to inform you that a rumour had been spread, and had reached his ears, that he only carried on the prosecution as a *public* prosecutor, but without the concurrence of his own judgment; and, therefore, to add the just weight of his *private* character to his public duty, and to repel what he thinks a calumny, he tells you that he should have deserved to have been driven from society if he had not arraigned the work and the author before you. Here, too, we stand in situations very different. I have no doubt of the existence of such a rumour, and of its having reached his ears, because he says so; but for the narrow circle in which any rumour, personally implicating my learned friend's character, has extended, I might appeal to the multitudes who surround us, and ask, which of them all, except the few connected in office with the Crown, ever heard of its existence? But with regard to myself, every man within hearing at this moment, nay, the whole people of England, have been witnesses to the calumnious clamour that, by every art, has been raised and kept up against me: in every place where business or pleasure collect the public together, day after day my name and character have been the topics of injurious reflection. And for what? Only for not having shrunk from the discharge of a duty which no personal advantage recommended, and which a thousand difficulties repelled. But, gentlemen, I have no complaint to make, either against the printers of these libels, or even against their authors: the greater part of them, hurried perhaps away by honest prejudices, may have believed they were serving their *country* by rendering *me* the object of its suspicions and contempt; and if there had been amongst them others who have mixed in it from personal malice and unkindness, I thank God I can forgive *them* also. Little, indeed, did they know me, who thought that such calumnies would influence my conduct. I will for ever, at all hazards, assert the dignity, independence, and integrity of the ENGLISH BAR, without which impartial justice, the most valuable part of the English constitution, can have no existence. From the moment that any advocate can be permitted to say that he *will* or will *not* stand between the Crown and the subject arraigned in the court where he daily sits to practise, from that moment the liberties of England are at an end. If the advocate refuses to defend, from what *he may think* of the charge or of the defence, he assumes the character of the Judge; nay, he assumes it before the hour of judgment; and, in proportion to his rank and reputation, puts the heavy influence of, perhaps, a mistaken opinion into the scale against the accused, in whose favour the benevolent principle of English law makes all presumptions, and which commands the very Judge to be his counsel.

Gentlemen, it is now my duty to address myself without digression to the defence.

The first thing which presents itself in the discussion of any subject is to state distinctly, and with precision, what the question is, and, where prejudice and misrepresentation have been exerted, to distinguish it accurately from what it is NOT. The question, then, is NOT whether the constitution of our fathers—under which we live, under which I present myself before you, and under which alone you have any jurisdiction to hear me—be or be not preferable to the constitution of America or France, or any other human constitution. For upon what principle can a court, constituted by the authority of any Government, and administering a positive system of law under it, pronounce a decision against the constitution which creates its authority, or the rule of action which its jurisdiction is to enforce? The common sense of the most uninformed person must revolt at such an absurd supposition.

I have no difficulty, therefore, in admitting that, if by accident some or all of you were alienated in opinion and affection from the forms and principles of the English Government, and were impressed with the value of that unmixed representative constitution which this work recommends and inculcates, you could not *on that account* acquit the defendant. Nay, to speak out plainly, I freely admit that even if you were avowed enemies to monarchy, and devoted to republicanism, you would be nevertheless bound by your oaths, as a jury sworn to administer justice according to the English law, to convict the author of *The Rights of Man*, if it were brought home to your consciences that he had exceeded those widely-extended bounds which the ancient wisdom and liberal policy of the English constitution have allotted to the range of a free press. I freely concede this, because you have no jurisdiction to judge either the author or the work by any rule but that of English law, which is the source of your authority. But having made this large concession, it follows, by a consequence so inevitable as to be invulnerable to all argument or artifice, that if, on the other hand, you should be impressed (which I know you to be) not only with a dutiful regard, but with an enthusiasm, for the whole form and substance of your own Government; and though you should think that this work, in its circulation amongst classes of men unequal to political researches, may tend to alienate opinion; still you cannot, *upon such grounds*, without a similar breach of duty, convict the defendant of a libel—unless he has clearly stepped beyond that extended range of communication which the same ancient wisdom and liberal policy of the British constitution has allotted for the liberty of the press.

Gentlemen, I admit, with the Attorney-General, that in every case where a court has to estimate the quality of a writing, the *mind* and *intention* of the writer must be taken into the account, —the *bona* or *mala fides*, as lawyers express it, must be examined, —for a writing may undoubtedly proceed from a motive, and be directed to a purpose, not to be deciphered by the mere construction of the thing written. But wherever a writing is arraigned as seditious or slanderous, not upon its ordinary construction in language, nor from the necessary consequences of its publication, under *any* circumstances, and at *all* times, but that the criminality springs from some *extrinsic matter*, not visible upon the page itself, nor universally operative, but capable only of being connected with it by evidence, so as to demonstrate the effect of the publication and the design of the publisher; such a writing, not libellous PER SE, cannot be arraigned as the author's work is arraigned upon the record before the court. I maintain, without the hazard of contradiction, that the law of England positively requires, for the security of the subject, that every charge of a libel complicated with *extrinsic facts and circumstances, dehors the writing*, must appear literally upon the record by an averment of such extrinsic facts and circumstances, that the defendant may know what crime he is called upon to answer, and how to stand upon his defence. What crime is it that the defendant comes to answer for to-day? —what is the notice that I, who am his counsel, have from this parchment of the crime alleged against him? I come to defend his having written *this book*. The record states nothing else:— the general charge of sedition in the introduction is notoriously paper and packthread; because the innuendoes cannot enlarge the sense or natural construction of the text. The record does not state any one *extrinsic fact or circumstance* to render the work criminal at one time more than *another;* it states no peculiarity of time or season or intention, not provable from the writing itself, which is the naked charge upon record. There is nothing, therefore, which gives you any jurisdiction beyond the construction of the *work itself ;* and you cannot be justified in finding it criminal because published at *this* time, unless it would have been a criminal publication under any circumstances, or at *any other* time.

The law of England, then, both in its forms and substance, being the only rule by which the author or the work can be justified or condemned, and the charge upon the record being the naked charge of a libel, the cause resolves itself into a question of the deepest importance to us all—THE NATURE AND EXTENT OF THE LIBERTY OF THE ENGLISH PRESS.

But before I enter upon it, I wish to fulfil a duty to the defendant, which, if I do not deceive myself, is at this moment peculiarly necessary to his impartial trial. If an advocate entertains sentiments injurious to the defence he is engaged in, he is not only justified, but bound in duty, to conceal them; so, on the other hand, if his own genuine sentiments, or anything connected with his character or situation, can add strength to his professional assistance, he is bound to throw them into the scale. In addressing myself, therefore, to gentlemen not only zealous for the honour of English Government, but *visibly* indignant at any attack upon its principles, and who would, perhaps, be impatient of arguments from a suspected quarter, I give my client the benefit of declaring that I am, and ever have been, attached to the genuine principles of the British Government; and that, however the Court or you may reject the application, I defend him upon principles not only consistent with its permanence and security, but without the establishment of which it never could have had an existence.

The proposition which I mean to maintain as the basis of the liberty of the press, and without which it is an empty sound, is this: that every man, not intending to mislead, but seeking to enlighten others with what his own reason and conscience, however erroneously, have dictated to him as truth, may address himself to the universal reason of a whole nation, either upon the subject of governments in general, or upon that of our own particular country: that he may analyse the principles of its constitution, point out its errors and defects, examine and publish its corruptions, warn his fellow-citizens against their ruinous consequences, and exert his whole faculties in pointing out the most advantageous changes in establishments which he considers to be radically defective, or sliding from their object by abuse. All this every subject of this country has a right to do, if he contemplates only what he thinks would be for its advantage, and but seeks to change the public mind by the conviction which flows from reasonings dictated by conscience.

If, indeed, he writes *what he does not think* ; if, contemplating the misery of others, he wickedly condemns what his own understanding approves; or, even admitting his real disgust against the Government or its corruptions, if he *calumniates living magistrates*, or holds out to individuals that they have a right to run before the public mind in their *conduct* ; that they may oppose by contumacy or force what private reason only disapproves; that they may disobey the law, because their judgment condemns it; or resist the public will, because they honestly wish to change it—he is then a criminal upon every principle of rational policy, as well as upon the immemorial precedents of English justice; because such a person seeks to disunite individuals from their duty to the whole, and excites to overt acts of *misconduct* in a part of the community, instead of endeavouring to change, by the impulse of reason, that universal assent which, in this and in every country, constitutes the law for all.

I have, therefore, no difficulty in admitting that if, upon an attentive perusal of this work, it shall be found that the defendant has promulgated any doctrines which excite individuals to withdraw from their subjection to the law by which the whole nation consents to be governed; if his book shall be found to have warranted or excited that unfortunate criminal who appeared here yesterday to endeavour to relieve himself from imprisonment by the destruction of a prison, or dictated to him the language of defiance which ran through the whole of his defence; if throughout the work there shall be found any syllable or letter which strikes at the security of property, or which hints that anything less than *the whole nation* can constitute the law, or that the law, be it what it may, is not the inexorable rule of action for every individual, I willingly yield him up to the justice of the Court.

Gentlemen, I say, in the name of Thomas Paine, and in his words as author of *The Rights of Man*, as written in the very volume that is charged with seeking the destruction of property—

"The end of all political associations is the preservation of the rights of man, which rights are liberty, property, and security; that the nation is the source of all sovereignty derived from it; the right of property being secured and inviolable, no one ought to be deprived of it, except in cases of evident public necessity, legally ascertained, and on condition of a previous just indemnity."

These are undoubtedly the rights of man—the rights for which all governments are established—and the only rights Mr. Paine contends for; but which he thinks (no matter whether right or wrong) are better to be secured by a republican constitution than by the forms of the English Government. He instructs me to admit that, when government is once constituted, no individuals, without rebellion, can withdraw their obedience from it; that all attempts to excite them to it are highly criminal for the most obvious reasons of policy and justice; that nothing short of the will of a WHOLE PEOPLE can change or affect the rule by which a nation is to be governed; and that no private opinion, however honestly inimical to the forms or substance of the law, can justify resistance to its authority, while it remains in force. The author of *The Rights of Man* not only admits the truth of all this doctrine, but he consents to be convicted, and I also consent for him, unless his work shall be found studiously and painfully to inculcate those great principles of government which it is charged to have been written to destroy.

Let me not, therefore, be suspected to be contending that it is lawful to write a book pointing out defects in the English Government, and exciting individuals to destroy its sanctions, and to refuse obedience. But, on the other hand, I do contend that it is lawful to address the English nation on these momentous subjects; for had it not been for this inalienable right (thanks be to God and our fathers for establishing it!), how should we have had this constitution which we so loudly boast of? If, in the march of the human mind, no man could have gone before the establishments of the time he lived in, how could our establishment, by reiterated changes, have become what it is? If no man could have awakened the public mind to errors and abuses in our Government, how could it have passed on from stage to stage, through reformation and revolution, so as to have arrived from barbarism to such a pitch of happiness and perfection, that the Attorney-General considers it as profanation to touch it further, or to look for any further amendment?

In this manner power has reasoned in every age; Government, in *its own estimation*, has been at all times a system of perfection; but a free press has examined and detected its errors, and the people have from time to time reformed them. This freedom has alone made our Government what it is; this freedom alone can preserve it; and therefore, under the banners of that freedom, to-day I stand up to defend Thomas Paine. But how, alas! shall this task be accomplished? How may I expect from you what human nature has not made man for the performance of? How am I to address your reasons, or ask them to pause, amidst the torrent of prejudice which has hurried away the public mind on the subject you are to judge.

Was any Englishman ever so brought as a criminal before an English court of justice? If I were to ask you, gentlemen of the jury, what is the choicest fruit that grows upon the tree of English liberty, you would answer, SECURITY UNDER THE LAW. If I were to ask the whole people of England the return they looked for at the hands of Government for the burdens under which they bend to support it, I should still be answered, SECURITY UNDER THE LAW; or, in other words, an impartial administration of justice. So sacred, therefore, has the freedom of trial been ever held in England; so anxiously does justice guard against every possible bias in her path, that if the public mind has been locally agitated upon any subject in judgment, the forum has either been changed, or the trial postponed. The circulation of any paper that brings, or can be supposed to bring, prejudice, or even well-founded knowledge, within the reach of a British tribunal, *on the spur of an occasion*, is not only highly criminal, but defeats itself, by leading to put off the trial which its object was to pervert. On this principle, the noble and learned Judge will permit me to remind him that on the trial of the Dean of St. Asaph for a libel, or rather when he was brought to trial, the circulation of books by a society favourable to his defence was held by his Lordship, as Chief-Justice of Chester, to be a reason for not trying the cause; although they contained no matter relative to the Dean, nor to the object of his trial; being only extracts from ancient authors of high reputation on the general rights of juries to consider the innocence as well as the guilt of the accused; yet still, as the recollection of these rights was pressed forward *with a view to affect the proceedings*, the proceedings were postponed.

Is the defendant, then, to be the only exception to these admirable provisions? Is the English law to judge *him*, stripped of the armour with which its universal justice encircles *all others* ? Shall we, in the very act of judging him for detracting from the English Government, furnish him with ample matter for just reprobation, instead of detraction? Has not his cause been prejudged through a thousand channels? Has not the work before you been daily and publicly reviled, and his person held up to derision and reproach? Has not the public mind been excited by crying down the very phrase and idea of *The Rights of Man* ? Nay, have not associations of gentlemen—I speak it with regret, because I am persuaded, from what I know of some of them, that they, amongst them at least, thought they were serving the public—yet have they not, in utter contempt and ignorance of that constitution of which they declare themselves to be the guardians, published the grossest attacks upon the defendant? Have they not, even while the cause has been standing here for immediate trial, published a direct protest against the very work now before you; advertising in the same paper, though under the general description of seditious libels, a reward on the conviction of any person who should dare to sell the book itself, to which their own publication was an answer? The Attorney-General has spoken of a forced circulation of this work; but how have these prejudging papers been circulated? We all know how. They have been thrown into our carriages in every street; they have met us at every turn-pike; and they lie in the areas of all our houses. To complete the triumph of prejudice, that high tribunal of which I have the honour to be a member (my learned friends know what I say to be true) has been drawn into this vortex of slander; and some of its members—I must not speak of the House itself—have thrown the weight of their stations into the same scale. By all these means I maintain that this cause has been pre-judged.

It may be said that I have made no motion to put off the trial for these causes, and that courts of themselves take no cognisance of what passes elsewhere, without facts laid before them. Gentlemen, I know that I should have had equal justice from the Court, if I had brought myself within the rule. But when should I have been better in the present aspect of things? And I only remind you, therefore, of all these hardships, that you may recollect that your judgment is to proceed upon that alone which meets you *here*, upon *the evidence* in the cause, and not upon suggestions destructive of every principle of justice.

Having disposed of these foreign prejudices, I hope you will as little regard some arguments that have been offered to you in court. The letter which has been so repeatedly pressed upon you ought to be dismissed even from your recollection. I have already put it out of the question, as having been written long subsequent to the book, and as being a libel on the King, which no part of the information charges, and which may hereafter be prosecuted as a distinct offence. I consider that letter, besides, and indeed have always heard it treated, as a forgery, contrived to injure the merits of the cause, and to embarrass *me personally* in its defence. I have a right so to consider it, because it is unsupported by anything similar at an earlier period. The defendant's whole deportment, previous to the publication, has been wholly unexceptionable: he properly desired to be given up as the author of the book if any inquiry should take place concerning it: and he is not affected in evidence, either directly or indirectly, with any illegal or suspicious conduct; not even with having uttered an indiscreet or taunting expression, nor with any one matter or thing inconsistent with the duty of the best subject in England. His *opinions* indeed were adverse to our system; but I maintain that OPINION is free, and that CONDUCT alone is amenable to the law.

You are next desired to judge of the author's mind and intention by the modes and extent of the circulation of his work. The FIRST part of *The Rights of Man* Mr. Attorney-General tells you he did not prosecute, although it was in circulation through the country for a year and a half together, because it seems it circulated only amongst what he styles the judicious part of the public, who possessed in their capacities and experience an antidote to the poison; but that, with regard to the SECOND part now before you, its circulation had been forced into every corner of society; had been printed and re-printed for cheapness even upon whited-brown paper, and had crept into the very nurseries of children as a wrapper for their sweetmeats.

In answer to this statement, which after all stands only upon Mr. Attorney-General's own assertion, unsupported by any kind of proof (no witness having proved the author's personal inter-ference with the sale), I still maintain that if he had the most anxiously promoted it, the question would remain exactly THE SAME: the question would still be, whether at the time when Paine composed his work, and promoted the most extensive purchase of it, he believed or disbelieved what he had written? —and whether he contemplated the happiness or the misery of the English nation, to which it is addressed? And whichever of these intentions may be evidenced to your judgments upon reading the book itself, I confess I am utterly at a loss to com-prehend how a writer can be supposed to mean something different from what he has written, by proof of an anxiety (common, I believe, to all authors) that his work should be generally read. Remember, I am not asking your opinions of the *doctrines themselves,*—you have given them already pretty visibly since I began to address you,—but I shall appeal not only to you, but to those who, without our leave, will hereafter judge, and without appeal, of all that we are doing to-day,— whether, upon the matter which I hasten to lay before you, you can refuse to pronounce that from his education,—from the accidents and habits of his life,—from the time and occasion of the publication,—from the circumstances attending it,—and from every line and letter of the work itself, and from all his other writings, his conscience and understanding (*no matter whether erroneously or not*) were deeply and solemnly impressed with the matters contained in his book?—that he addressed it to the reason of the nation at large, and not to the passions of individuals?—and that, in the issue of its influence, he con-templated only what appeared to *him* (*though it may not to us*) to be the interest and happiness of England, and of the whole human race? In drawing the one or the other of these con-clusions, the book stands first in order, and it shall now speak for itself.

Gentlemen, *the whole of it* is in evidence before you; the particular parts arraigned having only been read by my consent, upon the presumption that, on retiring from the court, you would carefully compare them with the context, and all the parts with the WHOLE VIEWED TOGETHER. You cannot indeed do justice without it. The most common letter, even in the ordinary course of business, cannot be read in a cause to prove an obligation for twenty shillings without THE WHOLE being read, that the writer's meaning may be seen without deception. But in a criminal charge, comprehending only four pages and a half, out of a work containing nearly two hundred, you cannot, with even the appearance of common decency, pronounce a judgment without the most deliberate and cautious comparison. I observe that the noble and learned Judge confirms me in this observation.

If any given part of a work be legally explanatory of every other part of it, the preface, *à fortiori*, is the most material; because the preface is the author's own key to his writing: it is *there* that he takes the reader by the hand and introduces him to his subject; it is there that the spirit and intention of the whole is laid before him by way of prologue. A preface is meant by the author as a clue to ignorant or careless readers; the author says by it, to every man who chooses to begin where he ought, Look at my plan,—attend to my distinctions,—mark the purpose and limitations of the matter I lay before you.

Let, then, the calumniators of Thomas Paine now attend to his preface, where, to leave no excuse for ignorance or misrepresentation, he expresses himself thus:—

" I have differed from some professional gentlemen on the subject of prosecutions, and I since find they are falling into my opinion, which I will here state as fully but as concisely as I can.

" I will first put a case with respect to any law, and then compare it with a government, or with what in England is or has been called a constitution.

" It would be an act of despotism, or what in England is called arbitrary power, to make a law to prohibit investigating the principles, good or bad, on which such a law, or any other, is founded.

" If a law be bad, it is one thing to *oppose the practice* of it, but it is quite a different thing to *expose its errors*, to *reason* on its defects, and to *show cause* why it should be repealed, or why another ought to be substituted in its place. I have always held it an opinion (making it also my practice), that it is better to obey a bad law, making use at the same time of every argument to show its errors and procure its repeal, than forcibly to violate it; because the precedent of breaking a bad law might weaken the force, and lead to a discretionary violation, of those which are good.

" The case is the same with principles and forms of governments, or to what are called constitutions, and the parts of which they are composed.

" It is for the good of nations, and not for the emolument or aggrandisement of particular individuals, that government ought to be established, and that mankind are at the expense of supporting it. The defects of every government and constitution, both as to principle and form, must, on a parity of reasoning, be as open to discussion as the defects of a law, and it is a duty which every man owes to society to point them out. When those defects and the means of remedying them are generally seen by a NATION, THAT NATION will reform its government or its constitution in the one case as the government repealed or reformed the law in the other."

Gentlemen, you must undoubtedly wish to deal with every man who comes before you in judgment as you would be dealt by; and surely you will not lay it down to-day as a law to be binding hereafter, even upon yourselves, that if you should publish any opinion concerning existing abuses in your country's government, and point out to the whole public the means of amendment, you are to be acquitted or convicted as any twelve men may happen to agree with you in your *opinions*. Yet this is precisely what you are asked to do to another—It is precisely the case before you. Mr. Paine expressly says, I obey a law until it is repealed; obedience is not only my principle but my practice, since my disobedience of a law, from thinking it *bad*, might apply to justify another man in the disobedience of a *good one ;* and thus individuals would give the rule for themselves, and not society for all. You will presently see that the same principle pervades the whole work; and I am the more anxious to call your attention to it, however repetition may tire you, because it unfolds the whole principle of my argument; for, if you find a sentence in the whole book that invests any individual, or any number of individuals, or any community short of the WHOLE NATION, with a power of changing any part of the law or constitution, I abandon the cause,—YES, I freely abandon it, because I will not affront the majesty of a court of justice by maintaining propositions which, even upon the surface of them, are false. Mr. Paine, pages 162-168, goes on thus—

" When a NATION changes its opinion and habits of thinking, it is no longer to be governed as before; but it would not only be wrong, but bad policy, to attempt by force what ought to be accomplished by reason. Rebellion consists in forcibly opposing the general will of a nation, whether by a party or by a government. There ought, therefore, to be, in every nation, a method of occasionally ascertaining the state of public opinion with respect to government.

"There is, therefore, no power but the voluntary will of the people that has a right to act in any matter respecting a general reform; and by the same right that two persons can confer on such a subject, a thousand may. The object in all such preliminary proceedings is to find out what the GENERAL SENSE OF A NATION is, and to be governed by it. If it prefer a bad or defective government to a reform, or choose to pay ten times more taxes than there is occasion for, it has a right so to do; and, so long as the majority do not impose conditions on the minority different to what they impose on themselves, though there may be much error, there is no injustice; neither will the error continue long. Reason and discussion will soon bring things right, however wrong they may begin. By such a process no tumult is to be apprehended. The poor, in all countries, are naturally both peaceable and grateful in all reforms in which their interest and happiness are included. It is only by neglecting and rejecting them that they become tumultuous."

Gentlemen, these are the sentiments of the author of *The Rights of Man;* and, whatever *his* opinions may be of the defects in our Government, it never can change ours concerning it, if our sentiments are just; and a writing can never be seditious, in the sense of the English law, which states that the Government leans on the UNIVERSAL WILL for its support. . . .

Gentlemen, let others hold their opinions, and change them at their pleasure; I shall ever maintain it to be the dearest privilege of the people of Great Britain to watch over everything that affects their happiness, either in the system of their government or in the practice, and that for this purpose THE PRESS MUST BE FREE. It has always been so, and much evil has been corrected by it. If Government finds itself annoyed by it, let it examine its own conduct, and it will find the cause; let it amend it, and it will find remedy.

Gentlemen, I am no friend to sarcasms in the discussion of grave subjects, but you must take writers according to the view of the mind at the moment; Mr. Burke, as often as anybody, indulges in it. Hear his reason, in his speech on reform, for not taking away the salaries from Lords who attend upon the British Court. "You would," said he, "have the Court deserted by all the nobility of the kingdom.

"Sir, the most serious mischiefs would follow from such a desertion. Kings are naturally lovers of low company; they are so elevated above all the rest of mankind, that they must look upon all their subjects as on a level: they are rather apt to hate than to love their nobility on account of the occasional resistance to their will, which will be made by their virtue, their petulance, or their pride. It must indeed be admitted that many of the nobility are as perfectly willing to act the part of flatterers, tale-bearers, parasites, pimps, and buffoons, as any of the lowest and vilest of mankind can possibly be. But they are not properly qualified for this object of their ambition. The want of a regular education, and early habits, with some lurking remains of their dignity, will never permit them to become a match for an Italian eunuch, a mountebank, a fiddler, a player, or any regular practitioner of that tribe. The Roman emperors, almost from the beginning, threw themselves into such hands; and the mischief increased every day till its decline and its final ruin. It is, therefore, of very great importance (provided the thing is not overdone) to contrive such an establishment as must, almost whether a prince will or not, bring into daily and hourly offices about his person a great number of his first nobility; and it is rather an useful prejudice that gives them a pride in such a servitude: though they are not much the better for a Court, a Court will be much the better for them. I have, therefore, not attempted to reform any of the offices of honour about the King's person."

What is all this but saying that a King is an animal so incurably addicted to low company as generally to bring on by it the ruin of nations; but, nevertheless, he is to be kept as a necessary evil, and his propensities bridled by surrounding him with a parcel of miscreants still worse, if possible, but better than those he would choose for himself. This, therefore, if taken by itself, would be a most abominable and libellous sarcasm on kings and nobility; but look at the whole speech, and you observe a great system of regulation; and no man, I believe, ever doubted Mr. Burke's attachment to monarchy. To judge, therefore, of any part of a writing, THE WHOLE MUST BE READ.

With this same view, I will read to you the beginning of Harrington's *Oceana;* but it is impossible to name this well-known author without exposing to just contempt and ridicule the ignorant or profligate misrepresentations which are vomited forth upon the public, to bear down every man as desperately wicked who in any age or country has countenanced a republic, for the mean purpose of prejudging this trial.

Mr. Erskine took up a book, but laid it down again without reading from it, saying something to the gentleman who sat near him, in a low voice, which the reporter did not hear.

Is this the way to support the English constitution? Are these the means by which Englishmen are to be taught to cherish it? I say, if the man upon trial were stained with blood instead of ink, if he were covered over with crimes which human nature would start at the naming of, the means employed against him would not be the less disgraceful.

For this notable purpose, then, Harrington, *not above a week ago*,[1] was handed out to us as a low, obscure wretch, involved in the murder of the monarch and the destruction of the monarchy, and as addressing his despicable works at the shrine of an usurper. Yet this very Harrington, this low blackguard, was descended (you may see his pedigree at the Heralds' Office for sixpence) from eight dukes, three marquises, seventy earls, twenty-seven viscounts, and thirty-six barons, sixteen of whom were knights of the Garter—a descent which I think would save a man from disgrace in any of the circles of Germany. But what was he besides? A BLOOD-STAINED RUFFIAN? Oh, brutal ignorance of the history of the country! He was the most affectionate servant of Charles the First, from whom he never concealed his opinions; for it is observed by Wood that the King greatly affected his company; but when they happened to talk of a commonwealth, he would scarcely endure it. " I know not," says Toland, " which most to commend: the King, for trusting an honest man, though a republican; or Harrington, for owning his principles while he served a king."

But did his opinions affect his conduct? Let history again answer. He preserved his fidelity to his unhappy prince to the very last, after all his fawning courtiers had left him to his enraged subjects. He stayed with him while a prisoner in the Isle of Wight; came up by stealth to follow the fortunes of his monarch and master; even hid himself in the boot of the coach

[1] A pamphlet had been published just before, putting Paine and Harrington on the same footing—as obscure blackguards.

when he was conveyed to Windsor; and, ending as he began, fell into his arms and fainted on the scaffold.

After Charles's death, the *Oceana* was written, and as if it were written from justice and affection to his memory; for it breathes the same noble and spirited regard, and asserts that it was not CHARLES that brought on the destruction of the *monarchy,* but the feeble and ill-constituted nature of monarchy *itself.*

But the book was a flattery to Cromwell. Once more and finally let history decide. The *Oceana* was seized by the Usurper as a libel, and the way it was recovered is remarkable. I mention it to show that Cromwell was a wise man in himself, and knew on what governments must stand for their support.

Harrington waited on the Protector's daughter to beg for his book, which her father had taken, and on entering her apartment, snatched up her child and ran away. On her following him with surprise and terror, he turned to her and said, "I know what you feel as a mother, feel then for ME; your father has got MY child"—meaning the *Oceana.* The *Oceana* was afterwards restored on her petition; Cromwell answering with the sagacity of a sound politician, "Let him have his book; if my government is made to stand, it has nothing to fear from PAPER SHOT." He said true. No GOOD government will ever be battered by paper shot. Montesquieu says that "In a free nation it matters not whether individuals reason well or ill; it is sufficient that they *do* reason. Truth arises from the collision, and from hence springs liberty, which is a security from the effect of reasoning." The Attorney-General has read extracts from Mr. Adams's answer to this book. Let others write answers to it, like Mr. Adams; I am not insisting upon the infallibility of Mr. Paine's doctrines; if they are erroneous, let them be answered, and truth will spring from the collision.

Milton wisely says that a disposition in a nation to this species of controversy is no proof of sedition or degeneracy, but quite the reverse. [I omitted to cite the passage with the others.] In speaking of this subject he rises into that inexpressibly sublime style of writing wholly peculiar to himself. He was indeed no plagiary from anything human; he looked up for light and expression, as he himself wonderfully describes it, by devout prayer to that great Being who is the source of all utterance and knowledge; and who sendeth out His seraphim with the hallowed fire of His altar to touch and purify the lips of whom He pleases. "When the cheerfulness of the people," says this mighty poet, "is so sprightly up as that it has not only wherewith to guard well its own freedom and safety, but to spare and to bestow upon the solidest and sublimest points of controversy and new invention, it betokens us not degenerated nor drooping to a fatal decay, but casting off the old and wrinkled skin of corruption, to outlive these pangs, and wax young again, entering the glorious ways of truth and prosperous virtue, destined to become great and honourable in these latter ages. Methinks I see, in my mind, a noble and puissant nation rousing herself, like a strong man after sleep, and shaking her invincible locks: methinks I see her as an eagle muing her mighty youth, and kindling her undazzled eyes at the full mid-day beam; purging and unscaling her long-abused sight at the fountain itself of heavenly radiance; while the whole noise of timorous and flocking birds, with those also that love the twilight, flutter about, amazed at what she means, and in their envious gabble would prognosticate a year of sects and schisms."

Gentlemen, what Milton only saw in his mighty imagination, I see in fact; what he expected, but which never came to pass, I see now fulfilling; methinks I see this noble and puissant nation, not degenerated and drooping to a fatal decay, but casting off the wrinkled skin of corruption to put on again the vigour of her youth. And it is because others as well as myself see this that we have all this uproar!—France and its constitution are the mere pretences. It is because Britons begin to recollect the inheritance of their own constitution, left them by their ancestors;—it is because they are awakened to the corruptions which have fallen upon its most valuable parts, that forsooth the nation is in danger of being destroyed by a single pamphlet. I have marked the course of this alarm: it began with the renovation of those exertions for the public which the alarmists themselves had originated and deserted; and they became louder and louder when they saw them avowed and supported by my admirable friend Mr. Fox, the most eminently honest and enlightened statesman that history brings us acquainted with: a man whom to name is to honour, but whom in attempting adequately to describe I must fly to Mr. Burke, my constant refuge when eloquence is necessary: a man who, to relieve the sufferings of the most distant nation, "put to the hazard his ease, his interest, his power, even his darling popularity, for the benefit of a people whom he had never seen." How much more then for the inhabitants of his native country!—yet this is the man who has been censured and disavowed in the manner we have lately seen.

Gentlemen, I have but a few more words to trouble you with: take my leave of you with declaring that all this freedom which I have been endeavouring to assert is no more than the ancient freedom which belongs to our own inbred constitution.   I have not asked you to acquit Thomas Paine upon any new lights, or upon any principle but that of the law, which you are sworn to administer;—my great object has been to inculcate that wisdom and policy, which are the parents of the government of Great Britain, forbid this jealous eye over her subjects; and that, on the contrary, they cry aloud in the language of the poet, adverted to by Lord Chatham on the memorable subject of America, *unfortunately without effect*—

> " Be to their faults a little blind,
>   Be to their virtues very kind,
>   Let all their thoughts be unconfined,
>   And clap your padlock on the mind."

Engage the people by their affections,—convince their reason,— and they will be loyal from the only principle that can make loyalty sincere, vigorous, or rational,—a conviction that it is their truest interest, and that their government is for their good. Constraint is the natural parent of resistance, and a pregnant proof that reason is not on the side of those who use it.   You must all remember Lucian's pleasant story: Jupiter and a countryman were walking together, conversing with great freedom and familiarity upon the subject of heaven and earth.   The countryman listened with attention and acquiescence, while Jupiter strove only to convince him; but happening to hint a doubt, Jupiter turned hastily round and threatened him with his thunder.   "Ah, ah!" says the countryman, "now, Jupiter, I know that you are wrong; you are always wrong when you appeal to your thunder."

This is the case with me— I can reason with the people of England, but I cannot fight against the thunder of authority.

Gentlemen, this is my defence for free opinions.   With regard to myself, I am, and always have been, obedient and affectionate to *the law*—to that rule of action, as long as I exist, I shall ever give my voice and my conduct; but I shall ever do as I have done to-day, maintain the dignity of my high profession, and perform, as I understand them, all its important duties.

ON THE DELIVERANCE OF EUROPE

WILLIAM PITT

HOUSE OF COMMONS: 7 JUNE, 1799

[The house having resolved itself into a Committee of Supply, his
Majesty's message, which had been referred to the committee the
preceding day, acquainting the House with the engagements entered
into between his Majesty and the Emperor of Russia, was read.

Mr. Pitt then rose, and in a short speech moved "that the sum of
825,000*l.* be granted to his Majesty, to enable his Majesty to fulfil his
engagements with Russia in such a manner as may be best adapted
to the exigencies of the case."

Mr. Tierney opposed the motion on the ground of its object being
undefined. He called upon ministers to declare what was the *common
cause* they talked of, and what was meant by the *deliverance of
Europe;* asserting, that he would not vote any sums for a purpose
which he did not understand, and in aid of a power whose object he
did not know, which might be appropriated to her own views exclusively, and to the injury instead of the welfare of England.]

I WISH, Sir, to offer such an explanation on some of the
topics dwelt upon by the honourable gentleman[1] who just sat
down, as will, I think, satisfy the committee and the honourable
gentleman. The nature of the engagement to which the
message would pledge the house is simply, that, 1st, for the
purpose of setting the Russian army in motion, we shall
advance to that country 225,000*l.*, part of which by instal-
ments, to accompany the subsidy to be paid when the army is
in actual service. And I believe no one, who has been the
least attentive to the progress of affairs in the world, who can
appreciate worth, and admire superior zeal and activity, will
doubt the sincerity of the sovereign of Russia, or make a
question of his integrity in any compact. The 2d head of
distribution is 75,000*l.* per month, to be paid at the expiration
of every succeeding month of service; and, lastly, a subsidy of
37,500*l.* to be paid after the war, on the conclusion of a peace
by common consent. Now, I think it strange that the honourable gentleman should charge us with want of prudence, while
it cannot be unknown to him that the principal subsidies are
not to be paid until the service has been performed, and that
in one remarkable instance the present subsidy differs from
every other, inasmuch as a part of it is not to be paid until

[1] Mr. Tierney.

after the conclusion of a peace by common consent. I think gentlemen would act more consistently if they would openly give their opposition on the principle that they cannot support the war under any circumstances of the country and of Europe, than in this equivocal and cold manner to embarrass our deliberations, and throw obstacles in the way of all vigorous co-operation. There is no reason, no ground to fear that that magnanimous prince will act with infidelity in a cause in which he is so sincerely engaged, and which he knows to be the cause of all good government, of religion and humanity, against a monstrous medley of tyranny, injustice, vanity, irreligion, ignorance, and folly. Of such an ally there can be no reason to be jealous; and least of all have the honourable gentlemen opposite me grounds of jealousy, considering the nature and circumstances of our engagements with that monarch. As to the sum itself, I think no man can find fault with it. In fact, it is comparatively small. We take into our pay 45,000 of the troops of Russia, and I believe, if any gentleman will look to all former subsidies, the result will be, that never was so large a body of men subsidized for so small a sum. This fact cannot be considered without feeling that this magnanimous and powerful prince has undertaken to supply at a very trifling expense a most essential force, and that for *the deliverance of Europe*. I still must use this phrase, notwithstanding the sneers of the honourable gentleman. Does it not promise the deliverance of Europe, when we find the armies of our allies rapidly advancing in a career of victory at once the most brilliant and auspicious that perhaps ever signalized the exertions of any combination? Will it be regarded with apathy, that that wise and vigorous and exalted prince has already, by his promptness and decision, given a turn to the affairs of the continent? Is the house to be called upon to refuse succours to our ally, who, by his prowess, and the bravery of his arms, has attracted so much of the attention and admiration of Europe?

The honourable gentleman says he wishes for peace, and that he approved more of what I said on this subject towards the close of my speech, than of the opening. Now what I said was, that if by powerfully seconding the efforts of our allies, we could only look for peace with any prospect of realizing our hopes, whatever would enable us to do so promptly and effectually would be true economy. I must, indeed, be much misunderstood, if generally it was not perceived that I meant, that whether the period which is to carry us to peace be shorter or longer, what we have to look to is not so much when we make peace, as whether we shall derive from it complete and solid security; and that whatever other nations may do, whether they shall persevere in the contest, or untimely abandon it, we have to look to ourselves for the means of defence, we are to look to the means to secure our constitution, preserve our character, and maintain our independence, in the virtue and perseverance of the people. There is a high-spirited pride, an elevated loyalty, a generous warmth of heart, a nobleness of spirit, a hearty, manly gaiety, which distinguish our nation, in which we are to look for the best pledges of general safety, and of that security against an aggressing usurpation, which other nations in their weakness or in their folly have yet nowhere found. With respect to that which appears so much to embarrass certain gentlemen—the deliverance of Europe—I will not say particularly what it is. Whether it is to be its deliverance from that under which it suffers, or that from which it is in danger; whether from the infection of false principles, the corroding cares of a period of distraction and dismay, or that dissolution of all governments, and that death of religion and social order which are to signalize the triumph of the French republic, if unfortunately for mankind she should, in spite of all opposition, prevail in the contest;—from whichsoever of these Europe is to be delivered, it will not be difficult to prove, that what she suffers, and what is her danger, are the power and existence of the French government. If any man says that the government is not a tyranny, he miserably mistakes the character of that body. It is an insupportable and odious tyranny, holding within its grasp the lives, the characters, and the fortunes of all who are forced to own its sway, and only holding these that it may at will measure out of each the portion, which from time to time it sacrifices to its avarice, its cruelty, and injustice. The French republic is dyked and fenced round with crime, and owes much of its present security to its being regarded with a horror which appals men in their approaches to its impious battlements.

The honourable gentleman says, that he does not know whether the Emperor of Russia understands what we mean by the deliverance of Europe. I do not think it proper here to dwell much at length on this curious doubt. But whatever may be the meaning which that august personage attaches to our phrase " the deliverance of Europe," at least he has shown that he is no stranger to the condition of the world; that whatever be the specific object of the contest, he has learnt rightly to consider the character of the common enemy, and shows by his public proceedings that he is determined to take measures of more than ordinary precaution against the common disturbers of Europe, and the common enemy of man. Will the honourable gentleman continue in his state of doubt? Let him look to the conduct of that prince during what has passed of the present campaign. If in such conduct there be not unfolded some solicitude for the deliverance of Europe from the tyranny of France, I know not, Sir, in what we are to look for it. But the honourable gentleman seems to think no alliance can long be preserved against France. I do not deny that unfortunately some of the nations of Europe have shamefully crouched to that power, and receded from the common cause, at a moment when it was due to their own dignity, to what they owed to that civilized community of which they are still a part, to persevere in the struggle, to reanimate their legions with that spirit of just detestation and vengeance which such inhumanity and cruelty might so well provoke. I do not say that the powers of Europe have not acted improperly in many other instances; and Russia in her turn; for, during a period of infinite peril to this country, she saw our danger advance upon us, and four different treaties entered into of offensive alliance against us, without comment, and without a single expression of its disapprobation. This was the conduct of that power in former times. The conduct of his present Majesty raises quite other emotions, and excites altogether a different interest. His Majesty, since his accession, has unequivocally declared his attachment to Great Britain, and, abandoning those projects of ambition which formed the occupation of his predecessor, he chose rather to join in the cause of religion and order against France, than to pursue the plan marked out for him to humble and destroy a power, which he was taught to consider as his common enemy. He turned aside from all hostility against the Ottoman Porte, and united his force to the power of that prince, the more effectually to check the progress of the common enemy. Will, then, gentlemen continue to regard with suspicion the conduct of that prince? Has he not sufficiently shown his devotion to the cause in which we are engaged, by the kind, and number, and value of his sacrifices, ultimately to prevail in the struggle against a tyranny which, in changing our point of vision, we everywhere find accompanied in its desolating progress by degradation, misery, and nakedness, to the unhappy victims of its power—a tyranny which has magnified and strengthened its powers to do mischief, in the proportion that the legitimate and venerable fabrics of civilized and polished society have declined from the meridian of their glory, and lost the power of doing good—a tyranny which strides across the ill-fated domain of France, its foot armed with the scythe of oppression and indiscriminate proscription, that touches only to blight, and rests only to destroy; the reproach and the curse of the infatuated people who still continue to acknowledge it. When we consider that it is against this monster the Emperor of Russia has sent down his legions, shall we say that he is not entitled to our confidence?

But what is the constitutional state of the question? It is competent, undoubtedly, to any gentleman to make the character of an ally the subject of consideration; but in this case it is not to the Emperor of Russia we vote a subsidy, but to his Majesty. The question, therefore, is, whether his Majesty's government affix any undue object to the message, whether they draw any undue inference from the deliverance of Europe. The honourable gentleman has told us, that his deliverance of Europe is the driving of France within her ancient limits—that he is not indifferent to the restoration of the other states of Europe to independence, as connected with the independence of this country; but it is assumed by the honourable gentleman, that we are not content with wishing to drive France within her ancient limits, that, on the contrary, we seek to overthrow the government of France; and he would make us say, that we never will treat with it as a republic. Now I neither meant anything like this, nor expressed myself so as to lead to such inferences. Whatever I may in the abstract think of the kind of government called a republic, whatever may be its fitness to the nation where it prevails, there may be times when it would not be dangerous to exist in its vicinity. But while the spirit of France remains what at present it is, its government despotic, vindictive, unjust, with a temper untamed, a character unchanged, if its power to do wrong at all remains, there does not exist any security for this country or Europe. In my view of security, every object of ambition and aggrandizement is abandoned. Our simple object is security, just security, with a little mixture of indemnification. These are the legitimate objects of war at all times; and when we have attained that end, we are in a condition to derive from peace its beneficent advantages; but until then, our duty and our interest require that we should persevere unappalled in the struggle to which we were provoked. We shall not be satisfied with a false security. War, with all its evils, is better than a peace in which there is nothing to be seen but usurpation and injustice, dwelling with savage delight on the humble, prostrate condition of some timid suppliant people. It is not to be dissembled, that in the changes and chances to which the fortunes of individuals, as well as of states, are continually subject, we may have the misfortune, and great it would be, of seeing our allies decline the contest. I hope this will not happen. I hope it is not reserved for us to behold the mortifying spectacle of two mighty nations abandoning a contest, in which they have sacrificed so much, and made such brilliant progress.

In the application of this principle, I have no doubt but the honourable gentleman admits the security of the country to be the legitimate object of the contest; and I must think I am sufficiently intelligible on this topic. But wishing to be fully understood, I answer the honourable gentleman when he asks, "Does the right honourable gentleman mean to prosecute the war until the French republic is overthrown? Is it his determination not to treat with France while it continues a republic?" —I answer, I do not confine my views to the territorial limits of France; I contemplate the principles, character, and conduct of France; I consider what these are; I see in them the issues of distraction, of infamy and ruin, to every state in her alliance; and therefore I say, that until the aspect of that mighty mass of iniquity and folly is entirely changed;—until the character of the government is totally reversed; until, by the common consent of the general voice of all men, I can with truth tell parliament, France is no longer terrible for her contempt of the rights of every other nation—she no longer avows schemes of universal empire—she has settled into a state whose government can maintain those relations in their integrity, in which alone civilized communities are to find their security, and from which they are to derive their distinction and their glory;—until in the situation of France we have exhibited to us those features of a wise, a just, and a liberal policy, I cannot treat with her. The time to come to the discussion of a peace can only be the time when you can look with confidence to an honourable issue; to such a peace as shall at once restore to Europe her settled and balanced constitution of general polity, and to every negotiating power in particular, that weight in the scale of general empire which has ever been found the best guarantee and pledge of local independence and general security. Such are my sentiments. I am not afraid to avow them. I commit them to the thinking part of mankind; and if they have not been poisoned by the stream of French sophistry, and prejudiced by her falsehood, I am sure they will approve of the determination I have avowed, for those grave and mature reasons on which I found it. I earnestly pray that all the powers engaged in the contest may think as I do, and particularly the Emperor of Russia, which, indeed, I do not doubt; and therefore I do contend, that with that power it is fit that the house should enter into the engagement recommended in his Majesty's message.

[Mr. Tierney, in reply, commented on the last speech of the Chancellor of the Exchequer, and contended that the explanation he had given made it clear, that it was not merely against the power of France we were struggling, but against her system;—not merely to repel her within her ancient limits, but to drive her back from her present to her ancient opinions;—in fact, to prosecute the war until the existing government of France should be overthrown. Upon which grounds he should refuse voting any subsidy for foreign service.

Mr. Pitt rose once more:]

Sir, I cannot agree to the interpretation the honourable gentleman has thought proper to give to parts of my speech. He has supposed that I said, we persevere in the war, and increase our activity, and extend our alliances, to impose a government on another country, and to restore monarchy to France. I never once uttered any such intention. What I said was, and the house must be in the recollection of it, that the France which now exists, affords no promise of security against aggression and injustice in peace, and is destitute of all justice and integrity in war. I observed also, and I think the honourable gentleman must agree with me when I repeat it, that the character and conduct of that government must enter into the calculation of security to other governments against wrong, and for the due and liberal observance of political engagements. The honourable gentleman says, that he has too much good sense, and that every man must have too much good sense, to suppose that territorial limits can, of themselves, be made to constitute the security of states. He does well to add his sanction to a doctrine that is as old as political society itself. In the civilized and regular community, states find their mutual security against wrong, not in territory only, they have the guarantee of fleets, of armies, of acknowledged integrity, and tried good faith; it is to be judged of by the character, the talents, and the virtues of the men who guide the councils of states, who are the advisers of princes: but what is it in the situation of the French republic, on which can be founded a confidence which is to be in itself some proof that she can afford security against wrong? She has territory, she has the remains of a navy, she has armies; but what is her character as a moral being? who is there to testify her integrity? The Swiss nation!—Who bears testimony to her good faith? The states she has plundered, under the delusive but captivating masks of deliverers from tyranny!—What is the character of her advisers? what the aspect of her councils? They are the authors of all that misery, the fountain-head of all those calamities, which, marching by the side of an unblushing tyranny, have saddened and obscured the fairest and the gayest portions of Europe, which have deformed the face of nature wherever their pestiferous genius has acquired an ascendency. In fine, we are to look for security from a government which is constantly making professions of different kinds of sentiments, and is constantly receding from every thing it professes;—a government that has professed, and in its general conduct still manifests, enmity to every institution and state in Europe, and particularly to this country, the best regulated in its government, the happiest in itself, of all the empires that form that great community.

Having said thus much on those matters, I shall now shortly notice a continued confusion in the honourable gentleman's ideas. On another occasion he could not understand what I meant by the deliverance of Europe; and in this second effort of his inquisitive mind he is not more happy. He tells us, he cannot see anything in the present principles of France but mere abstract metaphysical dogmas. What are those principles which guided the arms of France in their unprincipled attack on the independence of Switzerland, which the honourable gentleman has reprobated? Was the degradation, without trial, of the members of the assemblies of France—were, in short, those excesses, and that wickedness, in the contemplation of which the honourable gentleman says he first learnt to regard France as an odious tyranny—will he class the principles which could lead to all these things with the mere metaphysical obstructions of heated, over-zealous theorists? He will still persist, at least he has given the promise of considerable resistance to all arguments to the contrary, in saying that we have an intention to wage war against opinion. It is not so. We are not in arms against the opinions of the closet, nor the speculations of the school. We are at war with armed opinions; we are at war with those opinions which the sword of audacious, unprincipled, and impious innovation seeks to propagate amidst the ruins of empires, the demolition of the altars of all religion, the destruction of every venerable, and good, and liberal institution, under whatever form of polity they have been raised; and this, in spite of the dissenting reason of men, in contempt of that lawful authority which, in the settled order, superior talents and superior virtues attain, crying out to them not to enter on holy ground, nor to pollute the stream of eternal justice;—admonishing them of their danger, whilst, like the genius of evil, they mimic their voice, and, having succeeded in drawing upon them the ridicule of the vulgar, close their day of wickedness and savage triumph with the massacre and waste of whatever is amiable, learned, and pious, in the districts they have over-run. Whilst the principles avowed by France, and acted upon so wildly, held their legitimate place, confined to the circles of a few ingenious and learned men;—whilst these men continued to occupy those heights which vulgar minds could not mount; — whilst they contented themselves with abstract inquiries concerning the laws of matter or the progress of mind, it was pleasing to regard them with respect; for, while the simplicity of the man of genius is preserved untouched, if we will not pay homage to his eccentricity, there is, at least, much in it to be admired. Whilst these principles were confined in that way, and had not yet bounded over the common sense and reason of mankind, we saw nothing in them to alarm, nothing to terrify; but their appearance in arms changed their character. We will not leave the monster to prowl the world unopposed. He must cease to annoy the abode of peaceful men. If he retire into the cell, whether of solitude or repentance, thither we will not pursue him; but we cannot leave him on the throne of power.

I shall now give some farther instances of the confusion of the honourable gentleman's ideas. He says, that the French republic and liberty cannot exist together: therefore, as a friend to liberty, he cannot be a friend to France. Yet he tells us almost in the same breath, that he will not vote for anything that does not tend to secure the liberties of that country, though, to give him the benefit of his own proposition, not to wish the overthrow of France is not to wish for the preservation of English liberty. Indeed, he says, he will vote nothing for the purpose of overthrowing that tyranny, or, as he very strangely adds, the rights and liberties of others—the rights and liberties of France! But how will the gentleman maintain his character for consistency, while he will not vote for any measure that seeks to overthrow the power of a government, in the contemplation of which he has discovered a gulf in his mind between the ideas of its existence and the existence of liberty? It never, however, entered his mind to say that he made the overthrow of the French republic the *sine qua non.*

Here another example arises of that confusion of ideas into which, contrary to his usual custom, the honourable gentleman has fallen this evening:—he says he is one of those who think that a republic in France is not contrary to the safety of other countries, and not incongruous to the state of France itself. How strange is this! whilst we have it from the honourable gentleman, that liberty and the French republic cannot exist together. I am ready to say, that if the republican regimen was characterized by the sobriety of reason, affording nourishment, strength, and health to the members of the community; if the government was just and unambitious, as wisdom and sound policy dictate; if order reigned in her senates, morals in the private walk of life, and in their public places there were to be found the temples of their God, supported in dignity, and resorted to with pious awe and strengthening veneration by the people, there would be in France the reality of a well-regulated state, under whatever denomination, but *obruit male partum, male retentum, male gestum imperium.* Whilst republican France continues what it is, then I make war against republican France; but if I should see any chance of the return of a government that did not threaten to endanger the existence of other governments, far be it from me to breathe hostility to it. I must first see this change of fortune to France and to Europe make its progress with rapid and certain steps, before I relax in the assertion of those rights, which, dearer to Britons than all the world, because by them better understood and more fully enjoyed, are the common property, the links of union of the regular governments of Europe. I must regard as an enemy, and treat as such, a government which is founded on those principles of universal anarchy, and frightful injustice,

which, sometimes awkwardly dissembled, and sometimes inso-
lently avowed, but always destructive, distinguish it from every
other government of Europe.

ON PEACE WITH FRANCE

CHARLES JAMES FOX

HOUSE OF COMMONS: 3 FEB. 1800

MR. SPEAKER,—At so late an hour of the night I am sure
you will do me the justice to believe that I do not mean to go
at length into the discussion of this great question. Exhausted
as the attention of the House must be, and unaccustomed as I
have been of late to attend in my place, nothing but a deep
sense of my duty could have induced me to trouble you at all,
and particularly to request your indulgence at such an hour.
Sir, my hon. and learned friend has truly said that the present
is a new era in the war. The right hon. the Chancellor of the
Exchequer feels the justice of the remark; for by travelling
back to the commencement of the war, and referring to all the
topics and arguments which he has so often and so successfully
urged to the House, and by which he has drawn them on to the
support of his measures, he is forced to acknowledge that, at
the end of a seven years' conflict, we are come but to a new
era in the war, at which he thinks it necessary only to press all
his former arguments to induce us to persevere. All the topics
which have so often misled us—all the reasoning which has
so invariably failed—all the lofty predictions which have so
constantly been falsified by events—all the hopes which have
amused the sanguine, and all the assurances of the distress and
weakness of the enemy which have satisfied the unthinking,
are again enumerated and advanced as arguments for our
continuing the war. What! at the end of seven years of the
most burdensome and the most calamitous struggle that this
country was ever engaged in, are we again to be amused with
notions of finance and calculations of the exhausted resources
of the enemy as a ground of confidence and of hope?
Gracious God! Were we not told, five years ago, that France
was not only on the brink, but that she was actually in the
gulf of bankruptcy? Were we not told, as an unanswerable

argument against treating, that she could not hold out another campaign—that nothing but peace could save her—that she wanted only time to recruit her exhausted finances—that to grant her repose was to grant her the means of again molesting this country, and that we had nothing to do but persevere for a short time, in order to save ourselves for ever from the consequences of her ambition and her Jacobinism? What! after having gone on from year to year upon assurances like these, and after having seen the repeated refutations of every prediction, are we again to be seriously told that we have the same prospect of success on the same identical grounds? And without any other argument or security, are we invited, at this new era of the war, to carry it on upon principles which, if adopted, may make it eternal? If the right hon. gentleman shall succeed in prevailing on Parliament and the country to adopt the principles which he has advanced this night, I see no possible termination to the contest. No man can see an end to it; and upon the assurances and predictions which have so uniformly failed, are we called upon, not merely to refuse all negotiation, but to countenance principles and views as distant from wisdom and justice as they are in their nature wild and impracticable.

I must lament, Sir, in common with every friend of peace, the harsh and unconciliating language which ministers have held towards the French, and which they have even made use of in their answer to a respectful offer of negotiation. Such language has ever been considered as extremely unwise, and has ever been reprobated by diplomatic men. I remember with pleasure the terms in which Lord Malmesbury at Paris, in the year 1796, replied to expressions of this sort used by M. de la Croix. He justly said, " that offensive and injurious insinuations were only calculated to throw new obstacles in the way of accommodation, and that it was not by revolting reproaches, nor by reciprocal invective, that a sincere wish to accomplish the great work of pacification could be evinced." Nothing could be more proper nor more wise than this language; and such ought ever to be the tone and conduct of men entrusted with the very important task of treating with an hostile nation. Being a sincere friend to peace, I must say with Lord Malmesbury, that it is not by reproaches and by invective that we can hope for a reconciliation; and I am convinced in my own mind that I speak the sense of this House, and of a majority of the people of this country, when I lament that any unnecessary recriminations should be flung out by which obstacles are put in the way of pacification. I believe that it is the prevailing sentiment of the people that we ought to abstain from harsh and insulting language; and in common with them I must lament that both in the papers of Lord Grenville, and in the speeches of this night, such licence has been given to the invective and reproach. For the same reason I must lament that the right hon. gentleman has thought proper to go at such length, and with such severity of minute investigation, into all the early circumstances of the war, which, whatever they were, are nothing to the present purpose, and ought not to influence the present feelings of the House.

I certainly shall not follow him into all the minute detail, though I do not agree with him in many of his assertions. I do not know what impression his narrative may make on other gentlemen; but I will tell him, fairly and candidly, he has not convinced me. I continue to think, and until I see better grounds for changing my opinion than any that the right hon. gentleman has this night produced, I shall continue to think and to say, plainly and explicitly, that this country was the aggressor in the war. But with regard to Austria and Prussia —is there a man who for one moment can dispute that they were the aggressors? It will be vain for the right hon. gentleman to enter into long and plausible reasoning against the evidence of documents so clear, so decisive—so frequently, so thoroughly investigated. The unfortunate Louis XVI. himself, as well as those who were in his confidence, have borne decisive testimony to the fact that between him and the emperor there was an intimate correspondence, and a perfect understanding. Do I mean by this that a positive treaty was entered into for the dismemberment of France? Certainly not; but no man can read the declarations which were made at Mantua, as well as at Pilnitz, as they are given by M. Bertrand de Moleville, without acknowledging that there was not merely an intention, but a declaration of an intention, on the part of the great powers of Germany to interfere in the internal affairs of France, for the purpose of regulating the government against the opinion of the people. This, though not a plan for the partition of France, was, in the eye of reason and common sense, an aggression against France. The right hon. gentleman denies that there was such a thing as a treaty of Pilnitz. Granted. But was there not a declaration which amounted to an act of hostile aggression? The two powers, the Emperor of

Germany and the King of Prussia, made a public declaration that they were determined to employ their forces, in conjunction with those of the other sovereigns of Europe, " to put the King of France in a situation to establish, in perfect liberty, the foundations of a monarchical government equally agreeable to the rights of sovereigns and the welfare of the French." Whenever the other princes should agree to co-operate with them, " then, and in that case, their majesties were determined to act promptly, and by mutual consent, with the forces necessary to obtain the end proposed by all of them. In the meantime they declared that they would give orders for their troops to be ready for actual service." Now, I would ask gentlemen to lay their hands upon their hearts, and say what the fair construction of this declaration was—whether it was not a menace and an insult to France, since, in direct terms, it declared that whenever the other powers should concur, they would attack France, then at peace with them, and then employed only in domestic and internal regulations? Let us suppose the case to be that of Great Britain. Will any gentleman say, if two of the great powers should make a public declaration that they were determined to make an attack on this kingdom as soon as circumstances should favour their intention; that they only waited for this occasion; and that in the meantime they would keep their forces ready for the purpose; that it would not be considered by the parliament and people of this country as an hostile aggression? And is there an Englishman in existence who is such a friend to peace as to say that the nation could retain its honour and dignity if it should sit down under such a menace? I know too well what is due to the national character of England to believe that there would be two opinions on the case, if thus put home to our own feelings and understanding. We must, then, respect in others the indignation which such an act would excite in ourselves; and when we see it established on the most indisputable testimony, that both at Pilnitz and at Mantua declarations were made to this effect, it is idle to say that, as far as the Emperor and the King of Prussia were concerned, they were not the aggressors in the war.

" Oh! but the decree of the 19th of November 1792! that, at least," the right hon. gentleman says, " you must allow to be an act of aggression, not only against England, but against all the sovereigns of Europe." I am not one of those, Sir, who attach much interest to the general and indiscriminate provocations thrown out at random, like this resolution of the 19th of November 1792. I do not think it necessary to the dignity of any people to notice and to apply to themselves menaces flung out without particular allusion, which are always unwise in the power which uses them, and which it is still more unwise to treat with seriousness. But if any such idle and general provocation to nations is given, either in insolence or in folly, by any government, it is a clear first principle that an explanation is the thing which a magnanimous nation, feeling itself aggrieved, ought to demand; and if an explanation be given which is not satisfactory, it ought clearly and distinctly to say so. There ought to be no ambiguity, no reserve, on the occasion. Now we all know from documents on our table that M. Chauvelin did give an explanation of this silly decree. He declared in the name of his government "that it was never meant that the French government should favour insurrections; that the decree was applicable only to those people who, after having acquired their liberty by conquest, should demand the assistance of the republic; but that France would respect, not only the independence of England, but also that of her allies with whom she was not at war." This was the explanation given of the offensive decree. "But this explanation was not satisfactory!" Did you say so to M. Chauvelin? Did you tell him that you were not content with this explanation? And when you dismissed him afterwards, on the death of the king, did you say that this explanation was unsatisfactory? No; you did no such thing: and I contend that unless you demanded further explanations, and they were refused, you have no right to urge the decree of the 19th of November as an act of aggression. In all your conferences and correspondence with M. Chauvelin did you hold out to him what terms would satisfy you? Did you give the French the power or the means of settling the misunderstanding which that decree, or any other of the points at issue, had created? I contend that when a nation refuses to state to another the thing which would satisfy her, she shows that she is not actuated by a desire to preserve peace between them: and I aver that this was the case here. The Scheldt, for instance. You now say that the navigation of the Scheldt was one of your causes of complaint. Did you explain yourself on that subject? Did you make it one of the grounds for the dismissal of M. Chauvelin. Sir, I repeat it, a nation, to justify itself in appealing to the last solemn resort, ought to prove that it had taken every possible means, consistent with dignity, to demand the reparation which would be satisfactory, and if she refused to explain what would be satisfactory, she did not do her duty, nor exonerate herself from the charge of being the aggressor.

The right hon. gentleman has this night, for the first time, produced a most important paper—the instructions which were given to his Majesty's minister at the court of St. Petersburg about the end of the year 1792, to interest her Imperial Majesty to join her efforts with those of his Britannic Majesty to prevent, by their joint mediation, the evils of a general war. Of this paper, and of the existence of any such document, I for one was entirely ignorant; but I have no hesitation in saying that I completely approve of the instructions which appear to have been given; and I am sorry to see the right hon. gentleman disposed rather to take blame to himself than credit for having written it. He thinks that he shall be subject to the imputation of having been rather too slow to apprehend the dangers with which the French revolution was fraught, than that he was forward and hasty—" *Quod solum excusat, hoc solum miror in illo.*" I do not agree with him on the idea of censure. I by no means think that he was blameable for too much confidence in the good intentions of the French. I think the tenor and composition of this paper was excellent—the instructions conveyed in it wise; and that it wanted but one essential thing to have entitled it to general approbation— namely, to be acted upon. The clear nature and intent of that paper I take to be, that our ministers were to solicit the court of Petersburg to join with them in a declaration to the French government, stating explicitly what course of conduct, with respect to their foreign relations, they thought necessary to the general peace and security of Europe, and what, if complied with, would have induced them to mediate for that purpose— a proper, wise, and legitimate course of proceeding. Now I ask, Sir, whether, if this paper had been communicated to Paris at the end of the year 1792, instead of Petersburg, it would not have been productive of most seasonable benefits to mankind; and by informing the French in time of the means by which they might have secured the mediation of Great Britain, have not only avoided the rupture with this country, but have also restored general peace to the continent? The paper, Sir, was excellent in its intentions; but its merit was all in the composition. It was a fine theory, which ministers did not think proper to carry into practice. Nay, on the contrary, at the very time they were drawing up this paper they were insulting M. Chauvelin in every way, until about the 23rd or 24th of January 1793, when they finally dismissed him, without stating any one ground upon which they were willing to preserve terms with the French.

"But France," it seems, "then declared war against us; and she was the aggressor, because the declaration came from her." Let us look at the circumstances of this transaction on both sides. Undoubtedly the declaration was made by her; but is a declaration the only thing that constitutes the commencement of a war? Do gentlemen recollect that, in consequence of a dispute about the commencement of war, respecting the capture of a number of ships, an article was inserted in our treaty with France, by which it was positively stipulated that in future, to prevent all disputes, the act of the dismissal of a minister from either of the two courts should be held and considered as tantamount to a declaration of war? I mention this, Sir, because when we are idly employed in this retrospect of the origin of a war which has lasted so many years, instead of fixing our eyes only to the contemplation of the means of putting an end to it, we seem disposed to overlook everything on our own parts, and to search only for grounds of imputation on the enemy. I almost think it an insult on the House to detain them with this sort of examination. If, Sir, France was the aggressor, as the right hon. gentleman says she was throughout, why did not Prussia call upon us for the stipulated number of troops, according to the article of the defensive treaty of alliance subsisting between us, by which, in case either of the contracting parties was attacked, they had a right to demand the stipulated aid? And the same thing, again, may be asked when we were attacked. The right hon. gentleman might here accuse himself, indeed, of reserve; but it unfortunately happened that, at the time, the point was too clear on which side the aggression lay. Prussia was too sensible that the war could not entitle her to make the demand, and that it was not a case within the scope of the defensive treaty. This is evidence worth a volume of subsequent reasoning; for if, at the time when all the facts were present to their minds, they could not take advantage of existing treaties, and that, too, when the courts were on the most friendly terms with one another, it will be manifest to every thinking man that they were sensible they were not authorised to make the demand.

I really, Sir, cannot think it necessary to follow the right hon. gentleman into all the minute details which he has thought proper to give us respecting the first aggression; but that Austria and Prussia were the aggressors not a man in any country, who has ever given himself the trouble to think at all on the subject, can doubt. Nothing could be more hostile than their whole proceedings. Did they not declare to France that it was their internal concerns, not their external proceedings, which provoked them to confederate against her? Look back to the proclamations with which they set out. Read the declarations which they made themselves to justify their appeal to arms. They did not pretend to fear their ambition, their conquests, their troubling their neighbours; but they accused them of new-modelling their own government. They said nothing of their aggressions abroad; they spoke only of their clubs and societies at Paris.

Sir, in all this I am not justifying the French—I am not striving to absolve them from blame, either in their internal or external policy. I think, on the contrary, that their successive rulers have been as bad and as execrable, in various instances, as any of the most despotic and unprincipled governments that the world ever saw. I think it impossible, Sir, that it should have been otherwise. It was not to be expected that the French, when once engaged in foreign wars, should not endeavour to spread destruction around them, and to form plans of aggrandisement and plunder on every side. Men bred in the school of the House of Bourbon could not be expected to act otherwise. They could not have lived so long under their ancient masters without imbibing the restless ambition, the perfidy, and the insatiable spirit of the race. They have imitated the practice of their great prototype, and through their whole career of mischief and of crimes have done no more than servilely trace the steps of their own Louis XIV. If they have overrun countries and ravaged them, they have done it upon Bourbon principles. If they have ruined and dethroned sovereigns, it is entirely after the Bourbon manner. If they have even fraternised with the people of foreign countries, and pretended to make their cause their own, they have only faithfully followed the Bourbon example. They have constantly had Louis, the grand monarque, in their eye. But it may be said that this example was long ago, and that we ought not to refer to a period so distant. True, it is a distant period as applied to the man, but not so to the principle.

The principle was never extinct; nor has its operation been suspended in France, except, perhaps, for a short interval during the administration of Cardinal Fleury; and my complaint against the republic of France is, not that she has generated new crimes, not that she has promulgated new mischief, but that she has adopted and acted upon the principles which have been so fatal to Europe under the practice of the House of Bourbon. It is said that wherever the French have gone, they have introduced revolution; that they have sought for the means of disturbing neighbouring states, and have not been content with mere conquest. What is this but adopting the ingenious scheme of Louis XIV.? He was not content with merely overrunning a state;—whenever he came into a new territory he established what he called his Chamber of Claims; a most convenient device, by which he inquired whether the conquered country or province had any dormant or disputed claims, any cause of complaint, any unsettled demand upon any other state or province—upon which he might wage war upon such state, thereby discover again ground for new devastation, and gratify his ambition by new acquisitions. What have the republicans done more atrocious, more Jacobinical, than this? Louis went to war with Holland. His pretext was that Holland had not treated him with sufficient respect;—a very just and proper cause for war indeed! This, Sir, leads me to an example which I think seasonable, and worthy the attention of his Majesty's ministers. When our Charles II., as a short exception to the policy of his reign, made the triple alliance for the protection of Europe, and particularly of Holland, against the ambition of Louis XIV., what was the conduct of that great, virtuous, and most able statesman, M. de Witt, when the confederates came to deliberate on the terms upon which they should treat with the French monarch? When it was said that he had made unprincipled conquests, and that he ought to be forced to surrender them all, what was the language of that great and wise man? "No," said he; "I think we ought not to look back to the origin of the war so much as to the means of putting an end to it. If you had united in time to prevent these conquests, well; but now that he has made them, he stands upon the ground of conquest, and we must agree to treat with him, not with reference to the origin of the conquest, but with regard to his present posture. He has those places, and some of them we must be content to give up as the means of peace, for conquest will always successfully set up its claims to indemnification." Such was the language of this minister, who was the ornament of his time; and such, in my mind, ought to be the language of statesmen with regard to the French at this day. The same ought to have been said at the formation of the confederacy. It was true that the French had overrun Savoy; but they had overrun it upon Bourbon principles; and having gained this and other conquests before the confederacy was formed, they ought to have treated with her rather for future security than for past correction. States in possession, whether monarchical or republican, will claim indemnity in proportion to their success; and it will never be so much inquired by what right they gained possession as by what means they can be prevented from enlarging their depredations. Such is the safe practice of the world; and such ought to have been the conduct of the powers when the reduction of Savoy made them coalesce.

The right hon. gentleman may know more of the secret particulars of their overrunning Savoy than I do; but certainly, as they have come to my knowledge, it was a most Bourbon-like act. A great and justly celebrated historian, whom I will not call a foreigner—I mean Mr. Hume (a writer certainly estimable in many particulars, but who was a childish lover of princes)—talks of Louis XIV. in very magnificent terms; but he says of him that, though he managed his enterprises with skill and bravery, he was unfortunate in this, that he never got a good and fair pretence for war. This he reckons among his misfortunes! Can we say more of the republican French? In seizing on Savoy I think they made use of the words, " *convenances morales et physiques.*" These were their reasons. A most Bourbon-like phrase! And I therefore contend that as we never scrupled to treat with the princes of the House of Bourbon on account of their rapacity, their thirst of conquest, their violation of treaties, their perfidy, and their restless spirit, so we ought not to refuse to treat with their republican imitators. Ministers could not pretend ignorance of the unprincipled manner in which the French had seized on Savoy. The Sardinian minister complained of the aggression, and yet no stir was made about it. The courts of Europe stood by and saw the outrage; and our minister saw it. The right hon. gentleman will in vain, therefore, exert his powers to persuade me of the interest he takes in the preservation of the rights of nations, since, at the moment when an interference might have been made with effect, no step was taken, no remonstrance made, no mediation negotiated, to stop the career of conquest. All the pretended and hypocritical sensibility for the "rights of nations and for social order," with which we have since been stunned, cannot impose upon those who would take the trouble to look back to the period when this sensibility ought to have roused us into seasonable exertion. At that time, however, the right hon. gentleman makes it his boast that he was prevented by a sense of neutrality from taking any measures of precaution on the subject. I do not give the right hon. gentleman much credit for his spirit of neutrality on the occasion. It flowed from the sense of the country at the time, the great majority of which was clearly and decidedly against all interruptions being given to the French in their desire of regulating their own internal government.

But this neutrality, which respected only the internal rights of the French, and from which the people of England would never have departed but for the impolitic and hypocritical cant which was set up to rouse their jealousy and alarm their fears, was very different from the great principle of political prudence which ought to have actuated the councils of the nation, on seeing the first steps of France towards a career of external conquest. My opinion is, that when the unfortunate King of France offered to us, in the letter delivered by M. Chauvelin and M. Talleyrand, and even entreated us to mediate between him and the allied powers of Austria and Prussia, they ought to have accepted the offer and exerted their influence to save Europe from the consequence of a system which was then beginning to manifest itself. It was, at least, a question of prudence; and as we had never refused to treat and to mediate with the old princes on account of their ambition or their perfidy, we ought to have been equally ready now, when the same principles were acted upon by other men. I must doubt the sensibility which could be so cold and so indifferent at the proper moment for its activity. I fear that there was at that moment the germs of ambition rising in the mind of the right hon. gentleman, and that he was beginning, like others, to entertain hopes that something might be obtained out of the coming confusion. What but such a sentiment could have prevented him from overlooking the fair occasion that was offered for preventing the calamities with which Europe was threatened? What but some such interested principle could have made him forego the truly honourable task by which his administration would have displayed its magnanimity and its power? But for some such feeling would not this country, both in wisdom and in dignity, have interfered, and in conjunction with the other powers have said to France, "You ask for a mediation; we will mediate with candour and sincerity, but we will at the same time declare to you our apprehensions. We do not trust to your assertion of a determination to avoid all foreign conquest, and that you are desirous only of settling your own constitution, because your language is contradicted by experience and the evidence of facts. You are Frenchmen, and you cannot so soon have thrown off the Bourbon principles in which you were educated. You have already imitated the bad practice of your princes; you have seized on Savoy without a colour of right. But here we take our stand. Thus far you have gone, and we cannot help it; but you must go no farther. We will tell you distinctly what we shall consider as an attack on the balance and the security of Europe; and, as the condition of our interference, we will tell you also the securities that we think essential to the general repose." This ought to have been the language of his Majesty's ministers when their mediation was solicited; and something of this kind they evidently thought of when they sent the instructions to Petersburg which they have mentioned this night, but upon which they never acted. Having not done so, I say they have no claim to talk now about the violated rights of Europe, about the aggression of the French, and about the origin of the war in which this country was so suddenly afterwards plunged. Instead of this, what did they do? They hung back; they avoided explanation; they gave the French no means of satisfying them; and I repeat my proposition—when there is a question of peace and war between two nations, that government feels itself in the wrong which refuses to state with clearness and precision what she would consider as a satisfaction and a pledge of peace.

Sir, if I understand the true precepts of the Christian religion, as set forth in the New Testament, I must be permitted to say that there is no such thing as a rule or doctrine by which we are directed, or can be justified, in waging a war for religion. The idea is subversive of the very foundations upon which it stands, which are those of peace and good-will among men. Religion never was, and never can be, a justifiable cause of war; but it has been too often grossly used as the pretext and the apology for the most unprincipled wars.

I have already said, and I repeat it, that the conduct of the French to foreign nations cannot be justified. They have given great cause of offence, but certainly not to all countries alike. The right hon. gentlemen opposite to me have made an indiscriminate catalogue of all the countries which the French have offended, and, in their eagerness to throw odium on the nation, have taken no pains to investigate the sources of their several quarrels. I will not detain the House by entering into the long detail which has been given of their aggressions and their violences; but let me mention Sardinia as one instance which has been strongly insisted upon. Did the French attack Sardinia when at peace with them? No such thing. The King of Sardinia had accepted of a subsidy from Great Britain; and Sardinia was, to all intents and purposes, a belligerent power. Several other instances might be mentioned; but though perhaps in the majority of instances the French may be unjustifiable, is this the moment for us to dwell upon these enormities—to waste our time and inflame our passions by recriminating upon each other? There is no end to such a war. I have somewhere read, I think in Sir Walter Raleigh's *History of the World*, of a most bloody and fatal battle which was fought by two opposite armies, in which almost all the combatants on both sides were killed, "because," says the historian, "though they had offensive weapons on both sides, they had none for defence." So, in this war of words, if we are to use only offensive weapons, if we are to indulge only in invective and abuse, the contest must be eternal. If this war of reproach and invective is to be countenanced, may not the French with equal reason complain of the outrages and the horrors committed by the powers opposed to them? If we must not treat with the French on account of the iniquity of their former transactions, ought we not to be as scrupulous of connecting ourselves with other powers equally criminal? Surely, Sir, if we must be thus rigid in scrutinising the conduct of an enemy, we ought to be equally careful in not committing our honour and our safety with an ally who has manifested the same want of respect for the rights of other nations. Surely, if it is material to know the character of a power with whom you are only about to treat for peace, it is more material to know the character of allies, with whom you are about to enter into the closest connection of friendship, and for whose exertions you are about to pay.

Now, Sir, what was the conduct of your own allies to Poland?

Is there a single atrocity of the French in Italy, in Switzerland, in Egypt if you please, more unprincipled and inhuman than that of Russia, Austria, and Prussia in Poland? What has there been in the conduct of the French to foreign powers; what in the violation of solemn treaties; what in the plunder, devastation, and dismemberment of unoffending countries; what in the horrors and murders perpetrated upon the subdued victims of their rage in any district which they have overrun, worse than the conduct of those three great powers in the miserable, devoted, and trampled-on kingdom of Poland, and who have been, or are, our allies in this war for religion, social order, and the rights of nations? "Oh! but we regretted the partition of Poland!" Yes, regretted! you regretted the violence, and that is all you did. You united yourselves with the actors; you, in fact, by your acquiescence, confirmed the atrocity. But they are your allies; and though they overran and divided Poland, there was nothing, perhaps, in the manner of doing it which stamped it with peculiar infamy and disgrace. The hero of Poland, perhaps, was merciful and mild. He was "as much superior to Buonaparte in bravery, and in the discipline which he maintained, as he was superior in virtue and humanity! He was animated by the purest principles of Christianity, and was restrained in his career by the benevolent precepts which it inculcates." Was he? Let unfortunate Warsaw, and the miserable inhabitants of the suburb of Praga in particular, tell! What do we understand to have been the conduct of this magnanimous hero, with whom, it seems, Buonaparte is not to be compared? He entered the suburb of Praga, the most populous suburb of Warsaw; and there he let his soldiery loose on the miserable, unarmed, and unresisting people! Men, women, and children, nay, infants at the breast, were doomed to one indiscriminate massacre! Thousands of them were inhumanly, wantonly butchered! And for what? Because they had dared to join in a wish to meliorate their own condition as a people, and to improve their constitution, which had been confessed by their own sovereign to be in want of amendment. And such is the hero upon whom the cause of "religion and social order" is to repose! And such is the man whom we praise for his discipline and his virtue, and whom we hold out as our boast and our dependence, while the conduct of Buonaparte unfits him to be even treated with as an enemy!

But the behaviour of the French towards Switzerland raises

all the indignation of the right hon. gentleman and inflames his eloquence. I admire the indignation which he expresses (and I think he felt it) in speaking of this country, so dear and so congenial to every man who loves the sacred name of liberty. He who loves liberty, says the right hon. gentleman, thought himself at home on the favoured and happy mountains of Switzerland, where she seemed to have taken up her abode under a sort of implied compact, among all other states, that she should not be disturbed in this her chosen asylum. I admire the eloquence of the right hon. gentleman in speaking of this country of liberty and peace, to which every man would desire, once in his life at least, to make a pilgrimage. But who, let me ask him, first proposed to the Swiss people to depart from the neutrality which was their chief protection and to join the confederacy against the French? I aver that a noble relation of mine (Lord Robert Fitzgerald), then the minister of England to the Swiss Cantons, was instructed, in direct terms, to propose to the Swiss, by an official note, to break from the safe line they had laid down for themselves, and to tell them " in such a contest neutrality was criminal." I know that noble lord too well, though I have not been in habits of intercourse with him of late, from the employments in which he has been engaged, to suspect that he would have presented such a paper without the express instructions of his court, or that he would have gone beyond those instructions.

But was it only to Switzerland that this sort of language was held? What was our language also to Tuscany and to Genoa? An hon. gentleman (Mr. Canning) has denied the authenticity of a pretended letter which has been circulated and ascribed to Lord Harvey. He says it is all a fable and a forgery. Be it so; but is it also a fable that Lord Harvey did speak in terms to the grand duke which he considered as offensive and insulting? I cannot tell, for I was not present. But was it not, and is it not believed? Is it a fable that Lord Harvey went into the closet of the grand duke, laid his watch upon the table, and demanded in a peremptory manner that he should, within a certain number of minutes, I think I have heard within a quarter of an hour, determine, aye or no, to dismiss the French minister, and order him out of his dominions; with the menace that if he did not the English fleet should bombard Leghorn? Will the hon. gentleman deny this also? I certainly do not know it from my own knowledge; but I know that persons of the first credit, then at Florence, have stated these facts, and that they never have been contradicted. It is true that upon the grand duke's complaint of this indignity Lord Harvey was recalled; but was the principle recalled? Was the mission recalled? Did not ministers persist in the demand which Lord Harvey had made, perhaps ungraciously? Was not the grand duke forced, in consequence, to dismiss the French minister? and did they not drive him to enter into an unwilling war with the republic? It is true that he afterwards made his peace; and that, having done so, he was treated severely and unjustly by the French. But what do I conclude from all this but that we have no right to be scrupulous, we who have violated the respect due to peaceable powers ourselves in this war, which, more than any other that ever afflicted human nature, has been distinguished by the greatest number of disgusting and outrageous insults to the smaller powers by the great. And I infer from this also that the instances not being confined to the French, but having been perpetrated by every one of the allies, and by England as much as by the others, we have no right to refuse to treat with the French on this ground. Need I speak of your conduct to Genoa also? Perhaps the note delivered by Mr. Drake was also a forgery. Perhaps the blockade of the port never took place. It is impossible to deny the facts, which were so glaring at the time. It is a painful thing to me, Sir, to be obliged to go back to these unfortunate periods of the history of this war, and of the conduct of this country; but I am forced to the task by the use which has been made of the atrocities of the French as an argument against negotiation. I think I have said enough to prove that if the French have been guilty, we have not been innocent. Nothing but determined incredulity can make us deaf and blind to our own acts, when we are so ready to yield an assent to all the reproaches which are thrown out on the enemy, and upon which reproaches we are gravely told to continue the war.

"But the French," it seems, "have behaved ill everywhere. They seized on Venice, which had preserved the most exact neutrality, or rather," as it is hinted, "had manifested symptoms of friendship to them." I agree with the right hon. gentleman, it was an abominable act. I am not the apologist of, much less the advocate for, their iniquities; neither will I countenance them in their pretences for the injustice. I do not think that much regard is to be paid to the charges which a triumphant soldiery bring on the conduct of a people whom they have overrun. Pretences for outrage will never be wanting to the strong when they wish to trample on the weak; but when we accuse the French of having seized upon Venice, after stipulating for its neutrality and guaranteeing its independence, we should also remember the excuse that they made for violence—namely, that their troops had been attacked and murdered. I say I am always incredulous about such excuses; but I think it fair to hear whatever can be alleged on the other side. We cannot take one side of a story only. Candour demands that we should examine the whole before we make up our minds on the guilt. I cannot think it quite fair to state the view of the subject of one party as indisputable fact, without even mentioning what the other party has to say for itself. But, Sir, is this all? Though the perfidy of the French to the Venetians be clear and palpable, was it worse in morals, in principle, and in example than the conduct of Austria? My hon. friend (Mr. Whitbread) properly asked, " Is not the receiver as bad as the thief?" If the French seized on the territory of Venice, did not the Austrians agree to receive it? "But this," it seems, "is not the same thing." It is quite in the nature, and within the rule of diplomatic morality, for Austria to receive the country which was seized upon unjustly. "The emperor took it as a compensation: it was his by barter: he was not answerable for the guilt by which it was obtained." What is this, Sir, but the false and abominable reasoning with which we have been so often disgusted on the subject of the slave trade? Just in the same manner have I heard a notorious wholesale dealer in this inhuman traffic justify his abominable trade. "I am not guilty of the horrible crime of tearing that mother from her infants; that husband from his wife; of depopulating that village; of depriving that family of their sons, the support of their aged parent! No: thank heaven! I am not guilty of this horror; I only bought them in the fair way of trade. They were brought to the market; they had been guilty of crimes, or they had been made prisoners in war; they were accused of witchcraft, of obi, or of some other sort of sorcery; and they were brought to me for sale; I gave a valuable consideration for them; but God forbid that I should have stained my soul with the guilt of dragging them from their friends and families!" Such has been the precious defence of the slave trade; and such is the argument set up for Austria, in this instance of Venice. "I did not commit the crime of trampling on the independence of Venice. I did not seize on the city; I gave a *quid pro quo*. It was a matter of barter and indemnity; I gave half a million of human beings to be put under the yoke of France in another district, and I had these people turned over to me in return!" This, Sir, is the defence of Austria; and under such detestable sophistry as this is the infernal traffic in human flesh, whether in white or black, to be continued and even justified! At no time has that diabolical traffic been carried to a greater length than during the present war; and that by England herself as well as Austria and Russia.

"But France," it seems, "has roused all the nations of Europe against her;" and the long catalogue has been read to you to prove that she must have been atrocious to provoke them all. Is it true, Sir, that she has roused them all? It does not say much for the address of his Majesty's ministers if this be the case. What, Sir, have all your negotiations, all your declamation, all your money, been squandered in vain? Have you not succeeded in stirring the indignation and engaging the assistance of a single power? But you do yourselves injustice. I dare say the truth lies between you. Between their crimes and your money the rage has been excited; and full as much is due to your seductions as to her atrocities. My learned friend was correct, therefore, in his argument; for you cannot take both sides of the case: you cannot accuse them of having provoked all Europe, and at the same time claim the merit of having roused them to join you.

You talk of your allies. Sir, I wish to know who your allies are? Russia is one of them, I suppose. Did France attack Russia? Has the magnanimous Paul taken the field for social order and religion, on account of personal aggression? The Emperor of Russia has declared himself grand-master of Malta, though his religion is as opposite to that of the knights as ours is; and he is as much considered an heretic by the Church of Rome as we are. The King of Great Britain might, with as much propriety, declare himself the head of the order of the Chartreuse monks. Not content with taking to himself the commandery of this institution of Malta, Paul has even created a married man a knight, contrary to all the most sacred rules and regulations of the order. And yet this ally of ours is fighting for religion! So much for his religion: Let us see his regard to social order! How does he show his abhorrence of the principles of the French in their violation of the rights of other nations? What has been his conduct to Denmark? He says to Denmark—" You have seditious clubs at Copenhagen—

No Danish vessel shall enter the ports of Russia!" He holds a still more despotic language to Hamburg. He threatens to lay an embargo on their trade; and he forces them to surrender up men who are claimed by the French as their citizens—whether truly or not, I do not inquire. He threatens them with his own vengeance if they refuse, and subjects them to that of the French if they comply. And what has been his conduct to Spain? He first sends away the Spanish minister from Petersburg, and then complains as a great insult that his minister was dismissed from Madrid! This is one of our allies; and he has declared that the object for which he has taken up arms is to replace the ancient race of the House of Bourbon on the throne of France, and that he does this for the cause of religion and social order! Such is the respect for religion and social order which he himself displays; and such are the examples of it with which he coalesce!

No man regrets, Sir, more than I do, the enormities that France has committed; but how do they bear upon the question as it now stands? Are we for ever to deprive ourselves of the benefits of peace because France has perpetrated acts of injustice? Sir, we cannot acquit ourselves upon such ground. We have negotiated. With the knowledge of these acts of injustice and disorder, we have treated with them twice; yet the right hon. gentleman cannot enter into negotiation with them now; and it is worth while to attend to the reasons that he gives for refusing their offer. The revolution itself is no more an objection now than it was in 1796, when he did negotiate; for the government of France at that time was surely as unstable as it is now. The crimes of the French, the instability of their government, did not prevent him; and why are they to prevent him now? He negotiated with a government as unstable, and, baffled in that negotiation, he did not scruple to open another at Lisle in 1797. We have heard a very curious account of these negotiations this day, and, as the right hon. gentleman has emphatically told us, an "honest" account of them. He says he has no scruple in avowing that he apprehended danger from the success of his own efforts to procure a pacification, and that he was not displeased at its failure. He was sincere in his endeavours to treat, but he was not disappointed when they failed. I wish to understand the right hon. gentleman correctly. His declaration on the subject, then, I take to be this—that though sincere in his endeavours to procure peace in 1797, yet he apprehended greater danger from accomplishing his object than from the continuance of war; and that he felt this apprehension from the comparative views of the probable state of peace and war at that time. I have no hesitation in allowing the fact that a state of peace, immediately after a war of such violence, must, in some respects, be a state of insecurity; but does this not belong, in a certain degree, to all wars? And are we never to have peace, because that peace may be insecure? But there was something, it seems, so peculiar in this war and in the character and principles of the enemy, that the right hon. gentleman thought a peace in 1797 would be comparatively more dangerous than war. Why, then, did he treat? I beg the attention of the House to this—He treated, "because the unequivocal sense of the people of England was declared to be in favour of a negotiation." The right hon. gentleman confesses the truth, then, that in 1797 the people were for peace. I thought so at the time; but you all recollect that, when I stated it in my place, it was denied. "True," they said, "you have procured petitions; but we have petitions too: we all know in what strange ways petitions may be procured, and how little they deserve to be considered as the sense of the people." This was their language at the time; but now we find these petitions did speak the sense of the people, and that it was on this side of the House only that the sense of the people was spoken. The majority spoke a contrary language It is acknowledged, then, that the unequivocal sense of the people of England may be spoken by the minority of this House, and that it is not always by the test of numbers that an honest decision is to be ascertained. This House decided against what the right hon. gentleman knew to be the sense of the country; but he himself acted upon that sense against the vote of parliament.

The negotiation in 1796 went off, as my learned friend has said, upon the question of Belgium, or, as the right hon. gentleman asserts, upon a question of principle. He negotiated to please the people, but it went off " on account of a monstrous principle advanced by France incompatible with all negotiation." This is now said. Did the right hon. gentleman say so at the time? Did he fairly and candidly inform the people of England that they broke off the negotiation because the French had urged a basis that it was totally impossible for England at any time to grant? No such thing. On the contrary, when the negotiation broke off, they published a manifesto, " renewing in the face of Europe, the solemn declaration of that whenever the enemy should be disposed to enter on the work of a general pacification, in the spirit of conciliation and equity, nothing should be wanting on their part to contribute to the accomplishment of the great object." And accordingly, in 1797, notwithstanding this incompatible principle, and with all the enormities of the French on their heads, they opened a new negotiation at Lisle. They do not wait for any retractation of this incompatible principle; they do not wait even till overtures shall be made to them; but they solicit and renew a negotiation themselves. I do not blame them for this, Sir; I say only that it is an argument against the assertion of an incompatible principle. It is a proof that they did not then think as the right hon. gentleman now says they thought; but that they yielded to the sentiments of the nation, who were generally inclined to peace, against their own judgment; and, from a motive which I shall come to by-and-by, they had no hesitation, on account of the first rupture, to renew the negotiation—it was renewed at Lisle; and this the French broke off, after the revolution at Paris on the 4th of September. What was the conduct of the ministers upon this occasion? One would have thought that, with the fresh insult at Lisle in their minds, with the recollection of their failure the year before at Paris, if it had been true that they found an incompatible principle, they would have talked a warlike language, and would have announced to their country and to all Europe that peace was not to be obtained; that they must throw away the scabbard and think only of the means of continuing the contest. No such thing. They put forth a declaration in which they said that they should look with anxious expectation for the moment when the government of France would show a disposition and spirit corresponding with their own; and renewing before all Europe the solemn declaration that, at the very moment when the brilliant victory of Lord Duncan might have justified them in demanding more extravagant terms, they were willing, if the calamities of war could be closed, to conclude peace on the same moderate and equitable principles and terms which they had before proposed. Such was their declaration upon that occasion; and in the discussions which we had upon it in this House ministers were explicit. They said that by that negotiation there had been given to the world what might be regarded as an unequivocal test of the sincerity and disposition of government towards peace or against it; for those who refuse discussion show that they are disinclined to pacification; and it is therefore, they said, always to be considered as a test that the party who refuses to negotiate is the party who is disinclined to peace. This they themselves set up as the test. Try them now, Sir, by that test. An offer is made them. They rashly, and I think rudely, refuse it. Have they, or have they not, broken their own test?

But, they say, "we have not refused all discussion." They have put a case. They have expressed a wish for the restoration of the House of Bourbon, and have declared that to be an event which would immediately remove every obstacle to negotiation. Sir, as to the restoration of the House of Bourbon, if it shall be the wish of the people of France, I for one shall be perfectly content to acquiesce. I think the people of France, as well as every other people, ought to have the government which they like best themselves; and the form of that government, or the persons who hold it in their hands, should never be an obstacle with me to treat with the nation for peace, or to live with me in amity—but as an Englishman, and actuated by English feelings, I surely cannot wish for the restoration of the House of Bourbon to the throne of France. I hope that I am not a man to bear heavily upon any unfortunate family. I feel for their situation—I respect their distresses—but, as a friend of England, I cannot wish for their restoration to the power which they abused. I cannot forget that the whole history of the century is little more than an account of the wars and the calamities arising from the restless ambition, the intrigues, and the perfidy of the House of Bourbon.

I cannot discover, in any part of the laboured defence which has been set up for not accepting the offer now made by France, any argument to satisfy my mind that ministers have not forfeited the test which they held out as infallible in 1797. An hon. gentleman thinks that Parliament should be eager only to approach the throne with declarations of their readiness to support his Majesty in the further prosecution of the war, without inquiry; and he is quite delighted with an address, which he has found upon the journals, to King William, in which they pledged themselves to support him in his efforts to resist the ambition of Louis XIV. He thinks it quite astonishing how much it is in point, and how perfectly it applies to the present occasion. One would have thought, Sir, that in order to prove the application, he would have shown that an offer had been respectfully made by the grand monarque to King William to treat, which he had peremptorily and in very irritating terms refused; and that, upon this, the House of Commons had come forward, and with one voice declared their determination to stand by him, and their lives and fortunes, in prosecuting the just and necessary war. Not a word of all this; and yet the hon. gentleman finds it quite a parallel case, and an exact model for the House, on this day, to pursue. I really think, Sir, he might as well have taken any other address upon the Journals, upon any other topic, as this address to King William. It would have been equally in point, and would have equally served to show the hon. gentleman's talents for reasoning.

Sir, I cannot here overlook another instance of this hon. gentleman's candid style of debating, and of his respect for Parliament. He has found out, it seems, that in former periods of out history, and even in periods which have been denominated good times, intercepted letters have been published; and he reads from the *Gazette* instances of such publication. Really, Sir, if the hon. gentleman had pursued the profession to which he turned his thoughts when younger, he would have learnt that it was necessary to find cases a little more in point. And yet, full of his triumph on this notable discovery, he has chosen to indulge himself in speaking of a most respectable and a most honourable person as any that this country knows, and who is possessed of as sound an understanding as any man that I have the good fortune to be acquainted with, in terms the most offensive and disgusting, on account of words which he may be supposed to have said in another place.[1] He has spoken of that noble person and of his intellect in terms which, were I disposed to retort, I might say show the hon. gentleman to be possessed of an intellect which would justify me in passing over in silence anything that comes from such a man. Sir, that noble person did not speak of the mere act of publishing the intercepted correspondence; and the hon. gentleman's reference to the *Gazettes* of former periods is, therefore, not in point. The noble Duke complained of the manner in which these intercepted letters had been published, not of the fact itself of their publication; for, in the introduction and notes to those letters, the ribaldry is such that they are not screened from the execration of every honourable mind even by their extreme stupidity. The hon. gentleman says that he must treat with indifference the intellect of a man who can ascribe the present scarcity of corn to the war. Sir, I think there is nothing either absurd or unjust in such an opinion. Does not the war, necessarily, by

[1] The Duke of Bedford.

its magazines, and still more by its expeditions, increase consumption? But when we learn that corn is, at this very moment, sold in France for less than half the price which it bears here, is it not a fair thing to suppose that, but for the war and its prohibitions, a part of that grain would be brought to this country, on account of the high price which it would sell for, and that, consequently, our scarcity would be relieved from their abundance? I speak only upon report, of course; but I see that the price quoted in the French markets is less by one half than the prices in England. There was nothing, therefore, very absurd in what fell from my noble friend; and I would really advise the hon. gentleman, when he speaks of persons distinguished for every virtue, to be a little more guarded in his language. I see no reason why he and his friends should not leave to persons in another place, holding the same opinions as themselves, the task of answering what may be thrown out there. Is not the phalanx sufficient? It is no great compliment to their talents, considering their number, that they cannot be left to the task of answering the few to whom they are opposed; but perhaps the hon. gentleman has too little to do in this House, and is to be sent there himself. In truth, I see no reason why even he might not be sent, as well as some others who have been sent there.

To return to the subject of the negotiation in 1797. It is, in my mind, extremely material to attend to the account which the right hon. gentleman gives of his memorable negotiation of 1797, and of his motives for entering into it. In all questions of peace and war, he says, many circumstances must necessarily enter into the consideration; and that they are not to be decided upon the extremes: the determination must be made upon a balance and comparison of the evils or the advantages upon the one side and the other, and that one of the greatest considerations is that of finance. In 1797 the right hon. gentleman confesses he found himself peculiarly embarrassed as to the resources of the war, if they were to be found in the old and usual way of the funding system. Now, though he thought, upon his balance and comparison of considerations, that the evils of war would be fewer than those of peace, yet they would only be so provided, that he could establish a " new and solid system of finance " in place of the old and exhausted funding system; and to accomplish this it was necessary to have the unanimous approbation of the people. To procure this unanimity he pretended to be a friend to negotiation, though he did not wish for the success of that negotiation, but hoped only that through that means he should bring the people to argee to his new and solid system of finance. With these views, then, what does he do? Knowing that, contrary to his declarations in this House, the opinion of the people of England was generally for peace, he enters into a negotiation, in which, as the world believed at the time, and even until this day, he completely failed. No such thing, Sir—he completely succeeded,—for his object was not to gain peace; it was to gain over the people of this country to a " new and a solid system of finance "—that is, to the raising a great part of the supplies within the year, to the triple assessment, and to the tax upon income! And how did he gain them over? By pretending to be a friend of peace, which he was not; and by opening a negotiation which he secretly wished might not succeed. The right hon. gentleman says that in all this he was honest and sincere; he negotiated fairly, and would have obtained the peace if the French had shown a disposition correspondent to his own; but he rejoiced that their conduct was such as to convince the people of England of the necessity of concurring with him in the views which he had, and in granting him the supply which he thought essential to their posture at the time. Sir, I will not say that in all this he was not honest to his own purpose, and that he has not been honest in his declarations and confessions this night; but I cannot agree that he was honest to this House, or honest to the people of this country. To this House it was not honest to make them counteract the sense of the people, as he knew it to be expressed in the petitions upon the table; nor was it honest to the country to act in a disguise, and to pursue a secret purpose, unknown to them, while affecting to take the road which they pointed out. I know not whether this may not be honesty in the political ethics of the right hon. gentleman, but I know that it would be called by a very different name in the common transactions of society, and in the rules of morality established in private life. I know of nothing in the history of this country that it resembles, except, perhaps, one of the most profligate periods—the reign of Charles II., when the sale of Dunkirk might probably have been justified by the same pretence. Charles also declared war against France, and did it to cover a negotiation by which, in his difficulties, he was to gain a " solid system of finance."

But, Sir, I meet the right hon. gentleman on his own ground. I say that you ought to treat on the same principle on which you treated in 1797, in order to gain the cordial co-operation of the people. " We want experience and the evidence of facts."

Can there be any evidence of facts equal to that of a frank, open, and candid negotiation? Let us see whether Bounaparte will display the same temper as his predecessors. If he shall do so, then you will confirm the people of England in their opinion of the necessity of continuing the war, and you will revive all the vigour which you roused in 1797. Or will you not do this until you have a reverse of fortune? Will you never treat but when you are in a situation of distress, and when you have occasion to impose on the people?

"But," you say, "we have not refused to treat." You have stated a case in which you will be ready immediately to enter into a negotiation—viz., the restoration of the House of Bourbon; but you deny that this is a *sine quâ non;* and in your nonsensical language, which I do not understand, you talk of "limited possibilities" which may induce you to treat without the restoration of the House of Bourbon. But do you state what they are? Now, Sir, I say that if you put one case, upon which you declare that you are willing to treat immediately, and say that there are other possible cases which may induce you to treat hereafter, without mentioning what these possible cases are, you do state a *sine quâ non* of immediate treaty. Suppose I have an estate to sell, and I say my demand is £1000 for it—I will sell the estate immediately for that sum. To be sure, there may be other terms upon which I may be willing to part with it; but I say nothing of them. The £1000 is the only condition that I state now. Will any gentleman say that I do not make the £1000 the *sine quâ non* of the immediate sale? Thus, you say, the restoration of the princes is not the only possible ground; but you give no other. This is your *projet.* Do you demand a *contre projet?* Do you follow your own rule? Do you not do the thing of which you complained in the enemy? You seemed to be afraid of receiving another proposition; and by confining yourselves to this one point you make it in fact, though not in terms, your *sine quâ non.*

But the right hon. gentleman, in his speech, does what the official note avoids—he finds there the convenient words "experience and the evidence of facts"; upon these he goes into detail; and, in order to convince the House that new evidence is required, he goes back to all the earliest acts and crimes of the revolution—to all the atrocities of all the governments that have passed away; and he contends that he must have experience that these foul crimes are repented of, and that a purer and a better system is adopted in France, by which he may be sure that they shall be capable of maintaining the relations of peace and amity. Sir, these are not conciliatory words; nor is this a practical ground to gain experience. Does he think it possible that evidence of a peaceable demeanour can be obtained in war? What does he mean to say to the French Consul? "Until you shall in war behave yourself in a peaceable manner, I will not treat with you." Is there not something extremely ridiculous in this? In duels, indeed, we have often heard of this kind of language. Two gentlemen go out and fight; when, after discharging their pistols at one another, it is not an unusual thing for one of them to say to the other—"Now I am satisfied—I see that you are a man of honour and we are friends again." There is something, by-the-by, ridiculous even in this; but between nations it is more than ridiculous—it is criminal. It is a ground which no principle can justify, and which is as impracticable as it is impious. That two nations should be set on to beat one another into friendship is too abominable even for the fiction of romance; but for a statesman seriously and gravely to lay it down as a system upon which he means to act is monstrous. What can we say of such a test as he means to put the French government to, but that it is hopeless? It is in the nature of war to inflame animosity—to exasperate, not to soothe—to widen, not to approximate. And so long as this is to be acted upon, it is vain to hope that we can have the evidence which we require.

The right hon. gentleman, however, thinks otherwise; and he points out four distinct possible cases, besides the re-establishment of the Bourbon family, in which he would agree to treat with the French.

1. "If Buonaparte shall conduct himself so as to convince him that he has abandoned the principles which were objectionable in his predecessors, and that he shall be actuated by a more moderate system." I ask you, Sir, if this is likely to be ascertained in war? It is the nature of war not to allay but to inflame the passions; and it is not by the invective and abuse which have been thrown upon him and his government, nor by the continued irritations which war is sure to give, that the virtues of moderation and forbearance are to be nourished.

2. "If, contrary to the expectations of ministers, the people of France shall show a disposition to acquiesce in the government of Buonaparte." Does the right hon. gentleman mean to say that because it is an usurpation on the part of the present chief, therefore the people are not likely to acquiesce in it? I

have not time, Sir, to discuss the question of this usurpation, or whether it is likely to be permanent; but I certainly have not so good an opinion of the French, or of any people, as to believe that it will be short-lived, merely because it was an usurpation and because it is a system of military despotism. Cromwell was a usurper; and in many points there may be found a resemblance between him and the present chief consul of France. There is no doubt but that, on several occasions of his life, Cromwell's sincerity may be questioned, particularly in his self-denying ordinance—in his affected piety, and other things; but would it not have been insanity in France and Spain to refuse to treat with him because he was an usurper? No, Sir, these are not the maxims by which governments are actuated. They do not inquire so much into the means by which power may have been acquired, as into the fact of where power resides. The people did acquiesce in the government of Cromwell; but it may be said that the splendour of his talents, the vigour of his administration, the high tone with which he spoke to foreign nations, the success of his arms, and the character which he gave to the English name, induced the nation to acquiesce in his usurpation; and that we must not try Buonaparte by this example. Will it be said that Buonaparte is not a man of great abilities? Will it be said that he has not, by his victories, thrown a splendour over even the violence of the revolution, and that he does not conciliate the French people by the high and lofty tone in which he speaks to foreign nations? Are not the French, then, as likely as the English in the case of Cromwell to acquiesce in his government? If they should do so, the right hon. gentleman may find that this possible predicament may fail him. He may find that though one power may make war, it requires two to make peace. He may find that Buonaparte was as insincere as himself in the proposition which he made; and in his turn he may come forward and say—" I have no occasion now for concealment. It is true that in the beginning of the year 1800 I offered to treat, not because I wished for peace, but because the people of France wished for it; and besides, my old resources being exhausted, and there being no means of carrying on the war without a 'new and solid system of finance,' I pretended to treat, because I wished to procure the unanimous assent of the French people to this new and solid system. Did you think I was in earnest? You were deceived. I now throw off the mask; I have gained my point; and I reject your offers with scorn." Is it not a very possible case that he may use this language? Is it not within the right hon. gentleman's "knowledge of human nature"? But even if this should not be the case, will not the very test which you require—the acquiescence of the people of France in his government—give him an advantage-ground in the negotiation which he does not possess now? Is it quite sure that when he finds himself safe in his seat he will treat on the same terms as now, and that you will get a better peace some time hence than you might reasonably hope to obtain at this moment? Will he not have one interest less that at present? And do you not overlook a favourable occasion for a chance which is extremely doubtful? These are the considerations which I would urge to his Majesty's ministers against the dangerous experiment of waiting for the acquiescence of the people of France.

3. "If the allies of this country shall be less successful than they have every reason to expect they will be in stirring up the people of France against Buonaparte, and in the further prosecution of the war." And,

4. "If the pressure of the war should be heavier upon us than it would be convenient for us to continue to bear." These are the other two possible emergencies in which the right hon. gentleman would treat even with Buonaparte. Sir, I have often blamed the right hon. gentleman for being disengenuous and insincere. On the present occasion I certainly cannot charge him with any such thing. He has made to-night a most honest confession. He is open and candid. He tells Buonaparte fairly what he has to expect. "I mean," says he, "to do everything in my power to raise up the people of France against you. I have engaged a number of allies, and our combined efforts shall be used to incite insurrection and civil war in France. I will strive to murder you, or to get you sent away. If I succeed, well; but if I fail, then I will treat with you. My resources being exhausted, even my solid system of finance having failed to supply me with the means of keeping together my allies, and of feeding the discontents I have excited in France, then you may expect to see me renounce my high tone, my attachment to the House of Bourbon, my abhorrence of your crimes, my alarm at your principles; for then I shall be ready to own that, on the balance and comparison of circumstances, there will be less danger in concluding a peace than in the continuance of the war!" Is this a language for one state to hold to another? And what sort of a peace does the right hon. gentleman expect to receive in that case? Does he think

that Buonaparte would grant to baffled insolence, to humiliated
pride, to disappointment, and to imbecility the same terms
which he would be ready to give now? The right hon. gentleman cannot have forgotten what he said on another occasion—

> "——Potuit quæ plurima virtus
> Esse, fuit: toto certatum est corpore regni."

He would then have to repeat his words, but with a different
application. He would have to say: all our efforts are in vain—
we have exhausted our strength—our designs are impracticable
—and we must sue to you for peace.

Sir, what is the question this night? We are called upon
to support ministers in refusing a frank, candid and respectful
offer of negotiation, and to countenance them in continuing
the war. Now, I would put the question in another way.
Suppose ministers had been inclined to adopt the line of conduct
which they pursued in 1796 and 1797, and that to-night, instead
of a question on a war-address, it had been an address to his
Majesty to thank him for accepting the overture, and for opening
a negotiation to treat for peace: I ask the gentleman opposite—
I appeal to the whole 558 representatives of the people—
to lay their hands upon their hearts, and to say whether they
would not have cordially voted for such an address? Would
they, or would they not? Yes, Sir, if the address had breathed
a spirit of peace your benches would have resounded with rejoicings, and with praises of a measure that was likely to bring
back the blessings of tranquillity. On the present occasion, then,
I ask for the vote of none but of those who, in the secret confession of their conscience, admit, at this instant while they hear
me that they would have cheerfully and heartily voted with the
minister for an address directly the reverse of this. If every such
gentleman were to vote with me, I should be this night in
the greatest majority that ever I had the honour to vote with
in this House.

Sir, we have heard to-night a great many most acrimonious
invectives against Buonaparte, against the whole course of his
conduct, and against the unprincipled manner in which he
seized upon the reigns of government. I will not make his
defence—I think all this sort of invective, which is used only to
inflame the passions of this House and of the country, exceeding ill-timed and very impolitic—but I say I will not make his
defence. I am not sufficiently in possession of materials upon

which to form an opinion on the character and conduct of this extraordinary man. Upon his arrival in France he found the government in a very unsettled state, and the whole affairs of the republic deranged, crippled and involved. He thought it necessary to reform the government; and he did reform it, just in the way in which a military man may be expected to carry on a reform—he seized on the whole authority to himself. It will not be expected from me that I should either approve or apologise for such an act. I am certainly not for reforming governments by such expedients; but how this House can be so violently indignant at the idea of military despotism is, I own, a little singular, when I see the composure with which they can observe it nearer home; nay, when I see them regard it as a frame of government most peculiarly suited to the exercise of free opinion on a subject the most important of any that can engage the attention of a people. Was it not the system that was so happily and so advantageously established of late all over Ireland; and which, even now, the government may, at its pleasure, proclaim over the whole of that kingdom? Are not the persons and property of the people left in many districts at this moment to the entire will of military commanders? And is not this held out as peculiarly proper and advantageous at a time when the people of Ireland are free, and with unbiassed judgment, to discuss the most interesting question of a legislative union? Notwithstanding the existence of martial law, so far do we think Ireland from being enslaved, that we think it precisely the period and the circumstances under which she may best declare her free opinion! Now really, Sir, I cannot think that gentlemen who talk in this way about Ireland can, with a good grace, rail at military despotism in France.

But, it seems, "Buonaparte has broken his oaths. He has violated his oath of fidelity to the constitution of the year 3." Sir, I am not one of those who think that any such oaths ought ever to be exacted. They are seldom or ever of any effect; and I am not for sporting with a thing so sacred as an oath. I think it would be good to lay aside all such oaths. Who ever heard that, in revolutions, the oath of fidelity to the former government was ever regarded; or even when violated, that it was imputed to the persons as a crime? In times of revolution, men who take up arms are called rebels—if they fail, they are adjudged to be traitors. But who ever heard before of their being perjured? On the restoration of Charles II., those who had taken up arms for the Commonwealth were stigmatized as rebels and traitors, but not as men foresworn. Was the Earl of Devonshire charged with being perjured on account of the allegiance he had sworn to the House of Stuart, and the part he took in those struggles which preceded and brought about the Revolution? The violation of oaths of allegiance was never imputed to the people of England, and will never be imputed to any people. But who brings up the question of oaths? He who strives to make twenty-four millions of persons violate the oaths they have taken to their present constitution, and who desires to re-establish the House of Bourbon by such violation of their vows. I put it so, Sir, because, if the question of oaths be of the least consequence, it is equal on both sides. He who desires the whole people of France to perjure themselves, and who hopes for success in his project only upon their doing so, surely cannot make it a charge against Buonaparte that he has done the same.

"Ah! but Buonaparte has declared it as his opinion, that the two governments of Great Britain and of France cannot exist together. After the treaty of Campio Formio he sent two confidential persons, Berthier and Monge, to the Directory to say so in his name." Well, and what is there in this absurd and puerile assertion, if it was ever made? Has not the right hon. gentleman, in this House, said the same thing? In this, at least, they resemble one another. They have both made use of this assertion; and I believe that these two illustrious persons are the only two on earth who think it. But let us turn the tables. We ought to put ourselves at times in the place of the enemy, if we are desirous of really examining with candour and fairness the dispute between us. How may they not interpret the speeches of ministers and their friends in both Houses of the British Parliament? If we are to be told of the idle speech of Berthier and Monge, may they not also bring up speeches in which it has not been merely hinted, but broadly asserted, that "the two constitutions of England and France could not exist together?" May not these offences and charges be reciprocated without end? Are we ever to go on in this miserable squabble about words? Are we still, as we happen to be successful on the one side or other, to bring up these impotent accusations, insults, and provocations, against each other; and only when we are beaten and unfortunate to think of treating? Oh! pity the condition of man, gracious God! and save us from such a system of malevolence, in which all our old and venerated prejudices are to be done away, and by which we are taught to consider war as the natural state of man, and peace but as a dangerous and difficult extremity?

Sir, this temper must be corrected. It is a diabolical spirit and would lead to interminable war. Our history is full of instances that where we have overlooked a proffered occasion to treat, we have uniformly suffered by delay. At what time did we ever profit by obstinately persevering in war? We accepted at Ryswick the terms we had refused five years before, and the same peace which was concluded at Utrecht might have been obtained at Gertruydenberg. And as to security from the future machinations or ambition of the French, I ask you what security you ever had or could have? Did the different treaties made with Louis XIV. serve to tie up his hands, to restrain his ambition, or to stifle his restless spirit? At what period could you safely repose in the honour, forbearance, and moderation of the French Government? Was there ever an idea of refusing to treat because the peace might be afterwards insecure? The peace of 1763 was not accompanied with securities; and it was no sooner made than the French court began, as usual, its intrigues. And what security did the right hon. gentleman exact at the peace of 1783, in which he was engaged? Were we rendered secure by that peace? The right hon. gentleman knows well that soon after that peace the French formed a plan, in conjunction with the Dutch, of attacking our Indian possessions, of raising up the native powers against us, and of driving us out of India; as the French are desirous of doing now—only with this difference, that the cabinet of France entered into this project in a moment of profound peace, and when they conceived us to be lulled into perfect security. After making the peace of 1783, the right hon. gentleman and his friends went out, and I, among others, came into office. Suppose, Sir, that we had taken up the jealousy upon which the right hon. gentleman now acts, and had refused to ratify the peace which he had made. Suppose that we had said—" No; France is acting a perfidious part— we see no security for England in this treaty—they want only a respite, in order to attack us again in an important part of our dominions; and we ought not to confirm the treaty." I ask, would the right hon. gentleman have supported us in this refusal? I say that upon his reasoning he ought; but I put it fairly to him, would he have supported us in refusing to ratify the treaty upon such a pretence? He certainly ought not, and I am sure he would not, but the course of reasoning which he now assumes would have justified his taking such a ground. On the contrary, I am persuaded that he would have said—" This is a refinement upon jealousy. Security! You have security, the only security that you can ever expect to get. It is the present interest of France to make peace. She will keep it if it be her interest: she will break it if it be her interest; such is the state of nations; and you have nothing but your own vigilance for your security."

" It is not the interest of Buonaparte," it seems, " sincerely to enter into a negotiation, or, if he should even make peace, sincerely to keep it." But how are we to decide upon his sincerity? By refusing to treat with him? Surely if we mean to discover his sincerity, we ought to hear the propositions which he desires to make. " But peace would be unfriendly to his system of military despotism." Sir, I hear a great deal about the short-lived nature of military despotism. I wish the history of the world would bear gentlemen out in this description of military despotism. Was not the government erected by Augustus Cæsar a military despotism? and yet it endured for 600 or 700 years. Military despotism, unfortunately, is too likely in its nature to be permanent, and it is not true that it depends on the life of the first usurper. Though half the Roman emperors were murdered, yet the military despotism went on; and so it would be, I fear, in France. If Buonaparte should disappear from the scene, to make room, perhaps, for a Berthier, or any other general, what difference would that make in the quality of French despotism or in our relation to the country? We may as safely treat with a Buonaparte or with any of his successors, be they who they may, as we could with a Louis XVI., a Louis XVII., or a Louis XVIII. There is no difference but in the name. Where the power essentially resides, thither we ought to go for peace.

But, Sir, if we are to reason on the fact, I should think that it is the interest of Buonaparte to make peace. A lover of military glory, as that general must necessarily be, may he not think that his measure of glory is full—that it may be tarnished by a reverse of fortune, and can hardly be increased by any new laurels? He must feel that, in the situation to which he is now raised, he can no longer depend on his own fortune, his own genius, and his own talents, for a continuance of his success; he must be under the necessity of employing other generals, whose misconduct or incapacity might endanger his power, or whose triumphs even might affect the interest which he holds in the opinion of the French. Peace, then, would secure to him what he has achieved, and fix the inconstancy of fortune. But this will not be his only motive. He must see that France also requires a respite—a breathing interval to recruit her wasted strength. To procure her this respite would be, perhaps, the attainment of more solid glory, as well as the means of acquiring more solid power, than anything which he can hope to gain from arms and from the proudest triumphs. May he not then be zealous to gain this fame, the only species of fame, perhaps, that is worth acquiring? Nay, granting that his soul may still burn with the thirst of military exploits, is it not likely that he is earnestly disposed to yield to the feelings of the French people and to consolidate his power by consulting their interests? I have a right to argue in this way, when suppositions of his insincerity are reasoned upon on the other side. Sir, these aspersions are, in truth, always idle, and even mischievous. I have been too long accustomed to hear imputations and calumnies thrown out upon great and honourable characters to be much influenced by them. My learned friend has paid this night a most just, deserved, and honourable tribute of applause to the memory of that great and unparalleled character who has been so recently lost to the world. I must, like him, beg leave to dwell a moment on the venerable George Washington, though I know that it is impossible for me to bestow anything like adequate praise on a character which gave us, more than any other human being, the example of a perfect man; yet, good, great, and unexampled as General Washington was, I can remember the time when he was not better spoken of in this House than Buonaparte is now. The right hon. gentleman who opened this debate (Mr. Dundas) may remember in what terms of disdain, of virulence, and even of contempt, General Washington was spoken of by gentlemen on that side of the House. Does he not recollect with what marks of indignation any member was stigmatized as an enemy to his country who mentioned with common respect the name of General Washington? If a negotiation had then been proposed to be opened with that great man, what would have been said? "Would you treat with a rebel, a traitor! What an example would you not give by such an act!" I do not know whether the right hon. gentleman may not yet possess some of his old prejudices on the subject. I hope not. I hope by this time we are all convinced that a republican government, like that of America, may exist without danger or injury to social order or to established monarchies. They have happily shown that they can maintain the relations of peace and amity with other states: they have shown, too, that they are alive to the feelings of honour; but they do not lose sight of plain good sense and discretion. They have not refused to negotiate with the French, and they have accordingly the hopes of a speedy termination of every difference. We cry up their conduct, but we do not imitate it. At the beginning of the struggle we were told that the French were setting up a set of wild and impracticable theories, and that we ought not to be misled by them—we could not grapple with theories. Now we are told that we must not treat, because, out of the lottery, Buonaparte has drawn such a prize as military despotism. Is military despotism a theory? One would think that that is one of the practical things which ministers might understand, and to which they would have no particular objection. But what is our present conduct founded on but a theory, and that a most wild and ridiculous theory? What are we fighting for? Not for a principle; not for security; not for conquest even; but merely for an experiment and a speculation, to discover whether a gentleman at Paris may not turn out a better man than we now take him to be.

My hon. friend (Mr. Whitbread) has been censured for an opinion which he gave, and I think justly, that the change of property in France since the revolution must form an almost insurmountable barrier to the return of the ancient proprietors. "No such thing," says the right hon. gentleman; "nothing can be more easy. Property is depreciated to such a degree, that the purchasers would easily be brought to restore the estates." I very much differ from him in this idea. It is the character of every such convulsion as that which has ravaged France, that an infinite and indescribable load of misery is inflicted upon private families. The heart sickens at the recital of the sorrows which it engenders. No revolution implied, though it may have occasioned, a total change of property The restoration of the Bourbons does imply it; and there is the difference. There is no doubt but that if the noble families had foreseen the duration and the extent of the evils which were to fall upon their heads they would have taken a very different line of conduct. But they unfortunately flew from their country. The king and his advisers sought foreign aid. A confederacy was formed to restore them by military force; and as a means of resisting this combination, the estates of the fugitives were confiscated and sold. However, compassion may deplore the case, it cannot be said that the thing is unprecedented. The people have always resorted to such means of defence. Now the question is, how this property is to be got out of their hands? If it be true, as I have heard, that the purchasers of national and forfeited estates amount to 1,500,000 persons, I see no hope of their being forced to deliver up their property; nor do I even know that they ought. I question the policy, even if the thing were practicable; but I assert that such a body of new proprietors forms an insurmountable barrier to the restoration of the ancient order of things. Never was a revolution consolidated by a pledge so strong.

But, as if this were not of itself sufficient, Louis XVIII. from his retirement at Mittau puts forth a manifesto, in which he assures the friends of his house that he is about to come back with all the powers that formerly belonged to his family. He does not promise to the people a constitution which may tend to conciliate; but, stating that he is to come with all the *ancien régime*, they would naturally attach to it its proper appendages of bastiles, lettres de cachet, gabelle, etc. And the noblesse, for whom this proclamation was peculiarly conceived, would also naturally feel that if the monarch was to be restored to all his privileges, they surely were to be reinstated in their estates without a compensation to the purchasers. Is this likely to make the people wish for a restoration of loyalty? I have no doubt that there may be a number of Chouans in France, though I am persuaded that little dependence is to be placed on their efforts. There may be a number of people dispersed over France, and particularly in certain provinces, who may retain a degree of attachment to royalty; and how the government will contrive to compromise with that spirit I know not. I suspect, however, that Buonaparte will try; his efforts will be turned to that object; and, if we may believe report, he has succeeded to a considerable degree. He will naturally call to his recollection the precedent which the history of France itself will furnish. The once formidable insurrection of the Huguenots was completely stifled and the party conciliated by the policy of Henry IV., who gave them such privileges and raised them so high in the government as to make some persons apprehend danger therefrom to the unity of the empire. Nor will the French be likely to forget the revocation of the edict—one of the memorable acts of the House of Bourbon—an act which was never surpassed in atrocity, injustice, and impolicy, by anything that has disgraced Jacobinism. If Buonaparte shall attempt some similar arrangement to that of Henry IV. with the Chouans who will say that he is likely to fail? He will meet with no great obstacle to success from the influence which our ministers have established with the chiefs, or in the attachment and dependence which they have on our protection; for what has the right hon. gentleman told him, in stating the contingencies in which he will treat with Buonaparte? He will excite a rebellion in France —he will give support to the Chouans, if they can stand their ground; but he will not make common cause with them; for unless they can depose Buonaparte, send him into banishment, or execute him, he will abandon the Chouans, and treat with this very man, whom he describes as holding the reins and wielding the powers of France for purposes of unexampled barbarity.

Sir, I wish the atrocities of which we hear so much, and which I abhor as much as any man, were indeed unexampled. I fear that they do not belong exclusively to the French. When the right hon. gentleman speaks of the extraordinary successes of the last campaign, he does not mention the horrors by which some of those successes were accompanied. Naples, for instance, has been, among others, what is called "delivered"; and yet, if I am rightly informed, it has been stained and polluted by murders so ferocious, and by cruelties of every kind so abhorrent, that the heart shudders at the recital. It has been said, not only that the miserable victims of the rage and brutality of the fanatics were savagely murdered, but that, in many instances, their flesh was eaten and devoured by the cannibals who are the advocates and the instruments of social order! Nay, England is not totally exempt from reproach, if the rumours which are circulated be true. I will mention a fact to give ministers the opportunity, if it be false, of wiping away the stain that it must otherwise fix on the British name. It is said that a party of the republican inhabitants of Naples took shelter in the fortress of the Castel de Uova. They were besieged by a detachment from the Royal Army, to whom they refused to surrender; but demanded that a British officer should be brought forward, and to him they capitualted. They made terms with him under the sanction of the British name. It was agreed that their persons and property should be safe, and that they should be conveyed to Toulon. They were accordingly put on board a vessel; but before they sailed their property was confiscated, numbers of them taken out, thrown into dungeons, and some of them, I understand, notwithstanding the British guarantee, actually executed.

Where then, Sir, is this war, which on every side is pregnant with such horrors, to be carried? Where is it to stop? Not till you establish the House of Bourbon! And this you cherish the hope of doing, because you have had a successful campaign. Why, Sir, before this you have had a successful campaign. The situation of the allies, with all they have gained, is surely not to be compared now to what it was when you had taken Valenciennes, Quesnoy, Condé, etc., which induced some gentlemen in this house to prepare themselves for a march to Paris. With all that you have gained, you surely will not say that the prospect is brighter now than it was then. What have you gained but the recovery of a part of what you before lost? One campaign is successful to you—another to them; and in this way, animated by the vindictive passions of revenge, hatred, and rancour, which are infinitely more flagitious even than those of ambition and the thirst of power, you may go on for ever; as, with such black incentives, I see no end to human misery. And all this without an intelligible motive, all this because you may gain a better peace a year or two hence! So that we are called upon to go on merely as a speculation. We must keep Buonaparte for some time longer at war, as a state of probation. Gracious God, Sir, is war a state of probation? Is peace a rash system? Is it dangerous for nations to live in amity with each other? Is your vigilance, your policy, your common powers of observation, to be extinguished by putting an end to the horrors of war? Cannot this state of probation be as well undergone without adding to the catalogue of human sufferings? " But we must pause!" What! must the bowels of Great Britain be torn out—her best blood be spilt—her treasure wasted—that you may make an experiment? Put yourselves— oh! that you would put yourselves—in the field of battle, and learn to judge of the sort of horrors that you excite. In former wars a man might at least have some feeling, some interest, that served to balance in his mind the impressions which a scene of carnage and of death must inflict. If a man had been present at the Battle of Blenheim, for instance, and had inquired the motive of the battle, there was not a soldier engaged who could not have satisfied his curiosity, and even perhaps allayed his feelings—they were fighting to repress the uncontrolled ambition of the grand monarque. But if a man were present now at a field of slaughter, and were to inquire for what they are fighting— " Fighting!" would be the answer; "they are not fighting, they are pausing." "Why is that man expiring? Why is

that other writhing with agony? What means this implacable
fury?" The answer must be, "You are quite wrong, Sir; you
deceive yourself—they are not fighting—do not disturb them
—they are merely pausing!—this man is not expiring with
agony—that man is not dead—he is only pausing! Lord help
you, Sir! they are not angry with one another; they have now
no cause of quarrel—but their country thinks that there should
be a pause. All that you see, Sir, is nothing like fighting—
there is no harm, nor cruelty, nor bloodshed in it whatever—
it is nothing more than a *political pause!*—it is merely to try
an experiment—to see whether Buonaparte will not behave
himself better than heretofore; and in the meantime we have
agreed to a pause, in pure friendship!" And is this the way
Sir, that you are to show yourselves the advocates of order?
You take up a system calculated to uncivilize the world, to
destroy order, to trample on religion, to stifle in the heart, not
merely the generosity of noble sentiment, but the affections of
social nature; and in the prosecution of this system you spread
terror and devastation all around you.

Sir, I have done. I have told you my opinion. I think you
ought to have given a civil, clear and explicit answer to the
overture which was fairly and handsomely made you. If you
were desirous that the negotiation should have included all
your allies, as the means of bringing about a general peace, you
should have told Buonaparte so; but I believe you were afraid
of his agreeing to the proposal. You took that method before.
"Ay, but," you say, "the people were anxious for peace in
1797." I say they are friends to peace now; and I am confident that you will one day own it. Believe me, they are
friends to peace; although, by the laws which you have made
restraining the expression of the sense of the people, public
opinion cannot now be heard as loudly and unequivocally
as heretofore. But I will not go into the internal state of this
country. It is too afflicting to the heart to see the strides
which have been made, by means of, and under the miserable
pretext of this war, against liberty of every kind, both of speech
and of writing; and to observe in another kingdom the rapid
approaches to that military despotism which we affect to make
an argument against peace. I know, Sir, that public opinion,
if it could be collected, would be for peace, as much now as
in 1797, and I know that it is only by public opinion—not by
a sense of their duty—not by the inclination of their minds—
that ministers will be brought, if ever, to give us peace. I

conclude, Sir, with repeating what I said before; I ask for no gentleman's vote who would have reprobated the compliance of ministers with the proposition of the French government; I ask for no gentleman's support to-night who would have voted against ministers, if they had come down and proposed to enter into a negotiation with the French; but I have a right to ask—I know that, in honour, in consistency, in conscience, I have a right to expect the vote of every gentleman who would have voted with ministers in an address to his Majesty diametrically opposite to the motion of this night.

ON THE FALL OF NAPOLEON

GEORGE CANNING

LIVERPOOL: 10 JANUARY 1814

GENTLEMEN, as the representative of Liverpool, I am most happy in meeting my constituents again, after a year's experience of each other, and a year's separation; a year the most eventful in the annals of the world, and comprising within itself such a series of stupendous changes as might have filled the history of an age. You have been so good as to couple with my name the expression of your acknowledgments for the attention which I have paid to the interests of your town. You, gentlemen, I have no doubt, recollect the terms upon which I entered into your service; and you are aware, therefore, that I claim no particular acknowledgment at your hands for attention to the interests of Liverpool, implicated as they are with the general interests of the country. I trust, at the same time, that I have not been wanting to all or to any of you in matters of local or individual concern. But I should not do fairly by you, if I were not to take this opportunity of saying that a service (which certainly I will not pretend to describe as without some burden in itself) has been made light to me, beyond all example, by that institution which your munificence and provident care have established: I mean the office in London, through which your correspondence with your members is now carried on. I had no pretension, gentlemen, to this singular mark of your consideration; but neither will it, I hope, be thought presumptuous in me to confess, that I might not have been able to discharge the service which

I owe you, in a way which would have satisfied my own feelings as well as yours—that I might, in spite of all my endeavours, have been guilty of occasional omissions, if I had not been provided with some such medium of communication with my constituents. Of an absent and meritorious individual, it is as pleasing as it is just to speak well; and I do no more than justice to the gentleman [Mr. John Backhouse] whom you have appointed to conduct the office in question (with whom I had no previous acquaintance), in bearing public testimony to his merit, and in assuring you that it would be difficult to find any one who would surpass him in zeal, intelligence and industry.

Having despatched what it was necessary for me to say on these points, I know, gentlemen, that it is your wish, and I feel it to be my duty, that I should now proceed to communicate to you my sentiments on the state of public affairs, with the same frankness which has hitherto distinguished all our intercourse with each other. That duty is one which it does not now require any effort of courage to perform. To exhort to sacrifices, to stimulate to exertion, to shame despondency, to divert from untimely concession, is a duty of a sterner sort, which you found me not backward to discharge, at a period when, from the shortness of our acquaintance, I was uncertain whether my freedom might not offend you. My task of to-day is one at which no man can take offence. It is to mingle my congratulations with your rejoicings on the events which have passed and are passing in the world.

If, in contemplating events so widely (I had almost said so tremendously) important, it be pardonable to turn one's view for a moment to local and partial considerations, I may be permitted to observe, that, while to Great Britain, while to all Europe, while to the world and to posterity, the events which have recently taken place are matter of unbounded and universal joy, there is no collection of individuals who are better entitled than the company now assembled in this room (in great part, I presume, identically the same, and altogether representing the same interests and feelings as that of which I took leave, in this room, about fourteen months ago) to exalt in the present state of things, and to derive from it, in addition to their share of the general joy, a distinct and special satisfaction.

We cannot forget, gentlemen, the sinister omens and awful predictions under which we met and parted in October, 1812. The penalty denounced upon you for your election of me was embarrassment to the rich and famine to the poor. I was warned that, when I should return to renew my acquaintance with my constituents, I should find the grass growing in your streets. In spite of that denunciation, you did me the honour to elect me; in spite of that warning, I venture to meet you here again. It must be fairly confessed that this is not the season of the year to estimate correctly the amount of superfluous and unprofitable vegetation with which your streets may be teeming; but, without presuming to limit the power of productive nature, it is at least satisfactory to know that the fields have not been starved to clothe your quays with verdure; that it is not by economising in the scantiness of the harvest that nature has reserved her vigour for the pastures of your Exchange.

But, gentlemen, I am sure you feel, with me, that these are topics which I treat with levity only because they are not, nor were, at the time when they were seriously urged, susceptible of a serious argument; they did not furnish grounds on which any man would rest his appeal to your favour, or on which your choice of any man could be justified. If I have condescended to revert to them all, it is because I would leave none of those recollections untouched which the comparison of our last meeting with the present, I know, suggests to your minds as well as my own; and because I would, so far as in me lies, endeavour to banish from all future use, by exposing their absurdity, topics which are calculated only to mislead and to inflame. That the seasons would have run their appointed course, that the sun would have shone with as genial a warmth, and the showers would have fallen with as fertilizing a moisture, if you had not chosen me for your representative, is an admission which I make without much apprehension of the consequence. Nor do I wish you to believe that your choice of any other than me would have delayed the return of your prosperity, or prevented the revival of your commerce.

I make these admissions without fear, so far as concerns the choice between individuals. But I do not admit that it was equally indifferent upon what principles that choice should be determined. I do not admit that if the principles which it was then recommended to you to countenance had unfortunately prevailed in Parliament, and, through the authority of Parliament, had been introduced into the counsels of the country, they would not have interfered with fatal operation, not indeed to arrest the bounty of Providence, to turn back the course of the seasons, and to blast the fertility of the earth, but to stop that current of political events which, " taken at the flood," has placed England at the head of the world.

Gentlemen, if I had met you here again on this day in a state of public affairs as doubtful as that in which we took leave of each other; if confederated nations had been still arrayed against this country, and the balance of Europe still trembling in the scale, I should not have hesitated now, as I did not hesitate then, to declare my decided and unalterable opinion, that perseverance, under whatever difficulties, under whatever privations, afforded the only chance of prosperity to you, because the only chance of safety to your country, and the only chance of safety to the country, because the only chance of deliverance to Europe. Gentlemen, I should be ashamed to address you now in the tone of triumph, if I had not addressed you then in that of exhortation. I should be ashamed to appear before you shouting in the train of success, if I had not looked you in the face and encouraged you to patience under difficulties. It is because my acquaintance with you commenced in times of peril and embarrassment, and because then I neither flattered nor deceived you, that I now not only offer to you my congratulations, but put in my claim to yours, on the extinction of that peril, on the termination of that embarrassment, and on the glorious issue to which exertion and endurance have brought that great struggle in which our honour and our happiness were involved.

Gentlemen, during the course of a political life, nearly cœval with the commencement of the war, I have never given one vote, I have never uttered one sentiment, which had not for its object the consummation now happily within our reach.

I am not ashamed, and it is not unpleasing or unprofitable, to look back upon the dangers which we have passed, and to compare them with the scene which now lies before us. We behold a country inferior in population to most of her continental neighbours, but multiplying her faculties and resources by her own activity and enterprise, by the vigour of her constitution, and by the good sense of her people; we behold her, after standing up against a formidable foe throughout a contest, in the course of which every one of her allies, and at times all of them together, have fainted and failed—nay, have been driven to combine with the enemy against her—we behold her, at this moment, rallying the nations of Europe to one point, and leading them to decisive victory.

If such a picture were merely the bright vision of speculative philosophy, if it were presented to us in the page of the history of ancient times, it would stir and warm the heart.   But, gentlemen, this country is our own; and what must be the feelings which arise, on such a review, in the bosom of every son of that country? What must be the feelings of a community such as I am now addressing, which constitutes no insignificant part of the strength of the nation so described; which has suffered largely in her privations, and may hope to participate proportionably in her reward? What (I may be permitted to add) must be the feelings of one who is chosen to represent that community, and who finds himself in that honourable station at the moment of triumph only because he discountenanced despair in the moment of despondency?

From the contemplation of a spectacle so mighty and magnificent as this, I should disdain to turn aside to the controversies of party. Of principles, however, it is impossible not to say something; because our triumph would be incomplete, and its blessings might be transient, if we could be led astray by any sophistry; if we could consent, in a sort of compromise of common joy, to forget or to misstate the causes from which that triumph has sprung. All of one mind, I trust and believe we are, in exulting at the success of our country; all of one mind, I trust, we now are throughout this land, in determining to persevere if need be in strenuous exertion to prosecute, and, I hope, to perfect the great work so happily in progress. But we know that there are some of those who share most heartily in the public exaltation, who yet ascribe effects, which happily cannot be disputed, to causes which may justly be denied. No tenderness for disappointed prophecies, gentlemen, ought to induce us thus to disconnect effect and cause. It would lead to errors which might be dangerous, if unwarily adopted and generally received.

We have heard, for instance, that the war has now been successful, because the principles on which the war was undertaken have been renounced; that we are at length blessed with victory, because we have thrown away the banner under which we entered into the contest; that the contest was commenced with one set of principles, but that the issue has been happily brought about by the adoption of another. Gentlemen, I know of no such change. If we have succeeded, it has not been by the renunciation, but by the prosecution of our principles; if we have succeeded, it has not been by adopting new maxims of policy, but by upholding under all varieties of difficulty and discouragement, old, established, inviolable principles of conduct.

We are told that this war has of late become *a war of the people*, and that by the operation of that change alone the power of imperial France has been baffled and overcome. Nations, it is said, have at length made common cause with their sovereigns, in a contest which heretofore had been a contest of sovereigns only. Gentlemen, the fact of the change might be admitted, without therefore admitting the argument. It does not follow that the people were not at all times equally interested in the war (as those who think as I do have always contended that they were), because it may be and must be admitted that the people in many countries were for a time deluded. They who argue against us say that jarring interests have been reconciled. We say that gross delusions have been removed. Both admit the fact that sovereigns and their people *are* identified. But it is for them who contend that this has been effected by change of principles to specify the change. What change of principles or of government has taken place among the nations of Europe? We are the best judges of ourselves—what change has taken place *here?* Is the constitution other than it was when we were told (as we often were told in the bad times) that it was a doubt whether it were worth defending? Is the constitution other than it was when we were warned that peace on any terms must be made, as the only hope of saving it from popular indignation and popular reform?

There is yet another question to be asked. By what power, in what part of the world, has that final blow been struck which has smitten the tyrant to the ground? I suppose, by some enlightened republic; by some recently-regenerated government of pure philanthropy and uncorrupted virtue; I suppose by some nation which, in the excess of popular freedom, considers even a representative system as defective, unless each individual interferes directly in the national concerns; some nation of enlightened patriots, every man of whom is a politician in the coffee-house, as well as in the senate; I suppose it is from some such government as this that the conqueror of autocrats, the sworn destroyer of monarchical England, has met his doom. I look through the European world, gentlemen, in vain: I find there no such august community. But in another hemisphere I do find such a one, which, no doubt, must be the political David by whom the Goliath of Europe has been brought down. What is the name of that glorious republic, to which the gratitude of Europe is eternally due—which, from its innate hatred to tyranny, has so perseveringly exerted itself to liberate the world, and at last has successfully closed the contest? Alas, gentlemen, such a republic I do indeed find; and I find it enlisted, and (God be thanked!) enlisted alone, under the banner of the despot. But where was the blow struck? Where? Alas for theory! In the wilds of despotic Russia. It was followed up on the plains of Leipsic—by Russian, Prussian, and Austrian arms.

But let me not be mistaken. Do I, therefore, mean to contend—do I, therefore, give to our antagonists in the argument the advantage of ascribing to us the base tenet that an absolute monarchy is better than a free government? God forbid! What I mean is this, that, in appreciating the comparative excellence of political institutions, in estimating the force of national spirit, and the impulses of national feeling, it is idle—it is mere pedantry, to overlook the affections of nature. The order of nature could not subsist among mankind, if there were not an *instinctive* patriotism, I do not say unconnected with, but prior and paramount to, the desire of political amelioration. It may be very wrong that it should be so. I cannot help it. Our business is with fact. And surely it is not to be regretted that tyrants and conquerors should have learned, from the lessons of experience, that the first consideration suggested to the inhabitant of any country by a foreign invasion, is not whether the political constitution of the state be faultlessly perfect or not, but whether the altar at which he has worshipped—whether the home in which he has dwelt from his infancy—whether his wife and his children—whether the tombs of his forefathers—whether the place of the sovereign under whom he was born, and to whom he therefore owes (or, if it must be so stated, fancies that he therefore owes) allegiance—shall be abandoned to violence and profanation.

That, in the infancy of the French revolution, many nations in Europe were, unfortunately, led to believe and to act upon a different persuasion, is undoubtedly true; that whole countries were overrun by reforming conquerors, and flattered themselves with being proselytes till they found themselves victims. Even in this country, as I have already said, there have been times when we have been called upon to consider whether there was not something at home which must be mended before we could hope to repel a foreign invader with success.

It is fortunate for the world that this question should have been tried, if I may so say, to a disadvantage; that it should have been tried in countries where no man in his senses will say that the frame of political society is such as, according to the most moderate principles of regulated freedom, it ought to be; where, I will venture to say, without hazarding the imputation of being myself a visionary reformer, political society is not such as, after the successes of this war, and from the happy contagion of the example of Great Britain, it is sure gradually to become. It is fortunate for the world that this question should have been tried on its own merits; that, after twenty years of controversy, we should be authorized, by undoubted results, to revert to nature and to truth, and to disentangle the genuine feelings of the heart from the obstructions which a cold, presumptuous, generalizing philosophy had wound around them.

One of the most delightful poets of this country, in describing the various proportions of natural blessings and advantages dispensed by Providence to the various nations of Europe, turns from the luxuriant plains and cloudless skies of Italy to the rugged mountains of Switzerland, and inquires whether there also, in those barren and stormy regions, the " patriot passion " is found equally imprinted on the heart? He decides the question truly in the affirmative; and he says of the inhabitant of those bleak wilds:

> "Dear is that shed to which his soul conforms,
> And dear that hill which lifts him to the storms;
> And, as a child, when scaring sounds molest,
> Clings close and closer to the mother's breast,
> So the loud torrent and the whirlwind's roar,
> But bind him to his native mountains more."[1]

What Goldsmith thus beautifully applied to the physical varieties of soil and climate has been found no less true with respect to political institutions. A sober desire of improvement, a rational endeavour to redress error, and to correct imperfection in the political frame of human society, are not only natural, but laudable in man. But it is well that it should have been shown, by irrefragable proof, that these sentiments, even where most strongly and most justly felt, supersede not that devotion to native soil which is the foundation of national independence. And it is right that it should be understood and remembered, that the spirit of national independence alone, aroused where it had slumbered, enlightened where it had been deluded, and kindled into enthusiasm by the insults and outrages of an all-grasping invader, has been found sufficient, without internal changes and compromises of sovereigns or governments with their people— without relaxation of allegiance and abjurations of authority, to animate, as with one pervading soul, the different nations of the

Continent; to combine, as into one congenial mass, their various feelings, passions, prejudices; to direct these concentrated energies with one impulse against the common tyrant; and to shake (and, may we not hope? to overthrow) the *Babel* of his iniquitous power.

Gentlemen, there is another argument, more peculiarly relating to our own country, which has at times been interposed to discourage the prosecution of the war. That this country is sufficient to its own defence, sufficient to its own happiness, sufficient to its own independence; and that the complicated combinations of continental policy are always hazardous to our interests, as well as burdensome to our means, has been, at several periods of the war, a favourite doctrine, not only with those who, for other reasons, wished to embarrass the measures of the Government, but with men of the most enlightened minds, of the most benevolent views, and the most ardent zeal for the interests as well as the honour of their country. May we not flatter ourselves upon this point, also, experience has decided in favour of the course of policy which has been actually pursued.

Can any man now look back upon the trial which we have gone through, and maintain that, at any period during the last twenty years, the plan of insulated policy could have been adopted, without having in the event, at this day, prostrated England at the foot of a conqueror? Great, indeed, has been the call upon our exertions; great, indeed, has been the drain upon our resources; long and wearisome has the struggle been; and late is the moment at which peace is brought within our reach. But even though the difficulties of the contest may have been enhanced, and its duration protracted by it, yet is there any man who seriously doubts whether the having associated our destinies with the destinies of other nations be or be not that which, under the blessing of Providence, has eventually secured the safety of all?

It is at the moment when such a trial has come to its issue, that it is fair to ask of those who have suffered under the pressure of protracted exertion (and of whom rather than of those who are assembled around me—for by whom have such privations been felt more sensibly?)—it is now, I say, the time to ask whether, at any former period of the contest, such a peace could have been made as would at once have guarded the national interests and corresponded with the national character? I address myself now to such persons only as think the character of a nation an essential part of its strength, and consequently of its safety. But if, among persons of that description, there be one who, with all his zeal for the glory of his country, has yet at times been willing to abandon the contest in mere weariness and despair, of such a man I would ask, whether he can indicate the period at which he now wishes that such an abandonment had been consented to by the Government and the Parliament of Great Britain?

Is it when the Continent was at peace—when, looking upon the map of Europe, you saw one mighty and connected system, one great luminary, with his attendant satellites circulating around him; at that period could this country have made peace, and have remained at peace for a twelvemonth? What is the answer? Why, that the experiment was tried. The result was the renewal of the war.

Was it at a later period, when the Continental system had been established? When two-thirds of the ports of Europe were shut against you? When but a single link was wanting to bind the Continent in a circling chain of iron, which should exclude you from intercourse with other nations? At that moment peace was most earnestly recommended to you. At that moment, gentlemen, I first came among you. At that moment I ventured to recommend to you perseverance, patient perseverance; and to express a hope that, by the mere strain of an unnatural effort, the massive bonds imposed upon the nations of the Continent might, at no distant period, burst asunder. I was heard by you with indulgence—I know not whether with conviction. But is it now to be regretted that we did not at that moment yield to the pressure of our wants or of our fears? What has been the issue? The Continental system was completed, with the sole exception of Russia, in the year 1812. In that year the pressure upon this country was undoubtedly painful. Had we yielded, the system would have been immortal. We persevered, and, before the conclusion of another year, the system was at an end: at an end, as all schemes of violence naturally terminate, not by a mild and gradual decay, such as waits upon a regular and well-spent life, but by sudden dissolution; at an end, like the breaking up of a winter's frost. But yesterday the whole Continent, like a mighty plain covered with one mass of ice, presented to the view a drear expanse of barren uniformity; to-day, the breath of heaven unbinds the earth, the streams begin to flow again, and the intercourse of human kind revives.

Can we regret that we did not, like the fainting traveller, lie down to rest—but, indeed, to perish—under the severity of that inclement season? Did we not more wisely to bear up, and to wait the change?

Gentlemen, I have said that I should be ashamed, and in truth I should be so, to address you in the language of exultation, if it were merely for the indulgence, however legitimate, of an exuberant and ungovernable joy. But they who have suffered great privations have a claim not merely to consolation, but to something more. They are justly to be compensated for what they have undergone, or lost, or hazarded, by the contemplation of what they have gained.

We have gained, then, a rank and authority in Europe, such as, for the life of the longest liver of those who now hear me, must place this country upon an eminence which no probable reverses can shake. We have gained, or rather we have recovered, a splendour of military glory, which places us by the side of the greatest military nations in the world. At the beginning of this war, while there was not a British bosom that did not beat with rapture at the exploits of our navy, there were few who would not have been contented to compromise for that reputation alone; to claim the sea as exclusively our province, and to leave to France and the other Continental powers the struggle for superiority by land. That fabled deity, whom I see portrayed upon the wall, was considered as the exclusive patron of British prowess in battle; but in seeming accordance with the beautiful fiction of ancient mythology, our Neptune, in the heat of contest, smote the earth with his trident, and up sprang the fiery war-horse, the emblem of military power.

Let Portugal, now led to the pursuit of her flying conquerors—let liberated Spain—let France, invaded in her turn by those whom she had overrun or menaced with invasion, attest the triumphs of the army of Great Britain, and the equality of her military with her naval fame. And let those who, even after the triumphs of the Peninsula had begun, while they admitted that we had, indeed, wounded the giant in the heel, still deemed the rest of his huge frame invulnerable—let them now behold him reeling under the blows of united nations, and acknowledge at once the might of British arms and the force of British example.

I do not say that these are considerations with a view to which the war, if otherwise terminable, ought to have been purposely protracted; but I say that, upon the retrospect, we have good reason to rejoice that the war was not closed ingloriously and insecurely, when the latter events of it have been such as have established our security by our glory.

I say we have reason to rejoice, that, during the period when the Continent was prostrate before France—that, especially during the period when the Continental system was in force, we did not shrink from the struggle; that we did not make peace for present and momentary ease, unmindful of the permanent safety and greatness of this country; that we did not leave unsolved the momentous questions, whether this country could maintain itself against France, unaided and alone; or with the Continent divided; or with the Continent combined against it; whether, when the wrath of the tyrant of the European world was kindled against us with sevenfold fury, we could or could not walk unharmed and unfettered through the flames?

I say we have reason to rejoice that, throughout this more than *Punic* war, in which it has so often been the pride of our enemy to represent herself as the Rome, and England as the Carthage, of modern times (with at least this colour for the comparison, that the utter destruction of the modern Carthage has uniformly been proclaimed to be indispensable to the greatness of her rival), we have, I say, reason to rejoice that, unlike our assigned prototype, we have not been diverted by internal dissensions from the vigorous support of a vital struggle; that we have not suffered distress nor clamour to distract our counsels, or to check the exertions of our arms.

Gentlemen, for twenty years that I have sat in Parliament, I have been an advocate of the war. You knew this when you did me the honour to choose me as your representative. I then told you that I was the advocate of the war, because I was a lover of peace; but of a peace that should be the fruit of honourable exertion—a peace that should have a character of dignity—a peace that should be worth preserving, and should be likely to endure. I confess I was not sanguine enough, at that time, to hope that I should so soon have an opportunity of justifying my professions. But I know not why six weeks hence, such a peace should not be made as England may not only be glad, but proud to ratify. Not such a peace, gentlemen, as that of Amiens—a short and feverish interval of unrefreshing repose. During that peace, which of you went or sent a son to Paris, who did not feel or learn that an Englishman appeared in France shorn of the dignity of his country; with the mien of a suppliant, and the conscious prostration of a man who had consented to purchase his gain or his ease by submission? But let a peace be made to-morrow, such as the allies have now the power to dictate, and the meanest of the subjects of this kingdom shall walk the streets of Paris without being pointed out as the compatriot of Wellington; as one of that nation whose firmness and perseverance have humbled France and rescued Europe.

Is there any man that has a heart in his bosom who does not find, in the contemplation of this contrast alone, a recompense for the struggles and the sufferings of years?

But, gentlemen, the doing right is not only the most honourable course of action—it is also the most profitable in its results. At any former period of the war, the independence of almost all the other countries, our allies, would have been to be purchased with sacrifices profusely poured out from the lap of British victory. Not a throne to be re-established, not a province to be evacuated, not a garrison to be withdrawn, but this country would have had to make compensation out of her conquests for the concessions obtained from the enemy. Now, happily, this work is already done, either by our efforts or to our hands. The Peninsula free—the lawful commonwealth of European states already, in a great measure, restored, Great Britain may now appear in the congress of the world, rich in conquests, nobly and rightfully won, with little claim upon her faith or her justice, whatever may be the spontaneous impulse of her generosity or her moderation.

Such, gentlemen, is the situation and prospect of affairs at the moment at which I have the honour to address you. That you, gentlemen, may have your full share in the prosperity of your country, is my sincere and earnest wish. The courage with which you bore up in adverse circumstances eminently entitles you to this reward.

For myself, gentlemen, while I rejoice in your returning prosperity, I rejoice also that our connection began under auspices so much less favourable; that we had an opportunity of knowing each other's minds in times when the minds of men are brought to the proof—times of trial and difficulty. I had the satisfaction of avowing to you, and you the candour and magnanimity to approve, the principles and opinions by which my public conduct has uniformly been guided, at a period when the soundness of those opinions and the application of those principles was matter of doubt and controversy. I thought, and I said, at the time of our first meeting, that the cause of England and of civilized Europe must be ultimately triumphant, if we but preserved our spirit untainted and our constancy unshaken.   Such an assertion was, at that time, the object of ridicule with many persons: a single year has elapsed, and it is now the voice of the whole world.

Gentlemen, we may, therefore, confidently indulge the hope that our opinions will continue in unison; that our concurrence will be as cordial as it has hitherto been, if unhappily any new occasion of difficulty or embarrassment should hereafter arise.

At the present moment, I am sure, we are equally desirous to bury the recollection of all our differences with others in that general feeling of exultation in which all opinions happily combine.

CATHOLIC RIGHTS IN IRELAND

DANIEL O'CONNELL

DUBLIN : 23 FEBRUARY 1814

I WISH to submit to this meeting a resolution, calling on the different counties and cities in Ireland to petition for unqualified emancipation.   It is a resolution which has been already and frequently adopted; and when we persevered in our petitions, even at periods when we despaired of success; it becomes our pleasing duty to present them now that the symptoms of the times seemed so powerfully to promise an approaching relief.

Indeed, as long as truth or justice can be supposed to influence man; as long as man is admitted to be under the control of reason; so long must it be prudent and wise to procure discussions on the sufferings and the rights of the people of Ireland.   Truth has proclaimed the treacherous iniquity which deprived us of our chartered liberty; truth destroys the flimsy pretext under which this iniquity is continued; truth exposes our merits and our sufferings; whilst reason and justice combine to demonstrate our right—the right of every human being to freedom of conscience—a right without which every honest man must feel that to him, individually, the protection of government is a mockery, and the restriction of penal law a sacrilege.

Truth, reason and justice are our advocates; and even in England let me tell you that those powerful advocates have some authority.   They are, it is true, more frequently resisted there than in most other countries; but yet they have some sway among the English at all times. Passion may confound and prejudice darken the English understanding; and interested passion and hired prejudice have been successfully employed against us at former periods; but the present season appears singularly well calculated to aid the progress of our cause, and to advance the attainment of our important objects.

I do not make the assertion lightly. I speak after deliberate investigation, and from solemn conviction, my clear opinion that we shall, during the present session of Parliament, obtain a portion at least, if not the entire, of our emancipation. We cannot fail, unless we are disturbed in our course by those who graciously style themselves our friends, or are betrayed by the treacherous machinations of part of our own body.

Yes, everything, except false friendship and domestic treachery, forebodes success. The cause of man is in its great advance. Humanity has been rescued from much of its thraldom. In the states of Europe, where the iron despotism of the feudal system so long classed men into two species— the hereditary masters and the perpetual slaves; when rank supplied the place of merit, and to be humbly born operated as a perpetual exclusion:—in many parts of Europe man is reassuming his natural station, and artificial distinctions have vanished before the force of truth and the necessities of governors.

France has a representative government; and as the unjust privileges of the clergy and nobility are abolished; as she is blessed with a most wise, clear, and simple code of laws; as she is almost free from debt, and emancipated from odious prejudices, she is likely to prove an example and a light to the world.

In Germany the sovereigns who formerly ruled at their freewill and caprice are actually bribing the people to the support of their thrones, by giving them the blessings of liberty. It is a wise and a glorious policy. The Prince Regent has emancipated his Catholic subjects of Hanover, and traced for them the grand outlines of a free constitution. The other states of Germany are rapidly following the example. The people, no longer destined to bear the burdens only of society, are called up to take their share in the management of their own concerns, and in the sustentation of the public dignity and happiness. In short, representative government, the only rational or just government, is proclaimed by princes as a boon to their people, and Germany is about to afford many an example of the advantages of rational liberty. Anxious as some kings appear to be in the great work of plunder and robbery, others of them are now the first heralds of freedom.

It is a moment of glorious triumph to humanity; and even one instance of liberty, freely conceded, makes compensation for a thousand repetitions of the ordinary crimes of military monarchs. The crime is followed by its own punishment; but the great principle of the rights of man establishes itself now on the broadest basis, and France and Germany now set forth an example for England to imitate.

Italy, too, is in the paroxysms of the fever of independence. Oh, may she have strength to go through the disease, and may she rise like a giant refreshed with wine! One thing is certain, that the human mind is set afloat in Italy. The flame of freedom burns; it may be smothered for a season; but all the whiskered Croats and the fierce Pandours of Austria will not be able to extinguish the sacred fire. Spain, to be sure, chills the heart and disgusts the understanding. The combined Inquisition and the court—press upon the mind, whilst they bind the bodies in fetters of adamant. But this despotism is, thank God, as unrelentingly absurd as it is cruel, and there arises a darling hope of the very excess of the evil. The Spaniards must be walking corpses—they must be living ghosts, and not human beings, unless a sublime reaction be in rapid preparation. But let us turn to our own prospects.

The cause of liberty has made, and is making, great progress in states heretofore despotic. In all the countries in Europe, in which any portion of freedom prevails, the liberty of conscience is complete. England alone, of all the states pretending to be free, leaves shackles upon the human mind; England alone, amongst free states, exhibits the absurd claim of regulating belief by law, and forcing opinion by statute. Is it possible to conceive that this gross, this glaring, this iniquitous absurdity can continue? Is it possible, too, to conceive that it can continue to operate, not against a small and powerless sect, but against the millions, comprising the best strength, the most affluent energy of the empire?—a strength and an energy daily increasing, and hourly appreciating their own importance. The present system, disavowed by liberalized Europe, disclaimed by sound reason, abhorred by genuine religion, must soon and for ever be abolished.

Let it not be said that the princes of the Continent were

forced by necessity to give privileges to their subjects, and that England has escaped from a similar fate. I admit that the necessity of procuring the support of the people was the main-spring of royal patriotism on the Continent; but I totally deny that the ministers of England can dispense with a similar support. The burdens of the war are permanent; the dis-tresses occasioned by the peace are pressing; the financial system tottering, and to be supported in profound peace only by a war taxation. In the meantime, the resources of corruption are mightily diminished. Ministerial influence is necessarily diminished by one-half of the effective force of indirect bribery; full two-thirds must be disbanded. Peculation and corruption must be put upon half pay, and no allowances. The ministry lose not only all those active partisans; those outrageous loyalists, who fattened on the public plunder during the seasons of immense expenditure; but those very men will themselves swell the ranks of the malcontents, and probably be the most violent in their opposition. They have no sweet consciousness to reward them in their present privations; and therefore they are likely to exhaust the bitterness of their souls on their late employers. Every cause conspires to render this the period in which the ministry should have least inclination, least interest, least power, to oppose the restoration of our rights and liberties.

I speak not from mere theory. There exist at this moment practical illustrations of the truth of my assertions. Instances have occurred which demonstrate, as well the inability of the ministry to resist the popular voice, as the utility of re-echoing that voice, until it is heard and understood in all its strength and force. The ministers had determined to continue the property tax; they announced their determination to their partisans at Liverpool and in Bristol. Well, the people of England met; they petitioned; they repeated—they reiterated their petitions, until the ministry felt they could no longer resist; and they ungraciously, but totally, abandoned their determination; and the property tax now expires.

Another instance is also now before us. It relates to the Corn Laws. The success of the repetition of petitions in that instance is the more remarkable, because such success has been obtained in defiance of the first principles of political economy, and in violation of the plainest rules of political justice.

This is not the place to discuss *the merits of the Corn Laws;*

but I cannot avoid, as the subject lies in my way, to put upon public record my conviction of the INUTILITY AS WELL AS THE IMPROPRIETY OF THE PROPOSED MEASURE RESPECTING THOSE LAWS. *I expect that it will be believed in Ireland that I would not volunteer thus an opposition of sentiment to any measure, if I was not most disinterestedly, and in my conscience, convinced that* SUCH MEASURE WOULD NOT BE OF ANY SUBSTANTIAL OR PERMANENT UTILITY TO IRELAND.

As far as I am personally concerned, my interest plainly is to keep up the price of lands; but I am quite convinced that the measure in question will have an effect PERMANENTLY AND FATALLY INJURIOUS TO IRELAND. *The clamour respecting the Corn Laws has been fomented by parsons who were afraid that they would not get enough money for their tithes, and absentee landlords, who apprehended a diminution of their rack rents;* and if you observed the names of those who have taken an active part in favour of the measure, you will find amongst them many, if not all, the persons who have most distinguished themselves against the liberty and religion of the people. There have been, I know, many good men misled, and many clever men deceived, on this subject; but the great majority are of the class of oppressors.

There was formed, some time ago, an association of a singular nature in Dublin and the adjacent counties. Mr. Luke White was, as I remember, at the head of it. It contained some of our stoutest and most stubborn seceders; it published the causes of its institution; it recited that, whereas butcher's meat was dearer in Cork, and in Limerick, and in Belfast than in Dublin, it was therefore expedient to associate, in order that the people of Dublin should not eat meat too cheap. Large sums were subscribed to carry the patriotic design into effect, but public indignation broke up the ostensible confederacy; it was too plain and too glaring to bear public inspection. The indignant sense of the people of Dublin forced them to dissolve their open association; and if the present enormous increase of the price of meat in Dublin beyond the rest of Ireland be the result of secret combination of any individuals, there is at least this comfort, that they do not presume to beard the public with the open avowal of their design to increase the difficulties of the poor in procuring food.

Such a scheme as that, with respect to meat in Dublin—such a scheme, precisely, is the sought-for corn law. The only difference consists in the extent of the operation of both plans.

The *corn plan* is only more extensive, not more unjust in principle, but it is more *unreasonable in its operation*, because its *necessary tendency must be to destroy that very market of which it seeks the exclusive possession.* The *corn law men want, they say, to have the exclusive feeding of the manufacturers; but at present our manufacturers, loaded as they are with taxation, are scarcely able to meet the goods of foreigners* in the markets of the world. The English are already undersold in foreign markets; but *if to this dearness produced by taxation there shall be added the dearness produced by dear food,* is it not plain that it will be impossible to enter into a competition with foreign manufacturers, who have no taxes and cheap bread? Thus the corn laws will destroy our manufactures, and compel our manufacturers to emigrate in spite of penalties; and the corn law supporters will have injured themselves and destroyed others.

I beg pardon for dwelling on this subject. If I were at liberty to pursue it here, I would not leave it until I had satisfied every dispassionate man that the *proposed measure* is both USELESS AN DUNJUST; but this is not the place for doing so, and I only beg to record at least the honest dictates of my judgment on this interesting topic. My argument, of the efficacy of petitioning, is strengthened by the impolicy of the measure in question; because, if petitions, by their number and perseverance, succeed in establishing a proposition impolitic in principle, and oppressive to thousands in operation, what encouragement does it not afford to us to repeat our petitions for that which has justice for its basis, and policy as its support!

The great advantages of discussion being thus apparent, the efficacy of repeating, and repeating, and repeating again our petitions being thus demonstrated by notorious facts, the Catholics of Ireland must be sunk in criminal apathy if they neglect the use of an instrument so efficacious for their emancipation.

There is further encouragement at this particular crisis. Dissension has ceased in the Catholic body. Those who paralysed our efforts, and gave our conduct the appearance and reality of weakness, and wavering, and inconsistency, have all retired. Those who were ready to place the entire of the Catholic feelings and dignity, and some of the Catholic religion too, under the feet of every man who pleased to call himself our friend, and to prove himself our friend, by praising on every occasion, and upon no occasion, the oppressors of the Catholics, and by abusing the Catholics themselves; the men who would link the Catholic cause to this patron and to that, and sacrifice it at one time to the minister, and at another to the opposition, and make it this day the tool of one party, and the next the instrument of another party; the men, in fine, who hoped to traffic upon our country and our religion—who would buy honours, and titles, and places, and pensions, at the price of the purity, and dignity, and safety of the Catholic Church in Ireland; all those men have, thank God, quitted us, I hope for ever. They have returned into silence and secession, or have frankly or covertly gone over to our enemies. I regret deeply and bitterly that they have carried with them some few who, like my Lord Fingal, entertain no other motives than those of purity and integrity, and who, like that noble lord, are merely mistaken.

But I rejoice at this separation—I rejoice that they have left the single-hearted, and the disinterested, and the indefatigable, and the independent, and the numerous, and the sincere Catholics to work out their emancipation unclogged, unshackled, and undismayed. They have bestowed on us another bounty also —they have proclaimed the causes of their secession—they have placed out of doubt the cause of the diversions. It is not intemperance, for that we abandoned; it is not the introduction of extraneous topics, for those we disclaimed; it is simply and purely, veto or no veto—restriction or no restriction—no other words; it is religion and principle that have divided us; thanks, many thanks to the tardy and remote candour of the seceders, that has at length written in large letters *the cause of their secession—it is the Catholic Church of Ireland—it is whether that Church shall continue independent of a Protestant ministry or not. We are for its independence*—the seceders are for its dependence.

Whatever shall be the fate of our emancipation question, thank God we are divided for ever from those who would wish that our Church should crouch to the partisans of the Orange system. Thank God, secession has displayed its cloven foot, and avowed itself to be synonymous with vetoism.

Those are our present prospects of success. First, man is elevated from slavery almost everywhere, and human nature has become more dignified, and, I may say, more valuable. Secondly, England wants our cordial support, and knows that she has only to secede to us justice in order to obtain our affectionate assistance. Thirdly, this is the season of successful petition, and the very fashion of the times entitles our petition to succeed. Fourthly, the Catholic cause is disencumbered of hollow friends and interested speculators. Add to all these the native and inherent strength of the principle of religious freedom and the inert and accumulating weight of our wealth, our religion, and our numbers, and where is the sluggard that shall dare to doubt our approaching success?

Besides, even our enemies must concede to us that we act from principle, and from principle only. We prove our sincerity when we refuse to make our emancipation a subject of traffic and barter, and ask for relief only upon those grounds which, if once established, would give to every other sect the right to the same political immunity. All we ask is "a clear stage and no favour." We think the Catholic religion the most rationally consistent with the divine scheme of Christianity, and, therefore, all we ask is that everybody should be left to his unbiassed reason and judgment. If Protestants are equally sincere, why do they call the law, and the bribe, and the place, and the pension, in support of their doctrines? Why do they fortify themselves behind pains, and penalties, and exclusions, and forfeitures? Ought not our opponents to feel that they degrade the sanctity of their religion when they call in the profane aid of temporal rewards and punishments, and that they proclaim the superiority of our creed when they thus admit themselves unable to contend against it upon terms of equality, and by the weapons of reason and argument, and persevere in refusing us all we ask—" a clear stage and no favour."

Yes, Mr. Chairman, our enemies, in words and by actions, admit and proclaim our superiority. It remains to our friends alone, and to that misguided and ill-advised portion of the Catholics who have shrunk into secession — it remains for those friends and seceders alone to undervalue our exertions, and underrate our conscientious opinions.

Great and good God, in what a cruel situation are the Catholics of Ireland placed! If they have the manliness to talk of their oppressors as the paltry bigots deserve—if they have the honesty to express, even in measured language, a small portion of the sentiments of abhorrence which peculating bigotry ought naturally to inspire—if they condemn the principle which established the Inquisition in Spain and Orange lodges in Ireland, they are assailed by the combined clamour of those parliamentary friends and title-seeking, place-hunting seceders. The war-whoop of "*intemperance*" is sounded, and a persecution is instituted by our advocates and our seceders — against the Catholic who dares to be honest and fearless, and independent!

But I tell you what they easily forgive—nay, what our friends, sweet souls, would vindicate to-morrow in parliament, if the subject arose there. Here it is—here is the *Dublin Journal* of the 21st of February, printed just two days ago. In the administration of Lord Whitworth, and the secretary-ship of Mr. Peel, there is a government newspaper—a paper supported solely by the money of the people; for its circulation is little, and its private advertisements less. Here is a paper continued in existence like a wounded reptile—only whilst in the rays of the sun, by the heat and warmth communicated to it by the Irish administration. Let me read two passages for you. The first calls " *Popery the deadly enemy of pure religion and rational liberty.*" Such is the *temperate* description the writer gives of the Catholic faith. With respect to the purity of religion I shall not quarrel with him. I only differ with him in point of taste; but I should be glad to know what this creature calls rational liberty. I suppose such as existed at Lacedæmon—the dominion of Spartans over Helots —the despotism of masters over slaves, that is his rational liberty. We will readily pass so much by. But attend to this:—

" I will," says this moderate and temperate gentleman, " *lay before the reader such specimens of the* POPISH SUPERSTITION *as will convince him that the treasonable combinations cemented by oaths, and the* NOCTURNAL ROBBERY AND ASSASSINATION *which have prevailed for many years past in Ireland, and still exist in many parts of it, are produced as a necessary consequence by its intolerant and sanguinary principles.*"

Let our seceders—let our gentle friends who are shocked at our intemperance, and are alive to the mild and concili-ating virtues of Mr. Peel—read this passage, sanctioned I may almost say, certainly countenanced by those who do the work of governing Ireland. Would to God we had but one genuine, unsophisticated friend, one real advocate in the House of Commons! How such a man would pour down indignation on the clerks of the Castle, who pay for this base and vile defamation of our religion—of the religion of nine-tenths of the population of Ireland!

But perhaps I accuse falsely; perhaps the administration of Ireland are guiltless of patronizing these calumnies. Look at the paper and determine; it contains nearly five columns

of advertisements—only one from a private person—and even
that is a notice of an anti-Popery pamphlet, by a Mr. Cousins,
a Curate of the Established Church. Dean Swift has somewhere observed that the poorest of all the possible rats was
a curate—(*much laughing*); and if this rat be so, if he have
as usual a large family, a great appetite, and little to eat, I
sincerely hope that he may get what he wants—a fat living.
Indeed, for the sake of consistency, and to keep up the succession of bad pamphlets, he ought to get a living.

Well, what think you are the rest of the advertisements?
First, there are three from the worthy Commissioners of Wide
Streets; one dated 6th August 1813, announcing that they
would, the ensuing Wednesday, receive certain proposals.
Secondly, the Barony of Middlethird is proclaimed, as of the
6th of September last, for fear the inhabitants of that Barony
should not as yet know they were proclaimed. Thirdly, the
proclamation against the Catholic Board, dated only the 3rd
day of June last, is printed lest any person should forget
the history of last year. Fourthly, there is proclamation
stating that gunpowder was not to be carried *coastwise* for
six months, and this is dated the 5th of October last. But
why should I detain you with the details of State proclamations, printed for no other purpose than as an excuse for
putting so much of the public money into the pocket of a
calumniator of the Catholics. The abstract of the rest is
that there is one other proclamation, stating that Liverpool
is a port fit for importation from the East Indies; another
forbidding British subjects from serving in the American
forces during the present, that is, the past war; and another
stating that although we had made peace with France, we
are still at war with America, and that, therefore, no marine
is to desert; and to finish the climax, there is a column
and a half of extracts from several statutes; all this printed
at the expense of Government—that is, at the expense of the
people.

Look now at the species of services for which so enormous
a sum of our money is thus wantonly lavished! It consists
simply of calumnies against the Catholic religion—calumnies so
virulously atrocious as, in despite of the intention of the authors,
to render themselves ridiculous. This hireling accuses our
religion of being an enemy to liberty, of being an encourager
of treason, of instigating to robbery, and producing a system
of assassination. Here are libels for which no prosecution is

instituted. Here are libels which are considered worthy of encouragement, and which are rewarded by the Irish treasury. And is it for this—is it to supply this waste, this abuse of public money—is it to pay for those false and foul calumnies, that we are, in a season of universal peace, to be borne down with a war taxation? Are we to have two or three additional millions of taxes imposed upon us in peace, in order that this intestine war of atrocious calumny may be carried on against the religion of the people of Ireland with all the vigour of full pay and great plunder? Let us, agitators, be now taunted by jobbers in Parliament with our violence, our intemperance. Why, if we were not rendered patient by the aid of a dignified contempt, is there not matter enough to disgust and to irritate almost beyond endurance?

Thus are we treated by our friends, and our enemies, and our seceders; the first abandon, the second oppress, the third betray us, and they all join in calumniating us; in the last they are all combined. See how naturally they associate;—this libeller in the *Dublin Journal*, who calls the Catholic religion a system of assassination, actually praises in the same paper some individual Catholics; he praises, by name, Quarantotti, and my Lord Fingal (*much laughing*), and the respectable party (those are his words) who join with that noble lord.

Of Lord Fingal I shall always speak with respect, because I entertain the opinion that his motives are pure and honourable; but can anything else, or at least ought anything, place his secession in so strong a point of view to the noble lord himself as to find that he and his party are praised by the very man who, in the next breath, treats his religion as a system of assassination? Let that party have all the enjoyment which such praises can confer; but if a spark of love for their religion or their country remains with them, let them recollect that they could have earned those praises only by having, in the opinion of this writer, betrayed the one and degraded the other.

This writer, too, attempts to traduce Lord Donoughmore. He attacks his lordship in bad English, and worse Latin, for having, as he says, cried *peccavi* to Popish thraldom. But the ignorant trader in virulence knew not how to spell that single Latin word, because they do not teach Latin at the charter schools.

I close with conjuring the Catholics to persevere in their present course.

Let us never tolerate the slightest inroad on the discipline of our ancient, our holy Church. Let us never consent that she should be made the hireling of the ministry. *Our forefathers would have died, nay, they perished in hopeless slavery rather than consent to such degradation.*

Let us rest upon the barrier where they expired, *or go back into slavery rather than forward into irreligion and disgrace!* Let *us* also advocate our cause on the two great principles— first, that of an eternal separation in spirituals between our Church and the State; secondly, that of *the eternal right to freedom of conscience*—a right which, I repeat it with pride and pleasure, would exterminate the Inquisition in Spain and bury in oblivion the bloody orange flag of dissension in Ireland!

"THE IMMORTAL STATESMAN"

BROUGHAM v. PITT

LORD BROUGHAM

Election Speech at Liverpool: 8 Oct. 1812

Gentlemen,—I feel it necessary after the fatigues of this long and anxious day, to entreat, as I did on a former occasion, that you would have the goodness to favour me with as silent a hearing as possible, that I may not by over-exertion in my present exhausted state, destroy that voice which I hope I may preserve to raise in your defence once more hereafter.

Gentlemen, I told you last night when we were near the head of the poll, that I, for one at least, would never lose heart in the conflict, or lower my courage in fighting your battles, or despair of the good cause although we should be fifty, a hundred, or even two hundred behind our enemies. It has happened this day, that we have fallen short of them, not quite by two hundred, but we have lost one hundred and seventy votes: I tell you this with the deepest concern, with feelings of pain and sorrow which I dare not trust myself in attempting to express. But I tell it you without any sensation approaching to despondency. This is the only feeling which I have not now present in my breast. I am overcome with your unutterable affection towards me and my cause. I feel a wonder mingled with gratitude, which no language can even attempt to describe, at your faithful, unwearied, untameable exertions in behalf of our common object. I am penetrated with an anxiety for its success, if possible more lively than any of yourselves can know who are my followers in this mighty struggle—an anxiety cruelly increased by that which as yet you are ignorant of, though you are this night to hear it. To my distinguished friends who surround me, and connect me more closely with you, I am thankful beyond all expression. I am lost in admiration of the honest and courageous men amongst you who have resisted all threats as well as all bribes, and persevered in giving me their free unbought voices. For those unhappy persons who have been scared by imminent fear on their own and their children's behalf from obeying the impulse of their conscience, I feel nothing of resentment—nothing but pity and compassion. Of those who have thus opposed us, I think as charitably as a man can think in such circumstances. For this great town, (if it is indeed to be defeated in the contest, which I will not venture to suppose) for the country at large whose cause we are upholding—whose fight we are fighting — for the whole manufacturing and trading interests—for all who love peace—all who have no profit in war —I feel moved by the deepest alarm lest our grand attempt may not prosper. All these feelings are in my heart at this moment —they are various—they are conflicting—they are painful— they are burthensome—but they are not overwhelming! and amongst them all, and I have swept round the whole range of which the human mind is susceptible—there is not one that bears the slightest resemblance to despair. I trust myself once more into your faithful hands—I fling myself again on you for protection—I call aloud to you to bear your own cause in your hearts—I implore of you to come forth in your own defence— for the sake of this vast town and its people—for the salvation of the middle and lower orders—for the whole industrious part of the whole country—I entreat you by your love of peace—by your hatred of oppression—by your weariness of burthensome and useless taxation—by yet another appeal to which those must lend an ear who have been deaf to all the rest—I ask it for your families—for your infants—if you would avoid such a winter of horrors as the last! It is coming fast upon us—already it is near at hand—yet a few short weeks and we may be in the midst of those unspeakable miseries, the recollection of which now rend your very souls. If there is one freeman amongst this immense multitude who has not tendered his voice,—and if he can be deaf to this appeal,—if he can suffer the threats of our antagonists to frighten him away from the recollections of the last dismal winter,—that man will not vote for me. But if I have the happiness of addressing one honest man amongst you, who has a care left for his wife and children, or for other endearing ties of domestic tenderness, (and which of us is altogether without them?) that man will lay his hand on his heart when I now bid him do so, —and with those little threats of present spite ringing in his ear, he will rather consult his fears of greater evil by listening to the dictates of his heart, when he casts a look towards the dreadful season through which he lately passed—and will come bravely forward to place those men in Parliament whose whole efforts have been directed towards the restoration of peace, and the revival of trade.

Do not, gentlemen, listen to those who tell you the cause of freedom is desperate;—they are the enemies of that cause and of you,—but listen to me,—for you know me,—and I am one who has never yet deceived you,—I say, then, that *it will be* desperate if you make no exertions to retrieve it. I tell you that your languor alone can betray it,—that it can only be made desperate through your despair. I am not a man to be cast down by temporary reverses, let them come upon me as thick, and as swift, and as sudden as they may. I am not he who is daunted by majorities in the outset of a struggle for worthy objects,— else I should not now stand here before you to boast of triumphs won in your cause. If your champions had yielded to the force of numbers,—of gold—of power—if defeat could have dismayed them—then would the African Slave Trade never have been abolished—then would the cause of Reform, which now bids fair to prevail over its enemies, have been long ago sunk amidst the desertions of its friends,—then would those prospects of peace have been utterly benighted, which I still devoutly cherish, and which even now brighten in our eyes,—then would the Orders in Council which I overthrew by your support, have remained a disgrace to the British name, and an eternal obstacle to our best interests. I no more despond now than I have done in the course of those sacred and glorious contentions,—but it is for you to say whether to-morrow shall not make it my duty to despair. To-morrow is your last day,—your last efforts must then be made;—if you put forth your strength the day is your own—if you desert me, it is lost. To win it I shall be the first to lead you on, and the last to forsake you.

Gentlemen, when I told you a little while ago that there were new and powerful reasons to-day for ardently desiring that our cause might succeed, I did not sport with you,—yourselves shall now judge of them. I ask you,—Is the trade with America of any importance to this great and thickly peopled town? (cries of, Yes! yes!) Is a continuance of the rupture with America likely to destroy that trade? (loud cries of, It is! it is!) Is there any man who would deeply feel it, if he heard that the rupture was at length converted into open war? Is there a man present who would not be somewhat alarmed if he supposed that we should have another year without the American trade? Is there any one of nerves so hardy, as calmly to hear that our Government have given up all negociation—abandoned all hopes of speedy peace with America? Then I tell that man to brace up his nerves,—I bid you all be prepared to hear what touches you all equally. We are by this day's intelligence at war with America in good earnest,—our Government have at length issued letters of marque and reprisal against the United States! (universal cries of, God help us! God help us!) Aye, God help us! God of his infinite compassion take pity on us! God help and protect this poor town,—and this whole trading country!

Now, I ask you whether you will be represented in Parliament by the men who have brought this grievous calamity on your heads, or by those who have constantly opposed the mad career which was plunging us into it? Whether will you trust the revival of your trade—the restoration of your livelihood—to them who have destroyed it, or to me whose counsels, if followed in time, would have averted this unnatural war, and left Liverpool flourishing in opulence and peace? Make your choice,—for it lies with yourselves which of us shall be commissioned to bring back commerce and plenty,—they whose stubborn infatuation has chased those blessings away,—or we, who are only known to you as the strenuous enemies of their miserable policy, the fast friends of your best interests.

Gentlemen, I stand up in this contest against the friends and followers of Mr. Pitt, or, as they partially designate him, the immortal statesman now no more. *Immortal* in the miseries of his devoted country! Immortal in the wounds of her bleeding liberties! Immortal in the cruel wars which sprang from his cold miscalculating ambition! Immortal in the intolerable taxes, and countless loads of debt which these wars have flung upon us—which the youngest man amongst us will not live to see the end of! Immortal in the triumphs of our enemies, and the ruin of our allies, the costly purchase of so much blood and treasure! Immortal in the afflictions of England, and the humiliation of her friends, through the whole results of his twenty years' reign, from the first rays of favour with which a delighted Court gilded his early apostacy, to the deadly glare which is at this instant cast upon his name by the burning metropolis of our last ally![1] But may no such immortality ever fall to my lot— let me rather live innocent and inglorious; and when at last I cease to serve you, and to feel for your wrongs, may I have an humble monument in some nameless stone, to tell that beneath it there rests from his labours in your service, " *an enemy of the immortal statesman—a friend of peace and of the people.*"

Friends! you must now judge for yourselves, and act accordingly. Against us and against you stand those who call themselves the successors of that man. They are the heirs of his policy; and if not of his immortality too, it is only because their talents for the work of destruction are less transcendent than his. They are his surviving colleagues. His fury survives in them if not his fire; and they partake of all his infatuated principles, if they have lost the genius that first made those principles triumphant. If you choose them for your delegates, you know to what policy you lend your sanction—what men you exalt to power. Should you prefer me, your choice falls upon one who, if obscure and unambitious, will at least give his own age no reason to fear him, or posterity to curse him—one whose proudest ambition it is to be deemed the friend of Liberty and of Peace.

[1] The news of the burning of Moscow had arrived by that day's post.

ON PARLIAMENTARY REFORM

LORD MACAULAY

HOUSE OF COMMONS: 2 MARCH 1831

IT is a circumstance, Sir, of happy augury for the motion before
the House, that almost all those who have opposed it have
declared themselves hostile on principle to Parliamentary
Reform. Two members, I think, have confessed that, though
they disapprove of the plan now submitted to us, they are
forced to admit the necessity of a change in the representative
system. Yet even those gentlemen have used, as far as I have
observed, no arguments which would not apply as strongly to
the most moderate change as to that which has been proposed
by his Majesty's government. I say, Sir, that I consider this
as a circumstance of happy augury. For what I feared was,
not the opposition of those who are averse to all Reform, but
the disunion of reformers. I knew that, during three months,
every reformer had been employed in conjecturing what the
plan of the Government would be. I knew that every reformer
had imagined in his own mind a scheme differing doubtless in
some points from that which my noble friend, the Paymaster of
the Forces, has developed. I felt, therefore, great apprehension
that one person would be dissatisfied with one part of the Bill,
that another person would be dissatisfied with another part,
and that thus our whole strength would be wasted in internal
dissensions. That apprehension is now at an end. I have
seen with delight the perfect concord which prevails among all
who deserve the name of reformers in this House; and I trust
that I may consider it as an omen of the concord which will
prevail among reformers throughout the country. I will not,
Sir, at present express any opinion as to the details of the Bill;
but, having during the last twenty-four hours given the most
diligent consideration to its general principles, I have no
hesitation in pronouncing it a wise, noble, and comprehensive
measure, skilfully framed for the healing of great distempers,
for the securing at once of the public liberties, and of the public
repose, and for the reconciling and knitting together of all the
orders of the State.

The hon. Baronet who has just sat[1] down has told us

[1] Sir John Walsh.

that the Ministers have attempted to unite two inconsistent principles in one abortive measure. Those were his very words. He thinks, if I understand him rightly, that we ought either to leave the representative system such as it is, or to make it perfectly symmetrical. I think, Sir, that the Ministers would have acted unwisely if they had taken either course. Their principle is plain, rational, and consistent. It is this, to admit the middle class to a large and direct share in the representation, without any violent shock to the institutions of our country. I understand those cheers; but surely the gentlemen who utter them will allow that the change which will be made in our institutions by this Bill is far less violent than that which, according to the hon. Baronet, ought to be made if we make any reform at all. I praise the Ministers for not attempting, at the present time, to make the representation uniform. I praise them for not effacing the old distinction between the towns and the counties, and for not assigning Members to districts, according to the American practice, by the Rule of Three. The Government has, in my opinion, done all that was necessary for the removing of a great practical evil, and no more than was necessary.

I consider this, Sir, as a practical question. I rest my opinion on no general theory of government. I distrust all general theories of government. I will not positively say that there is any form of polity which may not, in some conceivable circumstances, be the best possible. I believe that there are societies in which every man may safely be admitted to vote. Gentlemen may cheer, but such is my opinion. I say, Sir, that there are countries in which the condition of the labouring classes is such that they may safely be intrusted with the right of electing members of the Legislature. If the labourers of England were in that state in which I, from my soul, wish to see them, if employment were always plentiful, wages always high, food always cheap, if a large family were considered not as an encumbrance but as a blessing, the principal objections to universal Suffrage would, I think, be removed. Universal Suffrage exists in the United States without producing any very frightful consequences; and I do not believe that the people of those States, or of any part of the world, are in any good quality naturally superior to our own countrymen. But, unhappily, the labouring classes in England, and in all old countries, are occasionally in a state of great distress. Some of the causes of this distress are, I fear, beyond the control of the Government. We know what effect distress produces, even on people more intelligent than the great body of the labouring classes can possibly be. We know that it makes even wise men irritable, unreasonable, credulous, eager for immediate relief, heedless of remote consequences. There is no quackery in medicine, religion, or politics which may not impose even on a powerful mind, when that mind has been disordered by pain or fear. It is, therefore, no reflection on the poorer class of Englishmen, who are not, and who cannot in the nature of things be, highly educated, to say that distress produces on them its natural effects, those effects which it would produce on the Americans, or on any other people, that it blinds their judgment, that it inflames their passions, that it makes them prone to believe those who flatter them, and to trust those who would serve them. For the sake, therefore, of the whole society, for the sake of the labouring classes themselves, I hold it to be clearly expedient that, in a country like this, the right of suffrage should depend upon a pecuniary qualification.

But, Sir, every argument which would induce me to oppose Universal Suffrage induces me to support the plan which is now before us. I am opposed to Universal Suffrage because I think that it would produce a destructive revolution. I support this plan because I am sure that it is our best security against a revolution. The noble Paymaster of the Forces hinted, delicately indeed and remotely, at this subject. He spoke of the danger of disappointing the expectations of the nation; and for this he was charged for threatening the House. Sir, in the year 1817, the late Lord Londonderry proposed a suspension of the Habeas Corpus Act. On that occasion he told the House that, unless the measures which he recommended were adopted, the public peace could not be preserved. Was he accused of threatening the House? Again, in the year 1819, he proposed the laws known by the name of the Six Acts. He then told the House that, unless the executive power were reinforced, all the institutions of the country would be overturned by popular violence. Was he then accused of threatening the House? Will any gentleman say that it is parliamentary and decorous to urge the danger arising from popular discontent as an argument for severity; but that it is unparliamentary and indecorous to urge that same danger as an argument for conciliation? I, Sir, do entertain great apprehension for the fate of my country. I do in my conscience believe that, unless the plan proposed, or some similar plan, be speedily adopted, great and terrible calamities will befall us. Entertaining this opinion, I think myself bound to state it, not as a threat, but as a reason. I support this bill because it will improve our institutions; but I support it also because it tends to preserve them. That we may exclude those whom it is necessary to exclude, we must admit those whom it may be safe to admit. At present we oppose the schemes of revolutionists with only one half, with only one quarter of our proper force. We say, and we say justly, that it is not by mere numbers, but by property and intelligence, that the nation ought to be governed. Yet, saying this, we exclude from all share in the government great masses of property and intelligence, great numbers of those who are most interested in preserving tranquillity, and who know best how to preserve it. We do more. We drive over to the side of revolution those whom we shut out from power. Is this a time when the cause of law and order can spare one of its natural allies?

My noble friend, the Paymaster of the Forces, happily described the effect which some parts of our representative system would produce on the mind of a foreigner, who had heard much of our freedom and greatness. If, Sir, I wished to make such a foreigner clearly understand what I consider as the great defects of our system, I would conduct him through that immense city which lies to the north of Great Russell Street and Oxford Street, a city superior in size and in population to the capitals of many mighty kingdoms; and probably superior in opulence, intelligence, and general respectability to any city in the world. I would conduct him through that interminable succession of streets and squares, all consisting of well-built and well-furnished houses. I would make him observe the brilliancy of the shops, and the crowd of well-appointed equipages. I would show him that magnificent circle of palaces which surrounds the Regent's Park. I would tell him that the rental of this district was far greater than that of the whole kingdom of Scotland at the time of the Union. And then I would tell him that this was an unrepresented district. It is needless to give any more instances. It is needless to speak of Manchester, Birmingham, Leeds, Sheffield, with no representation, or of Edinburgh and Glasgow, with a mock representation. If a property tax were now imposed on the principle that no person who had less than a hundred and fifty pounds a year should contribute, I should not be surprised to find that one-half in number and value of the contributors had no votes at all; and it would, beyond all doubt, be found that one-fiftieth part in number and value of the contributors had a larger share of the representation than the other forty-nine fiftieths. This is not government by property. It is government by certain detached portions and fragments of property, selected from the rest, and preferred to the rest, on no rational principle whatever.

To say that such a system is ancient is no defence. My hon. friend, the member for the University of Oxford,[1] challenges us to show that the Constitution was ever better than it is. Sir, we are legislators, not antiquaries. The question for us is, not whether the Constitution was better formerly, but whether we can make it better now. In fact, however, the system was not in ancient times by any means so absurd as it is in our age. One noble Lord[2] has to-night told us that the town of Aldborough, which he represents, was not larger in the time of Edward the First than it is at present. The line of its walls, he assures us, may still be traced. It is now built up to that line. He argues, therefore, that as the founders of our representative institutions gave members to Aldborough when it was as small as it now is, those who would disfranchise it on account of its smallness have no right to say that they are recurring to the original principle of our representative institutions. But does the noble Lord remember the change which has taken place in the country during the last five centuries? Does he remember how much England has grown in population, while Aldborough has been standing still? Does he consider, that in the time of Edward the First, the kingdom did not contain two millions of inhabitants? It now contains nearly fourteen millions. A hamlet of the present day would have been a town of some importance in the time of our early Parliaments. Aldborough may be absolutely as considerable a place as ever. But compared with the kingdom, it is much less considerable, by the noble Lord's own showing, than when it first elected burgesses. My hon. friend, the member for the University of Oxford, has collected numerous instances of the tyranny which the kings and nobles anciently exercised, both over this house and over the electors. It is not strange that, in times when nothing was held sacred, the rights of the people, and of the representatives

[1] Sir Robert Harry Inglis.
[2] Lord Stormont.

of the people, should not have been held sacred. The proceedings which my hon. friend has mentioned no more prove that by the ancient constitution of the realm this House ought to be a tool of the King and of the aristocracy, than the Benevolences and the Shipmoney prove their own legality, or than those unjustifiable arrests which took place long after the ratification of the great Charter and even after the Petition of Right, prove that the subject was not anciently entitled to his personal liberty. We talk of the wisdom of our ancestors; and in one respect at least they were wiser than we. They legislated for their own times. They looked at the England which was before them. They did not think it necessary to give twice as many members to York as they gave to London, because York had been the capital of Britain in the time of Constantius Chlorus; and they would have been amazed indeed if they had foreseen that a city of more than a hundred thousand inhabitants would be left without representatives in the nineteenth century, merely because it stood on ground which in the thirteenth century had been occupied by a few huts. They framed a representative system, which, though not without defects and irregularities, was well adapted to the state of England in their time. But a great revolution took place. The character of the old corporations changed. New forms of property came into existence. New portions of society rose into importance. There were in our rural districts rich cultivators, who were not freeholders. There were in our capital rich traders, who were not livery men. Towns shrank into villages. Villages swelled into cities larger than the London of the Plantagenets. Unhappily while the natural growth of society went on, the artificial polity continued unchanged. The ancient form of the representation remained; and precisely because the form remained, the spirit departed. Then came that pressure almost to bursting, the new wine in the old bottles, the new society under the old institutions. It is now time for us to pay a decent, a rational, a manly reverence to our ancestors, not by superstitiously adhering to what they in other circumstances did, but by doing what they, in our circumstances, would have done. All history is full of revolutions, produced by causes similar to those which are now operating in England. A portion of the community which had been of no account expands and becomes strong. It demands a place in the system, suited, not to its former weakness, but to its present power. If this is granted, all is well. If this is refused, then comes the struggle between the young energy of one class and the ancient privileges of another. Such was the struggle between the Plebeians and the Patricians of Rome. Such was the struggle of the Italian allies for admission to the full rights of Roman citizens. Such was the struggle of our North American colonies against the mother country. Such was the struggle which the Third Estate of France maintained against the aristocracy of birth. Such was the struggle which the Roman Catholics of Ireland maintained against the aristocracy of creed. Such is the struggle which the free people of colour in Jamaica are now maintaining against the aristocracy of skin. Such, finally, is the struggle which the middle classes in England are maintaining against an aristocracy of mere locality, against an aristocracy the principle of which is to invest a hundred drunken potwallopers in one place, or the owner of a ruined hovel in another, with powers which are withheld from cities renowned to the farthest ends of the earth for the marvels of their wealth and of their industry.

But these great cities, says my honourable friend the member for the University of Oxford, are virtually, though not directly, represented. Are not the wishes of Manchester, he asks, as much consulted as those of any town which sends members to Parliament? Now, Sir, I do not understand how a power which is salutary when exercised virtually can be noxious when exercised directly. If the wishes of Manchester have as much weight with us as they would have under a system which should give representatives to Manchester, how can there be any danger in giving representatives to Manchester? A virtual representative is, I presume, a man who acts as a direct representative would act; for surely it would be absurd to say that a man virtually represents the people of Manchester who is in the habit of saying No, when a man directly representing the people of Manchester would say Ay. The utmost that can be expected from virtual representation is that it may be as good as direct representation. If so, why not grant direct representation to places which, as everybody allows, ought, by some process or other, to be represented?

If it be said that there is an evil in change as change, I answer that there is also an evil in discontent as discontent. This, indeed, is the strongest part of our case. It is said that the system works well. I deny it. I deny that a system works well which the people regard with aversion. We may say here that it is a good system and a perfect system. But if any man were to say so to any six hundred and fifty-eight respectable farmers or shopkeepers, chosen by lot in any part of England, he would be hooted down, and laughed to scorn. Are these the feelings with which any part of the government ought to be regarded? Above all, are these the feelings with which the popular branch of the legislature ought to be regarded? It is almost as essential to the utility of a House of Commons that it should possess the confidence of the people, as that it should deserve that confidence. Unfortunately, that which is in theory the popular part of our government, is in practice the unpopular part. Who wishes to dethrone the King? Who wishes to turn the Lords out of their House? Here and there a crazy radical, whom the boys in the street point at as he walks along. Who wishes to alter the constitution of this House? The whole people. It is natural that it should be so. The House of Commons is, in the language of Mr. Burke, a check, not on the people, but for the people. While that check is sufficient, there is no reason to fear that the King or the nobles will oppress the people. But if that check requires checking, how is it to be checked? If the salt shall lose its savour, wherewith shall we season it? The distrust with which the nation regards this House may be unjust. But what then? Can you remove that distrust? That it exists cannot be denied. That it is an evil cannot be denied. That it is an increasing evil cannot be denied. One gentleman tells us that it has been produced by the late events in France and Belgium; another, that it is the effect of seditious works which have lately been published. If this feeling be of origin so recent, I have read history to little purpose. Sir, this alarming discontent is not the growth of a day or of a year. If there be any symptoms by which it is possible to distinguish the chronic diseases of the body politic from its passing inflammations, all those symptoms exist in the present case. The taint has been gradually becoming more extensive and more malignant, through the whole lifetime of two generations. We have tried anodynes. We have tried cruel operations. What are we to try now? Who flatters himself that he can turn this feeling back? Does there remain any argument which escaped the comprehensive intellect of Mr. Burke, or the subtlety of Mr. Windham? Does there remain any species of coercion which was not tried by Mr. Pitt and by Lord Londonderry? We have had laws. We have had blood. New treasons have been created. The Press has been shackled. The Habeas Corpus Act has been suspended. Public meetings have been prohibited. The event has proved that these expedients were mere palliatives. You are at the end of your palliatives. The evil remains. It is more formidable than ever. What is to be done?

Under such circumstances, a great plan of reconciliation, prepared by the ministers of the Crown, has been brought before us in a manner which gives additional lustre to a noble name, inseparably associated during two centuries with the dearest liberties of the English people. I will not say that this plan is in all its details precisely such as I might wish it to be. But it is founded on a great and a sound principle. It takes away a vast power from a few. It distributes that power through the great mass of the middle order. Every man, therefore, who thinks as I think is bound to stand firmly by ministers who are resolved to stand or fall with this measure. Were I one of them, I would sooner, infinitely sooner, fall with such a measure than stand by any other means that ever supported a Cabinet.

My hon. friend, the member for the University of Oxford, tells us that if we pass this law England will soon be a republic. The reformed House of Commons will, according to him, before it has sat ten years, depose the King and expel the Lords from their House. Sir, if my hon. friend could prove this, he would have succeeded in bringing an argument for democracy infinitely stronger than any that is to be found in the works of Paine. My hon. friend's proposition is in fact this : that our monarchical and aristocratical institutions have no hold on the public mind of England; that these institutions are regarded with aversion by a majority of the middle class. This, Sir, I say, is plainly deducible from his proposition; for he tells us that the representatives of the middle class will inevitably abolish royalty and nobility within ten years: and there is surely no reason to think that the representatives of the middle class will be more inclined to a democratic revolution than their constituents. Now, Sir, if I were convinced that the great body of the middle class in England look with aversion on monarchy and aristocracy, I should be forced, much against my will, to come to this conclusion, that monarchical and aristocratical institutions are unsuited to my country. Monarchy and aristocracy, valuable and useful as I think them, are still valuable and useful as means, and not as ends. The end of government is the happiness of the people; and I do not conceive that, in a country like this, the happiness of the people can be promoted by a form of government in which the middle classes place no confidence, and which exists only because the middle classes have no organ by which to make their sentiments known. But, Sir, I am fully convinced that the middle classes sincerely wish to uphold the Royal prerogatives and the constitutional rights of the Peers. What facts does my hon. friend produce in support of his opinion? One fact only; and that a fact which has absolutely nothing to do with the question. The effect of this Reform, he tells us, would be to make the House of Commons all-powerful. It was all-powerful once before, in the beginning of 1649. Then it cut off the head of the King, and abolished the House of Peers. Therefore, if it again has the supreme power, it will act in the same manner. Now, Sir, it was not the House of Commons that cut off the head of Charles the First; nor was the House of Commons then all-powerful. It had been greatly reduced in numbers by successive expulsions. It was under the absolute dominion of the army. A majority of the House was willing to take the terms offered by the King. The soldiers turned out the majority; and the minority, not a sixth part of the whole House, passed those votes of which my hon. friend speaks, votes of which the middle classes disapproved then, and of which they disapprove still.

My hon. friend, and almost all the gentlemen who have taken the same side with him in this debate, have dwelt much on the utility of close and rotten boroughs. It is by means of such boroughs, they tell us, that the ablest men have been introduced into Parliament. It is true that many distinguished persons have represented places of this description. But, Sir, we must judge of a form of government by its general tendency, not by happy accidents. Every form of government has its happy accidents. Despotism has its happy accidents. Yet we are not disposed to abolish all constitutional checks, to place an absolute master over us, and to take our chance whether he may be a Caligula or a Marcus Aurelius. In whatever way the House of Commons may be chosen, some able men will be chosen in that way who would not be chosen in any other way. If there were a law that the hundred tallest men in England should be Members of Parliament, there would probably be some able men among those who would come into the House by virtue of this law. If the hundred persons whose names stand first in the alphabetical list of the Court Guide were made Members of Parliament, there would probably be able men among them. We read in ancient history that a very able king was elected by the neighing of his horse; but we shall scarcely, I think, adopt this mode of election. In one of the most celebrated republics of antiquity, Athens, Senators and Magistrates were chosen by lot; and sometimes the lot fell fortunately. Once, for example, Socrates was in office. A cruel and unjust proposition was made by a demagogue. Socrates resisted it at the hazard of his own life. There is no event in Grecian history more interesting than that memorable resistance. Yet who would have officers appointed by lot, because the accident of the lot may have given to a great and good man a power which he would probably never have attained in any other way? We must judge, as I said, by the general tendency of a system. No person can doubt that a House of Commons chosen freely by the middle classes will contain very many able men. I do not say that precisely the same able men who would find their way into the present House of Commons will find their way into the reformed House; but that is not the question. No particular man is necessary to the State. We may depend on it that, if we provide the country with popular institutions, those institutions will provide it with great men.

There is another objection, which, I think, was first raised by the hon. and learned member for Newport[1] He tells us that the elective franchise is property; that to take it away from a man who has not been judicially convicted of malpractices is robbery; that no crime is proved against the voters in the close boroughs; that no crime is even imputed to them in the preamble of the bill; and that therefore to disfranchise them without compensation would be an act of revolutionary tyranny. The hon. and learned gentleman has compared the conduct of the present Ministers to that of those odious tools of power who, towards the close of the reign of Charles the Second, seized the charters of the Whig Corporations. Now, there was another precedent, which I wonder that he did not recollect, both because it is much more nearly in point than that to which he referred, and because my noble friend, the Paymaster of the Forces, had previously alluded to it. If the elective franchise is property, if to disfranchise voters without a crime proved, or a compensation given, be robbery, was there ever such an act of robbery as the disfranchising of the Irish forty-shilling freeholders?

[1] Mr. Horace Twiss.

Was any pecuniary compensation given to them? Is it declared in the preamble of the bill which took away their franchise that they had been convicted of any offence? Was any judicial inquiry instituted into their conduct? Were they even accused of any crime? Or if you say that it was a crime in the electors of Clare to vote for the hon. and learned gentleman who now represents the County of Waterford, was a Protestant freeholder in Louth to be punished for the crime of a Catholic freeholder in Clare? If the principle of the hon. and learned member for Newport be sound, the franchise of the Irish peasantry was property. That franchise the Ministers under whom the hon. and learned member held office did not scruple to take away. Will he accuse those Ministers of robbery? If not, how can he bring such an accusation against their successors?

Every gentleman, I think, who has spoken from the other side of the House has alluded to the opinions which some of his Majesty's Ministers formerly entertained on the subject of Reform. It would be officious in me, Sir, to undertake the defence of gentlemen who are so well able to defend themselves. I will only say that, in my opinion, the country will not think worse either of their capacity or of their patriotism because they have shown that they can profit by experience, because they have learned to see the folly of delaying inevitable changes. There are others who ought to have learned the same lesson. I say, Sir, that there are those who, I should have thought, must have had enough to last them all their lives of that humiliation which follows obstinate and boastful resistance to changes rendered necessary by the progress of society, and by the development of the human mind. Is it possible that those persons can wish again to occupy a position which can neither be defended nor surrendered with honour? I well remember, Sir, a certain evening in the month of May, 1827. I had not then the honour of a seat in this House, but I was an attentive observer of its proceedings. The right hon. Baronet opposite,[1] of whom personally I desire to speak with that high respect which I feel for his talents and his character, but of whose public conduct I must speak with the sincerity required by my public duty, was then, as he is now, out of office. He had just resigned the seals of the Home Department, because he conceived that the recent ministerial arrangements had been too favourable to the Catholic claims. He rose to ask whether

[1] Sir Robert Peel.

it was the intention of the new Cabinet to repeal the Test and Corporation Acts, and to reform the Parliament. He bound up, I well remember, those two questions together; and he declared that if the Ministers should either attempt to repeal the Test and Corporation Acts, or bring forward a measure of Parliamentary Reform, he should think it his duty to oppose them to the utmost. Since that declaration was made, four years have elapsed; and what is now the state of the three questions which then chiefly agitated the minds of men? What is become of the Test and Corporation Acts? They are repealed. By whom? By the right hon. Baronet. What has become of the Catholic disabilities? They are removed. By whom? By the right hon. Baronet. The question of Parliamentary Reform is still behind. But signs, of which it is impossible to misconceive the import, do most clearly indicate that unless that question also be speedily settled, property and order, and all the institutions of this great monarchy, will be exposed to fearful peril. Is it possible that gentlemen long versed in high political affairs cannot read these signs? Is it possible that they can really believe that the Representative system of England, such as it now is, will last to the year 1860? If not, for what would they have us wait? Would they have us wait merely that we may show to all the world how little we have profited by our own recent experience? Would they have us wait that we may once again hit the exact point where we can neither refuse with authority nor concede with grace? Would they have us wait that the numbers of the discontented party may become larger, its demands higher, its feelings more acrimonious, its organization more complete? Would they have us wait till the whole tragi-comedy of 1827 has been acted over again? till they have been brought into office by a cry of "No Reform," to be reformers, as they were once before brought into office by a cry of "No Popery," to be emancipators? Have they obliterated from their minds — gladly, perhaps, would some among them obliterate from their minds — the transactions of that year? And have they forgotten all the transactions of the succeeding year? Have they forgotten how the spirit of liberty in Ireland, debarred from its natural outlet, found a vent by forbidden passages? Have they forgotten how we were forced to indulge the Catholics in all the licence of rebels, merely because we chose to withhold from them the liberties of subjects? Do they wait for associations more formidable than that of the Corn Exchange, for contributions larger than the Rent, for agitators more violent than those who, three years ago, divided with the King and the Parliament the sovereignty of Ireland? Do they wait for that last and most dreadful paroxysm of popular rage, for that last and most cruel test of military fidelity? Let them wait, if their past experience shall induce them to think that any high honour or any exquisite pleasure is to be obtained by a policy like this. Let them wait, if this strange and fearful infatuation be indeed upon them, that they should not see with their eyes, or hear with their ears, or understand with their heart. But let us know our interest and our duty better. Turn where we may, within, around, the voice of great events is proclaiming to us, Reform, that you may preserve. Now, therefore, while everything at home and abroad forebodes ruin to those who persist in a hopeless struggle against the spirit of the age; now, while the crash of the proudest throne of the Continent is still resounding in our ears; now, while the roof of a British palace affords an ignominious shelter to the exiled heir of forty kings; now, while we see on every side ancient institutions subverted and great societies dissolved; now, while the heart of England is still sound; now, while old feelings and old associations retain a power and a charm which may too soon pass away; now, in this your accepted time; now, in this your day of salvation, take counsel, not of prejudice, not of party spirit, not of the ignominious pride of a fatal consistency, but of history, of reason, of the ages which are past, of the signs of this most portentous time. Pronounce in a manner worthy of the expectation with which this great debate has been anticipated, and of the long remembrance which it will leave behind. Renew the youth of the State. Save property, divided against itself. Save the multitude, endangered by its own ungovernable passions. Save the aristocracy, endangered by its own unpopular power. Save the greatest, and fairest, and most highly civilized community that ever existed from calamities which may in a few days sweep away all the rich heritage of so many ages of wisdom and glory. The danger is terrible. The time is short. If this bill should be rejected, I pray to God that none of those who concur in rejecting it may ever remember their votes with unavailing remorse amidst the wreck of laws, the confusion of ranks, the spoliation of property, and the dissolution of social order.

REPEAL OF THE CORN LAWS

SIR ROBERT PEEL

HOUSE OF COMMONS: 15 MAY 1846

SIR,—I believe it is nearly three months since I first proposed, as the organ of her Majesty's Government, the measure which, I trust, is about to receive to-night the sanction of the House of Commons; and considering the lapse of time, considering the frequent discussions, considering the anxiety of the people of this country that these debates should be brought to a close, I feel that I should be offering an insult to the House if I were to condescend to bandy personalities upon such an occasion. Sir, I foresaw that the course which I have taken from a sense of public duty would expose me to serious sacrifices. I foresaw as its inevitable result, that I must forfeit friendship which I most highly valued, that I must interrupt political relations in which I felt a sincere pride; but the smallest of all the penalties which I anticipated, were the continued venomous attacks of the member for Shrewsbury.[1]   Sir, I will only say of that honourable gentleman that if he, after reviewing the whole of my public life, a life extending over thirty years previous to my accession to office in 1841, if he then entertained the opinion of me which he now professes, if he thought I was guilty of these petty larcenies from Mr. Horner and others, it is a little surprising that in the spring of 1841, after his long experience of my public career, he should have been prepared to give me his confidence. It is still more surprising that he should have been ready, as I think he was, to unite his fortunes with mine in office, thus implying the strongest proof which any public man can give of confidence in the honour and integrity of a minister of the Crown.

Sir, I have explained more than once what were the circumstances under which I felt it to be my duty to take this course. I did feel in November last that there was just cause for apprehension of scarcity and famine in Ireland. I am stating what were the apprehensions I felt at that time, what were the motives from which I acted; and those apprehensions, though they may be denied now, were at least shared then by those honourable

[1] Disraeli.

gentlemen who sit below the gangway. The honourable member for Somersetshire [1] expressly declared that, at the period to which I referred, he was prepared to acquiesce in the suspension of the Corn Laws. An honourable member also, a recent addition to this House, who spoke with great ability the other night, the honourable member for Dorsetshire,[2] distinctly declared, that he thought I should have abandoned my duty if I had not advised that, considering the circumstances of Ireland, the restrictions on the importation of foreign corn should be temporarily removed. I may have been wrong, but my impression was, first, that my duty towards a country threatened with famine required that that, which had been the ordinary remedy under all similar circumstances, should be resorted to, namely, that there should be free access to the food of man from whatever quarter it might come. I was prepared to give the best proof which public men generally can give of the sincerity of their opinions, by tendering my resignation of office, and devolving upon others the duty of proposing this measure; and, Sir, I felt this, that if these laws were once suspended, and there was unlimited access to food, the produce of other countries, I and those with whom I acted felt the strongest conviction that it was not for the interest of the agricultural party, that an attempt should be made permanently to reimpose restrictions on the importation of food.

I could not propose the re-establishment of the existing law with any guarantee for its permanence. As the noble lord says, I had acted with Mr. Huskisson in 1822, 1825, and 1826, in revising the commercial system, and applying to that system the principles of free trade. In 1842, after my accession to office, I proposed a revision of the Corn Laws. Had anything taken place at the election of 1844 which precluded that revision? Was there a public assurance given to the people of this country, at the election of 1841, that the existing amount of protection should be retained? [Yes, Yes.] There was, was there? Then, if there was, you were as guilty as I. What was the assurance given? If it was that the amount of protection to agriculture, which existed in 1843 and 1841, should be retained, opposition ought to have been made by you to the revision of 1842. Why was the removal of the prohibition on the importation of foreign meat and foreign cattle assented to? That removal must have been utterly at variance with any assurance that the protection to agriculture, which existed in 1840 and 1841, should be retained. Yet that removal was voted by the House by large majorities;

[1] Sir. T. Acland.   [2] Mr. Seymer.

and after the Bill of 1842, was I not repeatedly asked this question—" Now that you have passed this Bill establishing a new Corn Law, will you give a public assurance, that to that you will, at all times, adhere?" Did I not uniformly decline to give any such assurance? I said I had no intention of proposing an alteration of that law at the time when the question was put to me; but I distinctly declared that I would not fetter for ever my discretion by giving such a pledge. These things are on record. It was quite impossible for me, consistently with my own convictions, after a suspension of import duties, to propose the re-establishment of the existing law with any security for its continuance.

Well, then, the question which naturally arose was this:— Shall we propose some diminished protection to agriculture, or, in the state of public feeling which will exist after the suspension of the restriction, shall we propose a permanent and ultimate settlement of the question? To be of any avail, it must have been diminished greatly below its present standard, and that diminution, I believe, would have met with as much opposition from the agricultural body as the attempt finally to settle the question. And now, after all these debates, I am firmly convinced that it is better for the agricultural interest to contemplate the final settlement of this question, rather than to attempt the introduction of a law giving a diminished protection. My belief is, that a diminished protection would, in no respect, conciliate agricultural feeling: and this I must say, nothing could be so disadvantageous as to give an ineffectual protection and yet incur all the odium of giving an adequate one. What have we been told during this discussion? With scarcely an exception, I have listened attentively to every speech that has been made on this side of the House, and, admitting the talent that has been displayed, I confess they have, in no respect, altered the conviction upon which I have acted. You tell me it would have been possible, with such support as I should have received, to have continued the existing law. I believe it might have been. As far as the gratification of any personal object of ambition is concerned (interruption)—I am perfectly ready to listen to any reply that may be made to my observations, and I think it is hardly fair to attempt to interrupt me by such exclamations, but it has so far succeeded. (Sir Robert paused a few moments.) I am told that it would have been possible to continue this protection, but after the suspension of it, for I now assume that the suspension would have been assented to on account of the necessities of Ireland, the difficulty of maintaining it would have been greatly increased, because it would have been shown, after the lapse of three years, that, although it had worked tolerably well during the continuance of the abundance, or at least of average harvests, yet at the moment it was exposed to the severe trial of scarcity, it then ceased to effect the object for which it was enacted, and that, in addition to the state of public feeling with reference to restrictions on imports generally, would have greatly added to the difficulty of maintaining the law. There would have been public proof of its inefficiency for one of the great objects for which it was enacted.

But let me say, although it has not been brought prominently under consideration, that, without any reference to the case of Ireland, the working of the law, as far as Great Britain is concerned, during the present year, has not been satisfactory. You would have to contend not merely with difficulties arising from suspension on account of the case of Ireland, but it would have been shown to you that the rate of duty has been high on account of the apparent lowness in the price of corn, while that lowness of price has arisen not from abundance in quantity, but from deficient quality. It would have been shown, and conclusively, that there are greater disparities of price, in most of the principal markets of this country, between corn of the highest quality and of the lowest than have ever existed in former periods. It would have been proved that there never was a greater demand than there has been during the present year, for wheat of fine quality for the purpose of mixing with wheat of inferior quality, which forms the chief article brought for sale into our domestic markets. It would have been shown you that had there been free access to wheat of higher quality than they have assumed, the whole population of this country would for the last four months have been consuming bread of a better quality. My belief, therefore, is that, in seeking the re-enactment of the existing law after its suspension, you would have to contend with greater difficulties than you anticipate.

Still I am told, " You would have had a majority," I think a majority might have been obtained. I think you could have continued this law, notwithstanding these increased difficulties, for a short time longer; but I believe that the interval of its maintenance would have been but short, and that there would have been, during the period of its continuance, a desperate conflict between different classes of society; that your arguments in favour of it would have been weak; that you might have had no alternative at an early period, had the cycle of unfavourable harvests returned—and who can give an assurance that they would not? that you might, at an early period, have had no alternative but to concede an alteration of this law under circumstances infinitely less favourable than the present to a final settlement of the question.

The honourable gentleman the member for Dorsetshire said, "We can fight the League with their own weapons;" that is to say, finding that we cannot control by law those measures resorted to by the Anti-Corn-Law League, which I cannot defend, and which I very sincerely regret were ever resorted to—the establishment of voters in counties, not being naturally voters in those counties—the honourable gentleman said, "We can make faggot votes as well as they," and the landed interest, he said, by the greater facilities which they possess, would be able to beat the League. Well, but what a sad alternative is this! what a sad conflict to be carrying on! Even admitting that it would be necessary, and might be done from honest convictions of that necessity, could you do it without destroying the county constituencies? Surely it is wise to consider the alternative, and, believe me, you who are anxious for the maintenance of the aristocratic system, you who desire wisely, and justly desire, to discourage the infusion of too much of the democratic principle into the Constitution of the country, although you might, for a time, have relied on the faggot votes you created in a moment of excitement, yet the interval would not be long before that weapon would break short in your hands. You would find that those additional votes created for the purpose of combating the votes of the League, though when brought up at the first election under the influence of an excitement connected with the Corn Laws, they might have been true to your side, yet after the lapse of a short time, some exciting question connected with democratic feelings would arise, and then your votes and the votes of the League, not being subjected to legitimate influence, would unite, and you would find you had entailed on the country permanent evils, destroying the Constitution for the purpose of providing a temporary remedy. It was the foresight of these consequences, it was the belief that you were about to enter into a bitter and, ultimately, an unsuccessful struggle, that has induced me to think that for the benefit of all classes, for the benefit of the agricultural class itself, it was desirable to come to a permanent and equitable settlement of this question.

These are the motives on which I acted. I know the penalty

to which I must be subjected for having so acted, but I declare, even after the continuance of these debates, that I am only the more impressed with the conviction that the policy we advise is correct. An honourable gentleman, in the course of this evening, the honourable member for Sunderland,[1] informed us that he had heard that there was excitement about the Corn Laws; but he undertook to give a peremptory contradiction to that report, for he never recollected any public question being proposed involving such great interests which, on the whole, was received by all classes concerned, by the manufacturing and by the agricultural classes, with less excitement and with a greater disposition to confide in the wisdom of the decision of Parliament. Well if that be so, if this question is proposed at such a time (Mr. Hudson.—No, no). I certainly understood the honourable member to make that statement (Mr. Hudson.—I will explain after). I may be mistaken, and of course I am, if the honourable member says so; but I understood him to say, that so far from there being any undue excitement, he thought that there was much less than could have been expected, and that all parties were disposed to acquiesce in the decision of Parliament.

Mr. Hudson.—What I stated, I believe, was this: that there was no excitement in favour of the Bill—not that there was a deep feeling on the part of the agriculturists against it, but that there was no public excitement in its favour.

That varies very little from the expressions I used, and entirely justifies the inference which I drew. If there be no excitement in favour of the Bill, and no strong feeling on the part of agriculturists against it, it appears to me that this is not an unfavourable moment for the dispassionate consideration by Parliament of a subject otherwise calculated to promote excitement on the part of one class, and to cause great apprehension on the part of the other, and the honourable member's statement is a strong confirmation of my belief that it is wise to undertake the settlement of this question when there is such absence of excitement, rather than to wait until a period when unfavourable harvests and depressed manufactures may have brought about a state of things which may render it less easy for you to exercise a dispassionate judgment on the matter. Sir, I do not rest my support of this Bill upon the temporary ground of scarcity in Ireland. I do not rest my support of the Bill upon that temporary scarcity; but I believe that scarcity left no alternative

[1] Mr. Hudson.

to us but to undertake the consideration of this subject; and, that consideration being necessary, I think that a permanent adjustment of the question is not only imperative, but the best policy for all concerned. And I repeat now, that I have a firm belief that it is for the general benefit of all, for the best interests of the country, independent of the obligation imposed on us by temporary scarcity, it is for the general interests of the great body of the people that an arrangement should be made for a permanent removal of the restrictions upon the introduction of food.

I will assign my reasons for that opinion. I take my facts from the opponents of this measure. I take the speech of the honourable gentleman, the member for Oxfordshire,[1] a speech distinguished by all the ability and usual clearness and research of the honourable gentleman. We shall have no difference respecting our facts, for I shall take them from the opponents of this measure. The only question is as to the just inference to be drawn from these facts. The honourable gentleman said:—" Allowing that the facts and figures which we have produced for the last thirty years are correct, then I find that there has been a great increase in trade, that there has been a cheapening of commodities; but there has been no improvement in the social condition of the great masses of the people." Now, all of you admit that the real question at issue is the improvement of the social and moral condition of the masses of the population. We wish to elevate, in the gradation of society, that great class which gains its support by manual labour. That is agreed on all hands. The mere interest of the landlords, the mere interest of the occupying tenants, important as they are, are subordinate to the great question—what is calculated to increase the comforts, to improve the condition, and elevate the social character of the millions who subsist by manual labour, whether they are engaged in manufactures or in agriculture. What, then, says the honourable member for Oxfordshire? Take his statements to be correct, and they suggest matter for grave consideration. Here is a country in which wealth has increased, in which trade has increased, in which commodities have been cheapened; but, said the honourable gentleman, " the social condition of the people has not been raised. I have tried it by every test by which I can determine the fact, and the conclusion I come to is, that it has not." If that be so, is it not a formidable state of things? If increased wealth and enjoyment, if increased trade and cheaper commodities have not given the people more contentment, have

[1] Mr. J. W. Henley.

not elevated them in the moral scale; if the moral and social improvement of those who form the foundation and platform of society has not advanced, is that not a subject of serious reflection? He says, " I look to the state of crime, it has increased. I look to the great articles, not of consumption, but of luxury, which have become necessities; I look to sugar, to tea, and to other articles of a similar nature, and I find there has been no corresponding increase of consumption." He says, " I draw my inferences from the facts and the statistics of the last thirty years." Well, let us go back to the period at which the thirty years commence, that is the year 1815; then began the present system of protection to agriculture.

You say you have carefully considered this state of things, that you have looked at them for the last thirty years, and you find increased wealth, increased trade, but a deteriorated condition of the people. With what do you compare the condition of the people for the last thirty years? With what preceding period do you institute the comparison? Take any period of the last century. Let us exclude the war; because, during the war which began in 1793, there was a great dislocation of capital, and a great derangement of social interest. Our comparison, to take a period of peace similar to that of the last thirty years, must be a period which preceded the French war. We must go to the last century. Take what period you please; take the period from 1700 down to 1791; and now let us compare what was the state of the law when the people, according to your showing, were in a more prosperous condition than during the last thirty years. Let us compare the state of the law at this period, or at any part of this period, with that when protection to agriculture began in 1815. Why, for the first thirty-six years of the last century there was no impediment to the importation of corn. For the first sixty-six years of that century, this country was an exporting country. Let me ask you, what were the agriculturists of Croatia and Hungary at this time about? Why did they not send us corn? This country was exporting corn at that time: the price of corn was low and did not exceed 41s. What was the law passed in 1773? Why, foreign corn was admitted at a duty of 6d., when the price was above 49s. 6d.; and, under that law, for six years after it was passed, this country was an exporting country. And did agriculture suffer during that period? Why, sir, there were more enclosure bills passed during that period, when there was a free importation of foreign corn, when it might be brought in at a duty of 6d. if the price exceeded

49s., than ever before. There were not less than 1560 enclosure bills passed. You say, then, that the condition of the people was comparatively better in point of morality and comfort than since 1815. In 1815 the commencement of the period of thirty years, this law was passed, that foreign corn should not be imported into England, until after the price had arrived at 80s. There was a positive prohibition of foreign corn unless the price arrived at 80s. That was the perfection of protection. Was that to continue? You relaxed it. In 1822 you permitted the importation of foreign corn when the price exceeded 70s. You altered this law again, which the honourable member for Newcastle-under-Lyme [1] ranks with principles and ancient institutions. By the law of 1828, you subjected foreign corn, when the price was under 64s., to a duty of 23s. 8d.; when it was at 69s., you subjected it to a duty of 16s. 8d.; and that law remained in force till 1842. And it was under the influence of this law, until you altered it in 1842, that you have the admission of the honourable gentleman, the member of Oxfordshire, that the social and moral condition of the people has not improved. What also did we in 1815? We imposed enormous duties and positive prohibitions upon other articles, the produce of foreign countries. At that time the duty upon foreign butter and cheese was 2s. 6d. and 1s. 6d. respectively: we raised it to £1, and 10s. 6d. Therefore, we did in 1815 adopt the principle of strict protection to agriculture; and the honourable gentleman says that he finds crime increased, and the command over comforts and the moderate luxuries which partake of the nature of necessaries, lessened. He says that is the result of the inspection of thirty years. So much, then, for the condition of the great body of the people.

Now I come to the facts of the honourable member for the North Riding of Yorkshire.[2] I heard his speech. I was sorry to observe the indisposition under which he laboured, an indisposition which in no degree prevented the exercise of his intellectual faculties, or prevented him from speaking with his usual clearness and power. I ask you to take the facts of the honourable gentleman since 1815. I am quoting the very expressions he used. The account I am giving of agriculture since that period is not mine, but his. I followed him closely, and took down his account of the condition of agriculture under a state of almost perfect protection. In 1815 you had prohibition of foreign importation till corn exceeded 80s. And these are the historical annals of the honourable gentleman, the advocate of agricultural protection. In 1816 and 1817, he says, you had severe distress. [Mr. Cayley.—In 1815 and 1816.] I think it was after 1815 and 1816. I think it was in 1817 that a speech was made from the throne lamenting the state of society, and the efforts that were made by designing men to take advantage of the distress of the country. It was in 1817 that the Habeas Corpus Act was suspended, and the Seditious Meetings Bill was passed. In 1819, the honourable gentleman said that such was the distress that the six Acts [1] were passed. In 1822, he said, agricultural distress was so intense that a Committee was appointed for the purpose of devising a remedy. He said that at that time the price of wheat, of beautiful wheat, was 40s.; that a farmer stated, I think, that where there were 150 persons usually out of employment, there were then 300; and that he had the greatest difficulty, on account of the low price of wheat, in giving employment to the agricultural labourers. From 1822 the honourable gentleman advanced to 1830, and he said that in 1830, on account of the depressed state of agriculture, we had the Swing [2] fires. In 1833 agriculture was again so depressed that it was necessary to appoint a committee to consider that distress and to attempt to devise a remedy He said that there were thirty-five villages in the north of England with a population of 200,000 persons depending upon their labour, and their wages did not exceed 3s. 8½d. per week per man. In 1834, he said, the Preston operatives presented a petition to this House, in which they complained of poverty, of ignorance, and of vice. The year 1835, he said, was as bad as the year 1822, and the prices were so low that the ordinary employment of agriculture could not be afforded. 1836 and 1837, he said, were years of sudden prosperity; but that came to an end in 1838, and there was prostration and suffering from 1839 to 1842.

This is the account which the honourable member gives of the state of agriculture under that protection which was terminated by the Bill of 1842. Now, observe what the honourable member also said. He said that there was a constant alternation of high prices and low prices, and he said, differing from many who concur with him in their vote, that the low prices, though caused by favourable harvests, entailed the greatest suffering upon the

---

[1] The six Acts, called Gagging Acts, directed against seditious meetings, libels, and newspapers.

[2] Between 1830 and 1833 there occurred many incendiary fires, farmers' ricks and stacks being the most frequent objects of attack. These fires were laid to the charge of an imaginary person, " Swing."

agricultural classes, and that in 1822 and 1835, the farmer who had sold his wheat for less than 40s. complained on account of the lowness of prices that he could not give the usual employment. That lowness of price did not arise from competition with foreign corn. There was no foreign corn imported to reduce prices. That low price was caused by competition among the home-growers of corn. There was a glut arising from productive harvests, there was no outlet for it, and there was prostration and suffering of the agriculturists in consequence. That is the account which the honourable member gives of the result of high protection, not upon the manufacturing interest, but upon the agricultural; and when he had given that account, when he had detailed those sufferings on the part of the agriculturists, I was surprised to hear the honourable gentleman conclude with a quotation:—

> " Woodman, spare that tree! "

I beg pardon, I am afraid I should have to ask the honourable member to supply me with a verse, but the purport of it was that not a bough must be touched; that those whom it sheltered in youth ought to let it remain in their old age. After that account of the consequences of this high protection upon the agricultural interest, I was surprised to hear that advice which the honourable gentleman gave us, not to touch a bough of that tree, under the shade of which agriculture had so long flourished. If he had said,—

> Ille et nefasto te posuit die
>
> . . . agro qui statuit meo
> Te, triste lignum, te caducum
> In domini caput immerentis,—[1]

I think it would have been a more appropriate quotation.

But, now, is there no exception to be made from this period of thirty years? Did nothing occur at the latter part of that period of thirty years to exempt it from the stigma which the honourable gentleman cast upon the preceding part? There have been three years, 1843, 1844, 1845, during which you have had, from some cause or other, the benefits of plenty and of cheapness. During the last three of these thirty years, the average price of wheat a little exceeded 50s. And let us see

[1] That man on an ill-omened day placed thee

. . . who planted thee in my field,
Thee, sinister log, thee threatening to fall
On the head of thy innocent lord.

whether, during that period, that censure will apply which applies to the former period; let us see whether, during the last three years, there has been no increase of comfort, no improvement in morality, no abatement of seditious feeling or disaffection. I care not what may be the cause of the abundance which has prevailed during the last three years. You say the cause is not to be attributed to the tariff, but that good harvests have produced abundance. Be it so. But there has been comparative abundance. There has been a less outlay required for the purchase of articles of first necessity. You say there has been a demand for labour on railways. Why, that is an effect, and not a cause. It is on account of your prosperity that you are enabled to apply your capital to internal improvements, causing this demand for labour and giving increased wages. And do you believe if wheat had been at 70s. instead of 50s., there would have been the same stimulus to the application of capital? But grant that the tariff of 1842 had nothing to do with the abatement of price in 1843, 1844, and 1845. I will concede it to you that it is attributable to the favour of Providence, to good harvests. But let us see what has been the result of this abundance. I will take the tests of the honourable gentleman. He says, facts and figures show that there has been no increase of consumption. Now, I will show that during the last three years trade has flourished, capital has accumulated, but that you cannot say of the last three years what you can say of the preceding twenty-seven years, that there has been a deterioration in the social condition of the people. I will, first, take those articles which enter largely into consumption. I have here a statement of the quantities of certain articles entered for home consumption in the United Kingdom from 1839 to 1841 and from 1843 to 1846, showing the average quantity of each article in each of those periods. In the first three years, when the prices of provisions were high, the average consumption of sugar for the three years ending in 1841 was 3,826,000 cwt. The average consumption for the last three years ending the 1st January, 1846, had increased from 3,826,000 cwt. to 4,346,000 cwt. The average consumption of tea in the first three years was 34,685,000 lbs.; in the last three years it increased to 42,000,000 lbs. The average consumption of coffee during the first three years of high price was 27,941,000 lbs. annually; the average consumption of the last three years was 31,883,000 lbs. The consumption of cocoa in the first three years averaged 1,859,000 lbs. annually; in the last three years, 2,575,000 lbs.

Take another article which, though in a smaller degree, enters largely into the consumption of the poor, and which is not a bad test of their comfort. During the first three years the consumption of currants averaged 175,000 cwt.; in the last three years it had increased to 285,000 cwt. I take, then, the tests of the honourable member for Oxfordshire, the consumption of articles necessary to the comfort of the people, and I show him that comparative plenty has produced this change in the command of the working classes over the smaller luxuries of life.

I will next come to a more important point, the state of crime. You have now an official record, presented within a few days, of what has been the state of crime in this country during the last thirty years. Now, what was the state of crime during the first period of twenty-seven years? From the first record in 1805 down to 1842, when the commitments attained the maximum number hitherto recorded, the increase in crime progressed from year to year, until it had extended to above 60 per cent. In 1843 a change commenced. In that year the number of commitments decreased. Within the last six years, three years of great increase of crime have been followed by three years during which the decrease was so considerable, that the number of commitments in 1845 has been reduced to what it was seven years ago. In the three years of high prices, this was the state of crime in each year:—the number of commitments in the first year was 27,187; in the second, 27,760; and in the third, 31,309. During the last three years, the number of commitments has been, in the first year, 29,591; in the second, 26,542; and in the third, 24,303. Well, then, I take this other test of criminality and the extension of morality, and I ask whether we can resist the legitimate inference, that the comparative cheapness and plenty, which have existed during the last three years, have had their effect in producing this diminished criminality? The gentleman who drew up this return says:—" The decrease of commitments in England," for the last three years, " has, therefore, been general, continued and extensive, to a degree of which there is no recorded example in this kingdom." He says again:—" In the sixth class containing those offences which do not fall within the definitions of the foregoing classes " (violence to the person and offences against property) " there is a total absence of commitments for seditious riots or sedition."

A total absence of commitments for these offences! Why, can you have a stronger proof of the improvement of a country, apart from the command of comforts, than the fact that there should have been this progressive diminution in commitments, and a total absence of any commitment for sedition or seditious riots? I say, therefore, comparing the result of the three years when we have had diminished protection to agriculture and a reduced price of provisions with the twenty-seven preceding years, the inference is just, that the diminution of crime is attributable to an increased command over those articles which constitute the food of the people. But you say, " As this happy state of things has arisen during the existence of the present Corn Laws, as the present Corn Laws have been consistent with cheapness and plenty, on what principle do you seek to disturb this happy arrangement? You have proved that, co-existent with the Corn Laws, there have been cheapness and plenty. Why, then, do you now come forward to propose their alteration? " Why, if you can show me that those laws were the cause of this happiness and plenty, that would, no doubt, be a strong and powerful reason for their continuance. But it cannot be denied that, simultaneously with a reduced protection to agriculture, there has been not only no diminution in agricultural improvement, but increased exertions, an increased demand for agricultural products, and increased comforts for the people.

As you have proceeded downwards from 1815 to 1842, there has been a corresponding benefit from the abatement of protection. If we could anticipate that the law of 1842 would continue to produce all the advantages to which I have referred, that might be a conclusive reason for adhering to it. But you assert that favourable harvests have occasioned these advantages. Why, what guarantee have you for the continuance of favourable harvests? You have had comparatively favourable harvests for the last three years, and you say then, as a matter of necessity, that we ought to continue this law. Continue the law say I too, if you can prove that this particular law has been the cause of these benefits. If, however, you say that favourable harvests have been the cause, I say then that does not constitute any reason for continuing the law. Those who have observed attentively the vicissitudes of the seasons, have remarked that there are cycles of favourable and unfavourable years. There was an unfavourable cycle of years in 1839, 1840, and 1841, during which time there was great distress. There has been since a favourable cycle of years during which there has been comparative abundance. But supposing that this cycle of years, in which we have had unfavourable harvests, should again return, have we, I ask, any security that the law of 1842 will enable us to obtain an ample supply of food? Suppose, also, that consistent with those unfavourable harvests, we had also a depressed state of manufactures, shall we then be in a favourable position for making any alteration in the law? Remember how short a time has elapsed since we had the state of Paisley, of Sheffield, and of Stockport brought under our special notice. Now, if these times should again return, after this interval of comparative happiness, when the contrast of our misery will be considerably heightened by the preceding period of happiness which has prevailed, do you believe it would be possible to maintain in existence a law which leaves a duty of 16s. a quarter upon wheat when it had arrived at the price of 56s.? You may say, " Disregard the progress of public opinion; defy the League; enter into a combination against it; determine to fight the battle of protection, and you will succeed." My firm belief is, without yielding to the dictation of the League, or any other body [Oh, Oh!], yes, subjecting myself to that imputation, I will not hesitate to say my firm belief is, that it is most consistent with prudence and good policy, most consistent with the real interests of the landed proprietors themselves, most consistent with the maintenance of a territorial aristocracy, seeing by how precarious a tenure, namely, the vicissitude of the seasons, you hold your present protective system; I say it is my firm belief that it is for the advantage of all classes, in these times of comparative comfort and comparative calm, to anticipate the angry discussions which might arise, by proposing at once a final adjustment of the question.

I have stated the reasons which have induced me to take the present course. You may, no doubt, say that I am only going on the experience of three years, and am acting contrary to the principles of my whole life. Well, I admit that charge; I admit that I have defended the existence of the Corn Laws; yes, and that up to the present period, I have refused to acquiesce in the proposition to destroy them. I candidly admit all this. But, when I am told that I am acting inconsistently with the principles of my whole life by advocating free trade, I give this statement a peremptory denial. During the last three years I have subjected myself to many taunts on this question, and you have often said to me that Earl Grey had found out something indicating a change in my opinions. Did I not say I thought that we ought not hastily to disturb vested interests by any rash legislation? Did I not declare that the principle of political economy suggested the purchasing in the cheapest and the selling in the dearest market? Did I not say that I thought there was nothing so special in the produce of agriculture that should exempt it from the application of this principle which we have applied already to other articles? You have a right, I admit, to taunt me with any change of opinion upon the Corn Laws; but when you say that, by my adoption of the principle of free trade, I have acted in contradiction to those principles which I have always avowed during my whole life, that charge at least, I say, is destitute of foundation.

Sir, I will not enter at this late hour into the discussion of any other topic. I foresaw the consequences that have resulted from the measures which I thought it my duty to propose. We were charged with the heavy responsibility of taking security against a great calamity in Ireland. We did not act lightly. We did not form our opinion upon merely local information, the information of local authorities likely to be influenced by an undue alarm. Before I and those who agreed with me came to that conclusion, we had adopted every means, by local inquiry and by sending perfectly disinterested persons of authority to Ireland, to form a just and correct opinion. Whether we were mistaken or not, I believe we were not mistaken, but, even if we were mistaken, a generous construction should be put upon the motives and conduct of those who are charged with the responsibility of protecting millions of the subjects of the Queen from the consequences of scarcity and famine. Sir, whatever may be the result of these discussions, I feel severely the loss of the confidence of those from whom I heretofore received a most generous support. So far from expecting them, as some have said, to adopt my opinions, I perfectly recognise the sincerity with which they adhere to their own. I recognise their perfect right, on account of the admitted failure of my speculation, to withdraw from me their confidence. I honour their motives, but I claim, and always will claim, while entrusted with such powers and subject to such responsibility as the minister of this great country is entrusted with, and is subject to; I always will assert the right to give that advice which I conscientiously believe to be conducive to the general well-being. I was not considering, according to the language of the honourable member for Shrewsbury, what was the best bargain to make for a party. I was considering first what were the best measures to avert a great calamity and, as a secondary consideration, to relieve that interest, which I was bound to protect, from the odium of refusing to acquiesce in measures which I thought to be necessary for the purpose of averting that calamity. Sir, I cannot charge myself or my colleagues with having been unfaithful to the trust committed to us. I do not believe that the great institutions of this country have suffered during our administration of power.

The noble lord [1] says he hopes that the discussions which have threatened the maintenance of amicable relations with the United States [2] will be brought to a fortunate close. Sir, I think I can appeal to the course which we have pursued, against some obloquy, some misconstruction, some insinuations, that we were abandoning the honour of this country; I think I can appeal to the past experience of this Government, that it has been our earnest desire, by every effort consistently with the national honour, to maintain friendly relations with every country on the face of the globe. This principle, so long as we are entrusted with the management of public affairs, will continue to influence us in respect to the settlement of our unfortunate differences with the United States.

Sir, if I look to the prerogative of the Crown, if I look to the position of the Church, if I look to the influence of the aristocracy, I cannot charge myself with having taken any course inconsistent with Conservative principles, calculated to endanger the privileges of any branch of the Legislature, or any institutions of the country. My earnest wish has been, during my tenure of power, to impress the people of this country with a belief that the Legislature was animated by a sincere desire to frame its legislation upon the principles of equity and justice. I have a strong belief that the greatest object, which we or any other Government can contemplate, should be to elevate the condition of that class of the people with whom we are brought into no direct relationship by the exercise of the elective franchise. I wish to convince them that our object has been to apportion taxation, that we shall relieve industry and labour from any undue burden, and transfer it, so far as is consistent with the public good, to those who are better enabled to bear it. I look to the present peace of this country; I look to the absence of all disturbance, to the non-existence of any commitment for a seditious offence; I look to the calm that prevails in the public mind; I look to the absence of all disaffection; I look to the increased and growing public confidence on account of the course you have taken in relieving trade from restrictions and industry

[1] Lord J. Russell.
[2] Touching the Maine boundary and the Oregon territory.

from unjust burdens: and where there was dissatisfaction, I see contentment; where there was turbulence, I see there is peace; where there was disloyalty, I see there is loyalty: I see a disposition to confide in you, and not to agitate questions that are at the foundations of your institutions. Deprive me of power to-morrow, you can never deprive me of the consciousness that I have exercised the powers committed to me from no corrupt or interested motives, from no desire to gratify ambition, or attain any personal object; that I have laboured to maintain peace abroad consistently with the national honour and defending every public right, to increase the confidence of the great body of the people in the justice of your decisions, and by the means of equal law to dispense with all coercive powers, to maintain loyalty to the Throne and attachment to the Constitution, from a conviction of the benefit that will accrue to the great body of the people.

THE JEWISH DISABILITIES BILL

R. L. SHEIL

HOUSE OF COMMONS: 7 FEBRUARY 1848

SIR,—If the hon. the learned and exceedingly able gentleman who has just sat down (Mr. Walpole) had been a member of the House of Commons when the member for Tamworth brought forward the measure of Emancipation, the speech which he has this night pronounced against the Jews would have been fully as apposite upon that great historical occasion. With all his habits of fine forensic discrimination, I do not think that he can distinguish between the objections urged against the Catholic and against the Jew. He has, for example, strenuously insisted that, in the writ by which the sheriff is commanded to hold an election, a reference is made to the maintenance of the Anglican Church. That objection is nearly as strong when applied to the Unitarian, the Baptist, the Independent, and above all, to the professors of the religion to which it is my good fortune to belong. That men subject to all the duties should be deemed unworthy of the rights of Englishmen, appears to me to be a remarkable anomaly. The enjoyment of rights ought not to be dissociated from the liabilities to duties. A British subject ought in every regard to be considered a British citizen; and inasmuch as the professors of the most ancient religion in the world, which, as far as it goes, we not only admit to be true, but hold to be the foundation of our own, are bound to the performance of every duty which attaches to a British subject, to a full fruition of every right which belongs to a British citizen, they have, I think, an irrefragable title. A Jew born in England cannot transfer his allegiance from his Sovereign and his country; if he were to enter the service of a foreign Power engaged in hostilities with England, and were taken in arms, he would be accounted a traitor. Is a Jew an Englishman for no other purposes than those of condemnation? I am not aware of a single obligation to which other Englishmen are liable from which a Jew is exempt; and if his religion confers on him no sort of immunity, it ought not to affect him with any kind of disqualification.

It has been said, in the course of these discussions, that a Jew is not subject to penalties, but to privations. But what is privation but a synonym for penalty? Privation of life, privation of liberty, privation of property, privation of country, privation of right, privation of privilege—these are degrees widely distant indeed, but still degrees in the graduated scale of persecution. The Parliamentary disability that affects the Jew has been designated in the course of these debates by the mollified expressions to which men who impart euphemism to severity are in the habit of resorting; but most assuredly an exclusion from the House of Commons ought, in the House of Commons itself, to be regarded as a most grievous detriment. With the dignity, and the greatness, and the power of this, the first assembly in the world, the hardship of exclusion is commensurate. Some of the most prominent opponents of this measure are among the last by whom a seat in Parliament ought to be held in little account. On this branch of the case—the hardship of an exclusion from this House—I can speak as a witness, as well as an advocate. I belong to that great and powerful community which was a few years ago subject to the same disqualification that affects the Jew; and I felt that disqualification to be most degrading. Of myself I will not speak, because I can speak of the most illustrious person by whom that community was adorned. I have sat under the gallery of the House of Commons, by the side of Mr. O'Connell, during a great discussion on which the destiny of Ireland was dependent. I was with him when Plunket convinced, and Brougham surprised, and Canning charmed, and Peel instructed, and Russell exalted and improved. How have I seen him repine at his exclusion from the field of high intellectual encounter in those lists in which so many competitors for glory were engaged, and into which, with an injurious tardiness, he was afterwards admitted! How have I seen him chafe the chain which bound him down, but which, with an effort of gigantic prowess, he burst at last to pieces! He was at the head of millions of an organised and indissoluble people. The Jew comes here with no other arguments than those which reason and truth supply; but reason and truth are of counsel with him; and in this assembly, which I believe to represent, not only the high intelligence, but the highmindedness of England, reason will not long be baffled, and truth, in fulfilment of its great aphorism, will at last prevail.

I will assume that the exclusion from this House is a great privation, and I proceed to consider whether it be not a great wrong. Nothing but necessity could afford its justification; and of this plea we should be taught, by a phrase which has almost grown proverbial, to beware. Cardinal Caraffa relied upon necessity when he founded that celebrated tribunal whose practices are denounced by you, but upon whose maxims have a care lest you should unconsciously proceed. The sophistications of intolerance are refuted by their inconsistencies. If a Jew can choose, wherefore should he not be chosen? If a Jew can vote for a Christian, why should not a Christian vote for a Jew? Again, the Jew is admissible to the highest municipal employments; a Jew can be High Sheriff—in other words, he can empanel the jury by which the first Christian Commoner in England may be tried for his life. But if necessity is to be pleaded as a justification for the exclusion of the Jew, it must be founded on some great peril which would arise from his admission. What is it you fear? What is the origin of this Hebrewphobia? Do you tremble for the Church? The Church has something perhaps to fear from eight millions of Catholics, and from three millions of Methodists, and more than a million of Scotch seceders. The Church may have something to fear from the assault of sectaries from without, and still more to fear from a sort of spurious Popery, and the machinations of mitred mutiny from within; but from the Synagogue—the neutral, impartial, apathetic, and unproselytising Synagogue—the Church has nothing to apprehend. But it is said that the House will become unchristianised. The Christianity of the Parliament depends on the Christianity of the country, and the Christianity of the country is fixed in the faith, and inseparably intertwined with the affections of the people. It is as stable as England herself, and as long as Parliament shall endure, while the Constitution shall stand, until the great mirror of the nation's mind shall have been shattered to pieces, the religious feelings of the country will be faithfully reflected here. This is a security far better than can be supplied by a test which presents a barrier to an honest Jew, but which a scornful sceptic can so readily and so disdainfully overleap.

Reference has been made in the course of these discussions to the author of " The Decline and Fall of the Roman Empire." A name still more illustrious might have been cited. Was not the famous St. John—was not Bolingbroke, the fatally accomplished, the admiration of the admirable, to whom genius paid an almost idolatrous homage, and by whom a sort of fascination was exercised over all those who had the misfortune to approach him—was not the unhappy sceptic, by whom far more mischief to religion and morality must have been done than could be effected by half a hundred of the men by whom the Old Testament is exclusively received, a member of this House? Was he stopped by the test that arrests the Jew; or did he not trample upon it and ascend through this House to a sort of masterdom in England, and become the confidential and favourite adviser of his Sovereign? He was not only an avowed and ostentatious infidel, but he was swayed by a distempered and almost insane solicitude for the dissemination of his disastrous disbelief. Is it not then preposterous that a man by whom all revealed religion is repudiated, who doubts the immortality of the soul, doubts a future state of rewards and punishments, doubts in a superintending Providence, believes in nothing, fears nothing, and hopes for nothing, without any incentive to virtue, and without any restraint upon depravity excepting such as a sense of conventional honour or the promptings of a natural goodness may have given him—is it not, I say, preposterous, and almost monstrous, that such a man, for whom a crown of deadly nightshade should be woven, should be enabled, by playing the imposture of a moment and uttering a valueless formula at the table of the House, to climb to the pinnacle of power; and that you should slap the doors of the House with indignity upon a conscientious man who adheres to the faith in which he was born and bred; who believes in the great facts that constitute the foundation of Christianity; who believes in the perpetual existence of the nobler portion of our being; who believes in future retribution and in recompense to come; who believes that the world is taken care of by its almighty and everlasting Author; who believes in the mercy of God, and practises humanity to man; who fulfils the ten great injunctions in which all morality is comprised; whose ear was never deaf to the supplications of the suffering; whose hand is as open as day to charity; and whose life presents an exemplification of the precepts of the Gospel far more faithful than that of many a man by whom, in the name of the Gospel, his dishonouring and unchristian disabilities are most wantonly, most injuriously, and most opprobriously maintained? But where in the Scripture—in what chapter, in what text, in what single phrase—will you find an authority for resorting to the infliction of temporal penalty, or of temporal privation of any kind, as a means of propagating heavenly truth? You may

find an authority, indeed, in the writings of jurists and of
divines, and in the stern theology of those austere and haughty
churchmen by whom the Pharisaical succession, far better
than the Apostolical, is personally and demonstratively proved.
But you will not find it in the New Testament; you will not find
it in Matthew, nor in Mark, nor in Luke, nor in John, nor in the
espistles of the meek and humble men to whom the teaching
of all nations was given in charge; above all, you will not find
in it anything that was ever said, or anything that was ever
done, or anything that was ever suffered, by the Divine Author
of the Christian religion, who spoke the Sermon on the Mountain, who said that the merciful should be blessed, and who,
instead of ratifying the anathema which the people of Jerusalem
had invoked upon themselves, prayed for forgiveness for those
who knew not what they did, in consummating the Sacrifice
that was offered up for the transgressions of the world.

It was not by persecution, but despite of it—despite of
imprisonment, and exile, and spoliation, and shame, and death,
despite the dungeon, the wheel, the bed of steel, and the
couch of fire—that the Christian religion made its irresistible
and superhuman way. And is it not repugnant to common
reason, as well as to the elementary principles of Christianity
itself, to hold that it is to be maintained by means diametrically
the reverse of those by which it was propagated and diffused?
But, alas! for our frail and fragile nature, no sooner had the
professors of Christianity become the co-partners of secular
authority than the severities were resorted to which their perse-
cuted predecessors had endured. The Jew was selected as an
object of special and peculiar infliction. The history of that most
unhappy people is, for century after century, a trail of chains
and a trail of blood. Men of mercy occasionally arose to interpose in their behalf. St. Bernard—the great St. Bernard, the
last of the Latin Fathers—with a most pathetic eloquence took
their part. But the light that gleamed from the ancient turrets
of the Abbey of Clairvaux was transitory and evanescent. New
centuries of persecution followed; the Reformation did nothing
for the Jew. The infallibility of Geneva was sterner than the
infallibility of Rome. But all of us—Calvinists, Protestants,
Catholics—all of us who have torn the seamless garment into
pieces, have sinned most fearfully in this terrible regard.

It is, however, some consolation to know that in Roman
Catholic countries expiation of this guilt was commenced. In
France and in Belgium all civil distinction between the Pro-

testant and the Jew is at an end. To this Protestant country a great example will not have been vainly given. There did exist in England a vast mass of prejudice upon this question, which is, however, rapidly giving way. London, the point of Imperial centralisation, has been a noble manifestation of its will. London has advisedly, deliberately, and with benevolence aforethought, selected the most prominent member of the Jewish community as its representative, and united him with the first Minister of the Crown. Is the Parliament prepared to fling back the Jew upon the people, in order that the people should fling back the Jew upon the Parliament? That will be a dismal game, in the deprecation of whose folly and whose evils the Christian and the statesman should concur. But not only are the disabilities which it is the object of this measure to repeal at variance with genuine Christianity, but I do not hesitate to assert that they operate as impediments to the conversion of the Jews, and are productive of consequences directly the reverse of those for which they were originally designed. Those disabilities are not sufficiently onerous to be compulsory, but they are sufficiently vexatious to make conversion a synonym for apostacy, and to affix a stigma to an interested conformity with the religion of the State. We have relieved the Jew from the ponderous mass of fetters that bound him by the neck and by the feet; but the lines which we have left, apparently light, are strong enough to attach him to his creed, and make it a point of honour that he should not desert it.

There exists in this country a most laudable anxiety for the conversion of the Jews. Meetings are held, and money is largely subscribed for the purpose, but all these creditable endeavours will be ineffectual unless we make a restitution of his birthright to every Englishman, who professes the Jewish religion. I know that there are those who think that there is no such thing as an English, or a French, or a Spanish Jew. A Jew is but a Jew; his nationality, it is said, is engrossed by the hand of recollection and of hope, and the house of Jacob must remain for ever in a state of isolation among the strange people by whom it is encompassed. In answer to these sophistries I appeal to human nature. It is not wonderful that when the Jew was oppressed, and pillaged, and branded in a captivity worse than Babylonian, he should have felt upon the banks of the Thames, or of the Seine, or of the Danube, as his forefathers felt by the waters of the Euphrates, and that the psalm of exile should have found an echo in his heart. This is not strange; it would have been strange if it had been otherwise; but justice — even partial justice — has already operated a salutary change.

In the same measure in which we have already relaxed the laws against the Jews, that patriot instinct by which we are taught to love the land of our birth has been revised. British feeling has already taken root in the heart of the Jew, and for its perfect development nothing but perfect justice is required. To the fallacies of fanaticism give no heed. Emancipate the Jew—from the Statute-book of England be the last remnant of intolerance erased for ever; abolish all civil discriminations between the Christian and the Jew, fill his whole heart with the consciousness of country. Do this, and we dare be sworn that he will think, and feel, and fear, and hope as you do; his sorrow and his exultation will be the same; at the tidings of English glory his heart will beat with a kindred palpitation, and whenever there shall be need, in the defence of his Sovereign and of his country, his best blood, at your bidding, will be poured out with the same heroic prodigality as your own.

THE WAR WITH RUSSIA

RICHARD COBDEN

HOUSE OF COMMONS: 22 DECEMBER 1854

[*The then War Secretary, the Duke of Newcastle, had introduced a bill to raise a force of 15,000 foreigners, who were to be drilled in this country. Though opposed by the Conservative party, the bill was carried on December 22nd*].

To set myself right with those hon. gentlemen who profess to have great regard for liberty everywhere, I beg to state that I yield to no one in sympathy for those who are struggling for freedom in any part of the world; but I will never sanction an interference which shall go to establish this or that nationality by force of arms, because that invades a principle which I wish to carry out in the other direction—the prevention of all foreign interference with nationalities for the sake of putting them down. Therefore, while I respect the motives of those gentlemen, I cannot act with them. This admission, however, I freely make, that, were it likely to advance the cause of liberty, of constitutional freedom, and national independence, it would be a great inducement to me to acquiesce in the war, or, at all events, I should see in it something like a compensation for the multiplied evils which attend a state of war.

And now we come to what is called the statesman's ground for this war: which is, that it is undertaken to defend the Turkish empire against the encroachments of Russia—as a part of the scheme, in fact, for keeping the several states of Europe within those limits in which they are at present circumscribed. This has been stated as a ground for carrying on the present war with Russia; but, I must say, this view of the case has been very much mixed up with magniloquent phraseology, which has tended greatly to embarrass the question. The noble lord, the member for the city of London, was the first, I think, to commence these magniloquent phrases, in a speech at Greenock about last August twelvemonths, in which he spoke of our duties to mankind, and to the whole world; and he has often talked since of this war as one intended to protect the liberties of all Europe and of the civilised world. I remember, too, the phrases which the noble lord made use of at a city meeting, where he spoke of our being " engaged in a just and necessary war, for no immediate advantage, but for the defence of our ancient ally, and for the maintenance of the independence of Europe." Well, I have a word to say to the noble lord on that subject. Now, we are placed to the extreme west of a continent, numbering some 200,000,000 inhabitants; and the theory is, that there is great danger from a growing Eastern power, which threatens to overrun the Continent, to inflict upon it another deluge like that of the Goths and Vandals, and to eclipse the light of civilisation in the darkness of barbarism. But, if that theory be correct, does it not behove the people of the Continent to take some part in pushing back that deluge of barbarism? I presume it is not intended that England should be the Anacharsis Clootz of Europe; but that, at all events, if we are to fight for everybody, those, at least, who are in the greatest danger will join with us in resisting the common enemy. I am convinced, however, that all this declamation about the independence of Europe and the defence of civilisation will by-and-by disappear. I take it for granted then, that the statesman's object in this war is to defend Turkey against the encroachments of Russia, and so to set a barrier against the aggressive ambition of that great empire. That is the language of the Queen's speech. But have we not accomplished that object? I would ask, have we not arrived at that point? Have we not effected all that was proposed in the Queen's speech? Russia is now no longer within the Turkish territory; she has renounced all idea of invading Turkey; and now, as we are told by the noble lord, there have been put forward certain proposals from Russia, which are to serve as the basis of peace.

What are those proposals? In the first place, there is to be a joint protectorate over the Christians by the five great powers; there is to be a joint guarantee for the rights and privileges of the principalities; there is to be a revision of the rule laid down in 1841 with regard to the entrance of ships of war into the Bosphorus, and the Danube is to be free to all nations. These are the propositions that are made for peace, as we are told by the noble lord; and it is competent for us, I think, as a House of Commons, to offer an opinion as to the desirability of a treaty on those terms.

My first reason for urging that we should entertain those proposals is, that we are told that Austria and Prussia have agreed to them. Those two powers are more interested in this quarrel than England and France can be. Upon that subject I will quote the words of the noble lord the member for Tiverton, uttered in February last. The noble lord said:

" We know that Austria and Prussia had an interest in the matter more direct and greater than had either France or England. To Austria and Prussia it is a vital matter — a matter of existence—because, if Russia were either to appropriate any large portion of the Turkish territory, or even to reduce Turkey to the condition of a mere dependent state, it must be manifest to any man who casts a glance over the map of Europe, and who looks at the geographical position of these two powers with regard to Russia and Turkey, that any considerable accession of power on the part of Russia in that quarter must be fatal to the independence of action of both Austria and Prussia."

I entirely concur with the noble lord in his view of the interest which Austria and Prussia have in this quarrel, and what I want to ask is, Why should we seek greater guarantees and stricter engagements from Russia than those with which Austria and Prussia are content? They lie on the frontier of this great empire, and they have more to fear from its power than we can have; no Russian invasion can touch us until it has passed over them; and is it likely, if we fear, as we say we do, that Western Europe will be overrun by Russian barbarism—is it likely, I say, that since Austria and Prussia will be the first to suffer, they will not be as sensible to that danger as we can be? Ought we not rather to take it as a proof that we have somewhat exaggerated the danger which threatens Western Europe, when we find that Austria and Prussia are not so alarmed at it as we are? They are not greatly concerned about the danger, I think, or else they would join with England and France in a great battle to push it back. If, then, Austria and Prussia are ready to accept these proposals, why should not we be? Do you suppose that, if Russia really meditated an attack upon Germany—that if she had an idea of annexing the smallest portion of German territory, with only 100,000 inhabitants of Teutonic blood, all Germany would not be united as one man to resist her? Is there not a strong national feeling in that Germanic race?—are they not nearly 40,000,000 in number?—are they not the most intelligent, the most instructed, and have they not proved themselves the most patriotic people in Europe? And if they are not dissatisfied, why should we stand out for better conditions, and why should we make greater efforts and greater sacrifices to obtain peace than they? I may be told, that the people and the government of Germany are not quite in harmony on these points. (Cheers.) Hon. gentlemen who cheer ought to be cautious, I think, how they assume that governments do not represent their people. How would you like the United States to accept that doctrine with regard to this country? But I venture to question the grounds upon which that opinion is formed. I have taken some little pains to ascertain the feeling of the people in Germany on this war, and I believe that if you were to poll the population of Prussia—which is the brain of Germany—whilst nineteen-twentieths would say that in this quarrel England is right and Russia wrong; nay, whilst they would say they wished success to England as against Russia— yet, on the contrary, if you were to poll the same population as to whether they would join England with an army to fight against Russia, I believe, from all I have heard, that nineteen-twentieths would support their king in his present pacific policy.

But I want to know which is the advantage of having the vote of a people like that in your favour, if they are not inclined to join you in action? There is, indeed, a wide distinction between the existence of a certain opinion in the minds of a people and a determination to go to war in support of that opinion. I think we were rather too precipitate in transferring our opinion into acts; that we rushed to arms with too much rapidity; and that if we had abstained from war, continuing to occupy the same ground as Austria and Prussia, the result would have been that Russia would have left the principalities, and have crossed the Pruth, and that, without a single shot being fired, you would have accomplished the object for which you have gone to war. But what are the grounds on which we are to continue this war, when the Germans have acquiesced in the proposals of peace which have been made? Is it that war is a luxury? Is it that we are fighting—to use a cant phrase of Mr. Pitt's time—to secure indemnity for the past and security for the future? Are we to be the Don Quixotes of Europe, to go about fighting for every cause where we find that some one has been wronged? In most quarrels there is generally a little wrong on both sides; and, if we make up our minds always to interfere when any one is being wronged, I do not see always how we are to choose between the two sides. It will not do always to assume that the weaker party is in the right, for little states, like little individuals, are often very quarrelsome, presuming on their weakness, and not unfrequently abusing the forbearance which their weakness procures them. But the question is, on what ground of honour or interest are we to continue to carry on this war, when we may have peace upon conditions which are satisfactory to the great countries of Europe who are near neighbours of this formidable power? There is neither honour nor interest forfeited, I think, in accepting these terms, because we have already accomplished the object for which it was said this war was begun.

The questions which have since arisen, with regard to Sebastopol, for instance, are mere points of detail, not to be bound up with the original quarrel. I hear many people say, "We will take Sebastopol, and then we will treat for peace." I am not going to say that you cannot take Sebastopol—I am not going to argue against the power of England and France. I might admit, for the sake of argument, that you can take Sebastopol. You may occupy ten miles of territory in the Crimea for any time; you may build there a town; you may carry provisions and reinforcements there, for you have the command of the sea; but while you do all this, you will have no peace with Russia. Nobody who knows the history of Russia can think for a moment that you are going permanently to occupy any portion of her territory, and, at the same time, to be at peace with that empire. But admitting your power to do all this, is the object which you seek to accomplish worth the sacrifice which it will cost you? Can anybody doubt that the capture of Sebastopol will cost you a prodigious sacrifice of valuable lives; and, I ask you, is the object to be gained worth that sacrifice? The loss of treasure I will leave out of the question, for that may be replaced, but we can never restore to this country those valuable men who may be sacrificed in fighting the battles of their country—perhaps the most energetic, the bravest, the most devoted body of men that ever left these islands. You may sacrifice them, if you like, but you are bound to consider whether the object will compensate you for that sacrifice.

I will assume that you take Sebastopol; but for what purpose is it that you will take it, for you cannot permanently occupy the Crimea without being in a perpetual state of war with Russia? It is, then, I presume, as a point of honour, that you insist upon taking it, because you have once commenced the siege. The noble lord, speaking of this fortress, said: "If Sebastopol, that great stronghold of Russian power, were destroyed, its fall would go far to give that security to Turkey which was the object of the war." But I utterly deny that Sebastopol is the stronghold of Russian power. It is simply an outward and visible sign of the power of Russia; but, by destroying Sebastopol, you do not by any means destroy that power. You do not destroy or touch Russian power, unless you can permanently occupy some portion of its territory, disorder its industry, or disturb its government. If you can strike at its capital, if you can deprive it of some of its immense fertile plains, or take possession of those vast rivers which empty themselves into the Black Sea, then, indeed, you strike at Russian power; but, suppose you take Sebastopol, and make peace to-morrow; in ten years, I tell you, the Russian Government will come to London for a loan to build it up again stronger than before. And as for destroying those old, green fir-ships, you only do the emperor a service by giving him an opportunity for building fresh ones.

Is not the celebrated case of Dunkirk exactly in point? In 1713, at the treaty of Utrecht, the French king, under sore necessity, consented to destroy Dunkirk. It had been built under the direction of Vauban, who had exhausted his genius and the coffers of the state in making it as strong as science and money could make it. The French king bound himself to demolish it, and the English sent over two commissioners to see the fortress thrown to the ground, the jetties demolished and cast into the harbour, and a mole or bank built across the channel leading into the port; and you would have thought Dunkirk was destroyed once and for ever. There was a treaty binding the king not to rebuild it, and which on two successive occasions was renewed. Some years afterwards a storm came and swept away the mole or bank which blocked up the channel, by which accident ingress and egress were restored; and shortly afterwards, a war breaking out between England and Spain, the French Government took advantage of our being engaged elsewhere, and rebuilt the fortifications on the sea side, as the historian tells us, much stronger than before. The fact is recorded, that in the Seven Years' War, about forty years afterwards, Dunkirk, for all purposes of aggression by sea, was more formidable than ever. We had in that case a much stronger motive for destroying Dunkirk than we can ever have in the case of Sebastopol; for in the war which ended in the peace of Utrecht, there were 1600 English merchant vessels, valued at £1,250,000, taken by privateers which came out of Dunkirk.

Then again in the middle of the last century, we destroyed Cherbourg, and during the last war we held possession of Toulon; but did we thereby destroy the power of France? If we could have got hold of some of her fertile provinces—if we could have taken possession of her capital, or struck at her vitals, we might have permanently impoverished and diminished her power and resources; but we could not do it by the simple demolition of this or that fortress. So it would be in this case—we might take Sebastopol, and then make peace; but there would be the rankling wound—there would be venom in the treaty which would determine Russia to take the first opportunity of reconstructing this fortress. There would be storms, too, there, which would destroy whatever mole we might build across the harbour of Sebastopol, for storms in the Black Sea are more frequent, as we know, than in the Channel; but even if Sebastopol were utterly destroyed, there are many places on the coast of the Crimea which might be occupied for a similar purpose.

But then comes the question, Will the destruction of Sebastopol give security to the Turks? The Turkish empire will only be safe when its internal condition is secure, and you are not securing the internal condition of Turkey while you are at war; on the contrary, I believe you are now doing more to demoralise the Turks and destroy their government than you could possibly have done in time of peace. If you wish to secure Turkey, you must reform its government, purify its administration, unite its people, and draw out its resources; and then it will not present the spectacle of misery and poverty that it does now. Why, you yourselves have recognised the existing state of Turkey to be so bad that you intend to make a treaty which shall bind the five powers to a guarantee for the better treatment of the Christians. But have you considered well the extent of the principle in which you are embarking? You contemplate making a treaty, by which the five powers are to do that together which Russia has hitherto claimed to do herself. What sort of conclusion do you think disinterested and impartial critics—people in the United States, for instance—will draw from such a policy? They must come to the conclusion that we have been rather wrong in our dealings with Russia, if we have gone to war with her to prevent her doing that very thing which we ourselves propose to do, in conjunction with the other powers. If so much mischief has sprung from the protectorate of one power, Heaven help the Turks when the protectorate of the five powers is inaugurated! But, at this very moment, I understand that a mixed commission is sitting at Vienna, to serve as a court of appeal for the Danubian principalities; in fact, that Moldavia and Wallachia are virtually governed by a commission representing Austria, England, France, and Turkey.

Now, this is the very principle of interference against which I wish to protest. From this I derive a recognition of the exceptional internal condition of Turkey, which, I say, will be your great difficulty upon the restoration of peace. Well, then, would it not be more statesman-like in the Government, instead of appealing, with clap-trap arguments, to heedless passions out of doors, and telling the people that Turkey has made more progress in the career of regeneration during the last twenty years than any other country under the sun, at once to address themselves to the task before them—the reconstruction of the internal system of that empire? Be sure this is what you will have to do, make peace when you may; for everybody knows that, once you withdraw your support and your agency from her, Turkey must immediately collapse, and sink into a state of anarchy. The fall of Sebastopol would only make the condition of Turkey the worse; and, I repeat, that your real and most serious difficulty will begin when you have to undertake the management of that country's affairs, after you withdraw from it, and when you will have to re-establish her as an independent state. I would not have said a word about the condition of Turkey, but for the statement twice so jauntily made about her social progress by the noble lord the member for Tiverton. Why, what says the latest traveller in that country on this head? Lord Carlisle, in his recent work, makes the following remarks on the state of the Mahometan population, after describing the improving condition of the Porte's Christian subjects:

"But when you leave the partial splendours of the capital and the great state establishments, what is it you find over the broad surface of a land which nature and climate have favoured beyond all others, once the home of all art and all civilisation? Look yourself — ask those who live there — deserted villages, uncultivated plains, banditti-haunted mountains, torpid laws, a corrupt administration, a disappearing people."

Why, the testimony borne by every traveller, from Lamartine downwards, is, that the Mahometan population is perishing—is dying out from its vices, and those vices of a nameless character. In fact, we do not know the true social state of Turkey, because it is indescribable; and Lord Carlisle, in his work, says that he is constrained to avoid referring to it. The other day, Dr. Hadly, who had lately returned from Turkey, where he had a near relation who had been physician to the embassy for about thirty-five years, stated in Manchester that his relative told him that the population of Constantinople, into which there is a large influx from the provinces, has considerably diminished during the last twenty years, a circumstance which he attributes to the indescribable vices of the Turks. Now, I ask, are you doing anything to promote habits of self-reliance or self-respect among this people by going to war in their behalf? On the contrary, the moment your troops landed at Gallipoli, the activity and energy of the French killed a poor pacha there, who took to his bed, and died from pure distraction of mind; and from that time to this you have done nothing but humiliate and demoralise the Turkish character more than ever. I have here a letter from a friend, describing the conflagration which took place at Varna, in which he says, it was curious to see how our sailors, when they landed to extinguish the fire in the Turkish houses, thrust the poor Turks aside, exactly as if they had been so many infant-school children in England. Another private letter, which I recently received from an officer of high rank in the Crimea, states:

" We are degrading the Turk as fast as we can; he is now the scavenger of the two armies as far as he can be made so. He won't fight, and his will to work is little better; he won't be trusted again to try the former, and now the latter is all he is allowed to do. When there are entrenchments to be made, or dead to be buried, the Turks do it. They do it as slowly and lazily as they can, but do it they must. This is one way of raising the Turk; it is propping him up on one side to send him headlong down a deeper precipice on the other."

That is what you are doing by the process that is now going on in Turkey. I dare say you are obliged to take the whole command into your own hands, because you find no native power —no administrative authority in that country; and you cannot rely on the Turks for anything. If they send an army to the Crimea, the sick are abandoned to the plague or the cholera, and having no commissariat, their soldiers are obliged to beg a crust at the tents of our men. Why, sir, what an illustration you have in the facts relating to our sick and wounded at Constantinople of the helpless supineness of the Turks! I mention these things, as the whole gist of the Eastern question lies in the difficulty arising from the prostrate condition of this race.

Your troops would not be in this quarter at all, but for the anarchy and barbarism that reign in Turkey.

Well, you have an hospital at Scutari, where there are some thousands of your wounded. They are wounded Englishmen, brought there from the Crimea, where they have gone, 3000 miles from their own home, to fight the battles of the Turks. Would you not naturally expect that when these miserable and helpless sufferers were brought to the Turkish capital, containing 700,000 souls, those in whose cause they have shed their blood would at once have a friendly and generous care taken of them? Supposing the case had been that these wounded men had been fighting for the cause of Prussia, and that they had been sent from the frontiers of that country to Berlin, which has only half the population of Constantinople, would the ladies of the former capital, do you think, have allowed these poor creatures to have suffered from the want of lint or of nurses? Does not the very fact that you have to send out everything for your wounded prove either that the Turks despise and detest, and would spit upon you, or that they are so feeble and incompetent as not to have the power of helping you in the hour of your greatest necessity? The people of England have been grossly misled regarding the state of Turkey. I am bound to consider that the noble lord the member for Tiverton expressed his honest convictions on this point; but certainly the unfortunate ignorance of one in his high position has had a most mischievous effect on the public opinion of this country, for it undoubtedly has been the prevalent impression out of doors that the Turks are thoroughly capable of regeneration and self-government—that the Mahometan population are fit to be restored to independence, and that we have only to fight their battle against their external enemies, in order to enable them to exercise the functions of a great power. A greater delusion than this, however, I believe, never existed in any civilised state.

Well, if, as I say is the case, the unanimous testimony of every traveller—German, French, English, and American—for the last twenty years, attests the decay and helplessness of the Turks, are you not wasting your treasure and your men's precious lives before Sebastopol in an enterprise that cannot in the least aid the solution of your real difficulty? If you mean to take the Emperor of Russia eventually into your counsels—for this is the drift of my argument—if you contemplate entering into a quintuple alliance, to which he will be one of the parties, in order to manipulate the shattered remains of Turkey, to reconstitute or revise her internal polity, and maintain her independence, what folly it is to continue fighting against the power that you are going into partnership with; and how absurd in the extreme it is to continue the siege of Sebastopol, which will never solve the difficulty, but must envenom the state with which you are to share the protectorate, and which is also the nearest neighbour of the power for which you interpose, and your efforts to reorganise which, even if there be a chance of your accomplishing that object, she has the greatest means of thwarting! Would it not be far better for you to allow this question to be settled by peace than to leave it to the arbitrament of war, which cannot advance its adjustment one inch?

I have already adduced an illustration from the history of this country, as an inducement for your returning to peace. I will mention another. We all remember the war with America, into which we entered in 1812, on the question of the right of search, and other cognate questions relating to the rights of neutrals. Seven years before that war was declared, public opinion and the statesmen of the two countries had been incessantly disputing upon the questions at issue, but nothing could be amicably settled respecting them, and war broke out. After two years of hostilities, however, the negotiators on both sides met again, and fairly arranged the terms of peace. But how did they do this? Why, they agreed in their treaty of peace not to allude to what had been the subject-matter of the dispute which gave rise to the war, and the question of the right of search was never once touched on in that treaty. The peace then made between England and America has now lasted for forty years; and what has been the result? In the meantime, America has grown stronger, and we, perhaps, have grown wiser, though I am not quite so sure of that. We have now gone to war again with a European power, but we have abandoned those belligerent rights about which we took up the sword in 1812. Peace solved that difficulty, and did more for you than war ever could have done; for, had you insisted at Ghent on the American people recognising your right to search their ships, take their seamen, and seize their goods, they would have been at war with you till this hour, before they would have surrendered these points, and the most frightful calamities might have been entailed on both countries by a protracted struggle.

Now apply this lesson to the Eastern question. Supposing you agree to terms of peace with Russia, you will have your hands full in attempting to ameliorate the social and political system of Turkey. But who knows what may happen with regard to Russia herself in the way of extricating you from your difficulty? That difficulty, as respects Russia, is no doubt very much of a personal nature. You have to deal with a man of great, but, as I think, misguided energy, whose strong will and indomitable resolution cannot easily be controlled. But the life of a man has its limits; and certainly, the Emperor of Russia, if he survive as many years from this time as the duration of the peace between England and America, will be a most extraordinary phenomenon. You can hardly suppose that you will have a great many years to wait before, in the course of nature, that which constitutes your chief difficulty in the present war may have passed away. It is because you do not sufficiently trust to the influence of the course of events in smoothing down difficulties, but will rush headlong to a resort to arms, which never can solve them, that you involve yourselves in long and ruinous wars. I never was of opinion that you had any reason to dread the aggressions of Russia upon any other state. If you have a weak and disordered empire like Turkey, as it were, next door to another that is more powerful, no doubt that tends to invite encroachments; but you have two chances in your favour —you may either have a feeble or differently-disposed successor acceding to the throne of the present Czar of Russia, or you may be able to establish some kind of authority in Turkey that will be more stable than its present rule. At all events, if you effect a quintuple alliance between yourselves and the other great powers, you will certainly bind Austria, Prussia, and France to support you in holding Russia to the faithful fulfilment of the proposed treaty relating to the internal condition of Turkey. Why not, then, embrace that alternative instead of continuing the present war? because, recollect that you have accomplished the object which her Majesty in her gracious speech last session stated that she had in view in engaging in this contest. Russia is no longer invading the Turkish territory; you are now rather invading Russia's own dominions, and attacking one of her strongholds at the extremity of her empire, but, as I contend, not assailing the real source of her power. Now, I say you may withdraw from Sebastopol without at all compromising your honour.

By-the-by, I do not understand what is meant when you say that your honour is staked on your success in any enterprise of this kind. Your honour may be involved in your successfully rescuing Turkey from Russian aggression; but, if you have accomplished that task, you may withdraw your forces from before Sebastopol without being liable to reproach for the sacrifice of your national honour.

I have another ground for trusting that peace would not be again broken, if you terminate hostilities now. I believe that all parties concerned have received such a lesson, that they are not likely soon to rush into war again. I believe that the Emperor of Russia has learnt, from the courage and self-relying force displayed by our troops, that an enlightened, free, and self-governed people is a far more formidable antagonist than he had reckoned upon, and that he will not so confidently advance his semi-barbarous hordes to cope with the active energy and inexhaustible resources of the representatives of Western civilisation. England also has been taught that it is not so easy as she imagined to carry on war upon land against a state like Russia, and will weigh the matter well in future before she embarks in any such conflict. . . .

Now, what do you intend to do if your operations before Sebastopol should fail? The Secretary at War tells us that "Sebastopol must be taken this campaign, or it will not be taken at all." If you are going to stake all upon this one throw of the dice, I say that it is more than the people of England themselves had calculated upon. But if you have made up your minds that you will have only one campaign against Sebastopol, and that, if it is not taken then, you will abandon it, in that case, surely, there is little that stands between you and the proposals for peace on the terms I have indicated.

I think you will do well to take counsel from the hon. member for Aylesbury [Mr. Layard], than whom—although I do not always agree with him in opinion—I know nobody on whose authority I would more readily rely in matters of fact relating to the East. That hon. gentleman tells you that Russia will soon have 200,000 men in the Crimea; and if this be so, and this number is only to be " the beginning," I should say, now is the time, of all others, to accept moderate proposals for peace.

Now, mark, I do not say that France and England cannot succeed in what they have undertaken in the Crimea. I do not set any limits to what these two great countries may do, if they persist in fighting this duel with Russia's force of 200,000 men in the Crimea; and, therefore, do not let it be said that I offer any discouragement to my fellow-countrymen; but what I come back to is the question—what are you likely to get that will compensate you for your sacrifice? The hon. member for

Aylesbury also says, that " the Russians will, next year, overrun Asiatic Turkey, and seize Turkey's richest provinces "—they will probably extend their dominion over Asia Minor down to the sea-coast. The acquisition of these provinces would far more than compensate her for the loss of Sebastopol. I suppose you do not contemplate making war upon the plains in the interior of Russia, but wish to destroy Sebastopol; your success in which I have told you, I believe, will only end in that stronghold being rebuilt, ten years hence or so, from the resources of London capitalists. How, then, will you benefit Turkey—and especially if the prediction is fulfilled regarding Russia's overrunning the greater portion of Asiatic Turkey? I am told, also, that the Turkish army will melt away like snow before another year; and where, then, under all these circumstances, will be the wisdom or advantage in carrying on the war?

I have now, sir, only one word to add, and that relates to the condition of our army in the Crimea. We are all, I dare say, constantly hearing accounts, from friends out there, of the condition, not only of our own soldiers, but also of the Turks, as well as of the state of the enemy. What I have said about the condition of the Turks will, I am sure, be made as clear as daylight, when the army's letters are published and our officers return home. But as to the state of our own troops, I have in my hand a private letter from a friend in the Crimea, dated the 2nd of December last, in which the writer says:

" The people of England will shudder when they read of what this army is suffering—and yet they will hardly know one-half of it. I cannot imagine that either pen or pencil can ever depict it in its fearful reality. The line, from the nature of their duties, are greater sufferers than the artillery, although there is not much to choose between them. I am told, by an officer of the former, not likely to exaggerate, that one stormy, wet night, when the tents were blown down, the sick, the wounded, and the dying of his regiment, were struggling in one fearful mass for warmth and shelter."

Now, if you consult those brave men, and ask what their wishes are, their first and paramount desire would be to fulfil their duty. They are sent to capture Sebastopol, and their first object would be to take that strong fortress, or perish in the attempt. But, if you were able to look into the hearts of these men, to ascertain what their longing, anxious hope has been, even in the midst of the bloody struggle at Alma or at Inkerman, I believe you would find it has been, that the conflict in which they were engaged might have the effect of sooner restoring them again to their own hearths and homes. Now, I say that the men who have acted so nobly at the bidding of their country are entitled to that country's sympathy and consideration; and if there be no imperative necessity for further prosecuting the operations of the siege, which must—it will, I am sure, be admitted by all, whatever may be the result—be necessarily attended with an immense sacrifice of precious lives—unless, I say, you can show that some paramount object will be gained by contending for the mastery over those forts and ships, you ought to encourage her Majesty's Government to look with favour upon the propositions which now proceed from the enemy; and then, if we do make mistakes in accepting moderate terms of peace, we shall, at all events, have this consolation, that we are erring on the side of humanity.

ON THE EASTERN CRISIS & THE DANGER OF WAR

JOHN BRIGHT

BIRMINGHAM: 13 JANUARY 1878

[*The annual meeting of the members of the Borough of Birmingham was held this year at a somewhat earlier date than usual, in consequence of the fact that the session of Parliament began at an unusually early period. John Bright took occasion to dwell on the menacing appearance of affairs in Eastern Europe, and to contrast the popular sentiment which led to the Crimean war with the general determination of the English people to take no part in the existing complications.*]

THIS meeting, as you know, has been called some days earlier than was some time ago intended, and you know, also, that Parliament has been summoned about three weeks before the usual time. It is because Parliament has been summoned so early that this meeting has been called so early. In ordinary times the summoning of Parliament creates a considerable interest in the country, but, on the whole, I think it is an interest rather of a pleasurable kind. On this occasion the announcement that Parliament was to meet on the 17th of January had the effect of creating great anxiety; in some cases I have heard it described as consternation, and in all the centres of trade it has caused a certain depression which has been sensibly felt. I am driven to the conclusion, at which I think a large portion of the people have arrived, that the cause of all this is not a fear of Parliament, but a want of confidence in the Administration. We have been passing through something like a crisis, and we have had no decisive voice from the Government. In point of fact, if one body of men has said that the Government has spoken in a particular way, the next body of men that you meet would tell you that the Government intended something entirely different. Of one thing, however, we may be quite sure, that the question which fills the mind of the people at this hour, and which has filled it for a long time back, is the great and solemn question of peace or war—and I doubt whether it would be possible to submit to any people a greater question than that.

There are many in this hall who remember a period, about twenty-three years ago, when the same question was submitted to the nation which the nation at this moment is considering, and that is, whether peace or war is the true policy and the true interest of this people. At that time the conclusion to which the people came was a conclusion in favour of war. They followed a Government that, unwisely as I thought then, and as most people think now, threw them into war. I think we may take some lesson from that war. I read a short time ago in a very influential newspaper—a newspaper which had supported the war of 1854—that it was a pity to go back at all to that question, that circumstances had entirely changed, and that men who were in favour of that war might very justly and properly be against a repetition of it. Now, for my share, I believe the arguments at the present moment for war are as strong as they were in 1854—and in point of fact, as I believe the war then had no just argument in its support, so I think that now there is no sound argument that can be brought forward to induce this people to countenance any entrance into the existing conflict. As to not going back to the past, what is common with individuals? Nothing is more common and nothing more wise than to look back. One of our poets has said:

> "'Tis greatly wise to talk with our past hours
> And ask them what report they bore to Heaven."

And how does a man become wiser as he grows older but by looking back upon the past, and by learning from the mistakes that he has made in his earlier years? And that which is true of an individual must surely also be true of a nation with regard to its foreign policy.

At that time the public mind was filled with falsehoods, and it was in a state which we might describe by saying that it became almost drunk with passion. With regard to Russia, you recollect, many of you, what was said of her power, of her designs, of the despotism which ruled in Russia, of the danger which hung over all the freedom of all the countries of Europe. And the error was not confined to a particular class. It spread from the cottage to all classes above, and it did not even spare those who were within the precincts of the throne. It was not adopted by the clergy of the Church of England only, but by the ministers of the Nonconformist bodies also. The poison had spread everywhere. The delusion was all-pervading. The mischief

seemed universal, and, as I know to my cost, it was scarcely
worth while to utter an argument or to bring forth a fact against
it. Well, we had a war for two years, and we know what was
its result; at least we know something of it. We know that the
naval arsenal at Sebastopol was to a large extent destroyed—
that the Russian fleet was sunk in the harbour of Sebastopol.
We know that when the treaty of peace came to be negotiated
in 1856 Russia was forced to consent to a limitation of her fleet
in the Black Sea, in order that she might never in future have
a fleet that could menace the security of Turkey. Now, there
was a certain cost that was necessarily paid for these things.
Some people consider that the cost, when they are going into a
war or when they are in it, is not of much consequence. I take
a different view. I think the loss of 40,000 men in the prime of
life, in their full powers—40,000 men killed in battle, dying
from wounds, dying from horrible maladies in horrible hospitals
—I think that is something, and I think the payment of
100,000,000*l*. sterling—and that war cost us far more—is a
serious thing for a country where there are so many poor people
and so many families who live only to-day on the produce of
the labour of yesterday. But then the loss we suffered was a
very small loss compared to the whole loss. I saw the other day
a note in a work to which I will refer by and by, which said that
90,000 Russians were buried on the north side of the city of
Sebastopol during that siege, and it was stated in the House
of Lords—I think by Lord Lansdowne during the war—that up
to the time of the death of the Emperor of Russia—the Emperor
Nicholas—240,000 Russians had died or been killed, and it is
stated upon good authority that the whole loss in men to the
Russians during that two years' war was not less than 500,000.
So that by adding our loss, and the French loss, and the Turkish
loss, and the Sardinian loss, Mr. Kinglake reckons that the whole
cost of the two years of that war was little if any less than
1,000,000 human lives.

Now, it cannot be wrong, and it cannot be unwise, that we
should look back and see what that war cost and what it gained.
The result of it was that Russia, for the time and in that particular part of her empire in the Crimea, was vanquished, and
a treaty of peace was agreed to at Paris in the year 1856. Now
I want to show you just for a moment how mistaken were some
of the opinions that were expressed at the time. I will only
give you two little extracts. In February of 1854 the *Times*
newspaper, which may be taken to be a wide representation, a

fair representation, of a vast amount of opinion in this country, said:

"To destroy Sebastopol is nothing less than to demolish the entire fabric of Russian ambition in those very regions where it is most dangerous to Europe. This feat, and this only, would have really promoted the solid and durable objects of the war."

Now, Sebastopol was destroyed, and the Russian fleet then existing was sunk by the Russians to bar the entrance to the harbour of Sebastopol, and Russia was limited for the future so that she should never have a fleet that could be a menace or be any danger to Turkey. Well, the *Times* was not the only authority which made a statement of this kind. There is a work, published lately, to which I will for a moment refer—that is, the third volume of the "Life of the Prince Consort." It is a book which I have read with intense interest, many parts of it with a painful interest. It is a book which gives you an exalted and, I believe, a true picture of the greatness and the nobleness of the character of the late Prince Consort. It is a book to which no doubt her Majesty the Queen has contributed the main portion of the facts and of the contents. In this work she has built up a monument, which probably will last as long as our language, of the greatness and the nobleness of the Prince. I doubt not it will last longer than any of those monuments of bronze or marble by which it has been sought to commemorate his name and his character.

Well, in this book there are things, I have said, of painful interest. I have seen some criticisms upon it which go the length of saying that they think the book had better not have been published now, as it is calculated to excite unfriendly feelings to Russia. I have learned rather a different lesson from it. I think it is impossible for anybody of intelligent and impartial judgment to read the book through without coming to the conclusion that the occurrence of that war was an enormous error on the part of our statesmen, and that we are bound now by all regard for our country utterly to condemn it. I will give you just one paragraph from one of the Prince's letters, or, rather, from a memorandum that was submitted to the Government, I think in 1854. He was referring to certain expectations held out to the House of Commons by Lord John Russell as to what the war should result in, and he says:

"I find that the impossibility of allowing Russia to retain her threatening armaments in the Crimea was one of the most prominent of these expectations and the one which gave most satisfaction to the House. Now that vast treasure and the best English blood have been profusely expended towards obtaining that object, the nation has a right to expect that any peace contemplated by the Government should fully and completely realise it."

He admits afterwards during the negotiations that the peace was not such a peace as they would have wished to have had, but it was a peace which was much better than continuing the war with the complications there were then in Europe. But what happened when you had destroyed Sebastopol, and when the fleet was sunk, and when you had limited their fleet in the future by the Treaty of Paris? If you will step over to the year 1871 you will find that the main article of the treaty—the limitation of the Russian fleet in the Black Sea, the article to which the Russians were, I suppose, more opposed than to any other, because they considered it was more humiliating—that article was surrendered by our Government and by other Governments of Europe—I will not say actually without remonstrance, though I think I might almost say so, but without any strong remonstrance, and without anything like a blow; so that everything has failed. You destroyed a large number of lives, you spent the money, and you disturbed the peace of Europe, and the end of it was that nothing whatsoever was gained, because fifteen years afterwards everything was relinquished, or nearly everything, for which war had been waged. The Russian fleet is no longer limited in the Black Sea. Turkey, for which you made war, is not only not safe, but is in much greater danger than she ever was before; and it is obvious, from what we have seen, that, in comparison with Turkey, Russia is just as powerful as if the war of 1854 had never taken place, and at that time we had, as you recollect, a great ally in the Emperor of the French.

Now, I should like to tell you what sort of an ally he was; fortunately we have not one of that kind now. France never was in favour of the war. The Emperor went into the war, not because he cared about Turkey or cared about Russia, but because he wanted to associate himself with respectable old monarchical institutions—with a respectable old monarchically governed country. He thought that some things that had taken place in his career might be forgotten, and that he would come out able to enter the very high society of the sovereigns of Europe. Now, what the Prince says about this is as follows: writing to his uncle Leopold, the late King of the Belgians, in December, 1855, he says, " I really believe there is not a single soul in France who ever gave himself the smallest concern about the maintenance of the Turkish empire." And he says further, in the year 1856, in February, " We know that England is hated all over the Continent, that even in France it is the Emperor, and the Emperor alone, who is with us body and soul; " and he added, " Our position in the Conference "—the Conference preceding the treaty of peace—" will be one of extreme difficulty, for, except the Emperor Napoleon, we have no one on our side." Therefore, whilst we were fighting the despotism of the Emperor Nicholas, we had as our principal ally the despotism of the Emperor Napoleon, and we had none of the sympathy of that great nation the French. More than 40,000 Frenchmen laid down their lives in the Crimea in alliance with us for a cause in which they had no interest, and in which their country had no sympathy.

At that time Europe was not with us, and, as you know, Europe is not with us now. In 1855, in May, the Prince says this: " The Crimea was chosen by France and England, forsaken by the rest of Europe, as the only vulnerable point of attack," and he says further, in 1854, " If there were a Germany, and a German sovereign in Berlin, it [that is, the calamity of this war] would never have happened." There is now a Germany, and there is a German Emperor in Berlin, yet the war has not been prevented. You will see, therefore, from this slight sketch that there is nothing but failure, nothing but disappointment in this page of the history of our country; and I want to ask you to-night, and to ask all those of my countrymen who may condescend to read what I am saying, I want to ask them whether they are willing to write such another page in our history—what shall I say?—shockingly terrible and bloody, and as utterly fruitless? Forsaken by Europe! We are forsaken by Europe now. Germany is not with us, Austria is not with us, Italy is not with us, France is not with us—we are alone. We only are constantly meddling, constantly doing or saying something which is supposed to be pleasant to the Turk, and which it is hoped, some people say—which it is often hoped—may be unpleasant to the Emperor of Russia.

Now I must ask you to consider for a moment why it is that

we are in this position, so different from the positions of the other nations of Europe. What interest have we at the east end of the Mediterranean which the other nations of Europe have not? We have only one point of interest, and they have it too, only we have it in a greater degree, and that is in the constant free maintenance of the passage through the Suez Canal. We have a vast dependency in India, and, therefore, in regard to military passage, and also in regard to trade—we, I suppose, furnish nearly three-fourths of all the shipping which passes through the canal—we have a greater interest in the canal being kept open than any other country in Europe has. That, of course, I admit. What a strange history has that canal? It is enough to teach us that we ought to examine carefully the declarations of great statesmen and Prime Ministers before we adopt a policy which they recommend to us. I recollect hearing Lord Palmerston denounce that canal. He condemned it as a thing not only of no advantage, but rather to be disliked by England; and he did not believe, if it was ever made, that it could be kept open. And he quoted, I think, the opinion of a distinguished railway engineer with a view to strengthen his argument. The consequence was that the canal was made almost entirely by French money, through the energy of M. Lesseps, who is a very eminent Frenchman, and I am not sure whether a single share in that company was held originally, or has been held from the beginning, by any native of this country.

I maintain that all Europe is interested in the canal, and all Europe would protest against any Power, be it the Khedive of Egypt or the Sultan of Turkey, or perhaps what is most unlikely of all, the Czar of Russia, that took any steps to prevent the free passage through the canal, or even dreamed of doing so. As a proof of it, it is, I believe, well known that all the Powers of Europe would be willing to combine with us and with the French company and with France for the purpose of declaring this canal not only a great national or European but a great world's work, and that under no conceivable circumstances shall any Power, or combination of Powers, be permitted to interfere with it. M. Lesseps, the French promoter of the canal, has over and over again made suggestions of this kind. They have been made to our Government, and I think it is a great misfortune, and have always thought so, that that plan was not adopted, and that the canal was not put in a condition of safety.

I think it is in a condition of safety now; but I mean in a condition of safety so clear and distinct and unquestionable that nobody could make use of it for the political objects for which it has been made use of lately. Now, why is it we cannot do this, why is it that at this moment, when talking about the canal in connection with Russia, that Mr. Cross in the House of Commons, among the interests he specified as those which England must maintain, mentioned this interest of the canal? I have heard a very eminent person on this side of the House say, and acknowledge to me, " As for the canal, I think that of the two the canal is in rather more danger from Turkey than it is from Russia." All this arises from an ignorance and, in some quarters, an ignorant jealousy of Russia. That ignorant jealousy has existed in this country for forty years past.

I was reading the other day a book of singular interest to me, the memoirs and correspondence of the late Senator Charles Sumner, a Senator of Massachusetts, in the United States. Charles Sumner was a personal friend of mine, and he corresponded with me for many years. In looking over his memoirs I came upon what I thought was a remarkable passage, which you will permit me to read to you. It is written in one of his letters from England in 1839. It was just previous to that time that there had been so much excitement in this country about Russia, and some people had really so nearly approached to a condition fit for Bedlam that they believed that the Russians were likely to come through the Baltic and to invade the east coast of England, and they persuaded the Government of that day— always too ready to be persuaded on things of this kind—to add 5000 men to the navy in order that the panic might be put an end to. It is like putting a plaster upon a sore. When people get into a panic of this kind they vote two millions or five millions of money, five thousand men to the navy, or five thousand men to the army, and then go to their beds and sleep soundly. All there is in it is that next morning they have the tax-gatherer, and they pay. At that time there was living in England a very eminent man, the late Lord Durham. He was a member of the Reform Cabinet; he was one of the members of the committee of that Cabinet who drew up the first Reform Bill. He was a man of very Liberal views; he wished the Cabinet of Lord Grey not to give us a 10l. franchise, but household franchise, and to accompany it with the ballot. I will tell you what sort of man he was. He had been Ambassador at the Court

of the Czar, at St. Petersburg, and Mr. Sumner says this of him,—
"I ventured to ask him what there was in the present reports with
regard to the hostile intentions of Russia towards England." "Not
a word of truth," he said, "I will give you leave to call me idiot if
there is a word of truth." He said that Russia was full of friendly
regard for England, and he pronounced the late Mr. Urquhart,
who died during the last autumn, somewhere in the South of
France, who was then going about the kingdom preaching
against Russia, a madman. Well, I have known Mr. Urquhart in
the House of Commons. I would not like to say a word against
him now that he is not here to answer for himself, but this I may
say without wrong, that he was a man so possessed of certain
notions that it was scarcely possible to believe him in a condition
for fairly reasoning upon them. He believed that the Czar
Nicholas managed the whole world by his diplomacy; he believed
Lord Palmerston was bribed by the Russian Government to sell
the liberties of Europe and the interests of this country to
Russia; he believed—and I have heard him say it in the most
positive manner—that the war in the Crimea was waged, not to
save Turkey, but to place Turkey in the hands of Russia, and
that if we would leave Turkey alone, and leave her to fight
Russia alone, Turkey was perfectly safe, and Russia would be
easily and finally vanquished. These were the views of Mr.
Urquhart, which I believe he held honestly, for he devoted years
of his life in preaching them, and Lord Durham said that Mr.
Urquhart, in preaching them, was acting like a madman, and
was utterly ignorant of the true state of things in Russia.

No nation, I believe, has been in disposition more friendly to
this nation than Russia. There is no nation on the Continent
of Europe that is less able to do harm to England, and there
is no nation on the Continent of Europe to whom we are less
able to do harm than we are to Russia. We are so separated
that it seems impossible that the two nations, by the use of
reason or common sense at all, could possibly be brought into
conflict with each other. We have India, and men tell you
that India is in jeopardy from Russia. I recollect a speech
made last session by Mr. Laing, who has been out to India as
Financial Minister, that was conclusive upon that point. But
there is one thing that Russia can do in India, and that may be
troublesome to us in another way, not in the way of war or of
conquest, but in the way of certain irritation and trouble. You
persuade the people of India by the writings of the press and

the speeches of public men in this country, that we run great hazard from the advance of Russia, and if you have enemies in India of course you feed their enmity by this language, and you make them, if they wish to escape from the government of England, turn naturally and inevitably to Russia as the Power that can help them. The interest of this country with regard to Russia in connection with India is an unbroken amity, and I am sure that that unbroken amity might be secured if we could get rid of the miserable jealousy that afflicts us.

I thought some time ago that we were approaching, and I trust still we are approaching, a better time. The present Emperor of Russia is not the one with whom we made the war. He is a man not given to military display. He is a man whose reign before this war was signalised chiefly by the grand act of the liberation of twenty millions of his people. He at least was willing to forget the unfortunate past. He consented that his only daughter, the loved child of his heart, should marry the son of the English Queen. And I thought that this was a great sign of a permanent reconciliation, and a very blessed promise of a prolonged peace; and although that has not borne in this political respect all the fruit one could have wished for, still I am delighted to believe that there is a great change growing, and a change for the better, and a change which I believe will be accelerated by what will take place when this unfortunate war comes to an end.

There are still the traditions of the Foreign Office. I once expressed—I was very irreverent towards such an ancient institution—the wish that the Foreign Office might some day be burned down; and at least, correcting myself, that if it should be burned down, that I hoped all its mad, and baneful, and wicked traditions would be burned with it. But these traditions still linger in the Foreign Office, and Lord Derby—to whom they are foreign—endeavouring to fill that eminent office, I believe with a true intention to serve his country, and to do right—has been made the victim of the traditions he finds in the office which he has filled for the last four or five years. But I say the heart of the nation is gradually changing. I met at dinner at a friend's house in Salford only the night before last an old friend of mine, and he came up to me and said, " Do you recollect me twenty-three or twenty-four years ago? You know I walked down Market Street with you that day when you came out of the Town Hall, where you had been hissed and hooted and maltreated, and where you were not allowed to speak to the constituents you were endeavouring to serve, and when you were not allowed to pass down the street without gross insult? " Well, now, a man may have an opinion in favour of peace, and the " dogs of war " will scarcely bark at him.

But still we cannot disguise from ourselves the fact that there is something of a war party in this country, and that it has free access to some, and indeed to not a few, of the newspapers of the London press. If there is any man here who thinks the question of our policy doubtful, if there is any man in the country who shall read what I say now who is in doubt, I ask him to look back to the policy of twenty-three years ago, and to see how it was then tried, and how it succeeded, or how it failed. The arguments were the same then exactly as they are now. The falsehoods were the same. The screechings and howlings of a portion of the press were just about the same. But the nation now—and if nations learned nothing, how long could they be sustained?—has learned something, and it has risen above this. I am persuaded that there is a great difference of opinion as to Russian policy in the main, or Turkish policy in this war, and men may pity especially the suffering on the one side or the suffering on the other—for my share, I pity the sufferings of both sides,—and whatever may be our differences of opinion, I think it is conclusively proved that the vast bulk of all the opinion that is influential in this country upon this question leads to this—that the nation is for a strict and rigid neutrality throughout this war.

It is a painful and terrible thing to think how easy it is to stir up a nation to war. Take up any decent history of this country from the time of William III until now—for two centuries, or nearly so—and you will find that wars are always supported by a class of arguments which, after the war is over, the people find were arguments they should not have listened to. It is just so now, for unfortunately there still remains the disposition to be excited on these questions. Some poet, I forget which it is, has said:

> "Religion, freedom, vengeance, what you will,
> A word's enough to raise mankind to kill;
> Some cunning phrase by faction caught and spread,
> That guilt may reign, and wolves and worms be fed."

" Some cunning phrase by faction caught and spread " like the

cunning phrase of "The balance of power," which has been
described as the ghastly phantom which the Government of this
country has been pursuing for two centuries and has never yet
overtaken. "Some cunning phrase" like that we have now of
"British interests." Lord Derby has said the wisest thing
that has been uttered by any member of this Administration
during the discussions on this war when he said that the greatest
of British interests is peace. And a hundred, far more than a
hundred, public meetings have lately said the same; and millions
of households of men and women have thought the same. To-
night we shall say "Amen" to this wise declaration. I am
delighted to see this grand meeting in this noble hall. This
building is consecrated to peace and to freedom. You are here
in your thousands, representing the countless multitudes outside. May we not to-night join our voices in this resolution,
that, so far as we are concerned, the sanguinary record of the
history of our country shall be closed—that we will open a new
page, on which shall henceforth be inscribed only the blessed
message of mercy and of peace?

FRANCHISE AND REFORM

BENJAMIN DISRAELI (LORD BEACONSFIELD)

House of Commons: 1867

*[Debate on the Third Reading of the Reform Bill passed in
that year.]*

Sir,—The debate of this evening commenced with what may be
described as two very violent speeches—that is, speeches very
abusive of the measure before the House, and very abusive of
the ministers who have introduced it. I am more anxious to
vindicate the measure than to defend the Government. But
it necessarily happens in questions of this character, which
have occupied the attention of Parliament for a long term of

years, that it is practically impossible to distinguish the measure from the ministry in any observations upon it. So much depends upon personal character and engagements, and upon the necessity of the time and the temper of the country, when a minister is called upon definitively to act, that it is perhaps impossible to separate, in the remarks which I have to offer to the House, a consideration of the conduct of the Government from the nature of the Bill which we now ask leave to read a third time. It is very easy for the noble lord the member of Stamford, while he treats of a question which has occupied the attention of Parliament for more than fifteen years, to quote some ambiguous expression which was used early in that period of fifteen years by Lord Derby, and then to cite some small passage in a speech made by myself in the year 1866. But I think that honourable gentlemen on both sides of the House will admit that to arrive at a just judgment of the conduct of public men, and of the character of the measures they propose, it is necessary to take larger and fuller views. Measures of this importance, and the conduct of those who may recommend them, are not to be decided by the quotation of a speech made in 1852, or of the remarks made in 1866. Now, Sir, I accept the challenge made by the noble lord. I will take that very term which he has himself fixed upon as the test of our conduct and our policy. I will throw my vision back over those fifteen years—to that very term of 1852, when we were called upon to undertake the responsibility of administration.

The question of Parliamentary Reform was becoming very rife in 1849 and 1850 and 1851. If I recollect right, it occupied the attention of Parliament when it first met in 1852, when we were sitting in Opposition, and therefore when we acceded to office, and to office for the first time, in the year 1852, although the question was not one which upon reflection men who were responsible for the conduct of affairs would have deemed necessary to treat, yet it was one upon which it was absolutely necessary that a cabinet should have some definite conclusions, and upon which it was quite certain the moment they acceded to office they would be called to express their opinion. It happened in that wise, for I think that within a month after we acceded to office Mr. Hume brought forward, as he was accustomed to do, the whole question of Parliamentary Reform in a very comprehensive manner; referring, not only to the franchise, but to the redistribution of seats, and many other matters connected with it. The cabinet had to meet and to decide upon the spirit in which they would encounter the motion of Mr. Hume, and I was the organ to express their opinions on the subject. The opinions I expressed upon that occasion from this very place were such as do not justify the remarks of the right honourable gentleman. They may not be fresh in the recollection of the House, but I will say only that upon that occasion, with the full authority of a unanimous Cabinet, expressing the opinion of Lord Derby's Government with regard to the question of Parliamentary Reform, I expressed our opinion that if the subject were again opened—and its immediate re-opening we deprecated—the fault which had been committed in 1832 in neglecting to give a due share of the representation to the working classes ought to be remedied. That was in the year 1852, when, with the full authority of the Cabinet, I said that no measure of Parliamentary Reform could be deemed satisfactory which did not remedy the great fault of the settlement of 1832. And I then contended, as I have done since, that before the settlement of 1832 franchises existed which were peculiar to the working classes, and that although the precise character of those franchises could not, perhaps, have been entirely defended, they should certainly not have been destroyed without the invention of fresh franchises more adapted to the times in which we live, and to the requirements of the classes concerned.

Therefore, it is quite clear that in 1852 our opinions upon Parliamentary Reform—for many of the members of that cabinet are members of the present—were such that the expressions of the right honourable gentleman opposite and the noble lord cannot for a moment be justified.

And, what Sir, occurred afterwards? When we were in Opposition for several years this question was constantly brought under the consideration of Parliament, and it continued to be patronised and encouraged by the then ministers of the Crown, who yet would not deal with it until the very last year of their existence as a cabinet; and then, after an official life of some six or seven years, they did introduce the subject to the consideration of Parliament, and left a Bill upon the table when they resigned their seals of office. It therefore became necessary for us in 1858 to consider the subject, and we did not conceal from ourselves for a moment the difficulties in treating it that we should have to encounter. But such was the situation of the question, such the state of the country with regard to it, such even the private counsel and encouragement of the

most influential of our predecessors in office, that we engaged
to consider the question, and to bring forward some measure
which we hoped might remove the difficulties that stood in
the way of general legislation, and to disembarrass political
life. We had then to consider the great question of the borough
franchise. It was proposed upon that occasion in the cabinet
of Lord Derby that the borough franchise should be founded
upon the principle of household suffrage. It is very true that
that proposition was not adopted, but it was not opposed, so
far as I can charge my memory, on any political ground; it
was not adopted by many members of the cabinet, because they
believed that if a scheme of that kind were brought forward it
would receive no support, generally speaking, in the country.
That opinion of Lord Derby's Government I may say was
ultimately formed on no mean knowledge; elaborate machinery
was had recourse to in order to obtain the information necessary
to form an accurate opinion on the subject, and the general
tenor of the information which reached us certainly forced us
to the conclusion that there was an insuperable objection on
the part of the constituencies at that time against any reduction
of the borough franchise whatever. That that was a true conclusion, and that the information which led to that conclusion
was correct, there can be no doubt, for although we were forced
to quit office by a resolution declaring that a reduction of the
borough franchise was expedient, those who succeeded us failed
in carrying any measure of that kind, and remained in office
for years without at all departing from their inaction.

But there is another feature in the policy of the Government
of 1859 with regard to this question which I have a right to
refer to, and, indeed, am bound to refer to, in vindication of
the conduct of the Government. Whatever difference of
opinion might have existed in the cabinet of Lord Derby, in
1859, on the question of establishing the borough franchise
on the principle of rated household suffrage, there was no
difference upon one point; the cabinet was unanimous, after
the utmost deliberation and with the advantage of very large
information upon the subject, that if we attempted to reduce
the borough qualification which then existed we must have
recourse to household suffrage, whatever might be the condition.
Upon that conclusion we acted, and I am at a loss to discover,
in the conduct of public men who have acted in the way I
have described, any foundation for the somewhat frantic attacks
which have been made upon us by the right honourable gentle-

man opposite, and for the bitter, though more temperately expressed, criticisms of the noble lord the member for Stamford. As probably the majority of the present House sat in the late Parliament, the House is well acquainted with the fortunes of the question of Parliamentary Reform during the years which followed the retirement of Lord Derby in 1859.

The question was unsuccessfully treated by the most powerful and popular minister this country has possessed for many years —by one, indeed, who at various times after 1859 apparently occupied a commanding position with reference to any question with which he proposed to deal; and it has so happened that every leading statesman of the day, every party representing any important section of power and opinion in the country who approached this subject, have all of them equally failed. Lord Russell failed, Lord Aberdeen failed, Lord Palmerston failed, Lord Derby failed, and we were called upon to reconsider the question when we came into office after a fresh failure by Lord Russell. It is said that we have brought forward a measure stronger than the one we opposed. If that be the case, it is no argument against our measure if it be one adapted to the requirements of the times. But, Sir, we who believe that there should be no reduction of the borough franchise other than what we propose, because there can be no sound resting-place between it and the present qualification, were perfectly justified in hesitating to accept a reduction of the franchise which might have disturbed the machinery of the State, and have resulted in consequences far more perilous than we believe can ensue from the measure we ask you to adopt. There had been for a considerable time a much-favoured plan before the public, and the object, or rather, I should say, the consequence of this plan, which may be described as a moderate reduction of the borough franchise, was the enfranchisement of a certain favoured portion of the working classes, who are always treated in this House and everywhere else publicly in terms of great eulogium, who are

Fed by soft dedication all day long,

and assured that they are very much superior to every other portion of the working classes. These were to be invested with the franchise on the implied condition that they were to form a certain Prætorian guard, and prevent every other portion of the working classes of this country from acquiring the privilege, and thus those other portions would be shut out from what is called the pale of the Constitution. This proposal, in different states and different degrees, was constantly before Parliament. We were greatly opposed to it, since we believed it was a dangerous policy, and we saw greater peril to the institutions of the country in admitting a small and favoured section of that kind into the political arena than in appealing to the sympathies of the great body of the people. The working classes will now probably have a more extensive sympathy with our political institutions, which, if they are in a healthy state, ought to enlist popular feeling because they should be embodiments of the popular requirements of the country.

It appeared to us that if this great change were made in the constitutional body there would be a better chance of arriving at the more patriotic and national feelings of the country than by admitting only a favoured section, who, in consideration of the manner in which they were treated, and the spirit in which they were addressed, together with the peculiar qualities which were ascribed to them, would regard themselves as marked out, as it were, from the rest of their brethren and the country, and as raised up to be critics rather than supporters of the Constitution. These were our views, and we retain the conviction that guided us in 1859, and from which if we have deviated, it was only for a moment, and because we thought that on this question it was impossible to come to any solution except in the spirit of compromise and mutual concession. We still adhered to the policy of 1859, and believed if you reduced the borough quali-fication — and some reduction was now inevitable — there was no resting-place until you came to a rating household suffrage.

Well, Sir, under these circumstances we acceded to power last year, and we found it was absolutely necessary to deal with this question; we came into power unpledged, and I have heard with some astonishment reproaches in regard to our change of opinion. I am not here to defend, to vindicate, or even to mitigate every expression I may have used on this subject during the course of many years, but I can appeal to the general tenor of the policy we have recommended. I have always said that the question of Parliamentary Reform was one which it was quite open to the Conservative party to deal with. I have said so in this House, and on the hustings, in the presence of my countrymen, a hundred times. I have always said, and I say so now, that when you come to a settlement of this question, you cannot be bound to any particular scheme, as if you were settling the duties on sugar, but dealing with the question on great constitutional principles, and which I hope to show have not been deviated from, you must deal with it also with a due regard to the spirit of the time and the requirements of the country. I will not dwell upon the excitement which then prevailed in the country, for I can say most sincerely that, without treating that excitement with contempt, or in any spirit analogous to contempt, we considered this question only with reference to the fair requirements of the country. But having to deal with this question, and being in office with a large majority against us, and finding that ministers of all colours of party and politics with great majorities, had failed to deal with it successfully, and believing that another failure would be fatal not merely to the Conservative party, but most dangerous to the country, we resolved to settle it if we could. Having accepted office unpledged, what was the course we adopted? Believing that it was a matter of the first state necessity that the question should be settled; knowing the majority was against us, and knowing the difficulties we had to deal with, being in a minority—and even with a majority our predecessors had not succeeded—after due deliberation we were of opinion that the only mode of arriving at a settlement was to take the House into council with us, and by our united efforts, and the frank communication of ideas, to attain a satisfactory solution.

I am in the recollection of the House: I ask whether that is not a faithful account of the situation? It was in harmony with these views that I placed resolutions on the table. It is very true that at that time—in the month of March or February it may be —you derided those resolutions and ridiculed the appeal; but reflection proved the policy was just, and you have adopted it. We have pursued the course which we felt to be the only one to bring this question to a happy termination, and your own good sense, or reflection, has convinced you that the original sneers were not well founded. You have all co-operated with us, and it is by that frank and cordial co-operation that we have arrived at the third reading. The noble lord the member for Stamford says that the Bill is no longer our Bill—that it has been enormously changed in consequence of our having accepted the ten conditions of the right honourable gentleman the member for South Lancashire, which he also informed the House the right honourable gentleman had so imperiously dictated. At the time there was some complaint of the imperious dictation of the right honourable gentleman; but it did not come from me: I can pardon those in Opposition who are inclined to be imperious, but I have no fault to find with the conditions that the right

honourable gentleman insisted upon, and which the noble lord
says I obsequiously observed.

What were those conditions? Let me recall them to the
House. In the first place, the right honourable gentleman
insisted—imperiously insisted—that the dual vote should be
given up. He declared his implacable hostility to the dual vote,
and the noble lord says the dual vote was thereupon given up.
It so happened, however, that the dual vote was given up one
fortnight before those conditions were so imperiously insisted
upon by the right honourable gentleman, and it was given up in
consequence of the unanimous reprobation of that political device
by the Conservative party: not a single gentleman on our side of
the House was in favour of it. That opinion was expressed in
writing and in this House by the right honourable member for
Oxfordshire; and, I will not say in consequence of his imperious
dictation, but because he expressed the unanimous feeling of our
friends, we took the earliest opportunity of signifying that the
dual vote should not be insisted on. Then the noble lord says
we gave up one of the bristling securities of the Bill—that of the
two years' residence. Well, we did not give that up obsequiously
because we divided the House upon it, and were defeated by a
large majority. Some of our friends voted against us, a great
many left the House, and the rest supported us under protest;
so that we had no very great Conservative encouragement to
stand up for these securities that we are told bristled round our
measure. I think the noble lord and the right honourable
gentleman have mistaken the character and spirit of the Conservative party when they describe the Government as leading
the party, when, as I believe, the party on this question has
always been in advance of the Government. There is not a
security that we have proposed that has not been objected to
by the Conservative party. I would recall to the recollection of
the House a celebrated meeting which took place in halls
supposed to be devoted to the conservation of the institutions of
the country, at which resolutions were absolutely passed——
(Mr. Sandford: No, No!) Well, passed with very little opposition. (Mr. Sandford: No, No!) Well, were they not passed at
all? (No!) Then am I to understand that the assembly broke
up in confusion with a unanimous reprobation of the policy of
Her Majesty's Government on this particular point of securities?

What was the next important condition imperiously dictated
and obsequiously accepted? It was the great reduction of the
county franchise. Now, what happened about the county

franchise? We proposed a £15 rating franchise. An honourable gentleman opposite proposed £10. I was prepared to vindicate the policy of the Government. A meeting of county gentlemen then took place, at which resolutions were certainly passed, because they were forwarded to me. The Government were entreated by that meeting to accept the county franchise at a lower rate than we proposed. Is not this increased evidence that, instead of hurrying the party into this abyss of danger, it was with very great difficulty that we could keep them back? Then comes the great case of the compound-householder, and the noble lord said that the right honourable gentleman (Mr. Gladstone) declared that there should be no difference between the compounder and non-compounder, and that I immediately and obsequiously gave that point up. But there is some very great mistake here. It is very true that the right honourable gentleman did object to the plans which we originally proposed with respect to the compounder; but when these terrible conditions were so imperiously dictated, the right honourable gentleman did not want the existing arrangements of this Bill to be adopted, but wished us to adopt the line of a £5 rating, which in our opinion would have entirely emasculated the Bill and destroyed its principle.

I have gone through the principal points referred to, because, to make up the ten conditions, the noble lord was obliged to go to the fancy franchises. We gave up the fancy franchises, because the lodger franchise had been accepted by the House, and it was quite unnecessary to have the fancy franchises when the lodger franchise was adopted. Was there any great deviation of principle, or anything astounding in our accepting the lodger franchise which was one of the propositions contained in the Bill we ourselves brought forward in 1859? Therefore, I think I have shown the noble lord that for that portentous statement of his, which seemed so to alarm the House—how this Bill had been enormously changed through the imperious dictation of the right honourable member for South Lancashire, and my obsequious yielding—there is very little foundation. And when I find that on the measure which I am now asking you to read the third time, there were twenty-six considerable divisions, in eighteen of which the right honourable member for South Lancashire voted against the Government, I fail to discover any evidence of that successful though imperious dictation of which we have heard so much. And, Sir, I think it cannot be said that this was a measure which bristled with securities and precautions that have been given up at the bidding of our opponents. That a great many of them have been given up I shall not deny; but they have been given up not always or in the greatest degree at the bidding of our opponents, and some of them have been given up to the general feeling of the House. Now, Sir, the noble lord says that by yielding to these ten same conditions, I have virtually altered the whole character of the Bill. Now, is that true? Is the whole character of the Bill altered? I contend on the contrary, that the Bill, though adapted of course to the requirements of the year in which we are legislating, is at the same time in harmony with the general policy which we have always maintained. This is a question which cannot be settled by a jeer or a laugh, but by facts, and by facts and results which many of you deprecate and deplore at this moment, and in consequence of which you tell us that you mean to reopen the agitation—a thing which I defy you to do.

I begin with what the honourable gentleman who smiles so serenely may regard as the most difficult question for us—namely, that of the borough franchise—and I say that, if we could not maintain the £10 borough franchise, which members of the Liberal party seem now much to deplore, but which they opposed in 1859, it was perfectly in harmony with the general expression of our opinions, and certainly with our policy as a party, that we should accept such a franchise as we are now recommending to you by this Bill. You declined, the House of Commons declined, and especially the Liberal party declined, to take their stand upon the £10 franchise. You will not deny that; you will not carp at that. Well, but has there been no question since that time between the £10 franchise, upon the merits of which the right honourable gentleman the member for Calne is always dilating, saying it has existed—as he told us to-night in a kind of rhetorical *crescendo*, which becomes more and more surprising—for at least 200 years; has there, I say, been no question, since the Government of 1859, between retaining the £10 borough franchise and accepting household suffrage? Have you not had the alternative offered of a multitude of schemes? Have you not heard of a franchise to be fixed at £8, £7, £6, and all sorts of pounds?

The question, therefore, for us practically to consider was—whether we were to accept this settlement of the borough franchise, we will say at £5, or whether we should adhere to the conviction at which we had arrived in 1859—namely, that if you reduced the qualification there was no safe resting-place until you came to a household rating franchise? The noble lord says that immense dangers are to arise to this country because we have departed from the £10 franchise. (Viscount Cranbourne: No!) Well, it was something like that, or because you have reduced the franchise. The noble lord is candid enough to see that if you had reduced it after what occurred in 1859, as you ought according to your pledges to have done, you would have had to reduce it again by this time. It is not likely that such a settlement of the difficulty would have been so statesmanlike that you could have allayed discontent or satisfied any great political demands by reducing the electoral qualification by 40s. or so. Then the question would arise—is there a greater danger from the number who would be admitted by a rating household franchise than from admitting the hundreds of thousands—the right honourable gentleman the member for South Lancashire calculated them at 300,000—who would come in under a £5 franchise? I think that the danger would be less, that the feeling of the large number would be more national than by only admitting what I call the Prætorian guard, a sort of class set aside, invested with peculiar privileges, looking with suspicion on their superiors, and with disdain on those beneath them, with no friendly feelings towards the institutions of their country and with great confidence in themselves. I think you would have a better chance of touching the popular heart, of evoking the national sentiment by embracing the great body of those men who occupy houses and fulfil the duties of citizenship by the payment of rates, than by the more limited and, in our opinion, more dangerous proposal.

So much for the franchise. I say that if we could not carry out our policy of 1859, the logical conclusion was that in settling the question we should make the proposition which you, after due consideration, have accepted, and which I hope you will to-night pass. Let us look at the other divisions of the subject. I will not test by little points the question of whether we have carried substantially the policy which we recommended. I say look to the distribution of seats. I am perfectly satisfied on the part of Her Majesty's Government with the distribution of seats which the House in its wisdom has sanctioned. I think it is a wise and prudent distribution of seats. I believe that upon reflection it will satisfy the country. It has been modified in one instance, to a certain degree, in favour of views which in principle we do not oppose; but we have succeeded in limiting the application of that principle; and, on the whole, the policy which is embodied in the distribution of seats, which by reading this Bill a third time I hope you are going to adopt, is the policy of redistribution which on the part of the Conservative party I have now for nearly twenty years impressed on this House. And what is that policy? That you should completely disfranchise no single place; that it would be most unwise without necessity to disfranchise any centre of representation; that you should take the smaller boroughs with two members each and find the degree of representation which you wanted to supply in their surplus and superfluity of representation. You have acted upon that principle. But, above all, year after year I have endeavoured to impress on this House the absolute necessity of your doing justice to those vast, I may almost say, unrepresented millions, but certainly most inadequately represented millions, who are congregated in your counties. You may depreciate what you have agreed to, but in my opinion you have agreed to a very great measure. At any rate it is the first, and it is a very considerable, attempt to do justice in regard to the representation of the counties.

Then although I am the last person in any way to underrate the value of the assistance which Her Majesty's Government have received from the House in the management of this measure; although I believe there is no other example in the annals of Parliament when there has been such a fair interchange of ideas between the two sides of the House, and when, notwithstanding some bitter words and burning sentiments which we have occasionally listened to—and especially to-night —there has been, on the whole, a greater absence of party feeling and party management than has ever been exhibited in the conduct of a great measure; although personally I am deeply grateful to many honourable gentlemen opposite for the advice and aid I have received from them, yet I am bound to say that in the carrying of this measure with all that assistance, and with an unaffected desire on our part to defer to the wishes of the House wherever possible, I do think the Bill embodies the chief principles of the policy that we have professed, and which we have always advocated.

Well, but there is a right honourable gentleman who has to-night told us that he is no prophet, but who for half an hour indulged in a series of the most doleful vaticinations that were ever listened to. He says that everything is ruined, and he begins with the House of Lords. Such a singular catalogue of political catastrophes, and such a programme of the injurious consequences of this legislation, were never heard of. The right honourable gentleman says, " There is the House of Lords; it is not of the slightest use now, and what do you think will happen to it when this Bill passes? " That was his argument. Well, my opinion is, if the House of Lords is at present in the position which the right honourable gentleman describes—and I am far from admitting it—then the passing of the Bill can do the House of Lords no harm, and it is very likely may do it a great deal of good. I think the increase of sympathy between the great body of the people and their natural leaders will be more likely to incite the House of Lords to action and to increased efforts to deserve and secure the gratitude and good feeling of the nation. " But," says the right honourable gentleman, " what is most terrible about the business of carrying this Bill is the treachery by which it has been accomplished." What I want to know from the right honourable gentleman is, when did the treachery begin? The right honourable gentleman thinks that a measure of Parliamentary Reform is an act of treachery, in consequence of what took place last year, when those who now bring it forward were in frequent council and co-operation with those who then and now oppose it. I can only say, for myself, that I hear of these mysterious councils for the first time. But if a compact was entered into last year, when we were in Opposition, that no measure of Parliamentary Reform should pass, or any proposal with that object be made by us—if such a proposal is an act of treason, then the noble lord the member for Stamford and his friends are as guilty of treachery as we who sit on these benches. Really I should have supposed that the right honourable gentleman would have weighed his words a little more; that when he talks of treachery he would have tried to define what he means, and that he would have drawn some hard and straight line to tell us where this treachery commenced. The right honourable gentleman, however, throws no light on the subject. He made a speech to-night which reminded me of the production of some inspired schoolboy, all about the battles of Chæronea and of Hastings. I think he said that the people of England should be educated, but that the quality of the education was a matter of no consequence as compared with the quantity. Now, the right honourable gentleman seems to be in doubt as to what may be his lot in the new Parliament, and what I should recommend him to be—if he will permit me to give him advice—is the school-master abroad. I should think that with his great power of classical and historical illustration the right honourable gentle-

man might soon be able to clear the minds of the new constituency
of all " perilous stuff," and thus render them as soundly Conservative as he himself could desire.

I must, however, remind the right honourable gentleman
when he tells us of the victims at Chæronea, to whom he likens
himself, that they died for their country, and died expressing
their proud exultation that their blood should be shed in so
sacred a cause.   But this victim of Chæronea takes the earliest
opportunity, not of expressing his glory in his achievements and
his sacrifice, but of absolutely announcing the conditions on
which he is ready to join with those who have brought upon him
so disgraceful a discomfiture.   He has laid before us a programme
to-night of all the revolutionary measures which he detests, but
which in consequence of the passing of this Bill he is now prepared to adopt.   The right honourable gentleman concluded his
attack upon us by accusing us of treachery, and by informing
us that he is going to support all those measures which he has
hitherto opposed in this House—though I believe he advocated
them elsewhere—and that he will recur, I suppose, to those
Australian politics which rendered him first so famous.

The right honourable gentleman told us that in the course
we are pursuing there is infamy.   The expression is strong;
but I never quarrel with that sort of thing, nor do I like on that
account to disturb an honourable gentleman in his speech,
particularly when he happens to be approaching his peroration.
Our conduct, however, according to him, is infamous—that is
his statement—because in office we are supporting measures of
Parliamentary Reform which we disapprove, and to which we
have hitherto been opposed.   Well, if we disapprove the Bill
which we are recommending the House to accept and sanction
to-night, our conduct certainly would be objectionable.   If we,
from the bottom of our hearts do not believe that the measure
which we are now requesting you to pass is on the whole the
wisest and best that could be passed under the circumstances,
I would even admit that our conduct was infamous.   But I
want to know what the right honourable gentleman thinks of
his own conduct when, having assisted in turning out the Government of Lord Derby in 1859, because they would not reduce
the borough franchise, he—if I am not much mistaken, having
been one of the most active managers in that intrigue—the right
honourable gentleman accepted office in 1860 under the Government of Lord Palmerston, who, of course, brought forward a
measure of Parliamentary Reform which, it would appear, the

right honourable gentleman also disapproved of, and more than disapproved, inasmuch as, although a member of the Government, he privately and successfully solicited his political opponents to defeat it. And yet this is the right honourable gentleman who talks of infamy!

Sir, the prognostications of evil uttered by the noble lord I can respect, because I know that they are sincere; the warnings and prophecies of the right honourable gentleman I treat in another spirit. For my part, I do not believe that the country is in danger. I think England is safe in the race of men who inhabit her; that she is safe in something much more precious than her accumulated capital—her accumulated experience; she is safe in her national character, in her fame, in the traditions of a thousand years, and in that glorious future which I believe awaits her.

ELECTION SPEECH IN MIDLOTHIAN

WILLIAM EWART GLADSTONE

Music Hall, George Street, Edinburgh: 25 Nov. 1879

My Lords and Gentlemen,—All will feel who are present, and all who, being absent, give any heed to the proceedings of to-day will feel that this is not an ordinary occasion. It is not an ordinary occasion which brings you and me together—me as a candidate for your Parliamentary suffrages, and you, I will not say as solicited by me, for by me you have not been solicited—but you as the spontaneous and gracious offerers to me of a trust which I deem it a high duty under these circumstances to seek, and which I shall deem it the highest honour to receive. It is not an ordinary occasion, gentlemen, because, as we all know, the ordinary rule is that in county representation it is customary, though not invariably the rule—it is customary to choose some one who, by residence, by property, by constant intercourse, is identified with the county that he is asked to represent. In these respects I come among you as a stranger. It is not the first time that such a combination has been known. On the contrary, it has been, I may say, not unfrequent for important counties, and especially for metropolitan

counties, to select those who, in that sense, are strangers to their
immediate locality to be their candidates or to be their representatives in Parliament, but always with a special purpose in
view, and that purpose has been the rendering of some emphatic
testimony to some important public principle.   It is not, gentlemen, for the purpose of gratuitously disturbing your county
that I am come among you, for before I could think it my duty
to entertain the wishes so kindly pressed upon me, I used the
very best exertions in my own power, and called in the very
best and most experienced advice at my command, in order
that I might be assured that I was not guilty of creating that
wanton disturbance—in truth, that I was to come among you
not as an intruder, not as a voluntary provoker of unnecessary
strife, but as the person who, according to every reasonable
principle of evidence, was designated by the desires of the
decided majority of electors as their future representative.

Then, my lords and gentlemen, neither am I here, as I can
truly and cheerfully say, for the purpose of any personal conflict.   I will begin this campaign, if so it is to be called,—and a
campaign, and an earnest campaign I trust it will be,—I will
begin by avowing my personal respect for my noble opponent
and for the distinguished family to which he belongs.   Gentlemen, I have had the honour—for an honour I consider it—to
sit as a colleague with the Duke of Buccleuch in the Cabinet
of Sir Robert Peel.   This is now nearly forty years ago.   Since
that time I frankly avow that I have changed various opinions;
I should say that I have learned various lessons.   But I must
say, and express it as my distinct and decided conviction, that
that noble Duke, who was then my colleague under Sir Robert
Peel, has changed like myself, but in an opposite direction, and
I believe that on this great occasion he is farther from his old
position than I am.   Let me, gentlemen, in the face of you who
are Liberals, and determined Liberals, let me render this tribute
to the memory of Sir Robert Peel.   I never knew a more conscientious public man; I never knew   in far the greater portion
of questions that concerned the public interest—a more enlightened statesman.   And this opinion I give with confidence,
in the face of the world, founded upon many years of intimate
communication with him upon every subject of public interest;
that, could his valuable life have been prolonged to this moment,
could he have been called upon to take part, as we are now
called upon to take part, in the great struggle which is com-
mencing in this country, Sir Robert Peel would have been found

contending along with you against the principles which now specially place you in determined opposition to the Government of the day. I render to the Duke of Buccleuch as freely as to Lord Dalkeith this tribute, that he—given and presupposed the misfortune of his false political opinions—is in all respects what a British nobleman ought to be, and sets to us all an example in the active and conscientious discharge of duty, such as he believes duty to be, which we shall do well, from our very different point of view, to follow.

And now I hope I have spoken intelligibly upon that subject, and I will pass on to another which is far less agreeable. I thought when the invitation of the electors of Midlothian was sent to me, that the matter in controversy was one of sufficient breadth and complication, and I then was not aware that it would become still more enhanced and still more entangled by a question which, in its first aspect, was local, but which, in its ulterior aspect, is of the deepest importance, embraces in its scope the whole country, and descends to the very roots of our institutions. I thought that in one thing at least my noble opponent and myself were agreed—that is to say, that we were agreed in making a common appeal to the true and legitimate electors of Midlothian. I am grieved to find that that is not to be the case; that, mistrusting the body to whom the constitution and the law had given the power of choice between candidates for Midlothian, an attempt has been made to import into the county a body of strangers, having no natural interest in the county, gifted with colourable qualifications invented by the chicanery of law, and that it is on this body that reliance is placed, in order, perchance, to realise some faint hope of overbearing the true majority of the constituency. I won't dilate, gentlemen, upon that subject—I won't now expatiate upon it,—but this I must say, that if anything was wanting to make me feel it more than ever a duty to endeavour to fight the battle with energy and determination, this most unfortunate act was the very thing destined for that purpose. Why, gentlemen, quite apart from every question of principle, nothing, I venture to say, can be so grossly imprudent as that which is familiarly known in homely but most accurate phrase as the manufacture of faggot votes. Those who manufacture faggot votes provoke investigation into the whole state of the law, and of those provisions of the law which at the present moment are framed with such liberality towards the possessors of property.

Why, sir, is it not enough that the man who happens to have

property in six or ten counties can give a vote in respect of that property, in conformity with the rules of the Constitution, in every one of those counties? Is it not enough that he who, after all, has only the interests of a citizen in the wellbeing of the country, shall be permitted, by the free assent of all parties, without dishonour, without evasion, to multiply his own individual existence, and to contribute to the issue of six or ten electioneering contests, instead of one? Is not this enough? Is not this sufficiently liberal to the rich man as compared with the poor man, who hardly ever, though he may be a voter, can by possibility have more than a single vote? Ought not the Duke of Buccleuch and his friends to be satisfied with that state of law? Is it not the fact that in this country, although the law refuses to give a double vote in respect of a larger qualification, yet is it not the fact that it is the rarest thing in the world to meet a poor voter who has more than one vote, whereas it is the rarest thing in the world to meet a gentleman voter, as he is called, who has not got more than one vote? Why are they not content with that state of things? Why do they determine upon adding to that lawful multiplication of power, which, I must say, is based upon a remarkable liberality towards the possessors of property? why, in addition to that, are they determined to aim at an unlawful multiplication of power, and to bring in upon you, the genuine voters of Midlothian, those guests, those foreigners—for foreigners they are— foreigners they are in respect of the concerns of this county —its political concerns—for the purpose of overbearing the genuine and true sense of the constituency? Gentlemen, my anticipation is that this extraordinary manœuvre will utterly, certainly, and miserably fail of its purpose. I have not been surprised to be assured by those among you who have interested themselves specially in the affairs of the coming election, that we stand quite as well as we did, or better than we did, before the introduction of these faggot votes. We are divided into parties in this country, and the division is a healthy one. But there is always, at the same time, a certain margin of gentlemen who will have regard to other than party considerations, where they think that some great public principle is at stake; and my belief is that there will be, and must be, many in Midlothian who will not consent to compromise a principle more sacred and more important than any of the ordinary differences of party, namely this, that the representative of each county shall be chosen by the county itself, and shall not be chosen by importations of gentlemen from abroad, brought in to overbear its true and native sense.

Well, gentlemen, I pass on from that subject, which you are very capable of handling, and which, I daresay, you will find a good deal to say upon before we have brought this business to a conclusion—I pass on to other matters, and I wish to say a word upon the subject—having thus far spoken of my own personal appearance and its grounds—upon the subject of the time at which I appear before you. Why do I come here to trouble you at this time? Are we going to have a dissolution? There is a question of great interest. I won't pretend, gentlemen, to answer it. My belief is that there has been a good deal of consultation in high quarters upon that subject; and observe the reason why there should be, and why there must have been consultation. The reason is plain. It is this: we have arrived at the time wherein, according to the fixed and invariable practice, I think, of the entire century, nay, even of more than the entire century, there ought to be a dissolution. The rule, and the wise rule, of our governors in other times has been, that although the law allows a duration of seven years to Parliament, it should not sit to transact more than the regular business of six sessions. And you will see, gentlemen, the good sense, I think, of such a rule. It appears to be founded upon this, that the operations of the seventh session would be likely to descend as to their moral level below the standard of the earlier portions of a Parliament; that the interests of the country would be more liable to be compromised by personal inducements, and personal inducements not in relation to the country at large, but in relation to particular groups and cliques of persons—in relation to what are sometimes called harassed interests. And matters of that kind would be likely to bring about a bartering and trafficking in public interests for personal ends if it were made absolutely certain that in so many weeks, or in two or three months, the Parliament must be dissolved. Now, out of this has grown a rule; I am far from saying that rule is a rule mathematical or inflexible; for some great public or national reason it is perfectly justifiable to depart from it—but what is the public or national reason for departing from it now? None at all. I defy the most ingenious man to suggest to me any reason whatever for departing from this rule, which has been in use through the whole of our lifetime—I believe even through the lifetime of your fathers and grandfathers. I don't believe the wit of man

can give a reason for departing from it except this, that it is
thought to be upon the whole for the interests of Her Majesty's
Government. That, I say at once, is not a legitimate reason
for departing from the constitutional rule. They have no right
to take into view the interests of the Government in respect
to a question whether a Parliament shall be prolonged beyond
the period fixed by long and unbroken usage. They are bound
to decide that question upon national and imperial considerations, and if no national or imperial consideration dictates a
departure from the rule, they are bound to adhere to the rule.
Well, now we are told they mean to break the rule. I can't
say I shall be surprised at their breaking the rule of usage, for
this Government, which delights in the title of Conservative,
or rather which was not satisfied with the title of Conservative,
but has always fallen back upon the title of Tory—this Tory
Government, from which we have the right to expect—I would
almost say to exact—an extraordinary reverence for everything
that was fixed—reverence which has been paid in many instances
whether it is good or bad — yet this Tory Government has
undoubtedly created a greater number of innovations, broken
away from a greater number of precedents, set a greater number
of new-fangled examples to mislead and bewilder future generations, than any Government which has existed in my time.
Therefore I am not at all surprised that they should have
broken away from a rule of this kind so far as regards the
respect due to an established and, on the whole, a reasonable and a useful custom; but at the same time they would
not break away without some reason—an illegitimate reason,
because one connected with their interests; a strange reason
because one would have thought that a Government whose
proceedings, as will be admitted on all hands, have been of
so marked a character, ought to have been anxious at the
earliest period permitted by usage to obtain the judgment of
the country.

And why, gentlemen, are they not anxious to obtain the judgment of the country? It is surely plain that they are not anxious.
If they were anxious, they would follow the rule, and dissolve
the Parliament. It is plain, therefore, that they are not anxious.
Why are they not anxious? Have they not told us all along
that they possess the confidence of the people? Have they
not boasted right and left that vast majorities of the nation
are in the same sense with themselves? Oh, gentlemen, these
are idle pretexts! It is an instinct lying far deeper than those

professions that teaches them that the country is against them. And it is because they know that the country is against them that they are unwilling to appeal to the country. Why, gentlemen, a dissolution, an appeal to the public judgment, when there is a knowledge beforehand on the part of those who make the appeal that the answer will be favourable, gives additional strength to those who make the appeal. If it be true, as they still say, that the country is in their favour, I say that after the favourable reply that they would receive to their appeal, they would come back to Parliament far stronger for the purpose of giving effect to the principles that they hold to be true, than they are at this moment. They know perfectly well that a favourable appeal would strengthen their hands; they know perfectly well that an unfavourable answer will be the end of their ministerial existence; and it therefore requires no great wit on our part to judge why, when they have reached the usual, and what I may almost call constitutional period, they don't choose to make an appeal at all.

There are some reasons, gentlemen, why they ought to make that appeal which bear on their own party interests. They will not have a very pleasant operation to perform when they produce their next Budget. I am not going to enter into that subject now. You must excuse me if I do not attempt on this occasion to cover the whole of the enormously wide field that is open before me; but I promise, especially as the Chancellor of the Exchequer says it is most agreeable to him that the question of finance should be discussed, and, in fact, he has chosen the most extraordinary opportunity, for the first time that I can recollect, for discussing it—namely, at the Lord Mayor's dinner—but as he is so desirous it should be discussed, I, having every disposition to comply with his wishes as far as I can, will certainly endeavour to enter into that matter, and set out the main facts of the case as well as I am able. I do not think there is a great anxiety to produce that Budget; and this of itself would recommend a dissolution.

I tell you, gentlemen, what I think, and that is what has led me to dwell at length on the subject of dissolution. It is because it is not a theoretical, but a practical consideration. It is this: we are told by "whippers-in," and gentlemen who probably have an inspiration that sometimes flows from the higher quarters into those peculiar and favoured channels—we are told that they think there will not be a dissolution for twelve months. Twelve months, gentlemen! There is what is called a " chapter of accidents," and by postponing the dissolution for twelve months you get your twelve months of the exercise of power. Now, I am not going to impute to this Government, or any Government, sordid motives for the desire to retain power. In my opinion, imputations of that kind, which are incessantly made upon me, and incessantly made upon the Liberal party generally, and especially upon the leaders of the Liberal party—in my opinion, imputations of that kind are disgraceful only to those who make them.

I pass on. The love of power is something much higher. It is the love, of course, of doing what they think good by means of power. Twelve months would be secured in that sense—something more would be secured. There would be the chance of striking some new theatrical stroke. There would be the chance of sending up some new rocket into the sky— the chance of taking some measure which again would carry misgiving and dismay to the hearts of the sober-minded portion of the nation—as I believe, at this time the great majority of the nation but which, appealing to pride and passion, would always in this, as in every country, find some loud-voiced minority ready to echo back its ill-omened sounds, and again to disturb the world, to destroy confidence, to unsettle business and the employments of life, to hold out false promises of greatness, but really to alienate from this country the sympathies of the civilised world, and to prepare for us the day of misfortune and of dishonour.

Now, gentlemen, I am not saying that which is peculiar to persons of my political creed. It was only upon the 10th of November that the Prime Minister gave to the world the assurance that he thought peace might be maintained. I thought that matter had been settled eighteen months ago, when he came back from Berlin and said he had got " peace with honour." Now he says, " I think peace may be maintained, and I think it is much more likely now than it was twelve months ago "—more likely than it was five months or four months after he had come back from Berlin and announced " peace with honour." That is what he says—he thinks it may be maintained. But on the very next morning, I read what I consider by far the cleverest of all the journals that have been used to support the foreign policy of the Ministry in the metropolis, viz. the *Pall Mall Gazette*. In it I read a passage to this effect: " We have before us ample evidence, in the tone of the foreign press, of the alarm which is felt upon the Continent at the supposed projects of the English Government." Rely upon it, gentlemen, there are more of these projects in the air. For the last two years their whole existence has been a succession of these projects. As long as Lord Derby and Lord Carnarvon were among them there was an important obstacle placed in their way in the character of these men. But since that time we have had nothing but new projects, one more alarming and more dangerous than another.

They began with sending their fleet to the Dardanelles without the consent of the Sultan, and in violation of the Treaty of Paris, which gave them no right to send it. After that they went on by bringing their Indian troops into Europe against the law of the country. After that they proceeded to make their Anglo-Turkish Convention, without the knowledge of Europe, when for six months they had been contending, I may say, at the point of the sword, that it was Europe, and Europe alone, that had a right to manage the concerns of the Turkish Empire. It is difficult, gentlemen, human memory will hardly avail, to bring up all these cases. I have got now as far as the Anglo-Turkish Convention. What is the next? The next is Afghanistan. A war was made in Afghanistan to the surprise and astonishment — I might almost say to the horror — of this country, upon which I shall have occasion, either to-day or on another day, to enlarge more than I can do at the present moment. I am now only illustrating to you the manner in which a series of surprises, a series of theatrical expedients, calculated to excite, calculated to alarm, calculated to stir pride and passion, and calculated to divide the world, have been the daily employment and subsistence, the established dietary of the present Government. Afghanistan, gentlemen, was not the last. Having had a diversion of that kind in Asia, the next turn was to be in Africa. But there a different course was adopted. The practice which in other circles is well known by the name of " hedging " was brought into play, and Sir Bartle Frere was exhorted and instructed as to affairs in Africa with infinite skill, and in terms most accurately constructed in such a way that if they turned out well, the honour and the glory would redound to this patriotic Government; but if they turned out ill, the responsibility and the burden would fall on the shoulders of Sir Bartle Frere.

Well, these came one after another, gentlemen, and now we have not done. We end where we began, and again it is a question of sending the fleet to the Dardanelles. Whether it is on its way there we do not know at this moment. We know that the officers—at least that is the last account I have seen—that the officers are only allowed to be within call at two hours' notice. When the catalogue of expedients is exhausted, it is just like a manager with his stock of theatrical pieces—after he has presented them all he must begin again—and so we are again excited, and I must say alarmed, and I believe that Europe is greatly disquieted and disturbed, by not knowing what is to be the next quasi-military operation of the Government.

These are not subjects, gentlemen, upon which I will dilate at the present moment, but this I will say, that in my opinion, and in the opinion which I have derived from the great states-men of the period of my youth, without any distinction of party, but, if there was any distinction of party, which I have learned more from Conservative statesmen than from Liberal statesmen, the great duty of a Government, especially in foreign affairs, is to soothe and tranquillise the minds of the people, not to set up false phantoms of glory which are to delude them into calamity, not to flatter their infirmities by leading them to believe that they are better than the rest of the world, and so to encourage the baleful spirit of domination; but to proceed upon a principle that recognises the sisterhood and equality of nations, the absolute equality of public right among them; above all, to endeavour to produce and to maintain a temper so calm and so deliberate in the public opinion of the country, that none shall be able to disturb it. The maxim of a Government ought, gentlemen, to be that which was known in ancient history as the appeal from Philip drunk to Philip sober. But the conduct of the present Government, and their resort one after another to these needless, alarming, and too frequently most discreditable measures, has been exactly the reverse. Their business has been to appeal to pride and to passion, to stir up those very feelings which every wise man ought to endeavour to allay, and in fact, constantly to appeal from Philip sober to Philip drunk.

Gentlemen, I have come into this county to repeat, with your permission, the indictment which I have to the best of my ability endeavoured to make many times elsewhere against Her Majesty's Government. It is a very serious indictment. It is well in these things that men should be held to the words that they utter, should be made to feel that they are responsible for them, and therefore you will perhaps allow me to read a sentence which I embodied in the letter written in reply to your most flattering and most obliging invitation. My sentence was this: "The management of finance, the scale of expenditure, the constantly growing arrears of legislation, serious as they are, only lead up to still greater questions. I hold before you, as I have held in the House of Commons, that the faith and honour of the country have been gravely compromised in the foreign policy of the Ministry; that by the disturbance of confidence, and lately even of peace, which they have brought about, they have prolonged and aggravated the public distress; that they have augmented the power and influence of the Russian Empire, even while estranging the feelings of its population; that they have embarked the Crown and people in an unjust war (the Afghan war), full of mischief if not of positive danger to India; and that by their use of the treaty-making and war-making powers of the Crown they have abridged the just rights of Parliament and have presented prerogative to the nation under an unconstitutional aspect which tends to make it insecure." Not from one phrase, not from one syllable of that indictment do I recede. If, gentlemen, in addressing this constituency there be any part of it upon which at the close I shall not seem to have made good the original statement, most glad shall I be to attend to the legitimate appeal of those who may think fit to challenge me upon the point, and to bring forward the matter —alas! only too abundant—by which every one of them can be substantiated before the world. Those, certainly, gentlemen, are charges of the utmost gravity.

But we are met with preliminary objections, and we are told, we are incessantly told, that there is no fault in the Government, that this is all a spirit of faction on the part of the Liberal party. I need not quote what you know very well; that that is the stock and standing material of invective against us —it is all our faction. The Government is perfectly innocent, but we are determined to blacken them because of the selfish and unjust motives by which we are prompted. Now that charge, standing as it usually does stand, in the stead of argument upon the acts of the Government themselves, and being found far more convenient by our opponents than the justification of those acts upon the merits, I wish to try that charge. I will not try it by retorting imputations of evil motive. I have already said what I think of them. And to no man will I, for one, impute a want of patriotism in his public policy. It is a charge continually made against us. So far as I am concerned it never shall be made against our opponents. But I am going to examine very shortly this charge of a spirit of faction on the part of the Liberal party. I do not condescend to deal with it by a mere counter-assertion, by a mere statement that we are innocent of it, nor will I endeavour to excite you—as probably a Tory speaker would excite you—as a thousand Tory speakers have excited their hearers, by drawing forth their uninformed cheers through assertions of that kind. But I will come to facts, and I will ask whether the facts of the case bear out, or whether they do not absolutely confute that assertion.

Now, the great question of dispute between the two parties, and the question out of which almost every other question has grown collaterally, has been what is known as the Eastern Question.

And what I want to point out to you is this—the date at which the Eastern Question, and the action of the Government upon the Eastern Question, began, and the date at which the action of the Liberal party, as a party, upon the Eastern Question began. The Eastern Question began, that is, its recent phase and development began, in the summer of 1875, and it immediately assumed great importance. In the winter of 1875 the Powers of Europe endeavoured to arrange for concerted action on the Eastern Question by what was called the Andrassy Note.

They had first endeavoured to arrange for concerted action by their consuls. The British Government stated that they objected on principle to any interference between the Sultan and his subjects. Nevertheless, they were willing to allow their consuls to act, provided it were done in such a way that no interference should be contemplated. Of course this failed. Then came the Andrassy Note. The Government objected on principle to the Andrassy Note, but they finally agreed to it, because the Turk wished them to agree to it—that is to say, that the Turk, who has very considerable astuteness, saw that he had better have in the councils of Europe some Power on which he could rely to prevent these councils from coming to practical effect, rather than to leave the Continental Powers of Europe to act alone.

In the spring of 1876, the Andrassy Note having been frustrated of its effect, not owing to the Government, who finally concurred in it, but owing to circumstances in Turkey, the Powers of Europe again endeavoured more seriously to arrange for concerted action, and produced what they called the Berlin Memorandum. The British Government absolutely and flatly refused to support the Berlin Memorandum. We have now arrived, gentlemen, at the end of the session of 1876. Now, mind, the charge is that the Liberal party has been cavilling at the foreign policy of the Government in the East from a spirit of faction. What I point out to you is this—that down to the end of the session 1876, although the Government had been adopting measures of the utmost importance in direct contradiction to the spirit and action of the rest of the Powers of Europe, there was not one word of hostile comment from the Liberal party.

On the 31st July 1876, at the very end of the session, there was a debate in the House of Commons. In that debate I took part. I did censure the conduct of the Government in refusing the Berlin Memorandum without suggesting some alternative to maintain the concert of Europe, and Lord Beaconsfield—I am now going to show you the evidence upon which I speak—Lord Beaconsfield, in reply to me on the debate, said that the right honourable gentleman, meaning myself, was the only person who has assailed the policy of the Government. Now I ask you, was it faction in the Liberal party to remain silent during all these important acts, and to extend their confidence to the Government in the affairs of the Turkish Empire, even when that Government was acting in contradiction to the whole spirit, I may say, of civilised mankind— certainly in contradiction to the united proposals of the five Great Powers of the continent of Europe?

Far more difficult is it to justify the Liberal party upon the other side. Why did we allow the East to be thrown into confusion? Why did we allow the concert of Europe to be broken up? Why did we allow the Berlin Memorandum to be thrown behind the fire, and no other measure substituted in its place? Why did we allow that fatal progression of events to advance, unchecked by us, so far, even after the fields of Bulgaria had flowed with blood, and the cry of every horror known and unknown had ascended to heaven from that country? Why did we remain silent for such a length of time? Gentlemen, that is not all.

It is quite true that there was, soon after, a refusal of the great human heart of this country, not in Parliament, but outside of Parliament, to acquiesce in what was going on, and to maintain the ignominious silence which we had maintained on the subject of the Bulgarian massacres.

In August and September 1876 there was an outburst, an involuntary outburst, for the strain could no longer be borne, from the people of this country, in every quarter of the country, denouncing those massacres. But that, gentlemen, was not by the action of the Liberal party. It was admitted by the Government themselves to be the expression of the country—misled, as they said, but still the expression of the country. It is true that it was said with reference to me that any man who made use of the susceptibilities of the country for the purpose of bringing himself back to office was worse than those who had perpetrated the Bulgarian massacres. But that was only a remark which hit one insignificant individual, nor was he very deeply wounded by it. But the Liberal party was not, as a party, in the field. Nay, more; that national feeling produced its effects. It produced the Conference at Constantinople. That was eighteen months after the Eastern Question had been opened. Down to the date of that Conference, the Liberal party had taken no step for any purpose prejudicial to the action of the Government; and when Lord Salisbury went to the Conference at Constantinople, he went, I say it without fear of contradiction, carrying with him the goodwill, carrying with him the favourable auspices, carrying with him, I will even say, the confidence of the Liberal party as to the result and the tendency of his exertions. And it was not till after nearly two years—viz. late in the spring, or during the spring of 1877—it was not until nearly two years after the Government had been busy with the Eastern Question that the Liberal party first began somewhat feebly to raise its voice in the House of Commons, and to protest against the course that had been adopted, which was evidently, as we thought, a course tending to bring about war, bloodshed, and disturbance, that might very easily have been avoided.

Now, gentlemen, I think I have shown you that it requires some audacity to charge with faction in this matter a party which maintained such a silence for nearly two years; which was even willing to acquiesce in the rejection of the Berlin Memorandum, and which heartily accompanied with its goodwill and confidence Lord Salisbury when he went to the Conference at Constantinople. I do not hesitate to say this, gentlemen, that when Lord Salisbury went to Constantinople—I believe with a perfectly upright and honourable intention—he carried with him a great deal more confidence from the Liberal party than he carried with him from some among his own colleagues.

But now, gentlemen, I can only say that if the Liberal party are governed by a factious spirit, they are great fools for their pains. What means a factious spirit but the action of an ungovernable desire to get into office? And it is alleged that the Liberal party are under the influence of such a desire. Well, gentlemen, if they are, all I can say is that there is no disputing about tastes; but men must be men of a very extraordinary taste who desire to take such a succession as will be left by the present Government.

I hope the verdict of the country will give to Lord Granville and Lord Hartington the responsible charge of its affairs.

But I must say I think them much to be pitied on the day when that charge is committed to their hands. Never, gentlemen, never in the recollection of living man has such an entangled web been given over to any set of men to unravel. Did they receive a similar inheritance from us when we went out of power? Did we give over to them that which will be given over by them to their successors? Gentlemen, I make no boast. We simply gave over to them what every Government has usually given over to its successors. Let us do them justice. Do not let us allow party feelings to lead us to suppose that there never has been prudence and discretion and right principle on the part of a Conservative Government, at least so far as to make sure that any evils for which they were responsible would be tolerable evils, and would not greatly disturb the general stability of the country. We did, merely to the best of our ability, what others had done before us.

But still, when we shall have so largely to consider the state of things to which the action of the present Government has brought the affairs of this country, it is absolutely necessary that I should briefly recall to your minds the nature of the starting-point from which they set out. What was their starting-place, gentlemen, in finance? The starting-point in finance was this, that we handed over to them a surplus which, in our hands, I will venture to say, would have been a surplus closely approaching six millions of money. Now, I have spoken of the manner in which they carry on this warfare, and you will believe that their scribes, with a pertinacious activity, feeling the difficulties of their case, have been very very hard driven to know how to deal with this question of the surplus. It has been necessary for them to get rid of it in some way or other, and some of them have actually had the cool audacity to say— I have read it in various newspapers; I have read it in a Sheffield newspaper, which, however, I won't name; it would not be delicate in reference to the feelings of the high-minded gentleman who wrote it—but they have asserted that we left to them £3,000,000 of Alabama payment, which we ought to have made, but which we handed over to them to pay. The only objection to this is that, if you consult the accounts, you will find that that £3,000,000 was paid by us in the year before we left office.

Then it is said this surplus was not a "realised surplus." What is meant by a realised surplus? According to them, there never has been such a thing in this country as a realised surplus. The law of this country provides, and most wisely provides, that when for the current year there is a certain surplus of revenue over expenditure, the money shall, in fixed proportions, be then and there applied to the reduction of debt. That, of course, was done in the last year of our Government. But what we left was the prospect of the incoming revenue for the following year. That was the prospect, which distinctly showed that there would be a surplus of £5,000,000 to £6,000,000, and that was the prospect we handed over to them; and if they choose to say it was not a realised surplus—undoubtedly it was no more realised than the Duke of Buccleuch's rents for next year are realised; but if, as is not likely, the Duke of Buccleuch has occasion to borrow on the security of his rents for next year, I suspect he will find many people quite ready to lend to him. Well, gentlemen, that is the only explanation I need give you. But I do assure you that such has been the amount of Tory assertion on this subject of the surplus, that I have been pestered for the last two or three years of my life with letters from puzzled Liberals, who wrote to say they had believed there was a surplus of £5,000,000 or £6,000,000, but the Tories would not admit it, and they begged me, for their own individual enlightenment, to explain to them how it was. Our surplus was like every other real and *bona fide* surplus, which the law of this country contemplates or permits, and the effect of it was that the Tories, who have since done nothing but add to the burdens of the people, were able to commence their career with a large remission of taxation. That was the case with finance.

How did we leave the army? because one of the favourite assertions of their scribes is that we ruined the army. Well, gentlemen, undoubtedly we put the country to very heavy expense on account of the army; but we put them to heavy expense for objects which we thought important. We found that the army, through the system of purchase, was the property of the rich. We abolished purchase, and we tried to make it, and in some degree, I hope, have made it, the property of the nation. But we have been told that we weakened and reduced the army. Weakened and reduced the army! Why, we for the first time founded a real military reserve—that reserve under which, in 1878, there happened an event previously quite unknown to our history—namely, that, upon the stroke of a pen sent forth by the Minister to the country, almost in a day five-and-thirty thousand trained men were added to the ranks of the army. That was the result of the system of reserve; and the system of reserve, along with many other great and valuable reforms, the country owes to Lord Cardwell, the Secretary of War under the late Government.

Well, gentlemen, you know—I need not enter into details— what was the general state of our foreign relations. The topic of our foreign relations can be disposed of in one minute. It is constantly said, indeed, by the scribes of the Government, and it was intimated by Lord Salisbury,—to whom I will return in greater detail at a future time,—that the foreign policy of the late Government was discreditable. Well, but here I have got a witness on the other side. I have got the witness of Lord Beaconsfield's Foreign Secretary at the time when he took office. At the time when he took office in the House of Lords, Lord Derby, then enjoying the full undivided confidence of the Conservative party, used these words on the 19th March 1874: "At the present moment the condition of the country in regard to our foreign relations is most satisfactory. There is no State whatever with which our relations are not most cordial." Now, our unfortunate friends and fellow-citizens, the Tories, are constantly called upon to believe that at the time they took office the state of the country, in regard to foreign relations, was most unsatisfactory, and that with no State were our relations most cordial, because by every State we were undervalued and despised. Gentlemen, there was not a cloud upon the horizon at the time when the charge of foreign affairs was handed over to Her Majesty's present Government. Does that imply that there was nothing serious to be done? Oh no, gentlemen, depend upon it, and you will find it to your cost before you are five years older, you will know it better than you do to-day; depend upon it that this Empire is an Empire, the daily calls of whose immense responsibilities, the daily inevitable calls of whose responsibilities, task and overtask the energies of the best and ablest of her sons. Why, gentlemen, there is not a country in the history of the world that has undertaken what we have undertaken; and when I say "what we have undertaken," I don't mean what the present Government have undertaken—that I will come to by and by—but what England in its traditional established policy and position has undertaken.

There is no precedent in human history for a formation like the British Empire. A small island at one extremity of the globe peoples the whole earth with its colonies. Not satisfied with that, it goes among the ancient races of Asia and subjects two hundred and forty millions of men to its rule. Along with all this it disseminates over the world a commerce such as no imagination ever conceived in former times, and such as no poet ever painted. And all this it has to do with the strength that lies within the narrow limits of these shores. Not a strength that I disparage; on the contrary, I wish to dissipate, if I can, the idle dreams of those who are always telling you that the strength of England depends, sometimes they say upon its prestige, sometimes they say upon its extending its Empire, or upon what it possesses beyond these shores. Rely upon it the strength of Great Britain and Ireland is within the United Kingdom. Whatever is to be done in defending and governing these vast colonies with their teeming millions; in protecting that unmeasured commerce; in relation to the enormous responsibilities of India—whatever is to be done, must be done by the force derived from you and from your children, derived from you and from your fellow-electors, throughout the land, and from you and from the citizens and people of this country. And who are they? They are, perhaps, some three-and-thirty millions of persons,—a population less than the population of France; less than the population of Austria; less than the population of Germany; and much less than the population of Russia. But the populations of Austria, of Russia, of Germany, and of France find it quite hard enough to settle their own matters within their own limits. We have undertaken to settle the affairs of about a fourth of the entire human race scattered over all the world. Is not that enough for the ambition of Lord Beaconsfield? It satisfied the Duke of Wellington and Mr. Canning, Lord Grey and Sir Robert Peel; it satisfied Lord Palmerston and Lord Russell, ay, and the late Lord Derby. And why cannot it satisfy—I do not want to draw any invidious distinction between Lord Beaconsfield and his colleagues; it seems to me that they are all now very much of one mind, that they all move with harmony amongst themselves; but I say, why is it not to satisfy the ambition of the members of the present Government? I affirm that, on the contrary, strive and labour as you will in office—I speak after the experience of a lifetime, of which a fair portion has been spent in office—I say that strive and labour as you will in Parliament and in office, human strength and human thought are not equal to the ordinary discharge of the calls and duties appertaining to Government in this great, wonderful, and world-wide Empire. And therefore, gentlemen, I say it is indeed deplorable that in addition to these calls, of which we have evidence in a thousand forms, and of our insufficiency to meet which we have evidence in a thousand forms—when, in addition to these calls, all manner of gratuitous, dangerous, ambiguous, impracticable, and impossible engagements are contracted for us in all parts of the world.

And that is what has lately been happening. I am not now going to discuss this question upon the highest grounds. I assail the policy of the Government on the highest grounds of principle. But I am now for a few moments only about to test it on the grounds of prudence. I appeal to you as practical men, I appeal to you as agriculturists, I appeal to you as tradesmen —I appeal to you in whatever class or profession you may be, and ask whether it is not wise to have some regard to the relation between means and ends, some regard to the relation between the work to be done and the strength you possess in order to perform it. I point to the state of our legislation, our accumulated and accumulating arrears constantly growing upon us; I point to the multitude of unsolved problems of our Government, to the multitude of unsolved problems connected with the administration of our Indian Empire—enough, God knows, to call forth the deepest and most anxious reflection of the most sober-minded; and even the most sanguine man, I say, might be satisfied with those tasks.

But what has been the course of things for the last three years? I will run them over almost in as many words. We have got an annexation of territory—I put it down merely that I might not be incomplete—an annexation of territory in the Fiji Islands, of which I won't speak, because I don't consider the Government is censurable for that act, whether it were a wise act or not. Nobody could say that that was their spontaneous act. But now let us look at what have been their spontaneous acts. They have annexed in Africa the Transvaal territory, inhabited by a free European, Christian, republican community, which they have thought proper to bring within the limits of a monarchy, although out of 8000 persons in that republic qualified to vote upon the subject, we are told, and I have never seen the statement officially contradicted, that 6500 protested against it. These are the circumstances under which we undertake to transform republicans into subjects of a monarchy. We have made war upon the Zulus. We have thereby become responsible for their territory; and not only this, but we are now, as it appears from the latest advices, about to make war upon a chief lying to the northward of the Zulus; and Sir Bartle Frere, who was the great authority for the proceedings of the Government in Afghanistan, has announced in South Africa that it will be necessary for us to extend our dominions until we reach the Portuguese frontier to the north. So much for Africa.

I come to Europe. In Europe we have annexed the island of Cyprus, of which I will say more at another time. We have assumed jointly with France the virtual government of Egypt; and possibly, as we are to extend, says Sir Bartle Frere, our southern dominions in Africa till we meet the southern frontier of the Portuguese possibly one of these days we may extend our northern dominions in Africa till we meet the northern frontier of the Portuguese. We then, gentlemen, have undertaken to make ourselves responsible for the good government of Turkey in Asia—not of Asia Minor, as you are sometimes told, exclusively, but of the whole of that great space upon the map, including the principal part of Arabia, which is known geographically as Turkey in Asia. Besides governing it well, we have undertaken to defend the Armenian frontier of Turkey against Russia, a country which we cannot possibly get at except either by travelling over several hundreds of miles by land, including mountain-chains never adapted to be traversed by armies, or else some thousands of miles of sea, ending at the extremity of the Black Sea, and then having to effect a landing. That is another of our engagements.

Well, and as if all that were not enough, we have, by the most wanton invasion of Afghanistan, broken that country into pieces, made it a miserable ruin, destroyed whatever there was in it of peace and order, caused it to be added to the anarchies of the Eastern world, and we have become responsible for the management of the millions of warlike but very partially civilised people whom it contains, under circumstances where the application of military power, and we have nothing but military power to go by, is attended at every foot with enormous difficulties.

Now, gentlemen, these are proceedings which I present to you at the present moment in the view of political prudence only. I really have but one great anxiety. This is a self-governing country. Let us bring home to the minds of the people the state of the facts they have to deal with, and in Heaven's name let them determine whether or not this is the way in which they like to be governed. Do not let us suppose this is like the old question between Whig and Tory. It is nothing of the kind. It is not now as if we were disputing about some secondary matter—it is not even as if we were disputing about the Irish Church, which no doubt was a very important affair. What we are disputing about is a whole system of Government, and to make good that proposition that it is a whole system of Government will be my great object in any addresses that I may deliver in this country. If it is acceptable, if it is liked by the people—they are the masters—it is for them to have it. It is not particularly pleasant for any man, I suppose, to spend the closing years of his life in vain and unavailing protest; but as long as he thinks his protest may avail, as long as he feels that the people have not yet had their fair chance and opportunity, it is his duty to protest, and it is to perform that duty, gentlemen, that I come here.

I have spoken, gentlemen, of the inheritance given over to the present Government by their predecessors, and of the inheritance that they will give over to those who succeed them. Now, our condition is not only, in my judgment, a condition of embarrassment, but it is one of embarrassment we have made for ourselves; and before I close, although I have already detained you too long, I must give a single illustration of the manner in which we have been making our own embarrassments. Why did we quarrel with the present Government about Turkey? I have shown that we were extremely slow in doing it. I believe we were too slow, and that, perhaps, if we had begun sooner our exertions might have availed more; but it was from a good motive. Why did we quarrel? What was the point upon which we quarrelled?

The point upon which we quarrelled was this: Whether coercion was under any circumstances to be applied to Turkey to bring about the better government of that country. Now that will not be disputed, or if it is disputed, and in order that it may not be disputed, for it is very difficult to say what won't be disputed—in order that it may not be disputed I will read from two conclusive authorities. That is my point. The foundation of the policy of the present Government was that coercion was not to be applied to Turkey. Here is what Lord Cranbrook, who stated the case of the Government in the House of Commons, said: " We have proclaimed, and I proclaim again, in the strongest language, that we should be wrong in every sense of the word if we were to endeavour to apply material coercion against Turkey; " that was what Lord Cranbrook said on the 15th February 1877, nor had he repented in April, for in April he said: " Above all, we feel that we, who have engaged ourselves by treaty, at least in former times, who have had no personal wrong done to us, have no right and no commission, either as a country, or, as I may say, from Heaven, to take upon ourselves the vindication by violence of the rights of the Christian subjects of the Porte, however much we may feel for them." Higher authority, of course, still than Lord Cranbrook, but in perfect conformity with him, was Lord Beaconsfield himself, who, on the 20th February 1877, after a speech of Lord Granville's, said this: " The noble Lord and his friends are of opinion that we should have coerced the Porte into the acceptation of the policy which we recommended. That is not a course which we can conscientiously profess or promote, and I think, therefore, when an issue so broad is brought before the House, it really is the duty of noble Lords to give us an opportunity to clear the mind of the country by letting it know what is the opinion of Parliament upon policies so distinct, and which in their consequences must be so different." Now, you see plainly that coercion in the extreme case that had arisen was recommended by the Liberal party. Coercion was objected to on the highest grounds by the Tory party; and Lord Beaconsfield virtually said, " Such is the profound difference between these policies that I challenge you to make a motion in Parliament, and to take the opinion of Parliament in order that we may know which way we are to move." That was not all, for after the English Government had disclaimed coercion, and after that terribly calamitous Russo-Turkish war had been begun and ended, Lord Beaconsfield declared that if the Government had been entirely consistent, they would not have rested satisfied with protesting against the action of Russia, so sacred was this principle of non-coercion in their eyes, but that they ought to have warned Russia that if she acted she must be prepared to encounter the opposition of England. I will read a very short passage from a letter of Sir Henry Layard which refers to that declaration. Sir Henry Layard, on the 18th April 1879, wrote or spoke as follows, I am not quite sure which; I quote it from an unexceptionable authority, the *Daily Telegraph* of April 19: " I agree with the remark of Lord Beaconsfield when he returned from the Berlin Congress, that if England had shown firmness in the first instance the late war might have been avoided. That is my conviction, and everything I have seen tends to confirm it." If England had shown firmness—that is to say, if she had threatened Russia. There is no other meaning applicable to the words. I have shown you, therefore, gentlemen, what it is upon which we went to issue—whether Turkey should be coerced, or whether she should not.

But there is an important limitation. We had never given countenance to single-handed attempts to coerce Turkey. We felt that single-handed attempts to coerce Turkey would probably lead to immediate bloodshed and calamity, with great uncertainty as to the issue. The coercion we recommended was coercion by the united authority of Europe, and we always contended that in the case where the united authority of Europe was brought into action, there was no fear of having to proceed to actual coercion. The Turk knew very well how to measure strength on one side and the other, and he would have yielded to that authority. But no, there must be no coercion under any circumstances. Such was the issue, gentlemen. Well, where do we stand now? We know what has taken place in the interval. We know that a great work of liberation has been done, in which we have had no part whatever. With the traditions of liberty which we think we cherish, with the recollection that you Scotchmen entertain of the struggles in which you have engaged to establish your own liberties here, a great work of emancipation has been going on in the world, and you have been prevented by your Government from any share in it whatever. But bitter as is the mortification with which I for one reflect upon that exclusion, I thank God that the work has been done. It has been done in one sense, perhaps, by the most inappropriate of instruments; but I rejoice in the result, that six or seven millions of people who were in partial subjection have been brought into total independence, and many millions more who were in absolute subjection to the Ottoman rule have been brought into a state which, if not one of total independence, yet is one of practical liberation actually attained, or very shortly to be realised—practical liberation from the worst of the evils which they suffered.

But what happens now? Why, it appears the Turk is going

to be coerced after all. But is not it a most astounding fact that the Government, who said they would on no consideration coerce the Turk, and who said that if Europe attempted to coerce the Turk nothing but misery could result, now expects to coerce the Turk by sending an order to Admiral Hornby at Malta, and desiring him to sail with his fleet into the east of the Mediterranean? Now, gentlemen, neither you nor I are acquainted with the whole of the circumstances attendant upon these measures. We don't know the reasons of State that have brought about this extraordinary result. But what I have pointed out to you is this, that Her Majesty's Government have in matter of fact come round to the very principle upon which they compelled the Liberals to join issue with them two or three years ago—the very principle which they then declared to be totally inadmissible, and for urging which upon them, their agents and organs through the country have been incessantly maintaining that nothing but the spirit of faction could have induced us to do anything so monstrous. That which nothing but the spirit of faction could have induced us to do, is embraced in principle by Her Majesty's Government. But is it embraced in the same form? No. We said: Let coercion be applied by the united authority of Europe—that is to say, for it is not an exaggeration so to put it, by the united authority of the civilised world applicable to this case. Our American friends have too remote an interest in it to take part. God forbid I should exclude them from the civilised world; but it was by the united authority of Europe that we demanded it. It is now attempted by the single authority and by the single hand of England. Will it succeed? All I can say is this, if it be directed to good and honest ends, to practical improvement, with all my heart I hope it may; but it may not, and then where is the responsibility? Where is the responsibility of those who refused to allow all Europe to act in unison, and who then took upon themselves this single-handed action? If it fails, they incur an immense responsibility. If it succeeds, it only becomes the more plain that had they but acceded to the advice which was at first so humbly tendered by the Liberal party, and which only after a long time was vigorously pressed—had they then acceded to the view of the Liberal party, and allowed Turkey to be dealt with as she ought to have been dealt with at the close of the Constantinople Conference, Turkey would have given way at once. The Power which yields to one State would still more readily have yielded to the united voice of the six great States. The concessions to be made by her would then have been made, and the horrors and the bloodshed, the loss of life and treasure, the heartburnings, the difficulties, the confusion, and the anarchy that have followed, would all of them have been saved.

Therefore, gentlemen, I say that our present embarrassments are of our own creation. It would be a very cruel thing to hold the present Government responsible for the existence of an Eastern Question that from time to time troubles Europe. I have not held them so responsible. I hold them responsible for having interrupted that concerted action which, it is as evident as considerations of sense and policy can make it— which could not have failed to attain its effect; and for now being driven to make the same effort, with diminished resources, in greater difficulties, and after the terrible penalties of an almost immeasurable bloodshed had been paid.

Now, gentlemen, all this, and a great deal more than this, has to be said, which cannot be said now. Neither your patience nor my strength could enable me to say it. I have detained you at great length. I have only opened, as it were, these questions. I have not even touched the great number of important subjects in which you naturally, as men of Scotland and men of Midlothian, feel very special interest. I will, however, gentlemen, for this day bid you farewell. But I shall say one word in closing, and it is this. It is constantly said by the Government, and it is a fair claim on their part, that they have been supported by large majorities in the House of Commons. It is a very fair claim, indeed, for a certain purpose. I should, indeed, have something to say upon the other side— viz. this, that you will find in no instance that I am aware of in history, neither in the American War nor in the great Revolutionary War, nor at any period known to me, has objection been taken, persistently and increasingly taken, by such large fractions of the House of Commons—not less, at any rate, than two-fifths of the House, sometimes more—to the foreign policy of the Government, as during this great controversy. The fact is, gentlemen, that in matters of foreign policy it does require, and it ought to require, very great errors and very great misdeeds on the part of the Government to drive a large portion of Parliament into opposition. It is most important to maintain our national unity in the face of the world. I, for my part, have always admitted, and admit now, that our responsibility in opposing the Government has been immense, but their responsibility in refusing to do right has been still greater. Still they are right in alleging that they have been supported by large majorities. Pray, consider what that means. That is a most important proposition; it is a proposition that ought to come home to the mind of every one here. It means this, that though I have been obliged all through this discourse to attack the Government, I am really attacking the majority of the House of Commons. Please to consider that you might, if you like, strike out of my speech all reference to the Government, all reference to any name, all reference to the body.

It is no longer the Government with which you have to deal. You have to deal with the majority of the House of Commons. The majority of the House of Commons has completely acquitted the Government. Upon every occasion when the Government has appealed to it, the majority of the House of Commons has been ready to answer to the call. Hardly a man has ever hesitated to grant the confidence that was desired, however outrageous in our view the nature of the demand might be. Completely and bodily, the majority of the House of Commons has taken on itself the responsibility of the Government—and not only the collective majority of the House of Commons, gentlemen. If you had got to deal with them by a vote of censure on that majority in the lump, that would be a very ineffective method of dealing. They must be dealt with indi-vidually. That majority is made up of units. It is the unit with which you have got to deal. And let me tell you that the occasion is a solemn one; for as I am the first to aver that now fully and bodily the majority of the House of Commons has, in the face of the country, by a multitude of repeated and deliberate acts, made itself wholly and absolutely responsible in the whole of these transactions that I have been commenting upon, and in many more; and as the House of Commons has done that, so upon the coming general election will it have to be determined whether that responsibility, so shifted from an Administration to a Parliament, shall again be shifted from a Parliament to a nation. As yet the nation has had no oppor-tunity. Nay, as I pointed out early in these remarks, the Government do not seem disposed to give them the opportunity. To the last moment, so far as we are informed by the best authorities, they intend to withhold it. The nation, therefore, is not yet responsible. If faith has been broken, if blood has been needlessly shed, if the name of England has been discredited and lowered from that lofty standard which it ought to exhibit to the whole world, if the country has been needlessly distressed, if finance has been thrown into confusion, if the foundations of the Indian Empire have been impaired, all these things as yet are the work of an Administration and a Parliament; but the day is coming, and is near at hand, when that event will take place which will lead the historian to declare whether or not they are the work, not of an Administration and not of a Parliament, but the work of a great and a free people. If this great and free and powerful people is disposed to associate itself with such transactions, if it is disposed to assume upon itself what some of us would call the guilt, and many of us must declare to be the heavy burden, of all those events that have been passing before our eyes, it rests with them to do it. But, gentlemen, let every one of us resolve in his inner conscience, before God and before man—let him resolve that he at least will have no share in such a proceeding; that he will do his best to exempt himself; that he will exempt himself from every participation in what he believes to be mischievous and ruinous misdeeds; that, so far as his exertions can avail, no trifling, no secondary consideration shall stand in the way of them, or abate them; that he will do what in him lies to dissuade his countrymen from arriving at a resolution so full of mischief, of peril, and of shame.

Gentlemen, this is the issue which the people of this country will have to try. Our minds are made up. You and they have got to speak. I for my part have done and will do the little that rests with me to make clear the nature of the great controversy that is to be decided; and I say from the bottom of my soul, " God speed the right."

IMPERIAL FEDERATION

RT. HON. JOSEPH CHAMBERLAIN

LONDON: 6 NOVEMBER 1895

MR. CHAIRMAN AND GENTLEMEN:—I thank you sincerely for the hearty reception you have given to this toast, and appreciate very much the warmth of your welcome. I see in it confirmation of the evidence which is afforded by the cordial and graceful telegram from the Premier of Natal, which has been read by your chairman, and by the other public and private communications we have received, that any man who makes it his first duty, as I do, to draw closer together the different portions of the British Empire will meet with hearty sympathy, encouragement, and support. I thank my old friend and colleague, Sir Charles Tupper, for the kind manner in which he has spoken of me. He has said much, no doubt, that transcends my merits, but that is a circumstance so unusual in the life of a politician that I do not feel it in my heart to complain.

I remember that Dr. Oliver Wendell Holmes, who was certainly one of the most genial Americans who ever visited these shores, said that when he was young he liked his praise in teaspoonfuls, that when he got older he preferred it in table-spoonfuls, and that in advanced years he was content to receive it in ladles. I confess that I am arriving at the period when I sympathise with Dr. Oliver Wendell Holmes.

Gentlemen, the occasion which has brought us together is an extremely interesting one. We are here to congratulate Natal, its Government and its people, and to congratulate ourselves on the completion of a great work of commercial enterprise and civilisation, which one of our colonies, which happens to be the last to have been included in the great circle of self-governing communities, has brought to a successful conclusion, giving once more a proof of the vigour and the resolution which have distinguished all the nations that have sprung from the parent British stock.

This occasion has been honoured by the presence of the representatives of sister colonies, who are here to offer words of sympathy and encouragement; and, in view of the representative character of the gathering, I think, perhaps, I may be permitted, especially as this is the first occasion upon which I have publicly appeared in my capacity as Minister for the Colonies, to offer a few words of a general application.

I think it will not be disputed that we are approaching a critical stage in the history of the relations between ourselves and the self-governing colonies. We are entering upon a chapter of our colonial history, the whole of which will probably be written in the next few years, certainly in the lifetime of the next generation, and which will be one of the most important in our colonial annals, since upon the events and policy which it describes, will depend the future of the British Empire. That Empire, gentlemen, that world-wide dominion to which no Englishman can allude without a thrill of enthusiasm and patriotism, which has been the admiration, and perhaps the envy, of foreign nations, hangs together by a thread so slender that it may well seem that even a breath would sever it.

There have been periods in our history, not so very far distant, when leading statesmen, despairing of the possibility of maintaining anything in the nature of a permanent union, have looked forward to the time when the vigorous communities to which they rightly entrusted the control of their own destinies would grow strong and independent, would assert their independence, and would claim entire separation from the parent stem. The time to which they looked forward has arrived sooner than they expected. The conditions to which they referred have been more than fulfilled; and now these great communities, which have within them every element of national life, have taken their rank amongst the nations of the world; and I do not suppose that any one would consider the idea of compelling them to remain within the empire as within the region of intelligent speculation. Yet although, as I have said, the time has come, and the conditions have been fulfilled, the results which these statesmen anticipated have not followed. They felt, perhaps, overwhelmed by the growing burdens of the vast dominions of the British Crown. They may well have shrunk from the responsibilities and the obligations which they involve; and so it happened that some of them looked forward not only without alarm, but with hopeful expectation, to a severance of the union which now exists.

But if such feelings were ever entertained they are entertained no longer. As the possibility of separation has become greater, the desire for separation has become less. While we on our part are prepared to take our share of responsibility, and to do all that may fairly be expected from the mother country, and while we should look upon a separation as the greatest calamity that could befall us, our fellow-subjects on their part see to what a great inheritance they have come by mere virtue of their citizenship; and they must feel that no separate existence, however splendid, could compare with that which they enjoy equally with ourselves as joint heirs of all the traditions of the past, and as joint partakers of all the influence, resources, and power of the British Empire.

I rejoice at the change that has taken place. I rejoice at the wider patriotism, no longer confined to this small island, which embraces the whole of Greater Britain and which has carried to every clime British institutions and the best characteristics of the British race. How could it be otherwise? We have a common origin, we have a common history, a common language, a common literature, and a common love of liberty and law. We have common principles to assert, we have common interests to maintain. I said it was a slender thread that binds us together. I remember on one occasion having been shown a wire so fine and delicate that a blow might break it; yet I was told that it was capable of transmitting an electrical energy that would set powerful machinery in motion. May it not be the same with the relations which exist between the colonies and ourselves; and may not that thread of union be capable of carrying a force of sentiment and of sympathy which will yet be a potent factor in the history of the world.

There is a word which I am almost afraid to mention, lest at the very outset of my career I should lose my character as a practical statesman. I am told on every hand that Imperial Federation is a vain and empty dream. I will not contest that judgment, but I will say this: that that man must be blind, indeed, who does not see that it is a dream which has vividly impressed itself on the mind of the English-speaking race, and who does not admit that dreams of that kind, which have so powerful an influence upon the imagination of men, have somehow or another an unaccountable way of being realised in their own time. If it be a dream, it is a dream that appeals to the highest sentiments of patriotism, as well as to our material interests. It is a dream which is calculated to stimulate and to inspire every one who cares for the future of the Anglo-Saxon people. I think myself that the spirit of the time is, at all events, in the direction of such a movement. How far it will carry us no man can tell; but, believe me, upon the temper and the tone in which we approach the solution of the problems which are now coming upon us depend the security and the maintenance of that world-wide dominion, that edifice of Imperial rule, which has been so ably built for us by those who have gone before.

Gentlemen, I admit that I have strayed somewhat widely from the toast which your chairman has committed to my charge. That toast is "The Prosperity of South Africa and the Natal and Transvaal Railway." As to South Africa, there can be no doubt as to its prosperity. We have witnessed in our own time a development of natural and mineral wealth in that country altogether beyond precedent or human knowledge; and what we have seen in the past, and what we see in the present, is bound to be far surpassed in the near future. The product of the mines, great as it is at present, is certain to be multiplied many fold, and before many years are over the mines of the Transvaal may be rivalled by the mines of Mashonaland or Matabeleland; and in the train of this great, exceptional, and wonderful prosperity, in the train of the diamond digger and of the miner, will come a demand for labour which no man can measure—a demand for all the products of agriculture and of manufacture, in which not South Africa alone, but all the colonies and the mother country itself must have a share.

The climate and soil leave nothing to be desired, and there is only one thing wanted—that is, a complete union and identity of sentiment and interest between the different States existing in South Africa. Gentlemen, I have no doubt that that union will be forthcoming, although it may not be immediately established. I do not shut my eyes to differences amongst friends which have unfortunately already arisen, and which have not yet been arranged. I think these differences, if you look below the surface, will be found to be due principally to the fact that we have not yet achieved in South Africa that local federation which is the necessary preface to any serious consideration of the question of Imperial federation. But, gentlemen, in these differences, my position, of course, renders it absolutely necessary that I should take no side. I pronounce no opinion, and it would not become me to offer any advice; although, if the good offices of my department were at any time invoked by those who are now separated, all I can say is that they would be heartily placed at their service.

Gentlemen, I wish success to the Natal Railway, and to

every railway in South Africa. There is room for all. There is prosperity for all—enough to make the mouth of an English director positively water. There is success for all, if only they will not waste their resources in internecine conflict. I have seen with pleasure that a conference is being held in order to discuss, and I hope to settle, these differences. I trust that they may be satisfactorily arranged. In the meantime I congratulate our chairman, as representing this prosperous colony, upon the enterprise they have displayed, upon the difficulties they have surmounted, and on the success they have already achieved. And I hope for them—confidently hope—the fullest share in that prosperity which I predict without hesitation for the whole of South Africa.

THE POWER AND RESPONSIBILITY OF THE PRESS

EARL OF ROSEBERY

LONDON: 12 APRIL 1913

MR. CHAIRMAN AND GENTLEMEN:—I have become so rusty in the art of speaking that I feel to-night as though I were delivering my maiden speech. I had indeed hoped to have done with speaking, but remember that years ago your club honoured me with an invitation at the time when I owned a residence near Naples, and I was guiltily conscious of the fact that I preferred going to Naples to attending the dinner. I therefore felt that, if you wished to claim it, you had a mortgage upon my services. Nevertheless, I don't feel in high spirits when approaching an audience which I regard as by far the most difficult that I have ever addressed—a collection of the cream (if that were not a confusion of metaphor) of that great confraternity, that great freemasonry, which is called the Press, and which is composed of the most critical, almost cynical (if that adjective were not offensive), and the most *blasé* listeners to speeches of which any audience is composed.

My only comfort is this — that, owing to circumstances, I occupy a humble place on the slope of the mountain of on-lookers of which you occupy the top. You are critical, you are dispassionate; you sound occasionally the bugle notes of war and strife from the top of the mountain, but in the secluded spot which I occupy I have no wish to stir up strife, and I observe the whole drama in an atmosphere to which you cannot aspire. During the Crimean War, while fighting took place on the heights of Alma, it was stated that a hermit lived near the foot and was totally unconscious for a long time that any war had been going on. While those present inspired and conducted the contending forces I am the hermit. It is all very well to be a hermit, but it does not make the position the less formidable when one has to address an audience of journalists.

One terror at any rate has been removed. The great terror of every public speaker in his time has been the reporter. So far as I can make out, the reporter has largely disappeared. He has ceased to report the speeches to which it was understood the whole community were looking forward with breathless interest. He has turned his pencil into a ploughshare; what he has done with it, I do not exactly know. At any rate, he has ceased to be that terror to public speakers that he was in my time; and he no longer reports—except the great lions of the Front Benches, every wag of whose tail it is necessary for every citizen to observe.

But at present, outside the proceedings of those great men, reports have ceased, to the infinite relief, if I may say so, of the speakers. I speak with feeling as a speaker. No conscientious speaker ever rose in the morning and read his morning newspaper without having a feeling of pain, to see in it, reported verbatim, with agonising conscientiousness, things which he would rather not have said, and things which he thought ought not to bear repetition. The agonising conscientiousness of the reporter caused a reaction in the speaker which no words can describe, except the testimony of one who had experienced it. Then let me take the point of view of the reader, which is now my only point of view. Does any reader of the last twenty years ever read the speeches that are reported? I have no doubt that those whose duty it is to criticise, laud, or rebuke the speakers in the public Press feel it their painful duty to read the speeches. But does anybody else? Does any impartial reader of the newspapers, the man who buys a paper on his way to the City in the morning, and an evening paper in the evening—does he ever read the speeches? I can conscientiously say, having been a speaker myself, that I never could find anybody who read my speeches. It was quite different in the time when I was young, when practically the whole family sat down after breakfast and read the whole debate through. But the present age is in too great a hurry for that. They take the abstract; they may possibly read the abstract of speeches; but I appeal to an intelligent audience when I assert with confidence that not one man in a hundred ever read the speeches which were so largely reported in the Press. Their removal from the Press gave space to other matters of greater interest, and is one of the greatest reliefs the newspaper reader ever experienced.

I always find it a little difficult to know what to say, because the Press, like a great steam engine, is a little sensitive in relation to itself. If the Press were not sensitive it would not have the sympathy of the public—it could not speak the voice of the nation. Those who would speak to journalists have only one safe course; they must adhere to certain principles. They must assert the power of the Press, they must assert the potentiality of the Press, they must assert the responsibility of the Press, and, fourthly, they must assert in the strongest language possible that the British Press is the best and cleanest in the world. To all those four principles I give my conscientious adherence. I believe in the power of the Press. I believe in the potentiality of the Press even more. I believe even more in the responsibility of the Press; and I believe most of all that the British Press is the best and cleanest in the world. But I am not quite sure that that covers the whole ground. There are two other things to be observed. One is (and it is no new one) the enormous monopoly which is now exercised by the Press. The great daily newspapers have such a monopoly, owing to the enormous cost of founding new ones, which is obvious to you all. I do not know what the cost is, but I have heard it put at from a half to three-quarters of a million, and even then with indifferent chances of success. Owing to the monopoly which is possessed and exercised by the principal daily newspapers of this country, their responsibility is greater than that of the newspaper of forty or fifty years ago.

Secondly, I would point out the great development of the Press. As far as I have been able to trace the origin of the Press, it dates from the threat of the Spanish Armada in 1588. It was then a mere fly-sheet, but it showed what was necessary or interesting to the people of this country. Now, every day journalists produce, not a newspaper, but a library, a huge production of information and knowledge upon every kind of subject. It may not be invidious to refer to one particular newspaper, though I know it will be a thorny subject. Take *The Times*, when it issued its South American Supplement. It was a weighty business—I have not perused it myself, but it contains, I imagine, every possible fact that could ever be known about South America. It weighed about one hundredweight. That is an extreme case, but it appealed to me on more than one occasion. If you consider that prodigious mass of information, that huge concretion of knowledge, launched upon the British public as a newspaper—and that is what the British public now expects—and just contrast that with anything that was known before these days, and I think it involves a great responsibility, that Niagara of information which is poured upon the British public every day, as well as conferring some benefit. The Press enables us to know, as far as it is possible, everything about everybody and everywhere. Let me take my point about the responsibility of the Press with regard to its omniscience. We hear a great deal about the apathy of the population about great questions. I think it is perfectly true. There is a profound apathy. People have no time to bother about anything except their own concerns and the last football match.

But is not that due to the prodigious amount of news, startling news very often, which the Press affords every inhabitant of these islands who buys a newspaper? Is it not the fact that it must be so—one feels that it must—that if a great number of impressions are hastily and successively made on the receptivity of the brain, those impressions are blunted, until the mental constitution becomes apathetic about other pieces of news? Do you not yourselves feel that, except, possibly, the blowing up of the Tower of London, there is hardly anything in the world to-night that could make you feel that anything great had occurred? How is it possible that a population, nurtured and fed on that perfect journalism, should have the slightest interest in any possible event that might occur on the morrow?

A hundred years ago there were two wars, one a great war and the other not so great, but very galling—the one with the United States of America and the other the great struggle to try to beat down the superman Napoleon. Then the public had no interest in the world, nothing reported, except with regard to those two wars. I think that if we realised the difference between the journalism of those days and the journalism of the present day we should feel that the responsibility for the apathy of the country as regards public questions is largely due to the perfection to which journalism has been brought. In those far-off days there was the meagre sheet, which was issued two or three times a week, and the demands of war had practically shut three continents out from our purview altogether, whereas now we hear daily and hourly every item of news about every country and every person all over the world. Therefore, I say that the responsibility for the apathy of our people about public events must rest largely with the perfection of the Press. That being the case, at any rate this could be done—the influence of the great newspapers of this country could be made the best and most beneficent for the people who receive them.

Gentlemen, I do not wish to detain you, but it is perhaps the last time I shall address an assembly of journalists—or perhaps any assembly at all. I do not think I should choose an assembly of journalists, with that critical eye, for the one I should habitually address, but I wish to say one word more, in case I should never have again an opportunity to address an assembly of journalists. I speak very warmly and very sincerely when I say that your power and potentialities appeal to me more than anything else with regard to journalism. Your power is obviously enormous and you must wish to exercise it with that conscientiousness and honour, as I believe you do exercise it; but the potentiality is something which I am not sure that even you always realise. I take it in regard to one question, the question of peace and war.

In some respects I do not suppose you have so much influence as Parliament; I do not suppose you have so much influence as Ministers. There was a famous saying attributed to a notable Scotsman two hundred years ago, that he knew a wise man who said that if they would let him have the writing of the ballads of the country he did not very much care who made the laws. Well, ballads do not matter much, but newspapers do, and I should agree with that sentiment if you substituted the word " newspapers " for " ballads." Your power is enormous. As you give to the people you receive back from the people mutual electricity, which gives you your power.

All that is a commonplace. But with regard to peace and war there is no commonplace. With regard to legislation and so forth, you probably have not so much power as Ministers

or members of Parliament, except when you embody the un-
mistakable voice of the people. With regard to peace and war,
upon those issues you have paramount influence—far greater
than any member of Parliament, as great as any Minister of
the Crown himself. When critical occasions arise you can either
magnify them or minimise them. I pray you in issues which
involve peace and war diminish them as much as possible.
Think what an awful responsibility is on you!

I think you have the power more than any other body of
men to promote or to avert the horrors of war. I am quite
sure that my humble advice is not needed by men who know
their business so much better than I can know it, but they
may sometimes, in the hurry of journalism—because it is a
hurried profession—forget the great principles which must
be inherent in the journalist. As they write, they may on
impulse of the moment, in defence against the aggressive
journalism from abroad, forget their obligation to their own
country. And I would ask them in these few last words, when
any such issue may occur, and God knows the atmosphere
is electrical enough at this moment, not to say a word that
may unnecessarily, or except in defence, bring about to their
fellow countrymen the innumerable catastrophes of war.

WORLD WAR SUPPLEMENT

A CALL TO ARMS

RT. HON. H. H. ASQUITH

At the Guildhall: 4 Sept. 1914

My Lord Mayor and Citizens of London,—It is three and
a half years since I last had the honour of addressing in this
hall a gathering of the citizens. We were then meeting under
the presidency of one of your predecessors men of all creeds
and parties, to celebrate and approve the joint declaration of
the two great English-speaking States that for the future any
differences between them should be settled, if not by agreement,
at least by judicial inquiry and arbitration, and never in any
circumstances by war. Those of us who hailed that great
eirenicon between the United States and ourselves as a land-

mark on the road of progress were not sanguine enough to think, or even to hope, that the era of war was drawing to a close. But still less were we prepared to anticipate the terrible spectacle which now confronts us—a contest, which for the number and importance of the Powers engaged, the scale of their armaments and armies, the width of the theatre of conflict, the outpouring of blood and loss of life, the incalculable toll of suffering levied upon non-combatants, the material and moral loss accumulating day by day to the higher interests of civilised mankind—a contest which in every one of these aspects is without precedent in the annals of the world. We were very confident three years ago in the rightness of our position when we welcomed the new securities for peace. We are equally confident in it to-day, when reluctantly, and against our will, but with clear judgment and a clean conscience, we find ourselves involved with the whole strength of this Empire in this bloody arbitrament between might and right. The issue has passed out of the domain of argument into another field. But let me ask you, and through you the world outside, what would have been our condition as a nation to-day, if through timidity, or through a perverted calculation of self-interest, or through a paralysis of the sense of honour and duty, we had been base enough to be false to our word, and faithless to our friends? Our eyes would have been turned at this moment with those of the whole civilised world to Belgium, a small State which has lived for more than seventy years under a several and collective guarantee to which we, in common with Prussia and Austria, were parties. We should have seen, at the instance and by the action of two of those guaranteeing Powers, her neutrality violated, her independence strangled, her territory made use of as affording the easiest and most convenient road to a war of unprovoked aggression against France. We, the British people, should at this moment have been standing by, with folded arms and with such countenance as we could command, while this small and unprotected State, in defence of her vital liberties, made a heroic stand against overweening and overwhelming force. We should have been admiring as detached spectators the siege of Liége, the steady and manful resistance of a small army, the occupation of Brussels with all its splendid traditions and memories, the gradual forcing back of the patriotic defenders of their fatherland to the ramparts of Antwerp, countless outrages suffered by them, buccaneering levies exacted from the unoffending civil population, and, finally, the greatest crime committed against civilisation and culture since the Thirty Years' War, the sack of Louvain, with its buildings, its pictures, its unique library, its unrivalled associations, a shameless holocaust of irreparable treasures, lit up by blind barbarian vengeance. What account could we, the Government and the people of this country, have been able to render to the tribunal of our national conscience and sense of honour, if, in defiance of our plighted and solemn obligations, we had endured, and had not done our best to prevent, yes, to avenge, these intolerable wrongs? For my part, I say that sooner than be a silent witness, which means in effect a willing accomplice, to this tragic triumph of force over law, and of brutality over freedom, I would see this country of ours blotted out of the pages of history.

That is only a phase, a lurid and illuminating phase, in the contest into which we have been called by the mandate of duty and of honour to bear our part. The cynical violation of the neutrality of Belgium was not the whole, but a step, a first step, in a deliberate policy of which, if not the immediate, the ultimate and not far distant aim was to crush the independence and the autonomy of the Free States of Europe. First Belgium, then Holland and Switzerland, countries like our own, imbued and sustained with the spirit of liberty, were, one after another, to be bent to the yoke. And these ambitions were fed and fostered by a body of new doctrine, a new philosophy, preached by professors and learned men. The free and full self-development which to these small States, to ourselves, to our great and growing Dominions over the seas, to our kinsmen across the Atlantic, is the well-spring and life-breath of national existence, that free self-development is the one capital offence in the code of those who have made force their supreme divinity, and upon its altars they are prepared to sacrifice both the gathered fruits and the potential germs of the unfettered human spirit. I use this language advisedly. This is not merely a material, it is also a spiritual conflict. Upon its issue everything that contains the promise of hope, that leads to emancipation and a fuller liberty for the millions who make up the mass of mankind, will be found sooner or later to depend.

Let me now turn for a moment to the actual situation in Europe. How do we stand? For the last ten years by what I believe to be happy and well-considered diplomatic arrangements we have established friendly and increasingly intimate relations with the two Powers, France and Russia, with whom in days gone by we have had in various parts of the world occasion for constant friction, and now and again for possible conflict. These new and better relations, based in the first instance upon business principles of give and take, matured into a settled temper of confidence and goodwill. They were never in any sense or at any time, as I have frequently stated in this hall, directed against other Powers.

No man in the history of the world has ever laboured more strenuously or more successfully than my right hon. friend Sir Edward Grey for that which is the supreme interest of the modern world—a general and abiding peace. It is, I venture to think, a very superficial criticism which suggests that under his guidance the policy of this country has ignored, still less that it has counteracted and hampered, the Concert of Europe. It is little more than a year ago when, under the stress and strain of the Balkan crisis, the Ambassadors of the Great Powers met here day after day and week after week, curtailing the area of possible differences, reconciling warring ambitions and aims, and preserving against almost incalculable odds the general harmony, and it was in the same spirit and with the same purpose when a few weeks ago Austria delivered her ultimatum to Servia that the Foreign Secretary—for it was he— put forward the proposal for a mediating conference between the four Powers not directly concerned—Germany, France, Italy, and ourselves. If that proposal had been accepted the actual controversy would have been settled with honour to everybody, and the whole of this terrible welter would have been avoided. And with whom does the responsibility rest for its refusal and for all the illimitable sufferings which now confront the world? One Power, and one Power only, and that Power is Germany. There is the foundation and origin of this world-wide catastrophe. We persevered to the end, and no one who has not been confronted, as we were, with the responsibility, which unless you had been face to face with it you could not possibly measure, the responsibility of determining the issues of peace and war—no one who has not been in that position can realise the strength, energy, and persistence with which we laboured for peace. We persevered by every expedient that diplomacy could suggest—straining almost to the breaking point our most cherished friendships and obligations—even to the last moment making effort upon effort, and indulging hope against hope. Then, and only then, when we were at last compelled to realise that the choice lay between honour and dishonour, between treachery and good faith—when we at last reached the dividing line which makes or mars a nation worthy of the name, it was then only that we declared for war.

Is there anyone in this hall, or in this United Kingdom, or in the vast Empire of which we here stand in the capital and centre, who blames us or repents our decision? If not, as I believe there is not, we must steel ourselves to the task, and, in the spirit which animated our forefathers in their struggle against the dominion of Napoleon, we must, and we shall, persevere to the end.

It would be a criminal mistake to underestimate either the magnitude, the fighting quality, or the staying power of the forces which are arrayed against us; but it would be equally foolish and equally indefensible to belittle our own resources whether for resistance or for attack. Belgium has shown us by memorable and glorious example what can be done by a relatively small State when its citizens are animated and fired by the spirit of patriotism.

In France and Russia we have as allies two of the greatest Powers in the world, engaged with us in a common cause, who do not mean to separate themselves from us any more than we mean to separate ourselves from them. We have upon the seas the strongest and most magnificent Fleet the world has ever seen. The Expeditionary Force which left our shores less than a month ago has never been surpassed, as its glorious achievements in the field have already made clear, not only in material equipment, but in the physical and moral quality of its constituent parts.

As regards the Navy, I am sure my right honourable friend Mr. Churchill, whom we are glad to see here, will tell you there is happily little more to be done. I do not flatter it when I say that its superiority is equally marked in every department and sphere of its activity. We rely on it with the most absolute confidence, not only to guard our shores against the possibility of invasion, not only to seal up the gigantic battleships of the enemy in the inglorious seclusion of their own ports, whence from time to time he furtively steals forth to sow the sea with murderous snares, which are more full of menace to neutral ships than to the British Fleet. Our Navy does all this, and while it is thirsting, I do not doubt, for that trial of strength in a fair and open fight which has so far been prudently denied it, it does a great deal more. It has hunted the German Mercantile Marine from the high seas. It has kept open our own stores of food supply, and largely curtailed those of the enemy, and when the few German cruisers which still infest the more distant ocean routes have been disposed of—as they will be very soon—it will achieve for British and neutral commerce, passing backwards and forwards, from and to every port of our Empire, a security as complete as it has ever enjoyed in the days of unbroken peace. Let us honour the memory of the gallant seamen who, in the pursuit of one or another of these varied and responsible duties, have already laid down their lives for their country.

In regard to the Army, there is a call for a new, a continuous, a determined, and a united effort. For, as the war goes on, we shall have not merely to replace the wastage caused by casualties, not merely to maintain our military power at its original level, but we must, if we are to play a worthy part, enlarge its scale, increase its numbers, and multiply many times its effectiveness as a fighting instrument. The object of the appeal which I have made to you, my Lord Mayor, and to the other Chief Magistrates of our capital cities, is to impress upon them the imperious urgency of this supreme duty.

Our self-governing Dominions throughout the Empire, without any solicitation on our part, demonstrated with a spontaneousness and unanimity unparalleled in history their determination to affirm their brotherhood with us, and to make our cause their own.

From Canada, from Australia, from New Zealand, from South Africa, and from Newfoundland, the children of the Empire assert, not as an obligation, but as a privilege, their right and their willingness to contribute money, material, and, what is better than all, the strength and sinews, the fortunes, and lives of their best manhood.

India, too, with not less alacrity, has claimed her share in the common task. Every class and creed, British and native, princes and people, Hindoos and Mohammedans, vie with one another in a noble and emulous rivalry. Two divisions of our magnificent Indian Army are already on their way. We welcome with appreciation and affection their proffered aid, and, in an Empire which knows no distinction of race or class, where all alike, as subjects of the King Emperor, are joint and equal custodians of our common interest and fortunes, we here hail with profound and heartfelt gratitude their association side by side and shoulder to shoulder with our home and Dominion troops, under the flag which is a symbol to all of a unity that the world in arms cannot dissever or dissolve.

With these inspiring appeals, and examples from our fellow-subjects all over the world, what are we doing, and what ought we to do at home? Mobilisation was ordered on the 4th August. Immediately afterwards, Lord Kitchener issued his call for 100,000 recruits for the Regular Army, which has been followed by a second call for another 100,000. The response up to to-day gives us between 250,000 and 300,000 men, and I am glad to say that London has done its share. The total number of Londoners accepted is not less than 42,000. I need hardly say that the appeal involves no disparagement or discouragement of the Territorial Force. The number of units in that force who have volunteered for foreign service is most satisfactory, and grows every day. We look to them with confidence to increase their numbers, to perfect their organisation in training, and to play the efficient part which has always been assigned to them, both offensive and defensive, in the military system of the Empire.

But to go back to the expansion of the Regular Army, we want more men, men of the best fighting quality, and if for the moment the number who offer and are accepted should prove to be in excess of those who can at once be adequately trained and equipped, do not let them doubt that appropriate provision will be made for incorporation of all willing and able men in the fighting forces of the King. We want first of all men, and we shall endeavour to secure that men desiring to serve together shall, wherever possible, be allotted to the same regiment or corps. The raising of battalions by counties or by municipalities with this object will be in every way encouraged, but we want not less urgently a larger supply of ex-non-commissioned officers, the pick of the men who have served their country in the past, and whom, therefore, in most cases, we shall be asking to give up regular employment in order that they may return to the work for the State which they alone are competent to do.

The appeal which we make is addressed quite as much to their employers as to the men themselves. They ought surely to be assured of reinstatement in their positions at the end of the war. Finally, there are numbers of commissioned officers now in retirement with large experience of handling troops, who have served their country in the past. Let them come forward, too, and show their willingness, if need be, to train bodies of men, for whom for the moment no regular cadres or units can be found. I have little more to say.

As to the actual progress of the war I will not say anything except that, in my judgment, in whatever direction we look there is abundant ground for pride and for comfort.

I say nothing more, because I think we should bear in mind, all of us, that we are at present watching the fluctuation of fortune only in the early stages of what is going to be a protracted struggle. We must learn to take long views and to cultivate above all other qualities—those of patience, endurance, and steadfastness.

Meanwhile, let us go, each one of us, to his or her appropriate part in the great common task.

Never had a people more or richer sources of encouragement and inspiration. Let us realise, first of all, that we are fighting as a United Empire, in a cause worthy of the highest traditions of our race. Let us keep in mind the patient and indomitable seamen who never relax for a moment, night or day, their stern vigil on the lonely sea. Let us keep in mind our gallant troops, who to-day, after a fortnight's continuous fighting under conditions which would try the mettle of the best army that ever took the field, maintain not only an undefeated but an unbroken front.

Finally, let us recall the memories of the great men and the great deeds of the past, commemorated some of them in the monuments which we see around us on these walls, not forgetting the dying message of the younger Pitt—his last public utterance, made at the table of your predecessor, my Lord Mayor, in this very hall, " England has saved herself by her exertions and will, as I trust, save Europe by her example." The England of those days gave a noble answer to his appeal and did not sheathe the sword until after nearly twenty years of fighting the freedom of Europe was secured. Let us go and do likewise.

" A SCRAP OF PAPER "

RT. HON. D. LLOYD GEORGE

QUEEN'S HALL, LONDON: 21 SEPT. 1914

[The German Chancellor, in conversation with the British Ambassador, remarked: " Are you going to war with us for a scrap of paper ? " meaning the treaty guaranteeing the neutrality of Belgium.]

THERE is no man in this room who has always regarded the prospect of our being engaged in a great war with greater reluctance, with greater repugnance than I have done throughout the

whole of my political life. There is no man more convinced that
we could not have avoided this war without national dishonour.
I am fully alive to the fact that every nation which has ever
engaged in any war has always invoked the sacred name of
honour. Many a crime has been committed in its name. There
are some crimes being committed now. All the same, national
honour is a reality, and any nation that disregards it is doomed.
Why is our honour as a country involved in this war? It is
because we are bound by honourable obligations to defend the
independence, the liberty, the integrity of a small neighbour.
She could not have compelled us. She was weak. But the
man who declines to discharge his duty because his creditor is
too poor to enforce it is a blackguard.

We entered into a solemn treaty to defend Belgium, but our
signatures did not stand alone there. Why are not Austria and
Germany performing the obligations of their bond? It is suggested that when we quote this treaty it is purely an excuse on
our part; it is our low craft and cunning to cloak our jealousy
of a superior civilisation which we are attempting to destroy.
Our answer is our action in 1870. We called then upon France
and Prussia to respect the treaty.

At that time the greatest danger to Belgium came from France,
and not from Germany, and we invited both belligerent Powers
to state that they had no intention of violating Belgian territory.
What was the answer given by Bismarck? He said it was
superfluous to ask Prussia such a question in face of the treaties
in force. France gave a similar answer. We received the thanks
of the Belgian people for our intervention in a remarkable
document addressed by the municipality of Brussels to Queen
Victoria. In 1870 the French army was wedged up against the
Belgian frontier, with every means of escape shut off by a ring of
flame from Prussian cannon. The one way out was by violating
the neutrality of Belgium, and the French preferred ruin and
humiliation to the breaking of their bond. The French Emperor,
the French marshals, a hundred thousand gallant Frenchmen preferred captivity rather than dishonour the name of their country.
When it was to the interest of France to break the treaty she did
not do it. It was the interest of Germany to-day to break it, and
Germany had done it.

She avows it with cynical contempt. She says that treaties
only bind you when it is to your interest to keep them. What
is a treaty, says the German Chancellor, but a scrap of paper?
Have you any £5 notes about you? Have you any of those neat

little Treasury one-pound notes? If you have, burn them. They are only scraps of paper. What are they made of? Rags! What are they worth? The whole credit of the British Empire! Scraps of paper! I have been dealing with scraps of paper in the last few weeks. We suddenly found the commerce of the world coming to a standstill. The machine had stopped. Why? The machinery of commerce was moved by bills of exchange. I have seen some of them; wretched, crinkled, scrawled over, blotted, frowzy; and yet those scraps of paper moved great ships, laden with thousands of tons of precious cargo, from one end of the world to the other. The motive power behind them was the honour of commercial men.

Treaties are the currency of international statesmanship. German merchants, German traders have the reputation of being as upright and straightforward as any traders in the world, but if the currency of German commerce is to be debased to the level of that of her statesmanship no trader from Shanghai to Valparaiso will ever look at a German signature again. That is the doctrine of the scrap of paper; that is the doctrine which is proclaimed by Bernhardi—that treaties only bind a nation as long as it is to its interest. It goes to the root of all public law. It is the straight road to barbarism. Just as if you removed the magnetic pole whenever it was in the way of a German cruiser, the whole navigation of the seas would become dangerous, difficult, impossible; the whole machinery of civilisation will break down if this doctrine wins in this war. We are fighting against barbarism. There is only one way of putting it right. If there are nations that say they will only respect treaties when it is to their interest to do so, we must make it to their interest to do so.

Germany's excuse was that she was compelled to break the treaty because rapidity of action was the great German asset. There was a greater asset for a nation, however, than rapidity of action, and that was honest dealing. Germany said that Belgium was plotting against her, and was engaged in a great conspiracy with Britain and France to attack her. Not merely was this not true, but Germany knew it was not true. Another excuse was that France meant to invade Germany through Belgium. That was absolutely untrue. France offered Belgium five army corps to defend her if she was attacked. Belgium said that she had got the word of the Kaiser. " Shall Cæsar send a lie? " All these tales about conspiracy had been vamped up since. A great nation ought to be ashamed to behave like a fraudulent bankrupt, perjuring its way through its obligations. Germany had deliberately broken this treaty, and we were in honour bound to stand by Belgium. Belgium had been treated brutally, how brutally we should not yet know. We knew already too much. What had she done? She was one of the most inoffensive little nations in the world, but her corn-fields had been trampled down, her villages had been burned to the ground, her art treasures had been destroyed, her men had been slaughtered—and her women and children, too. Hundreds of thousands of her people were now wandering homeless in their own land. And what was their crime? Their crime was that they trusted to the word of a Prussian king. No nation in future would commit that crime again. He was not going to enter into the tales of outrages. They were not always true. It was enough for him to have the story which the Germans themselves had admitted, proclaimed, and defended—the burnings, the massacres, the shooting down of homeless people, because, according to the Germans, they fired on German soldiers.

What business had the German soldiers there? Belgium was acting in pursuance of the most sacred right, the right to defend your own home. But the people were not in uniform, and they were shot. If a burglar broke into the Kaiser's palace at Potsdam, destroyed his furniture, shot down his servants, ruined his art treasures—especially those he has made himself, burned his precious manuscripts, do you think he would wait till he had got into uniform before he shot the burglar down? The Belgians were dealing with those who had broken into their households. But the perfidy of the Germans has already failed.

They entered Belgium to save time. The time has gone. They did not gain time, but they have lost their good name. Belgium is not the only little nation that has been attacked in this way, and I make no excuse for referring to the case of Servia. The history of Servia is not unblotted. Whose history in the category of nations is unblotted? The first nation that is without sin, let her cast a stone at Servia. Trained in a horrible school, she won her freedom with her tenacious valour, and she has maintained it by her courage. If any Servians were mixed up in the assassination of the Grand Duke they ought to be punished. Servia admits that. The Servian Government had nothing to do with it. Not even Austria claimed that. The Servian Prime Minister is one of the most capable and honoured men in Europe. Servia was willing to punish any one of her subjects who had been proved to have any complicity in that assassination. What more could you expect? She sympathised with her fellow-countrymen in Bosnia. That was one of her crimes. She must do so no more. Her newspapers were saying nasty things about Austria. They must do so no longer. That is the German spirit. You had it at Zabern. How dare you criticise a Prussian official? And if you laugh it is a capital offence.

Servia undertook to give orders to the newspapers not to criticise Austria in future, promised not to sympathise with Bosnia, said she would have no public meetings at which anything unkind was said about Austria. But that was not enough. She must dismiss from her army officers whom Austria should subsequently name. Those officers had emerged from a war where they were adding lustre to the Servian arms, and he wondered whether it was their guilt or efficiency that prompted Austria's action. The officers were not named. Servia was to undertake to dismiss them, and the names were to be sent on subsequently. Can you name a country in the world, the Chancellor said, that would have stood that? Supposing Germany or Austria had issued an ultimatum of that kind to this country. "You must dismiss from your army and navy all those officers whom we shall subsequently name." I think I can name them now. Lord Kitchener would go. Sir John French would be sent about his business. General Smith-Dorrien would go, and I am sure that Sir John Jellicoe would be one of them. There is another gallant old warrior who would go—Lord Roberts. It was a difficult situation for a small country. But how did Servia behave? It is not what happens to you in life that matters; it is the way in which you face it. Servia faced the situation with dignity. She said to Austria, " If any officers of mine have been guilty and are proved to be guilty I will dismiss them." Austria said, " That is not good enough for me." It was not guilt she was after, but capacity.

Then came Russia's turn. Russia had a special regard for Servia. Servia was a member of her family, and she could not see Servia maltreated. Austria knew that. Germany knew that. And Germany turned round to Russia and said, " Here, I insist that you shall stand by with your arms folded whilst Austria is strangling to death your little brother." What answer did the Russian Slav give? He gave the only answer that became a man. He turned to Austria and said, " You lay hands on that little fellow and I will tear your ramshackle Empire limb from limb." And he is doing it.

That is the story of the little nations. The world owes much to little nations and to little men. This theory of bigness—you must have a big empire and a big nation and a big man—well, long legs have their advantage in a retreat. Frederick the Great chose his warriors for their height, and that tradition has become a policy in Germany. Germany applies that ideal to nations. She will only allow six-foot-two nations to stand in the ranks; but all the world owes much to the little five-foot-five nations. The greatest art of the world was the work of little nations. The most enduring literature of the world came from little nations. The greatest literature of England came from her when she was a nation of the size of Belgium fighting a great empire. The heroic deeds that thrill humanity through generations were the deeds of little nations fighting for their freedom. Ah, yes, and the salvation of mankind came through a little nation. God has chosen little nations as the vessels by which He carries the choicest wines to the lips of humanity, to rejoice their hearts, to exalt their vision, to stimulate and to strengthen their faith, and if we had stood by when two little nations were being crushed and broken by the brutal hands of barbarism, our shame would have rung down through the everlasting ages.

But Germany insists that this is an attack by a low civilisation upon a higher. Well, as a mater of fact, the attack was begun by the civilisation which calls itself the higher one. Now I am no apologist for Russia. She has perpetrated deeds of which I have no doubt her best sons are ashamed. But what empire has not? And Germany is the last empire to point the finger of reproach at Russia. But Russia has made sacrifices for freedom—great sacrifices. You remember the cry of Bulgaria when she was torn by the most insensate tyranny that Europe has ever seen. Who listened to the cry? The only answer of the higher civilisation was that the liberty of Bulgarian peasants was not worth the life of a single Pomeranian soldier. But the rude barbarians of the North, they sent their sons by the thousand to die for Bulgarian freedom.

What about England? You go to Greece, the Netherlands, Italy, Germany, and France, and in all these lands I could point out to you places where the sons of Britain have died for the freedom of these countries. France has made sacrifices for the freedom of other lands than her own. Can you name a single country in the world for the freedom of which the modern Prussian has ever sacrificed a single life? The test of our faith, the highest standard of civilisation, is the readiness to sacrifice for others.

I would not say a word about the German people to disparage them. They are a great people; they have great qualities of head, of hand, and of heart. I believe, in spite of recent events, there is as great a store of kindness in the German peasant as in any peasant in the world. But he has been drilled into a false idea of civilisation. It is a hard civilisation; it is a selfish civilisation; it is a material civilisation. They could not comprehend the action of Britain at the present moment. " France," they say, " we can understand. She is out for vengeance, she is out for territory—Alsace-Lorraine. Russia, she is fighting for mastery; she wants Galicia." They can understand vengeance, they can understand you fighting for mastery, they can understand you fighting for greed of territory; they cannot understand a great Empire pledging its resources, pledging its might, pledging the lives of its children, pledging its very existence to protect a little nation that calls for its defence. God made man in IIis own image, high of purpose, in the region of the spirit. German civilisation would re-create him in the image of a Diesel engine—precise, accurate, powerful, with no room for the soul to operate. That is the higher civilisation.

What is their demand? Have you read the Kaiser's speeches? If you have not a copy, I advise you to buy it; they will soon be out of print, and you won't have any more of the same sort again. They are full of the chatter and bluster of German militarists— the mailed fist, the shining armour. Poor old mailed fist: its knuckles are getting a little bruised. Poor shining armour: the shine is being knocked out of it. But there is the same swagger and boastfulness running through the whole of the speeches. You saw that remarkable speech which appeared in the *British Weekly* this week. It is a very remarkable product, as an illustration of the spirit we have got to fight. It is his speech to the soldiers on the way to the front:—

" Remember that the German people are the chosen of God. On me, on me as German Emperor, the Spirit of God has descended. I am His weapon, His sword, and His Vice-gerent. Woe to the disobedient. Death to cowards and unbelievers."

There has been nothing like it since the days of Mahomet, Lunacy is always distressing—but sometimes it is dangerous, and when you get it manifested in the head of the State, and it has become the policy of a great Empire, it is about time that it should be ruthlessly put away. I do not believe he meant all these speeches; it was simply the martial straddle which he had acquired. But there were men around him who meant every word of it. That was their religion. Treaties? They tangle the feet of Germany in her advance. Cut them with the sword. Little nations? They hinder the advance of Germany. Trample them in the mire under the German heel. The Russian Slav? He challenges the supremacy of Germany in Europe. Hurl your legions at him and massacre him. Britain? She is a constant menace to the predominancy of Germany in the world. Wrest the trident out of her hand.

More than that, the new philosophy of Germany is to destroy Christianity. Sickly sentimentalism about sacrifice for others —poor pap for German digestion. We will have a new diet. We will force it on the world. It will be made in Germany, a diet of blood and iron. What remains? Treaties have gone; the honour of nations has gone; liberty gone; what is left? Germany! Germany is left—Deutschland uber Alles. That is what we have got to fight—that claim of the predominance of a civilisation, a material one, a hard one, a civilisation which if it once rules and sways the world, liberty goes, democracy vanishes, and unless Britain comes to the rescue, and her sons, it will be a dark day for humanity!

The Prussian Junker is the road-hog of Europe. Small nationalities in his way are flung to the roadside, bleeding and broken; women and children crushed under the wheel of his cruel car; Britain ordered out of his way. All I can say is this. If the old British spirit is alive in British hearts, that bully will be torn from his seat. Were he to win it would be the greatest catastrophe that had befallen democracy since the days of the Holy Alliance, and its ascendency. They think we cannot beat them. It will not be easy. It will be a long job. It will be a terrible war. But in the end we shall march through terror to triumph. We shall need all our qualities—every quality that Britain and its people possess—prudence in council, daring in action, tenacity in purpose, courage in defeat, moderation in victory, in all things faith, and we shall win.

It had pleased Germany to believe and to preach the belief that we were a decadent, degenerate, timorous, craven nation, but Germany was beginning to find out her mistake already. There were half a million men who had already registered their vow to cross the seas to hurl that insult against British courage against its perpetrators on the battlefields of France and of Germany.

Another half a million men were wanted. We should get them. But Wales must continue doing her duty.

I should like to see a Welsh army in the field. I should like to see what the race who faced the Normans for hundreds of years in their struggle for freedom, the race that helped to win the Battle of Crecy, the race that fought for a generation under Glendower—against the greatest captain in Europe—I should like to see that race give a good taste of its quality in this struggle in Europe; and they are going to do it.

It is a great opportunity. It only comes once in many centuries to the children of men. For most generations sacrifice comes in drab weariness of spirit to men. It has come to day to you, it has come to-day to us all, in the form of the glow and thrill of a great movement for liberty, that impels millions throughout Europe to the same noble end. It is a great war for the emancipation of Europe from the thraldom of a military caste, which has cast its shadow upon two generations of men, and which has now plunged the world into a welter of bloodshed. Some have already given their lives. There are some who have given more than their own lives. They have given the lives of those who are dear to them. I honour their courage, and may God be their comfort and their strength. But their reward is at hand. Those who have fallen have had consecrated deaths. They have taken their part in the making of a new Europe, a new world. I can see the sign of it coming in the glare of the battle-field. The people will gain more by this struggle in all lands than they comprehend at the present time.

But that is not all. There is something infinitely greater and more enduring which is emerging already out of this great conflict; a new patriotism, richer, nobler, more exalted than the old one. I can see a new recognition amongst all classes, high and low, shedding themselves of selfishness—a new recognition that the honour of a country does not depend merely on the maintenance of its glory in the stricken field, but in protecting its homes from distress as well. It is a new patriotism. It is bringing a new outlook for all classes. A great flood of luxury and of sloth which had submerged the land is receding, and a new Britain is appearing. We can see for the first time the fundamental things that matter in life, and that have been obscured from our vision by the tropical growth of prosperity.

May I tell you, in a simple parable, what I think this war is doing for us? I know a valley in North Wales, between the mountains and the sea, a beautiful valley, snug, comfortable, sheltered by the mountains from all the bitter blasts. It was very enervating, and I remember how the boys were in the habit of climbing the hills above the village to have a glimpse of the great mountains in the distance and to be stimulated and freshened by the breeze which came from the hilltops, and by the great spectacle of that great range.

We have been living in a sheltered valley for generations. We have been too comfortable, too indulgent, many, perhaps, too selfish. And the stern hand of fate has scourged us to an elevation where we can see the great everlasting things that matter for a nation, the great peaks of honour we had forgotten, duty and patriotism, and, clad in glittering white, the great pinnacle of sacrifice pointing like a rugged finger to Heaven. We shall descend into the valleys again, but as long as the men and women of this generation last they will carry in their hearts the image of these great mountain peaks, whose foundations are unshaken, though Europe rock and sway in the convulsions of a great war.

IRELAND AND THE WAR

JOHN REDMOND

HOUSE OF COMMONS: 3 AUGUST 1914

I HOPE the House will not think me impertinent to intervene in the debate, but I was moved to do so a great deal by that sentence of the Foreign Secretary in which he said the one bright spot in the situation was the changed feeling in Ireland.

Sir, in past times when this Empire has been engaged in these terrible enterprises it is true—and it would be the utmost affectation and folly on my part to deny it—that the sympathy of Nationalist Ireland, for reasons deep down in the centuries of history, has been estranged from this country. But allow me to say that what has occurred in recent years has altered the situation completely. I must not touch upon any controversial topic, but this I may be allowed to say: That a wider knowledge of the real facts of Irish history has altered the view of the democracy of this country towards the Irish, and I honestly believe that the democracy of Ireland will turn with the utmost anxiety and sympathy to this country in every trial and danger with which she is faced.

There is a possibility of history repeating itself. The House will remember that in 1778, at the end of the disastrous American War, when it might be said that the military power in this country was almost at its lowest ebb, the shores of Ireland were threatened with invasion. Then 100,000 Irish volunteers sprang into existence for the purpose of defending those shores.

At first, however (and how sad is the reading of the history of those days), no Catholic was allowed to be enrolled in that body of volunteers, yet from the first day the Catholics of the South and West of Ireland subscribed their money and sent it for the arming of their Protestant fellow countrymen.

Ideas widened as time went on, and finally the Catholics of the South were armed and enrolled as brothers in arms with their fellow countrymen. May history repeat itself.

To-day there are in Ireland two large bodies of volunteers, one of which has sprung into existence in the North and another in the South. I say to the Government that they may to-morrow withdraw every one of their troops from Ireland. Ireland will be defended by her armed sons from foreign invasion, and for that purpose the armed Catholics in the South will be only too glad to join arms with the armed Protestant Ulstermen.

Is it too much to hope that out of this situation a result may spring which will be good not merely for the Empire but for the future welfare and integrity of the Irish nation?

Whilst Irishmen are in favour of peace, and would desire to save the democracy of this country from all the horrors of war, whilst we will make any possible sacrifice for that purpose, still if dire necessity is forced upon this country we offer this to the Government of the day: They may take their troops away, and if it is allowed to us in comradeship with our brothers in the North, we will ourselves defend the coasts of Ireland.

EVERYMAN'S LIBRARY

A CLASSIFIED LIST OF THE 979 VOLUMES

In each of the thirteen classifications in this list (except BIOGRAPHY) the volumes are arranged alphabetically under the *authors' names*, but Anthologies and works by various hands are listed under titles. Where authors appear in more than one section, a cross-reference is given, viz.: (*See also* FICTION). The number at the end of each item is the number of the volume in the series.

BIOGRAPHY

Issued January 1945

The Publishers regret that, owing to wartime difficulties and shortages, some of the volumes may be found to be temporarily out of print.

BIOGRAPHY—*continued*

CLASSICAL

ESSAYS AND BELLES-LETTRES

ESSAYS AND BELLES-LETTRES—*continued*

FICTION

FICTION—*continued*

FICTION—*continued*

FICTION—*continued*

FICTION—continued

HISTORY

HISTORY—*continued*

Gibbon's Decline and Fall of the Roman Empire. Edited, with Introduction and Notes, by Oliphant Smeaton, M.A. 6 vols. 434-6, 474-6
   (*See also* BIOGRAPHY)
Green's Short History of the English People. Edited and Revised by L. Cecil Jane, with an Appendix by R. P. Farley, B.A. 2 vols. 727-8
Grote's History of Greece. Intro. by A. D. Lindsay. 12 vols. 186-97
Hallam's (Henry) Constitutional History of England. 3 vols. 621-3
Holinshed's Chronicle as used in Shakespeare's Plays. Introduction by Professor Allardyce Nicoll. 800
Irving's (Washington) Conquest of Granada. 478
   (*See also* ESSAYS *and* BIOGRAPHY)
Josephus' Wars of the Jews. Introduction by Dr. Jacob Hart. 712
Lutzow's Bohemia: An Historical Sketch. Introduction by President T. G. Masaryk. Revised edition. 432
Macaulay's History of England. 3 vols. 34-6
   (*See also* ESSAYS *and* ORATORY)
Maine's (Sir Henry) Ancient Law. 734
Merivale's History of Rome. (An Introductory vol. to Gibbon.) 433
Mignet's (F. A. M.) The French Revolution. 713
Milman's History of the Jews. 2 vols. 377-8
Mommsen's History of Rome. Translated by W. P. Dickson, LL.D. With a review of the work by E. A. Freeman. 4 vols. 542-5
Motley's Dutch Republic. 3 vols. 86-8
Parkman's Conspiracy of Pontiac. 2 vols. 302-3
Paston Letters, The. Based on edition of Knight. Introduction by Mrs. Archer-Hind, M.A. 2 vols. 752-3
Pilgrim Fathers, The. Introduction by John Masefield. 480
Pinnow's History of Germany. Translated by M. R. Brailsford. 929
Political Liberty, The Growth of. A Source-Book of English History. Arranged by Ernest Rhys. 745   [2 vols. 397-8
Prescott's Conquest of Mexico. With Intro. by Thomas Seccombe, M.A.
   „ Conquest of Peru. Intro. by Thomas Seccombe, M.A. 301
Sismondi's Italian Republics. 250
Stanley's Lectures on the Eastern Church. Intro. by A. J. Grieve. 251
Tacitus. Vol. I. Annals. Introduction by E. H. Blakeney. 273
   „ Vol. II. Agricola and Germania. Intro. E. H. Blakeney. 274
Thierry's Norman Conquest. Intro. by J. A. Price, B.A. 2 vols. 198-9
Villehardouin and De Joinville's Chronicles of the Crusades. Translated, with Introduction, by Sir F. Marzials, C.B. 333
Voltaire's Age of Louis XIV. Translated by Martyn P. Pollack. 780

ORATORY

Anthology of British Historical Speeches and Orations. Compiled by Ernest Rhys. 714
Bright's (John) Speeches. Selected, with Intro., by Joseph Sturge. 252
Burke's American Speeches and Letters. 340   (*See also* ESSAYS)
Demosthenes: Select Orations. 546
Fox (Charles James): Speeches (French Revolutionary War Period). Edited, with Introduction, by Irene Cooper Willis, M.A. 759
Lincoln's Speeches, etc. Intro. by the Rt. Hon. James Bryce. 206
   (*See also* BIOGRAPHY)
Macaulay's Speeches on Politics and Literature. 399
   (*See also* ESSAYS *and* HISTORY)
Pitt's Orations on the War with France. 145

PHILOSOPHY AND THEOLOGY

A Kempis' Imitation of Christ. 484
Ancient Hebrew Literature. Being the Old Testament and Apocrypha. Arranged by the Rev. R. B. Taylor. 3 vols. 253-6
Aquinas, Thomas: Selected Writings. Edited by Rev. Fr. D'Arcy. 953
Aristotle's Ethics. Translated by D. P. Chase. Introduction by Professor J. A. Smith. 547 (*See also* CLASSICAL)
Bacon's The Advancement of Learning. 719   (*See also* ESSAYS)

PHILOSOPHY AND THEOLOGY—*continued*

Berkeley's (Bishop) Principles of Human Knowledge, New Theory of Vision. With Introduction by A. D. Lindsay. 483

Boehme's (Jacob) The Signature of All Things, with Other Writings. Introduction by Clifford Bax. 569

Browne's Religio Medici, etc. Intro. by Professor C. H. Herford. 92

Bunyan's Grace Abounding and Mr. Badman. Introduction by G. B. Harrison. 815 (*See also* ROMANCE) [3 vols. 886–8

Burton's (Robert) Anatomy of Melancholy. Intro. by Holbrook Jackson.

Butler's Analogy of Religion. Introduction by Rev. Ronald Bayne. 90

Chinese Philosophy in Classical Times. Translated and edited by E. R. Hughes. 973

Descartes' (René) A Discourse on Method. Translated by Professor John Veitch. Introduction by A. D. Lindsay. 570

Ellis' (Havelock) Selected Essays. Introduction by J. S. Collis. 930

Gore's (Charles) The Philosophy of the Good Life. 924

Hindu Scriptures. Edited by Dr. Nicol Macnicol. Introduction by Rabindranath Tagore. 944

Hobbes's Leviathan. Edited, with Intro., by A. D. Lindsay, M.A. 691

Hooker's Ecclesiastical Polity. Intro. by Rev. H. Bayne. 2 vols. 201–2

Hume's Treatise of Human Nature, and other Philosophical Works. Introduction by A. D. Lindsay, M.A. 2 vols. 548–9

James (William): Selected Papers on Philosophy. 739

Kant's Critique of Pure Reason. Translated by J. M. D. Meiklejohn. Introduction by A. D. Lindsay, M.A. 909

Keble's The Christian Year. Introduction by J. C. Shairp. 690

King Edward VI. First and Second Prayer Books. Introduction by the Right Rev. E. G. S. Gibson. 448

Koran, The, Rodwell's Translation. 380

Latimer's Sermons. Introduction by Canon Beeching. 40

Law's Serious Call to a Devout and Holy Life. 91

Leibniz's Philosophical Writings. Selected and trans. by Mary Morris. Introduction by C. R. Morris, M.A. 905

Locke's Two Treatises of Civil Government. Introduction by Professor William S. Carpenter. 751

Malthus on the Principles of Population. 2 vols. 692–3

Mill's (John Stuart) Utilitarianism, Liberty, Representative Government. With Introduction by A. D. Lindsay, M.A. 482

,, Subjection of Women. (*See* Wollstonecraft, Mary, *under* SCIENCE)

More's Utopia. Introduction by Judge O'Hagan. 461

New Testament. Arranged in the order in which the books came to the Christians of the First Century. 93

Newman's Apologia pro Vita Sua. Intro. by Dr. Charles Sarolea. 636 (*See also* ESSAYS)

Nietzsche's Thus Spake Zarathustra. Trans. by A. Tille and M. M. Bozman.

Paine's Rights of Man. Introduction by G. J. Holyoake. 718 [892

Pascal's Pensées. Translated by W. F. Trotter. Introduction by T. S. Eliot. 874 [403

Ramayana and the Mahabharata, The. Translated by Romesh Dutt, C.I.E.

Renan's Life of Jesus. Introduction by Right Rev. Chas. Gore, D.D. 805

Robertson's (F. W.) Sermons on Christian Doctrine, and Bible Subjects. Each Volume with Introduction by Canon Burnett. 3 vols. 37–9

Robinson's (Wade) The Philosophy of Atonement and Other Sermons. Introduction by Rev. F. B. Meyer. 637

Rousseau's (J. J.) The Social Contract, etc. 660 (*See also* ESSAYS)

St. Augustine's Confessions. Dr. Pusey's Translation. 200

St. Francis: The Little Flowers, and The Life of St. Francis. 485

Seeley's Ecce Homo. Introduction by Sir Oliver Lodge. 305

Selection from St. Thomas Aquinas. Edited by The Rev. Father M. C. D'Arcy. 953

Spinoza's Ethics, etc. Translated by Andrew J. Boyle. With Introduction by Professor Santayana. 481

Swedenborg's (Emmanuel) Heaven and Hell. 379

,, ,, The Divine Love and Wisdom. 635

,, ,, The Divine Providence. 658

,, ,, The True Christian Religion. 893

POETRY AND DRAMA

Anglo-Saxon Poetry. Edited by Professor R. K. Gordon. 794
Arnold's (Matthew) Poems, 1840–66, including Thyrsis. 334
Ballads, A Book of British. Selected by R. B. Johnson. 572
Beaumont and Fletcher, The Select Plays of. Introduction by Professor Baker, of Harvard University. 506
Björnson's Plays. Vol. I. The Newly Married Couple. Leonardo, A Gauntlet. Trans. by R. Farquharson Sharp. 625
    ,,   ,,   Vol. II. The Editor, The Bankrupt, and The King. Translated by R. Farquharson Sharp. 696
Blake's Poems and Prophecies. Introduction by Max Plowman. 792
Browning's Poems, 1833–44. Introduction by Arthur Waugh. 41
    ,,   ,,   1844–64. 42
    ,,   Poems and Plays, 1871–90. 964
    ,,   The Ring and the Book. Intro. by Chas. W. Hodell. 502
Burns's Poems and Songs. Introduction by J. Douglas. 94
Byron's Poetical and Dramatic Works. 3 vols. 486–8
Calderon: Six Plays, translated by Edward FitzGerald. 819
Chaucer's Canterbury Tales. Edited by Principal Burrell, M.A. 307
Coleridge, Golden Book of. Edited by Stopford A. Brooke. 43
    (*See also* ESSAYS)
Cowper (William). Poems of. Edited by H. I'Anson Fausset. 872
    (*See also* BIOGRAPHY)
Dante's Divine Comedy (Cary's Translation). Specially edited by Edmund Gardner. 308
Donne's Poems Edited by H. I'Anson Fausset. 867 [Gardner. 308
Dryden's Poems. Edited by Bonamy Dobree. 910
Eighteenth-Century Plays. Edited by John Hampden. 818
Emerson's Poems. Introduction by Professor Bakewell, Yale, U.S.A. 715
English Galaxy of Shorter Poems, The. Chosen and edited by Gerald Bullett. 959
English Religious Verse. Edited by G. Lacey May. 937
Everyman and other Interludes, including eight Miracle Plays. Edited by Ernest Rhys. 381
FitzGerald's (Edward) Omar Kháyyám and Six Plays of Calderon. 819
Goethe's Faust. Parts I and II. Trans. and Intro. by A. G. Latham. 335
    (*See also* ESSAYS *and* FICTION)
Golden Book of Modern English Poetry, The. Edited by Thomas Caldwell. 921
Golden Treasury of Longer Poems, The. Edited by Ernest Rhys. 746
Goldsmith's Poems and Plays. Introduction by Austin Dobson. 415
    (*See also* ESSAYS *and* FICTION)
Gray's Poems and Letters. Introduction by John Drinkwater. 628
Hebbel's Plays. Translated, with an Introduction, by Dr. C. K. Allen. 694
Heine: Prose and Poetry. 911
Herbert's Temple. Introduction by Edward Thomas. 309
Herrick's Hesperides and Noble Numbers. Intro. by Ernest Rhys. 310
Ibsen's Brand. Translated by F. E. Garrett. 716
    ,,   Ghosts, The Warriors at Helgeland, and An Enemy of the People. Translated by R. Farquharson Sharp. 552
    ,,   Lady Inger of Östraat, Love's Comedy, and The League of Youth. Translated by R. Farquharson Sharp. 729
    ,,   Peer Gynt. Translated by R. Farquharson Sharp. 747
    ,,   A Doll's House, The Wild Duck, and The Lady from the Sea. Translated by R. Farquharson Sharp. 494
    ,,   The Pretenders, Pillars of Society, and Rosmersholm. Translated by R. Farquharson Sharp. 659
Jonson's (Ben) Plays. Intro. by Professor Schelling. 2 vols. 489–90
Kalidasa: Shakuntala. Translated by Professor A. W. Ryder. 629
Keats's Poems. 101
Kingsley's (Charles) Poems. Introduction by Ernest Rhys. 793
    (*See also* FICTION *and* FOR YOUNG PEOPLE)
Langland's (William) Piers Plowman. 571
Lessing's Laocoön, Minna von Barnhelm, and Nathan the Wise. 843
Longfellow's Poems. Introduction by Katherine Tynan. 382
Marlowe's Plays and Poems. Introduction by Edward Thomas. 383
Milton's Poems, Introduction by W. H. D. Rouse. 384 (*See also* ESSAYS)

POETRY AND DRAMA—*continued*

Minor Elizabethan Drama. Vol. I. Tragedy, Selected, with Introduction, by Professor Thorndike. Vol. II. Comedy. 491–2
Minor Poets of the 18th Century. Edited by H. I'Anson Fausset. 844
Minor Poets of the 17th Century. Edited by R. G. Howarth. 873
Modern Plays. By Somerset Maugham, R. C. Sherriff, A. A. Milne, Noel Coward, and Arnold Bennett and E. Knoblock. 942
Molière's Comedies. Introduction by Prof. F. C. Green. 2 vols. 830–1
New Golden Treasury, The. An Anthology of Songs and Lyrics. 695
Old Yellow Book, The. Introduction by Charles E. Hodell. 503
Omar Kháyyám (The Rubáiyát of). Trans. by Edward FitzGerald. 819
Palgrave's Golden Treasury. Introduction by Edward Hutton. 96
Percy's Reliques of Ancient English Poetry. 2 vols. 148–9
Poe's (Edgar Allan) Poems and Essays. Intro. by Andrew Lang. 791
    (*See also* FICTION)
Pope (Alexander): Collected Poems. Introduction by Ernest Rhys. 760
Proctor's (Adelaide A.) Legends and Lyrics. 150
Restoration Plays. A Volume of. Introduction by Edmund Gosse. 604
Rossetti's Poems and Translations. Introduction by E. G. Gardner. 627
Scott's Poems and Plays. Intro. by Andrew Lang. 2 vols. 550–1
    (*See also* BIOGRAPHY *and* FICTION)
Shakespeare's Comedies. 153
    ,,   Historical Plays, Poems, and Sonnets. 154
    ,,   Tragedies. 155
Shelley's Poetical Works. Introduction by A. H. Koszul. 2 vols. 257–8
Sheridan's Plays. 95
Spenser's Faerie Queene. Intro. by Prof. J. W. Hales. 2 vols. 443–4
    ,,   Shepherd's Calendar and Other Poems. Edited by Philip Henderson. 879
Stevenson's Poems, A Child's Garden of Verses, Underwoods, Songs of Travel, Ballads. 768   (*See also* ESSAYS, FICTION, *and* TRAVEL)
Swinburne's Poems and Prose. Selected and Edited by Richard Church.
Synge's (J. M.) Plays, Poems, and Prose. 968   [961
Tchekhov. Plays and Stories. 941
Tennyson's Poems. Vol. I. 1830–56. Introduction by Ernest Rhys. 44
    ,,   ,,   Vol. II. 1857–70. 626
Twenty One-Act Plays. Selected by John Hampden. 947
Webster and Ford. Plays. Selected, with Introduction, by Dr. G. B. Harrison. 899
Whitman's (Walt) Leaves of Grass (I), Democratic Vistas, etc. 573
Wilde (Oscar): Plays, Prose Writings, and Poems. 858
Wordsworth's Shorter Poems. Introduction by Ernest Rhys. 203
    ,,   Longer Poems. Note by Editor. 311

REFERENCE

Atlas of Ancient and Classical Geography. Many coloured and line Maps; Historical Gazetteer, Index, etc. 451
Biographical Dictionary of English Literature. 449
Biographical Dictionary of Foreign Literature. 900
Dates, Dictionary of. 554
Dictionary of Quotations and Proverbs. 2 vols. 809–10
Everyman's English Dictionary. 776
Literary and Historical Atlas. I. Europe, Many coloured and line Maps; full Index and Gazetteer. 496
    ,,   ,,   ,,   II. America.   Do.   553
    ,,   ,,   ,,   III. Asia.   Do.   633
    ,,   ,,   ,,   IV. Africa and Australia. Do.   662
Non-Classical Mythology, Dictionary of. 632
Reader's Guide to Everyman's Library. Revised edition, covering the first 950 vols. 889
Roget's Thesaurus of English Words and Phrases. 2 vols. 630–1
Smith's Smaller Classical Dictionary. Revised and Edited by E. H. Blakeney, M.A. 495
Wright's An Encyclopaedia of Gardening. 555

ROMANCE

Aucassin and Nicolette, with other Medieval Romances. 497

Boccaccio's Decameron. (Unabridged.) Translated by J. M. Rigg. Introduction by Edward Hutton. 2 vols. 845–6

Bunyan's Pilgrim's Progress. Introduction by Rev. H. E. Lewis. 204

Burnt Njal, The Story of. Translated by Sir George Dasent. 558

Cervantes' Don Quixote. Motteaux's Translation. Lockhart's Introduction. 2 vols. 385–6

Chrétien de Troyes: Eric and Enid. Translated, with Introduction and Notes, by William Wistar Comfort. 698

French Medieval Romances. Translated by Eugene Mason. 557

Geoffrey of Monmouth's Histories of the Kings of Britain. 577

Grettir Saga, The. Newly Translated by G. Ainslie Hight. 699

Gudrun. Done into English by Margaret Armour. 880

Guest's (Lady) Mabinogion. Introduction by Rev. R. Williams. 97

Heimskringla: The Olaf Sagas. Translated by Samuel Laing. Introduction and Notes by John Beveridge. 717

„ Sagas of the Norse Kings. Translated by Samuel Laing. Introduction and Notes by John Beveridge. 847

Holy Graal, The High History of the, 445

Kalevala. Introduction by W. F. Kirby, F.L.S., F.E.S. 2 vols. 259–60

Le Sage's The Adventures of Gil Blas. Intro. by Anatole Le Bras. 2 vols. 437–8

MacDonald's (George) Phantastes: A Faerie Romance. 732
(See also FICTION)

Malory's Le Morte d'Arthur. Intro. by Professor Rhys. 2 vols. 45–6

Morris (William): Early Romances. Introduction by Alfred Noyes. 261

„ „ The Life and Death of Jason. 575

Morte d'Arthur Romances, Two. Introduction by Lucy A. Paton. 634

Nibelungs, The Fall of the. Translated by Margaret Armour. 312

Rabelais' The Heroic Deeds of Gargantua and Pantagruel. Introduction by D. B. Wyndham Lewis. 2 vols. 826–7

Wace's Arthurian Romance. Translated by Eugene Mason. Layamon's Brut. Introduction by Lucy A. Paton. 578

SCIENCE

Boyle's The Sceptical Chymist. 559

Darwin's The Origin of Species. Introduction by Sir Arthur Keith. 811
(See also TRAVEL)

Eddington's (Sir Arthur) The Nature of the Physical World. Introduction by E. F. Bozman. 922

Euclid: the Elements of. Todhunter's Edition. Introduction by Sir Thomas Heath, K.C.B. 891

Faraday's (Michael) Experimental Researches in Electricity. 576

Galton's Inquiries into Human Faculty. Revised by Author. 263

George's (Henry) Progress and Poverty. 560

Hahnemann's (Samuel) The Organon of the Rational Art of Healing. Introduction by C. E. Wheeler. 663

Harvey's Circulation of the Blood. Introduction by Ernest Parkyn. 262

Howard's State of the Prisons. Introduction by Kenneth Ruck. 835

Huxley's Essays. Introduction by Sir Oliver Lodge. 47

„ Select Lectures and Lay Sermons. Intro. Sir Oliver Lodge. 498

Lyell's Antiquity of Man. With an Introduction by R. H. Rastall. 700

Marx's (Karl) Capital. Translated by Eden and Cedar Paul. Introduction by G. D. H. Cole. 2 vols. 848–9

Miller's Old Red Sandstone. 103

Owen's (Robert) A New View of Society, etc. Intro. by G. D. H. Cole. 799

Pearson's (Karl) The Grammar of Science. 939

Ricardo's Principles of Political Economy and Taxation. 590

Smith's (Adam) The Wealth of Nations. 2 vols. 412–13

Tyndall's Glaciers of the Alps and Mountaineering in 1861. 98

White's Selborne. Introduction by Principal Windle. 48

Wollstonecraft (Mary), The Rights of Woman, with John Stuart Mill's The Subjection of Women. 825

TRAVEL AND TOPOGRAPHY

A Book of the ' Bounty.' Edited by George Mackaness. 950
Anson's Voyages. Introduction by John Masefield. 510
Bates's Naturalist on the Amazon. With Illustrations. 446
Belt's The Naturalist in Nicaragua. Intro. by Anthony Belt, F.L.S. 561
Borrow's (George) The Gypsies in Spain. Intro. by Edward Thomas. 697
    ,,   ,,   The Bible in Spain. Intro. by Edward Thomas. 151
    ,,   ,,   Wild Wales. Intro. by Theodore Watts-Dunton. 49
     (See also FICTION)
Boswell's Tour in the Hebrides with Dr. Johnson. 387
     (See also BIOGRAPHY)
Burton's (Sir Richard) First Footsteps in East Africa. 500
Cobbett's Rural Rides. Introduction by Edward Thomas. 2 vols. 638-9
Cook's Voyages of Discovery. 99
Crèvecœur's (H. St. John) Letters from an American Farmer. 640
Darwin's Voyage of the Beagle. 104
     (See also SCIENCE)
Defoe's Tour through England and Wales. Introduction by G. D. H.
    Cole. 820-1   (See also FICTION)
Dennis' Cities and Cemeteries of Etruria. 2 vols. 183-4
Dufferin's (Lord) Letters from High Latitudes. 499
Ford's Gatherings from Spain. Introduction by Thomas Okey. 152
Franklin's Journey to the Polar Sea. Intro. by Capt. R. F. Scott. 447
Giraldus Cambrensis: Itinerary and Description of Wales. 272
Hakluyt's Voyages. 8 vols. 264, 265, 313, 314, 338, 339, 388, 389
Kinglake's Eothen. Introduction by Harold Spender, M.A. 337
Lane's Modern Egyptians. With many Illustrations. 315
Mandeville's (Sir John) Travels. Introduction by Jules Bramont. 812
Park (Mungo): Travels. Introduction by Ernest Rhys. 205
Peaks, Passes, and Glaciers. Selected by E. H. Blakeney, M.A. 778
Polo's (Marco) Travels. Introduction by John Masefield. 306
Roberts' The Western Avernus. Intro. by Cunninghame Grahame. 762
Speke's Discovery of the Source of the Nile. 50
Stevenson's An Inland Voyage, Travels with a Donkey, and Silverado
    Squatters. 766
     (See also ESSAYS, FICTION, and POETRY)
Stow's Survey of London. Introduction by H. B. Wheatley. 589
Wakefield's Letter from Sydney and Other Writings on Colonization. 828
Waterton's Wanderings in South America. Intro. by E. Selous. 772
Young's Travels in France and Italy. Intro. by Thomas Okey. 720

FOR YOUNG PEOPLE

Aesop's and Other Fables: An Anthology from all sources. 657
Alcott's Little Men. Introduction by Grace Rhys. 512
    ,,   Little Women and Good Wives. Intro. by Grace Rhys. 248
Andersen's Fairy Tales. Illustrated by the Brothers Robinson. 4
    ,,   More Fairy Tales. Illustrated by Mary Shillabeer. 822
Annals of Fairyland. The Reign of King Oberon. 365
    ,,   ,,   The Reign of King Cole. 366
Asgard and the Norse Heroes. Translated by Mrs. Boult. 689
Baker's Cast up by the Sea. 539
Ballantyne's Coral Island. 245
    ,,   Martin Rattler. 246
    ,,   Ungava. Introduction by Ernest Rhys. 276
Browne's (Frances) Granny's Wonderful Chair. Intro. by Dollie Radford.
Bulfinch's (Thomas) The Age of Fable. 472   [112
    ,,   ,,   Legends of Charlemagne. Introduction by Ernest
      Rhys. 556
Canton's A Child's Book of Saints. Illustrated by T. H. Robinson. 61
     (See also ESSAYS)
Carroll's Alice in Wonderland, Through the Looking-Glass, etc. Illus-
    trated by the Author. Introduction by Ernest Rhys. 836
Clarke's Tales from Chaucer. 537

FOR YOUNG PEOPLE—*continued*